Jury Selection Handbook

Jury Selection Handbook
The Nuts and Bolts of Effective Jury Selection

Ronald H. Clark
DISTINGUISHED PRACTITIONER IN RESIDENCE
SEATTLE UNIVERSITY SCHOOL OF LAW

Thomas M. O'Toole
PRESIDENT, SOUND JURY CONSULTING

A Lawyering Series Coursebook
Published in Collaboration with
Northeastern University School of Law

CAROLINA ACADEMIC PRESS
Durham, North Carolina

Library of Congress Cataloging-in-Publication Data

Names: Clark, Ronald H., author. | O'Toole, Thomas M., author.
Title: Jury selection handbook : the nuts and bolts of effective jury selection
    / Ronald H. Clark and Thomas M. O'Toole.
Description: Durham, North Carolina : Carolina Academic Press, LLC, [2017] |
    Includes bibliographical references and index.
Identifiers: LCCN 2017046266 | ISBN 9781531007973 (alk. paper)
Subjects: LCSH: Jury selection--United States. | Jury--United States.
Classification: LCC KF8979 .C53 2017 | DDC 347.73/752--dc23
LC record available at https://lccn.loc.gov/2017046266

e-ISBN 978-1-53100-798-0

CAROLINA ACADEMIC PRESS, LLC
700 Kent Street
Durham, North Carolina 27701
Telephone (919) 489-7486
Fax (919) 493-5668
www.cap-press.com

Printed in the United States of America

This book and we are dedicated:

To my family, Nancy, Brady, Soojin, Malachi, Riley,
Clancy, Kara, Beatrice, Samuel,
Colby, and Darren

Ronald H. Clark

To my family, my lovely wife Jodie, my parents, and
my phenomenal colleagues Jill, Scott, Joe, and "Missourah."

Thomas M. O'Toole

Contents

About the Series

Carolina Academic Press, in cooperation with Northeastern University School of Law, is pleased to offer a new series of teaching materials, the Lawyering Series.

Carolina Academic Press, an independent publisher, has a strong reputation for publishing innovative print and digital teaching materials for the law school community. Northeastern University School of Law has long been known as an innovator in legal education, with a national reputation for its Cooperative Legal Education (Co-op) Program and its rich clinical and externship offerings.

Over the last decade, the American Bar Association has urged American law schools to better prepare their students for the practice of law. Most recently, the ABA has enacted Standards that require all law students to complete a minimum of six credit hours of "experiential" courses. This requirement commenced for students beginning law school in fall 2016.

It is our sincere hope that the Lawyering Series will support law schools and law professors—both full-time and adjunct—as they search for more innovative and more practical teaching materials.

We welcome your comments and suggestions. Please contact Carolina Academic Press at manuscript@caplaw.com.

Acknowledgments

We are thankful to many individuals who provided insights and support: Laurie Sleeper Wells, administrative assistant; attorney at law Vonda M. Sargent; Kevin Boully, litigation consultant at Persuasion Strategies; and attorney at law Jonathan Barnard. A special thank you to Marilyn J. Berger and John B. Mitchell, Seattle University Professors Emeriti, for their friendship, guidance, and scholarship.

Many thanks for the support and assistance provided through Seattle University School of Law: Dean Annette C. Clark; Dean for Finance and Administration Richard Bird; Associate Dean for Academic Affairs John Eason; and Stephanie Wilson, the law school's Head of Reference Services.

And, we want to express our appreciation to our friends and professional colleagues at Carolina Academic Press: Keith Sipe, Publisher; Carol McGeehan, Senior Acquisitions Editor; Ryland Bowman, Managing Editor; and TJ Smithers, Production Associate.

About the Authors

Ronald H. Clark is a Distinguished Practitioner in Residence at Seattle University Law School, where he teaches Pretrial Advocacy, Trial Advocacy and Essential Lawyering Skills. He is a nationally known lecturer and author. His previous books include *Pretrial Advocacy, Trial Advocacy, Opening Statement and Closing Argument, Evidence: Skills and Strategies* and *Cross-Examination Handbook*. Mr. Clark has lectured for numerous bar and other associations across the country, as well as for the Department of Justice in Bosnia and Kosovo. Mr. Clark served in the King County Prosecutor's office in Seattle, Washington, as a senior deputy prosecutor, head of the trial teams, and, for ten years, as the Chief Deputy of the Criminal Division. Subsequently, Mr. Clark was the Senior Training Counsel at the National Advocacy Center in South Carolina.

Thomas O'Toole, Ph.D., is President of Sound Jury Consulting. He has practiced across the nation since 2003 in nearly every litigation type. He has consulted on matters as small as low-exposure medical malpractice claims and as large as "bet-the-company" MDL class actions and billion dollar environmental claims. He received his Ph.D. in litigation psychology and communication from the University of Kansas, which houses one of the nation's only doctoral programs designed to offer formal training for those entering the field of jury consulting.

Jury Selection Handbook

Chapter 1

Introduction to Book & Online Supplement

"No free man shall be captured, and or imprisoned, or disseised of his freehold, and or of his liberties, or of his free customs, or be outlawed, or exiled, or in any way destroyed, nor will we proceed against him by force or proceed against him by arms, but by the lawful judgment of his peers, and or by the law of the land."

Magna Carta, Article 39

"I'm no idealist to believe firmly in the integrity of our courts and in the jury system—that is no ideal to me, it is a living, working reality."

Atticus Finch in Harper Lee's
To Kill a Mockingbird, 234 (40th ann. ed.,
Harper Collins Publishers 1999) (1960)

A. Jury Selection — A Challenge and an Opportunity

You are about to engage in what can be viewed as the most difficult challenge in trial—jury selection. You are at counsel table in a courtroom as the court officer ushers in strangers who will be asked to render a verdict in your client's case. Generally, these citizens are unfamiliar with the law that they will be instructed to follow and about how to apply that law to the facts of your case. In fact, research shows they will struggle to understand the law and accurately apply it when finally instructed on it. They have no experience evaluating the credibility of witnesses. Some of them may harbor beliefs, expectations and biases that compromise their ability to apply the law to your client and your case impartially. Of course the group may include prospective jurors with some familiarity with the justice system, such as a lawyer or the person with prior jury service, but they are exceptions.

Jury selection also is the greatest challenge in trial because you do not know what these prospective jurors are going to say during jury selection and because at the outset you do not know everything you want to know about them even if you have been able to conduct a pretrial investigation of them, and/or they have completed a lengthy juror questionnaire. Instead, you are left to look for signs or indicators of how they might feel about the issues in the case, and these indicators are imperfect as they are always open to interpretation. Can you get them to reveal what you need to know about them during the jury selection? Further, during voir dire, the prospective jurors are forming an impression of you. Can you show them that you are the type of person they can trust and follow? Above all, jury selection is the most problematic part of trial, because you must decide with incomplete information who should not sit on the jury, a decision that can determine the outcome of the case. The unknowns and unpredictability inherent in jury selection might make you uneasy, but you are not alone. Most trial lawyers will readily admit that jury selection is their most uncomfortable phase of trial. Relax, this book is dedicated to showing you how to overcome these obstacles and concerns that jury selection presents and even enjoy the voir dire experience.

While jury selection presents a formidable challenge, it is also a great opportunity. Jury selection affords you a chance to engage in the only interchange that you are allowed to have with the jurors during trial. Jury selection is the only time you will get to learn what is on their minds until they reach a verdict or the judge declares a mistrial because they cannot reach a verdict. Your other communications to the jurors during the trial will be one-way, with you conveying information to the jurors and receiving nothing in return, with the exception of a few ambiguous nonverbal gestures and questions in trial venues that allow the practice of juror questions to witnesses.

Your colloquy with the prospective jurors during jury selection can accomplish at least five trial goals. First, you can elicit information from them that will help you determine whether you should seek to keep them off the jury by exercising either a challenge for cause or a peremptory challenge. Second, you can leave a favorable impression on the jurors so they will think you are sincere and trustworthy. Third, you can deal with case weaknesses and juror misconceptions. Fourth, you can gather information for your closing argument. Fifth, through your questioning and conversations with them, you can introduce them to your legal position, your case narrative, and your case theme and explore whether or not they will be receptive to it.

While the process is referred to as "jury selection," that does not mean by any stretch that you can select those jurors you would like to have hear the case. The only power you have is the power to remove jurors from the jury panel. If you want a particular prospective juror because it is apparent that the person favors your side, it is likely that your opponent will do what is necessary to keep the person off the jury. The best you can do is *deselect* prospective jurors whom you conclude you want off the jury with challenges. Rather, the phrase "jury selection" more aptly refers to the justice system's process of ultimately empaneling a jury that can fairly and impartially decide the case.

B. Jury Selection Book

Because jury selection poses such great challenges and opportunities, today's trial lawyers need to be fully prepared for, and adept at, conducting jury selection. This book is designed to fill those needs. *Jury Selection Handbook: The Nuts and Bolts of Effective Jury Selection* is intended for the full gamut of trial lawyers from fledgling to experienced trial lawyers as well as law students. It provides the tools for preparing and conducting effective jury selection. It can be utilized for trial advocacy seminars and law school trial advocacy courses and clinics. Any hard-working lawyer or law student can master the winning jury selection planning, strategies, and techniques presented here. Consequently, it is helpful for even the most experienced litigators to revisit this book as they prepare for jury selection in their own cases.

1. Examples — The Next Best Thing

The best thing to do in order to learn how to become a successful trial lawyer is to observe an experienced, skilled trial lawyer during trial, ideally as co-counsel, because then you can observe both the lawyer's preparation and performance. Of course, it is important to remember that there is a wide spectrum of jury selection philosophies and strategies practiced by different trial lawyers. It will be up to you to determine which methods make the most sense to borrow. The next best thing is to review transcripts of their trial work. Therefore, besides providing the law, procedures, strategies, and techniques, *Jury Selection Handbook: The Nuts and Bolts of Effective Jury Selection* illustrates how to effectively conduct jury selection with excerpts from trial transcripts. Whenever we present a trial transcript, we have edited it down to a segment that illustrates the strategies and techniques under discussion. You will be able to modify the attorney's remarks and patterns of questions in a transcript for use in your trials. Some of the finest trial work is the result of borrowing the best of the best from another trial lawyer.

Some of the transcript examples are from famous trials, such as the Dzhokhar Tsarnaev (Boston Marathon bomber) and the Engle Progeny (class action lawsuits against the tobacco industry) trials. Others are from carefully chosen civil and criminal cases from across the United States. Throughout this book, we will draw on jury selections from two antitrust trials, *In re TFT-LCD (Flat-Panel)*, held in the United States District Court, Northern District of California, and *Retractable Technologies, Inc. v. Becton, Dickinson and Company* conducted in the United States District Court, Eastern District of Texas, to illustrate various aspects of jury selection.[1] These two cases run like threads throughout the text. Other select *voir dires* include those from wrongful death, patent infringement, domestic violence, murder, sexual abuse, and negligence trials. Transcripts of voir dires from most of these trials are in the Appendices for this book which are contained on this book's companion online supplement at http://caplaw.com/jury.

Finally, all our editorial choices have been motivated by the same goal—to make jury selection come alive. We want you to feel a sense of excitement and creative challenge in formulating and conducting jury selection in your cases.

2. Book Overview

Jury Selection Handbook begins with Chapter 2 that discusses the law, rules and procedures governing jury selection. It also explains the selection process from the selection of the jury pool through the judge's and/or counsels' questioning of the prospective jurors. Beginning with Chapter 2 and throughout this book, we cover the necessary foundation of ethical, legal, and courtroom-custom boundaries of a proper jury selection.

Chapter 3 covers challenges to prospective jurors—challenges for cause and peremptory challenges—and how to exercise those challenges.

Chapter 4 focuses on how to prepare for jury selection, including such critical tasks as scouting the court, investigating the prospective jurors and developing specialized juror questionnaires.

---

1. *In re TFT-LCD (Flat-Panel) Antitrust Litigation*, No. 07-MDL-1827 SI, 10-CV-4572, 10-CV-5452, 10-CV-4114 (N.D. Cal. July 22, 2013), Appendix (hereafter App.1.1); *Retractable Techs., Inc. v. Becton, Dickinson and Co.*, 2:08cv16 E.D. (Tex. Sept. 3, 2013), App. 1.2.

Chapter 5 concentrates on how to get the most out of the services that a jury consultant can provide a trial lawyer in jury selection.

Chapter 6 discusses how to make a favorable impression on the jurors during your exchanges with them.

Chapter 7 is dedicated to an explanation of how to achieve the critical goal of obtaining useful information from the prospective jurors so that you can evaluate them and determine against whom you will exercise challenges.

In Chapter 8, we explore how to break the ice, opening the conversation with the prospective jurors, along with effective strategies and techniques for asking questions.

The next three chapters are devoted to explaining how to leave a favorable impression of your case with prospective jurors through your conversations with the panel as well as how to gather information that you can use to determine how to exercise challenges. Specifically, Chapter 9 explains methodologies for analyzing your case and for developing and introducing your case theme. Then, Chapters 10 and 11 explore how to present your legal position and case story and test whether or not the prospective jurors will be receptive them.

Chapter 12 deals with the important subject of how to address your case weaknesses and common juror misconceptions.

Chapter 13 examines the methods by which you can accomplish the central goal of evaluating the prospective jurors in order to intelligently exercise challenges.

Chapter 14 covers pretrial motions pertaining to jury selection and responses to those motions.

Finally, Chapter 15 provides role-play assignments that can be utilized in law school trial advocacy and clinic courses and in lawyer CLE or in-house law firm professional development training sessions.

Note that whenever we refer to a person as a "juror," we usually mean that the person is a prospective juror who has yet to be sworn in to serve on the jury for the trial.

C. Jury Selection Online Supplement

Jury Selection Handbook comes with a robust online supplement containing the book's Appendix. For example, in the online supplement at http:// caplaw.com/jury, you will find the following:

- Sample juror questionnaires, including questionnaires from *People of the State of California v. Orenthal James Simpson* (the O. J. Simpson

trial) and *United States v. Dzhokhar A. Tsarnaev* (the Boston
Marathon Bomber trial);
- Transcripts of a dozen complete jury selections in both federal and
  state courts and civil and criminal cases;
- Sample motions and responses relating to jury selection including:
  - motion for change of venue;
  - motion challenging the array;
  - motion for additional peremptory challenges;
  - motion for customized juror questionnaire;
  - motion to prohibit opposing counsel from asking improper questions during jury selection;
  - motion to provide reasonable time for attorney questioning; and
  - motion to permit counsel to question the panel.

A full list of the appendices can be found on pages 341–343.

Only by actually planning and doing jury selection can a lawyer fully understand voir dire and perfect the skills necessary to conduct an effective jury selection. Chapter 15 contains role-play assignments that can be used by practicing lawyers in continuing legal education workshops and students in law school trial advocacy classes and clinics. The assignments involve both a civil and criminal case and cover both the preparation for jury selection and conducting it.

The professor or instructor can tailor the number of assignments to the course, choosing to assign all or some of them. A Teacher's Manual containing teaching notes and supplementary materials is provided to any teacher who adopts the *Jury Selection Handbook*.

Chapter 2

Overview:
The Selection Process

"In all criminal prosecutions, the accused shall enjoy the right to a speedy and public trial, by an impartial jury of the State and district wherein the crime shall have been committed ..."

U.S. Const. amend. VI.

"In Suits at common law, where the value in controversy shall exceed twenty dollars, the right of trial by jury shall be preserved, and no fact tried by a jury, shall be otherwise re-examined in any Court of the United States, than according to the rules of the common law."

U.S. Const. amend. VII.

A. The Selection Process

To be fully prepared for jury selection, you should be well versed in how the people who arrive in the courtroom were selected and how they were oriented to what to expect during the proceedings and their jury service. It is essential that you understand every aspect of the selection process for at least three reasons. First, with this knowledge, you can protect your client's right to a fair and impartial jury comprised of a fair cross-section of the community. Second, when you adhere to the court's selection procedures, you will meet the judge's and jurors' expectations for proper conduct. Third, when you understand the jury selection process, you will feel more confident when engaged in it.

It is important to remember that the jury selection process varies from trial venue to trial venue and from judge to judge. In other words, it is not

9

necessarily the case that different judges within the same trial venue will adopt the same procedures. Often, the process that is used depends on the personal preferences of the judge. For example, some judges do not allow any attorney-conducted voir dire while others encourage lengthy sessions of attorney questioning. Consequently, it is important to know in advance of your trial exactly how the court plans to conduct jury selection.

In this chapter, we examine the complete jury selection process, including the rules, procedures and the roles played by the judge and attorneys at both the federal and state court levels. In this chapter, we also cover the Rules of Professional Conduct governing the responsibilities of counsel as they relate to the jury.

B. Jury Pool Selection

1. Summoned to Serve

Generally, the court administrator randomly selects members of the community in the court's venue, which is the county, judicial district composed of a combination of counties, or a locality where the trial will take place. The random selection processes typically involves drawing names from public records, such as those of citizens who have driver's licenses or are registered voters.

On the federal level, 28 U.S.C. § 1861 provides:

> It is the policy of the United States that all litigants in Federal courts entitled to trial by jury shall have the right to grand and petit juries selected at random from a fair cross section of the community in the district or division wherein the court convenes. It is further the policy of the United States that all citizens shall have the opportunity to be considered for service on grand and petit juries in the district courts of the United States, and shall have an obligation to serve as jurors when summoned for that purpose.[1]

The court administrator or court clerk issues summonses to those persons who have been randomly selected to serve in the jury pool. The summons commands the person to come to the courthouse at a specified date and time. The summons may explain grounds for being excused and how the person can contact the court about being excused.

The required period of time for jury service depends upon the practice in the jurisdiction. While in one jurisdiction, a person may be summoned to serve

---

1. 28 U.S.C. § 1861 (1968).

for a number of days, in another jurisdiction, a person may be summoned to serve for two days unless the person is seated on a jury, and then jury service runs until the end of the trial.

Accompanying the summons may be a juror badge and instructions to wear it when in and around the courthouse. Also, the summons package may contain a questionnaire regarding qualifications to be a juror for the recipient to fill out and return to the court. The court may also have a website where the person can fill out the questionnaire online.[2] Failure to return the questionnaire can result in a court order to appear and show cause why the questionnaire was not completed and returned, and failure to appear can be a misdemeanor.[3]

Jury service is a public duty. The law provides that failure to arrive at the courthouse when summoned can have serious ramifications. For example, the federal Jury Selection and Service Act provides:

> Any person summoned for jury service who fails to appear as directed may be ordered by the district court to appear forthwith and show cause for failure to comply with the summons. Any person who fails to show good cause for noncompliance with a summons may be fined not more than $1,000, imprisoned not more than three days, ordered to perform community service, or any combination thereof.[4]

Once that random group has been reduced by removal of persons who do not meet the *qualifications* to be a juror, those who are *exempt* from service and those who are *excused* from jury duty, the remainder is the "jury pool."

2. Juror Qualifications, Exemptions and Excuses

a. Federal Court

Prospective jurors for federal court are required to complete a juror qualification questionnaire, which is used by the court to decide if they are qualified for jury duty.[5]

---

2. *See, e.g., Jury Service: Complete Juror Questionnaire*, MINNESOTA JUDICIAL BRANCH, http://www.mncourts.gov/?page=3603 (Jan. 9, 2017).

3. *See e.g.*, MINN. STAT. § 593.40(4) (2016).

4. 28 U.S.C. § 1865 (2016).

5. 28 U.S.C. § 1864(a) (2016).

i. Qualified

Qualifications to be on a federal jury are spelled out in the federal Jury Act, which states that to be *qualified*, a person must:

- be a United States citizen;
- be at least 18 years of age;
- reside primarily in the judicial district for one year;
- be adequately proficient in English to satisfactorily complete the juror qualification form;
- have no disqualifying mental or physical condition;
- not currently be subject to felony charges punishable by imprisonment for more than one year; and
- never have been convicted of a felony (unless civil rights have been legally restored).

ii. Exempt

Under the federal Jury Act, the three groups that are *exempt* from federal jury service, and cannot serve even if they wish to, include:

- members of the armed forces on active duty;
- members of professional fire and police departments; and
- public officers of federal, state or local governments, who are actively engaged full-time in the performance of public duties.[6]

iii. Excused

Each federal district court has its own particular guidelines concerning who may be *excused* from jury service. Upon individual request from a summoned prospective juror, many courts permit a member of a designated group of persons or occupational classes, such as volunteer fire fighters and persons over 70 who have served on a federal jury within the previous two years, to be excused from jury duty.[7]

Additionally, in some cases, the federal court may follow state statutes that exclude certain classes for jurors. For example, in the state of Washington, the case law has determined that employees of the state cannot serve on civil juries in which the state is a party to the case.

---

6. 28 U.S.C. § 1863(b)(5)(B) (2016).

7. *Juror Qualifications*, U.S. COURTS (Jan. 9, 2017), http://www.uscourts.gov/services-forms/jury-service/juror-qualifications.

The Jury Act also authorizes a federal court or the court clerk under the court's supervision to excuse a juror from service at the time summoned on the grounds of "undue hardship or extreme inconvenience."[8]

b. State Court

States have statutes or court rules along the same lines as the federal laws regarding who is *qualified* to sit on a jury, who is automatically *exempt* and who may be *excused*. The following are two examples of state court rules regarding who is qualified for jury service and procedures for deciding who will be disqualified from service.

Ohio Juror Qualification Example: The Ohio Revised Code lists the qualifications to serve:

> Any person called as a juror for the trial of any cause shall be examined under oath or upon affirmation as to the person's qualifications. A person is qualified to serve as a juror if the person is eighteen years of age or older, is a resident of the county, and is an elector or would be an elector if the person were registered to vote, regardless of whether the person actually is registered to vote.[9]

Also, by Ohio statute, the court of common pleas or the commissioner of jurors may excuse a person who has been notified to serve for a number of reasons including, among others: the "juror's spouse or a near relative of the juror or the juror's spouse has recently died or is dangerously ill"; "[t]he juror is a cloistered member of a religious organization"; and "[t]he juror is over seventy-five years of age, and the juror requests to be excused."[10] Of those who are originally called for jury duty, a number will be excused or will have their jury duty postponed.

New York Juror Qualification Example: New York Judiciary Law Section 510 provides:

In order to qualify as a juror a person must:
1. Be a citizen of the United States, and a resident of the county.
2. Be not less than eighteen years of age.
3. Not have been convicted of a felony.
4. Be able to understand and communicate in the English language.

---

8. 28 U.S.C. § 1866(c)(1) (2016).
9. OHIO REV. CODE ANN. § 2313.17(A) (West 2012).
10. OHIO REV. CODE ANN. § 2313.14 (West 2012).

The commissioner of jurors or county clerk for each county in New York mails out a questionnaire for the prospective jurors to complete and submit. Based upon the responses in the questionnaires, the commissioner or clerk decides whether the persons are qualified to serve.[11]

3. Lawful Requirements for the Jury Pool

The jury pool must meet the constitutional requirement that it include a fair cross-section of the community, thereby affording the parties a fair and impartial jury. To constitute a fair cross-section of the community, the selection process for the jury pool must be a random one that does not purposely exclude any distinctive group in the community.[12] The federal Jury Act, codifying the constitutional protections, provides that each United States district court is required to have a plan for random selection of jurors "from a fair cross section of the community in the district or division wherein the court convenes."[13] According to the Jury Act, "No citizen shall be excluded from service as a … petit juror in the district courts of the United States or in the Court of International Trade on account of race, color, religion, sex, national origin, or economic status."[14]

4. Americans with Disabilities Act

Under the Americans with Disabilities Act, an individual with a disability cannot because of that disability be excluded from participation in activities of a public entity.[15] The United States District Court, District of Columbia held that the policy of the Superior Court of the District of Columbia to exclude blind persons from the jury pool violated the Americans with Disabilities Act.[16]

Most courthouses are equipped to accommodate persons with disabilities. For example, most courthouses can provide hearing aids, alternative seating arrangements and frequent breaks.

---

11. N.Y. Judiciary Laws §§ 509–10 (McKinney 1977).

12. *See, e.g.*, *Duren v. Missouri*, 439 U.S. 357, 360 (1979) (striking down a state law that excepted women from jury duty upon their request for exemption, holding that "such systematic exclusion of women that results in jury venires averaging less than 15% female violates the Constitution's fair-cross-section requirement"). *See also Taylor v. Louisiana*, 419 U.S. 522 (1975).

13. 28 U.S.C. § 1863 (2016).

14. 28 U.S.C. § 1862 (2016).

15. 42 U.S.C. § 12132.

16. *Galloway v. Superior Court of the D.C.*, 816 F. Supp. 12 (1993).

5. Number in the Jury Pool

The court administrator will issue summonses for the number of people that experience and judgment indicate will be needed to seat the number of jurors for the courts' trials plus a number of other persons that takes into account the likelihood that a significant number of those summoned will fail to appear despite the potential penalties for nonappearance.

In a sizeable courthouse with multiple courts, hundreds may be summoned to accommodate several jury trials being conducted simultaneously. For an extreme example, 3,000 summonses were issued for one death penalty case, resulting in 1,200 people responding to serve on a jury of 12 with five alternates. The pool was brought into court over a two-day period. The court advised this pool that the trial could take up to six months. Members of the pool were provided with a 21-page questionnaire to be filled out by each person, producing over 25,000 pages to be read.[17]

For the trial of rancher Ammon Bundy who was charged with impeding Interior Department employees from doing their jobs with a 41-day occupation of an Oregon bird sanctuary, the U.S. District Court sent out 1500 juror questionnaire and received 350 back. The court excused roughly 25% for hardship and bias.[18] Additionally, as an alternative to granting a change of venue, the Court summoned jurors from all divisions of the federal district rather than just the one where the Bundy case was being tried. These measures were taken as a result of requests submitted by the defense, so it is important to remember that you may have some influence over the pool of jurors that is brought into your trial venue beyond the standard change of venue request. These options will be discussed in greater detail later in this book.

If the number of persons who show up for jury duty does not meet the needs of the court, the court has the power to bring in more from the community. A federal court faced with an unanticipated shortage of jurors can have the federal marshal summon a number of jurors selected at random from voter or other acceptable lists.[19] If more prospective jurors respond than are needed, they will be sent home.

---

17. Interview with the Hon. Ronald Kessler, Judge King County Superior Court (ret.) (Oct. 14, 2014).

18. *Oregon Jury Pool Shrinks in Ammon Bundy Case*, Assoc. Press (Aug. 24, 2016), http://www.reviewjournal.com/news/bundy-blm/ammon-bundy-jury-pool-shrinks-oregon-eliminations.

19. 28 U.S.C. § 1866(f) (2016).

6. Jury Pool Orientation

Once the prospective jurors arrive at the courthouse, they usually congregate in a jury waiting room. This room is where tedium can set in as they wait to be sent out to a courtroom. It is a place where a good book or other distraction is needed. In some instances, jurors have waited a day or more before ever reaching a courtroom. When prospective jurors arrive in the jury waiting room, they may be given a juror pamphlet as reading material. Or, a pamphlet may have already been mailed to them along with the summons. To further educate the pool about the process, court personnel may show a video or lecture them about jury service.

During the juror's orientation, a juror pamphlet, video or lecture likely will cover matters such as:

- The right to trial by jury;
- Types of cases—civil vs. criminal, discussing burdens of proof;
- The process for jury selection;
- How to behave as a juror;
- Conduct in the jury room;
- Stages of trial; and
- Disabilities.[20]

It is helpful to know what the jurors have read, seen and been told about the process during their orientation because you can build that into your jury selection questions. For instance, you might preface a question with this: "As you might have noted in the Jury Booklet that you were given, it says that in a civil trial '[A]ny person unable to resolve a legal dispute with another is entitled to ask that it be decided in court.' ..."[21]

C. Jury Panel Selection

The *jury panel* (also called a *"venire panel"*) is that group of prospective jurors sent to a particular courtroom for a jury trial. The court administrator randomly picks members of the jury panel from the jury pool, and court personnel, ordinarily the bailiff, guides those people to the courtroom.

---

20. *Petit Juror Handbook*, Ill. Courts, http://www.state.il.us/court/CircuitCourt/Jury/Juror.asp (Jan. 9, 2017).

21. *Id.*

1. Number in the Jury Panel

Generally, the number selected for the jury panel is determined by the number of jurors and alternate jurors who will sit on the trial jury plus a number in excess of the number who could be disqualified or removed with challenges for cause or with peremptory challenges. For a trial by 14, 12 jurors and two alternates, the administrator may send a panel of 48 prospective jurors. The size of the venire depends upon the type of case, the extent of any media coverage, and the overall length of the trial. Judges typically request larger venires for cases that have received extensive pretrial publicity (as were the circumstances with the Ammon Bundy case) or cases that are expected to have long trials. For example, in one case in which one of the authors participated in jury selection, the judge requested a venire of 600 jurors due to the fact that the trial was expected to last over four months. Should the court run out of venire persons, the judge can ask for more to be sent from the jury pool.

2. Jury List

In most trial venues, once the initial venire panel has been randomly selected, the court staff provides the attorneys on each side with a numbered list of the venire members before the jury selection begins. Typically, the court adheres to the numerical order of the jurors on the list, meaning the first twelve jurors listed will be the first twelve jurors in the box. However, some courts randomly select jurors from the list when placing them in the box, providing attorneys with no predictability as to who will step into the box after a juror is removed.

3. Seating the Panel

Commonly, court personnel randomly choose prospective jurors, up to the number of jurors required for the type of case, to sit in the jury box. Other prospective jurors in the panel are seated in the spectator section of the courtroom. Another approach is to have them all be seated in the spectator section.

D. Number of Jurors for Trial

1. The Jury

[T]he fact that the jury at common law was composed of precisely 12 is a historical accident, unnecessary to effect the purposes of the jury system and wholly without significance "except to mystics."

So wrote Justice Byron White in *Williams v. Florida*, 99 U.S. 78, 102 (1970), which upheld a robbery conviction by a six-person jury, and left it to Congress and the states to determine the appropriate number of jurors as long as it resulted in a fair cross-section of the community and did not exclude any distinctive group in the community. In a later decision, the Supreme Court reaffirmed *Williams*, but held that research studies after *Williams* indicated that a reduction of a jury below six would impair the purpose and function of a jury and that therefore a five-person jury was inadequate.[22]

a. Federal Court

The Federal Rules of Civil Procedure provide that a federal jury for a civil case must have at least six jurors at the outset of the case and may have up to no more than 12. Unless the parties agree otherwise, the verdict must be unanimous and returned by a jury of at least six.[23]

For a federal criminal case, the Federal Rules of Criminal Procedure require a 12-person jury unless, before the verdict is rendered, the parties agree with the court's approval in writing that the jury may be smaller; or if the court finds it necessary to excuse a juror for good cause after the trial begins.[24] Also, even without the agreement of the parties, the judge may permit a jury of 11 persons to return a verdict if the court finds good cause to excuse a juror.[25] A unanimous verdict is required in any federal criminal case.[26]

b. State Court

State court rules and statutes set the jury's numerical size. However, the required number of jurors and how the number is reached varies from state to state. For example, civil rules may provide, as the New York rules do, that a

---

22. *Ballew v. Georgia*, 435 U.S. 223, 239 (1978).
23. FED. R. CIV. P. 48(a) and (b).
24. FED. R. CRIM. P. 23(b)(1) and (2).
25. FED. R. CRIM. P. 23(b)(3).
26. FED. R. CRIM. P. 31(a).

civil jury shall be composed of six people.[27] Or, for example, the state of Washington rules provide: "If before the case is called to be set for trial no party serves or files a demand that the case be tried by a jury of twelve, it shall be tried by a jury of six members with the concurrence of five being required to reach a verdict." Additionally, Washington rules provide that "[t]he parties may stipulate that the jury shall consist of any number less than 12 or that a verdict or a finding of a stated majority of the jurors shall be taken as the verdict or finding of the jury."[28]

A state court rule for criminal trials may dictate a 12-person jury unless prior to trial the defendants elect to have the case tried by a jury of not less than six persons. While most states require a unanimous verdict, a verdict of ten out of twelve has been held constitutional.[29] But, to be constitutional, the verdict of six jurors must be unanimous.[30]

2. Alternate Jurors

a. Federal Court

The practice of using alternate jurors in federal civil cases was abolished in 1991 because of dissatisfaction with the practice of having alternates sit through the trial without giving them the gratification of deliberating.[31] If a problem with a juror arises during trial or deliberations, the court for good cause may excuse the juror and that will not result in a mistrial.[32] Because at least six jurors are required to return a verdict, the court, particularly in a lengthy case, will select more than six jurors for a civil case. In other words, if the court seats a panel of ten jurors, all of those jurors will deliberate even though only six are required. This may have important implications for the parties, because it can be much more difficult to obtain ten unanimous votes than it is to obtain six.

---

27. N.Y. C.P.L.R. 4105 (McKinney 2015).

28. WASH. SUPERIOR COURT CIV. R. 38(b) and 48.

29. *Apodaca v. Oregon*, 406 U.S. 404 (1972).

30. *Burch v. Louisiana*, 441 U.S. 130 (1979).

31. Notes of the Advisory Committee on Rules on 1991 Amendment to FED. R. CRIM. P. 47.

32. Notes of the Advisory Committee on Rules on 1991 Amendment to FED. R. CRIM. P. 47(c): "This provision makes it clear that the court may in appropriate circumstances excuse a juror during the jury deliberations without causing a mistrial. Sickness, family emergency or juror misconduct that might occasion a mistrial are examples of appropriate grounds for excusing a juror. It is not grounds for the dismissal of a juror that the juror refuses to join with fellow jurors in reaching a unanimous verdict."

For a federal criminal case, the court can impanel up to six alternates.[33] Alternates must have the same qualifications as the other jurors and have the same authority as other jurors, and they are selected and sworn in the same way.[34] An alternate replaces a juror who is disqualified or unable to serve in the order in which the alternate was selected. For example, the alternate who was first seated replaces the first juror who leaves the jury box.[35] A court may retain the alternates after the jury begins deliberations in case a regular juror needs replacing, and if a replacement by an alternate occurs, the jury deliberations start over again.[36]

b. State Court

State court rules and statutes provide that the court may impanel alternate jurors in addition to the required number of jurors for both criminal and civil cases.[37] Alternates are available to replace regular jurors who are disqualified or prove unable to serve during the trial or jury deliberations. The number of alternates usually depends on the nature of the case and the expected length of trial.

E. The Public Trial and a Criminal Defendant's Right to Be Present

Under the Sixth and Fourteenth Amendments to the United States Constitution, a defendant in a criminal case has the rights to a public trial and to be present at all critical stages of trial, and that includes voir dire. The United States Supreme Court has affirmed that jury selection is "a critical stage of the criminal proceeding, during which the defendant has a constitutional right to be present."[38] In *Gomez v. United States*, 490 U.S. 858 (1989), the Supreme Court noted that jury selection is "the primary means by which a court may enforce a defendant's right to be tried by a jury free from ethnic, racial, or political prejudice, or predisposition about the defendant's culpability."

---

33. Fed. R. Crim. P. 24(c)(1).
34. Fed. R. Crim. P. 24(c)(2)(A) and (B).
35. Fed. R. Crim. P. 24(c)(2)(B).
36. Fed. R. Crim. P. 24(c)(3).
37. *See, e.g.*, Wash. Superior Court Civ. R. 47(b); Wash. State Superior Court Crim. R. 6.5.
38. *Gomez v. United States*, 490 U.S. 858, 873 (1989).

1. Right to a Public Trial

The right to a public trial exists at all critical stages of a criminal trial, which includes voir dire.[39] However, good reasons may exist to close the courtroom during voir dire, such as when sensitive matters need to be explored, and, thus, the right to a public trial is not an absolute right. If counsel wishes to have the courtroom closed for any portion of jury selection, the trial court must make findings specific enough to justify the closure. In *Waller v. Georgia*, 467 U.S. 39, 47 (1984), the Supreme Court reviewed a defendant's challenge to a closure order under the Sixth Amendment public trial right. In doing so, the Court quoted its earlier decision's standard from closure cases brought under the First Amendment's protection of public access to trials, as follows:

> The presumption of openness may be overcome only by an overriding interest based on findings that closure is essential to preserve higher values and is narrowly tailored to serve that interest. The interest is to be articulated along with findings specific enough that a reviewing court can determine whether the closure order was properly entered.[40]

The Washington State Supreme Court in *State v. Bone-Club* has held that a trial judge may close the courtroom after considering the following five criteria:

1. The proponent of closure or sealing must make some showing [of a compelling interest], and where that need is based on a right other than an accused's right to a fair trial, the proponent must show a "serious and imminent threat" to that right.
2. Anyone present when the closure motion is made must be given an opportunity to object to the closure.
3. The proposed method for curtailing open access must be the least restrictive means available for protecting the threatened interests.
4. The court must weigh the competing interests of the proponent of closure and the public.
5. The order must be no broader in its application or duration than necessary to serve its purpose.[41]

---

39. *Nebraska Press Ass'n. v. Stuart*, 427 U.S. 539 (1976); *Press-Enterprise v. Superior Court*, 464 U.S. 501 (1984); *Press Enterprise v. Superior Court*, 478 U.S. 1 (1986).

40. *Waller*, 467 U.S. at 45 (*quoting Press-Enterprise Co. v. Superior Court*, 464 U.S. 501 (1984).

41. *State v. Bone-Club*, 128 Wash. 2d 254, 258–59 (1995).

Failure by a trial court in the state of Washington to conduct an analysis under these criteria can result in reversal of a conviction. For example in *State v. Strode*, when the judge had jury members brought into judge's chambers to be questioned on sensitive topics with the judge, prosecuting attorney, defense counsel and the defendant present without doing an analysis under the five *Bone-Club* criteria, the Washington State Supreme Court held that the defendant's right to a public trial had been violated.[42]

In a civil case, *NBC Subsidiary, Inc. v. Superior Court*,[43] the California Supreme Court held that all court proceedings were to be open to the public, stating: "in general, the First Amendment provides a right of access to ordinary civil trials and proceedings, that constitutional standards governing closure of trial proceedings apply in the civil setting, and that section 124 must, accordingly, be interpreted in a manner compatible with those standards."

Regardless of whether or not parts of jury selection are closed to the public, courts will often seal personal information provided by jurors through questionnaires administered by the courts. In many instances, judges do not allow the attorneys to even leave the courtroom with the completed juror questionnaires.

It is essential that you be familiar with your local law regarding a public trial and voir dire. Some states have court rules governing procedures. For example, Minnesota Court Rule 26.01 Subd. 4 specifically addresses voir dire and public trial issues as follows:

(4) Exclusion of the Public From Voir Dire. In those rare cases where it is necessary, the following rules govern orders excluding the public from any part of voir dire or restricting access to the orders or to transcripts of the closed proceeding.

(a) Advisory. When it appears prospective jurors may be asked sensitive or embarrassing questions during voir dire, the court may on its own initiative or on request of either party, advise the prospective jurors that they may request an opportunity to address the court in camera, with counsel and defendant present, concerning their desire to exclude the public from voir dire when the sensitive or embarrassing questions are asked.

(b) In Camera Hearing. If a prospective juror requests an opportunity to address the court in camera during sensitive or em-

---

42. *See generally State v. Strode*, 167 Wash. 2d 222 (2009). A similar holding was reached in *State v. Wise*, 176 Wash. 2d 1 (2012).

43. *NBC Subsidiary, Inc. v. Superior Court*, 20 Cal. 4th 1178 (1999).

barrassing questioning, the request must be granted. The hearing must be on the record with counsel and the defendant present.

(c) Standards. In considering the request to exclude the public during voir dire, the court must balance the juror's privacy interests, the defendant's right to a fair and public trial, and the public's interest in access to the courts. The court may order voir dire closed only if it finds a substantial likelihood that conducting voir dire in open court would interfere with an overriding interest, including the defendant's right to a fair trial and the juror's legitimate privacy interests in not disclosing deeply personal matters to the public. The court must consider alternatives to closure. Any closure must be no broader than necessary to protect the overriding interest.

(d) Refusal to Close Voir Dire. If the court determines no overriding interest exists to justify excluding the public from voir dire, the voir dire must continue in open court on the record.

(e) Closure of Voir Dire. If the court determines that an overriding interest justifies closure of any part of voir dire, that part of voir dire must be conducted in camera on the record with counsel and the defendant present.

2. Right to Be Present

A defendant in a criminal case has the right to be present at all critical stages of trial.[44] This includes being present during jury selection and when the jury is impaneled.[45] For example, in *State v. Irby*, the Washington State Supreme Court held that the defendant's Fourteenth Amendment right to be present was violated when the trial court dismissed seven potential jurors by email in the absence of the defendant. That error was not harmless, and the conviction was reversed.[46]

A defendant may waive the constitutional right to be present at trial provided the waiver is voluntary, knowing and intelligent.[47] Therefore, the defendant should be present throughout voir dire unless the defendant has properly waived presence.

---

44. *Rushen v. Spain*, 464 U.S. 114, 117 (1983); *State v. Irby*, 170 Wash. 2d 874, 880–81 (2011).

45. *Diaz v. United States*, 223 U.S. 442, 455 (1912).

46. *State v. Irby*, 170 Wash. 2d 874, 877, 887 (2011).

47. *Taylor v. United States*, 414 U.S. 17, 19–20 (1973).

F. Swearing in the Panel

At the outset of jury selection, the judge swears in the panel of prospective jurors to fully and truthfully answer questions posed to them during jury selection. This is the first oath taken. Jurors who eventually are impaneled to hear the case take a second oath to well and truly try the case.

G. Judge's Introductory Remarks

The judge usually familiarizes the jury panel with the court, the procedures, and the case to be tried. During these remarks, the judge ordinarily will introduce the lower bench—clerk, bailiff and court reporter—and other court personnel, and call upon the lawyers to introduce themselves and their clients. When called upon, counsel should stand and say something like, "Thank you your honor, my name is…, and I represent Ms. Bigelow who is seated here on my right."

While the introductory remarks to the jury vary from judge to judge, some topics customarily covered in those remarks include: reading the charges in a criminal case; an abbreviated description of the nature of a civil case; a discussion of the juror's role; and an explanation of the jury selection process and the trial.

Judge's Introductory Remarks Example: Judge Leonard Davis in the antitrust case of *Retractable Technologies, Inc. v. Becton, Dickinson and Company* made the following remarks:

> THE COURT: All right. Very well.
>
> All right. Good morning, Ladies and Gentlemen of the Jury. I am United States District Judge Leonard Davis, and I want to welcome you to jury service in the Eastern District of Texas.
>
> Let me start by thanking you for your service here today. I know I can tell by some of the looks on your faces that on the Tuesday after Labor Day a lot of you would like to be some place other than where you are today.
>
> But I do want to just take a moment to remind you about our country and the right to trial by jury. And in this country we have that right. That is a right that is not enjoyed in hardly any other country in the world.

And I think we only have to turn on the evening news to see how disputes get settled in a lot of other countries in the world. So we are very fortunate to live in this country, to have this method of resolving disputes, which these two parties have between them; but it could not happen without you being here and being part of the process by being the jury that will decide this case.

So I hope even though you would probably rather be somewhere else this morning, that you will consider it a small price to pay for the freedoms that we enjoy in this country and look on it much—as your small contribution. Just as our military contributes to protect our freedoms, this is part of your small contribution to do that; and view it in that light.

So this is a civil lawsuit where the plaintiff, Retractable Technologies—which Mr. Carroll just announced for—and Mr. Thomas Shaw were the plaintiffs, Retractable, and Mr. Shaw accused the defendant, Becton Dickinson, of antitrust violations, false advertising, product disparagement, and tortious interference with prospective contract or business relations.

I and the parties will have much more to say about what the causes of action and the legal theories are involved in this dispute later, but I wanted you to have that basic knowledge of what the case is about.

I anticipate that the presentation of evidence in this case will take probably eight days. So this case is going to take up basically two weeks.

This morning we are selecting the jury, and that is all that we will do today. So—and I would guess that will take us until about noon today, and then all of you will be released at that time.

Eight of you will be selected to be on the jury in this case to decide that case. We will not hold court in this case any more this week. We are just picking the jury. And the eight of you that are selected will come back next Monday, and we will begin hearing evidence on next Monday. We will plan to go through Thursday. And we will take Friday off.

We normally go from about 9:00 in the morning until 4:00 in the afternoon. It is going to take, like I said, basically two weeks; I think eight days of testimony, so—seven to eight. So we will start on Monday, go through Thursday of next week, come back the next week, start on Monday, and probably go through Thursday or Friday and hopefully finish the case that week.

Right now, though, we are beginning the first stage of the trial, which is what we call Voir Dire Examination.

This is where the Court and the attorneys will be asking you some questions to help us evaluate you as a potential jury in this case. This will probably take about an hour or so.

Each side is then allowed to strike a certain number of jurors, and the first remaining eight jurors will be sworn in as the jury which will decide this case.

When we come back next Monday you will next hear the opening statements of the attorneys, which are what they believe that the evidence is going to show in the case. And then we will begin the presentation of the evidence.

The plaintiff will present their evidence first, testimony, exhibits. The defendant will cross-examine. And the defendant will have an opportunity to present evidence. And the plaintiff will have an opportunity to cross-examine. And then, finally, the plaintiff will have an opportunity to put on some rebuttal evidence. That will take up the majority of the time.

After all of the evidence is in, I will then give you what is called the Court's charge or jury instructions. That is where I will instruct you in detail on the law that you must follow in deciding the case.

After you have heard the Court's charge, then you will hear closing arguments by the attorneys for both sides. This is where they sum up or give a summation of what they believe that the evidence has shown in the case and what your verdict should be.

So that is an overview of what will be going on in the case. After you have heard the closing arguments, then the eight of you that are selected will retire to the jury room, begin your deliberations, and reach a verdict in the case.

Now, back to what we are doing today, voir dire.

The purpose of voir dire is to enable the Court to determine whether or not any prospective juror should be excused from jury service either by the Court, for what we call cause, or by counsel for the parties by way of what we call a preemptory challenge. That is a challenge for which no reason need be given.

"Voir dire" is a Latin phrase which means "to speak the truth," which I know each of you will do as you answer the questions which will be asked of you this morning.

Please listen very carefully to the questions asked of you, and do not be timid to speak up if they apply to you.

In other words, as you hear these questions if you are sitting there in the back of your mind going, well, I'm not sure whether that question applies to me or not, please go ahead and raise your hand and answer. We would rather have too much information than not enough information. And in answering these questions it is very important that you answer fully and completely.

If at any time there is a question that you would rather not discuss in front of everyone, just say: Judge, could I discuss that with you at the bench later? And I will be glad to do that with you.[48]

H. Questioning the Jurors

1. Judicial Discretion and Its Limits

The trial court has broad discretion in conducting jury selection. The United States Supreme Court in *Mu'Min v. Virginia* stated:

> This Court's cases have stressed the wide discretion granted to trial courts in conducting voir dire in the area of pretrial publicity and in other areas that might tend to show juror bias. For example, in holding that a trial court's voir dire questioning must "cover the subject" of possible juror racial bias, *Aldridge v. United States,* 283 U.S. 308, 311, the Court was careful not to specify the particulars by which this could be done.[49]

Because trial courts have wide discretion in how they structure jury selection, the process of who questions the prospective jurors, the time allotted for jury selection and how they are questioned varies from the federal to state and local court levels and at each level from courtroom to courtroom. In some courts, the judges do all the questioning, and in others, the attorneys freely engage in wide-ranging conversations with the prospective jurors. Indeed in some courts, some counsel will attempt to virtually try the case during jury selection. Some judges allow counsel to amble around the courtroom, but in others, judges require attorneys to stand behind a podium. Some judges have strict time limits for attorney questioning while other judges do not. Some judges allow attorneys to ask questions to the entire venire while others prefer that attorneys only ask questions to those jurors seated in the box.

---

48. Transcript of Proceedings at 1–2, *Retractable Techs., Inc. v. Becton, Dickinson and Co.,* 2:08cv16 E.D. (Tex. Sept. 3, 2013), App. 1.2.

49. *Mu'Min v. Virginia,* 500 U.S. 415, 415 (1991); *see also Rosales-Lopez v. United States,* 451 U.S. 189 (1981).

As counsel, you must know what the protocols are in your courtroom and what the judge expects of you. What may seem the most efficient and sensible is not always what the court will do. Consequently, it is important that you not make assumptions about how the jury selection process will proceed. If you know who your trial judge will be before the trial date and have not tried a case before the judge, it is good practice to watch the judge during jury selection. If that is not possible, speak with someone who is acquainted with the court's practices. Often, the court clerks are willing to provide guidance on how the judge prefers to conduct jury selection. Some judges describe their preferences for the jury selection process online or in a handout.

2. Questioning by Judge, Attorneys or Both

Who should question the jury? It has been argued that when only the judge questions the jurors, it conserves court time and eliminates attorney abuse of the process through such things as trying to ingratiate themselves with the jurors, indoctrinate them or even introduce evidence. It has also been argued that exclusive judicial questioning is as effective, if not more so, in seating a fair and impartial jury than when counsel is involved in questioning.

Others take the contrary position, arguing that because the attorneys know more about the case than the judge, the lawyers are able to extract more pertinent and reliable information. Also, from the attorney's perspective, it allows the attorney to gain some rapport with the jurors and to test out the prospective jurors' receptiveness to case theories. Finally, many judges impose limitations on the types of questions they will ask. For example, many judges limit their questions to past experiences of the jurors, relationships to the parties, and direct questions about specific biases against the parties, but are unwilling to ask questions about general case-related attitudes or beliefs.

The extent and content of the judge's questioning differs from judge to judge. The judge may just ask general questions as to juror qualifications or ask more specific questions regarding the case. And the judge may decide to ask follow-up questions if attorney questioning perks the judge's curiosity.

In most cases, it is beneficial for the attorneys to have the opportunity to ask questions of the jurors. It is rare that it would make sense for an attorney to give up the opportunity to directly question members of the jury panel.

a. Judge-Only Questioning

Federal judges have broad discretion in conducting jury selection, and may allow counsel to question the prospective jurors. Federal Rule of Civil Procedure 47(a) regarding selecting jurors states:

The court may permit the parties or their attorneys to examine prospective jurors or may itself do so. If the court examines the jurors, it must permit the parties or their attorneys to make any further inquiry it considers proper, or must itself ask any of their additional questions it considers proper.

The Federal Rule for criminal cases likewise grants the court authority to "examine prospective jurors or may permit the attorneys for the parties to do so."[50]

Under both the civil and criminal rules, a federal judge may conduct jury selection without any direct questioning by the lawyers. Under this approach, the attorneys submit questions to the federal judge to ask if the judge deems the questions proper.[51] The federal judge may require that counsel submit any questions in advance of the day of jury selection and require that the questions be close-ended and call for a "yes" or "no" answer.[52]

b. Attorney-Only Questioning

In some courts, the attorneys conduct the questioning of the prospective jurors with little or no judicial involvement except to protect against abuses. For example, in New York, the rule provides that, in civil cases, a party may apply for judicial presence during jury selection.[53]

c. Shared Questioning

In most state trial courts, questioning is shared between the judge and lawyers. Currently, the trend is towards federal judges allowing attorneys to directly share in the questioning of prospective jurors, rather than just submitting questions to the court. Although, in most cases, federal judges put greater limitations on the amount of time attorneys have to ask questions of the panel. In Chapter 14, we discuss making motions for follow-up questioning by counsel and for additional time to question the prospective jurors.

---

50. Fed. R. Crim. P. 24(a).

51. Fed. R. Civ. P. 47(a); Fed. R. Crim. P. 24(a).

52. Honorable Martha J. Pechman, *Voir Dire*, United District Court Western District of Washington, http://www.wawd.uscourts.gov/sites/wawd/files/PechmanVoirDire.pdf (Jan. 17, 2017).

53. N.Y. C.P.L.R. 4107 (McKinney 2011).

3. General Questions from the Bench

a. Hardship Questions

After making introductory remarks, the judge ordinarily will ask general questions directed at the whole panel. The judge's initial questioning will be fashioned to elicit claims by the prospective juror that they cannot serve because they have a hardship justifying being excused from jury service. The federal Jury Act provides that the court may excuse a prospective juror from service at the time summoned on the grounds of "undue hardship or extreme inconvenience."[54] State court rules provide for a similar approach and decision-making.[55] Hardship claims can include such things as medical, financial or employment difficulties. The judge will hear and decide upon each prospective juror's request.

While there is no set standard for determining "undue hardship or extreme inconvenience," the most common categories of individuals who are excused for hardship are those who are self-employed, those who have nonrefundable vacation plans, and those who will not be paid by their employer for the entire length of the trial.

As with many aspects of the jury selection process, the standards for granting hardship requests vary from judge to judge. Some judges are much more liberal when excusing jurors for hardship while others apply much higher standards that result in fewer jurors being excused.

The size of the jury panel may also influence the judge's willingness to excuse jurors for hardship. Judges try to remain conscious of how many panel members they will need to achieve the desired number of jurors. In some instances, judges deny hardship requests that they may have otherwise granted out of concern that they may "bust the panel," meaning they will be left with an insufficient number of jurors to complete the jury selection process.

Some judges will also seek input from the attorneys on each side about a hardship request, particularly when the judge is uncertain over whether or not she wants to grant the hardship request. These instances can often involve strategic moves by the attorneys. For example, if one side believes the bottom of the panel contains a lot of good jurors for them, they may urge the judge to release more jurors for hardship in order to reach that group of good jurors. Conversely, the other side may urge the judge to keep those jurors on the panel.

---

54. 28 U.S.C. § 1866(c)(1) (2008).
55. *See, e.g.,* WASH. CIV. R. 6.4(c)(1).

You need to pay close attention to and note the potential juror's hardship claim if the person remains on the panel, because that claim and how the court responded to it may affect the person's views and attitudes towards the trial and the players. The popular belief is that a plaintiff's attorney does not want a juror on the final panel who does not want to serve as a juror or who is inconvenienced by jury service. The plaintiff's attorney may believe that this juror will be less willing to award a large monetary figure if his jury service is creating a financial hardship. However, there is no research to support this common belief.

b. Other General Questions

In addition to questioning the prospective jurors about hardship, the judge usually will ask other general questions of the panel unless either the answers to the questions have been covered by the court's juror questionnaire, which was filled out in advance of voir dire, or the court's practice is to have the lawyers ask general questions. General questions are designed to help identify any person who might not be qualified to be a juror or should be excused, such as whether they know any of the parties or their counsel. These general questions can be answered "yes" or "no."

The following is an example of a Jury General Questioning chart, which a state trial judge sometimes provides to counsel to use when she poses her general questions to the jury. Each prospective juror is provided a card with a number on it. The judge instructs the panel that when she asks a general question, the panel members should hold up their cards if their answer is in the affirmative, and then the judge and lawyers can note their juror numbers on the chart. In the second column, counsel can write the number of the responding jurors seated in the jury box, and in the third column, they can write the numbers of other members of the panel who are seated in the spectator section.

This Jury General Questioning chart is a handy tool that you can use at trial because if these fundamental questions are neither asked by the judge nor otherwise put to the jurors, such as through a juror questionnaire, you can ask them to the panel.

If no chart or list of general questions is provided in your case, you will need a system for recording panel member responses, and suggested systems are discussed on pages 108–110.

Question	# in Jury Box	# on Jury Panel
1. Have you heard of this case before?		
2. Do you know any of the parties in this case, either the plaintiff or the defendant?		
3. Have any of you had any business dealings with either the plaintiff or the defendant companies?		
4. Have you had any business dealings with either the plaintiff or the defendant?		
5. The plaintiff is represented by _____ of the law firm of _____. Do any of you know _____ or have any of you had any contact with any members of his/her law firm?		
6. The defendant is represented by _____. of the law firm of _____. Do any of you know _____. or have any of you had any contact with any members of his/her law firm?		
7. Do any of you know any of the following individuals who may be called as witnesses in this case: (joint statement of evidence: witnesses)		
8. It is anticipated that the trial will last ____ days. Does this schedule present an undue hardship to any prospective juror?		
9. Do you or any of your relatives or close friends have any connection in any way with the court system or the administration of justice?		
10. Have any of you been a witness in a court proceeding?		
11. Have any of you served as a juror in a civil case?		
12. Have any of you served as a juror in a criminal case?		
13. Has any prospective juror ever studied or practiced law, medicine, or _____.?		
14. Do any of you have any ethical, moral or philosophical views that may cause you to feel uncomfortable sitting as a juror in a case where one party is asking for a money judgment against another?		

15. This case involves an _____. Have any of you or a close friend or relative had any experience with a similar or related type of case or incident?		
16. This case also involves an _____. Have any of you or a close friend or relative had any experience with a similar or related type of case or incident?		
17. Evidence may show that events in this case took place at or near _____. Are any prospective jurors particularly familiar with this location?		
18. Evidence presented in this case may discuss _____. Do any prospective jurors have such strong feelings about _____ that you would not be able to act impartially?		
19. Do any prospective jurors have an ailment that would make it uncomfortable to sit for several hours a day during trial (such as a bad back, etc.)?		
20. Does any prospective juror have any other ailment or disability that you believe would prevent you from sitting as a juror in this case?		

4. Questioning by the Lawyers

a. Preliminary Remarks

In a shared jury-selection process, after the court has questioned the panel, the judge turns questioning over to you and opposing counsel to ask questions. The extent to which you may make preliminary remarks to the panel before you begin asking question depends upon whether the judge permits any comments at all and, if so, what the court will allow counsel to say and for how long. Some judges may allow mini-openings, also referred to as "preliminary remarks" or "introductory remarks," before attorney voir dire begins. You need to determine what is permitted prior to trial. You do not want the judge to interrupt you in the middle of your introductory remarks with an admonishment that you should move along to questioning. See pages 196–197, 210, and 213–213 for a further discussion of introductory remarks and examples.

b. Time Allotted

The judge may set a reasonable time limit or number-of-questions limit for attorney questioning of the prospective jurors. For example, a trial judge may set time limits such as 30 minutes per round of attorney questioning of the prospective jurors. Typically, state court judges allow longer periods of time for attorney questioning than do federal judges.

However, when state law provides that counsel may orally question jurors during voir dire, the trial court cannot abuse its discretion by imposing unreasonable time limits that interfere with counsel's right to ascertain hidden juror prejudgments, and the court should give counsel reasonable advance notice of the time limit before commencement of trial. Failure to provide adequate time can result in reversal of the verdict.[56] At pages 319–320, we discuss a motion for reasonable amount of time for attorney questioning and provide a sample motion.

If the court does not impose a time limit, you should gauge the amount of time you spend asking questions based upon the complexity and seriousness of the case and both the judge's and the jury's tolerance level. Attorney questioning that unnecessarily goes on and on may send the message to the jury that you are inefficient, disorganized, and wasteful of their time.

c. Your Placement in the Courtroom

Generally, in federal court and in some state and municipal courts, you will be required to stand behind a podium. In other courts, you can move about the courtroom. However, if you stand behind a podium, it appears that you are lecturing instead of carrying on a conversation with the jurors. Therefore, to the extent that court protocol permits, position yourself away from the lectern and in a place where you are as visible as possible to the prospective jurors. If you are required to use the podium, you may be able to step to the side of the podium so the prospective jurors can see all of you.

While ideally you should be in close proximity to the jurors because that will enhance your communication with them, do not invade their space. To speak to prospective jurors in the spectator gallery, you may need to move about the courtroom.

---

56. *Campbell v. State*, 812 So. 2d 540, 541 (Fla. 4th DCA 2002); *Carver v. Niedermayer*, 920 So. 2d 123, 124–25 (Fla. Dist. Ct. App. 2006).

d. Questioning Process

When the judge and counsel share questioning, the judge may ask general questions and then allow counsel to ask general questions of the panel as well. Or, the judge may finish asking general questions and then turn it over to counsel who may intersperse general questions to the panel with questions directed to specific jurors. If the court has already asked and received responses to a question, you should not repeat the court's question, not only to avoid being repetitious but also because the judge is likely to interrupt you to point out the question has already been asked and answered. On the other hand, following up on a response to the court's questions is good practice.

For planning purposes, you need to ascertain where you are in the order of attorney questioning. Court procedure may call for the plaintiff to go first in questioning followed by the defendant, or the order may be the reverse with the defense commencing the questioning. Additionally, if there are multiple defendants, it is important to know which order the defense attorneys will go in for voir dire. The presence of multiple defendants can sometimes complicate the process. For example, the court may not allow the attorneys for each defendant their own allocation of voir dire time. Instead, the court may force the attorneys to share voir dire time and peremptory challenges, leaving it to the defense attorneys to determine how to best divide and use the time.

The court may well allow rounds of questioning. For instance, plaintiff's counsel has a round of questioning followed by the defense attorney and then another turn by plaintiff's counsel followed by a finishing round of questions by defense counsel. Sometimes, the court will predetermine how much time the attorneys have for each segment. In other instances, the court will provide a set amount of overall voir dire time and leave it up to the attorneys as to how they want to divide that time between their two rounds of questioning.

If you are first in the order of questioning, you can plan to ask the type of subjects listed in the forgoing Jury Questioning chart found at pages 32–33 if the judge does not inquire about them. Also, if the court permits, you may ask questions that introduce the panel to your case theory and theme. If the judge has inadvertently not introduced the court personnel (court reporter, bailiff, clerk), you can take the opportunity to make the introductions if you feel comfortable doing that or diplomatically bring this omission to the court's attention, allowing the judge to do the honors. It is a nice gesture towards these important people.

If you know you will be going second, you can plan to ask questions that probably will not have already been covered by the court and opposing counsel. Also, you can anticipate opposing counsel's questions and strategies and formulate introductory remarks and questions to counteract them.

Rather than addressing your questions to the panel, the court in which you appear might follow a procedure of individual-juror questioning. Under the individual-questioning approach, the attorneys question the prospective jurors one at a time with one lawyer asking questions followed by the opposing lawyer. After questioning the individual prospective juror, counsel either announces to the court "pass for cause" (not challenged for cause by the lawyer) or challenges the prospective juror. If challenged and removed by the court, the prospective juror's chair is filled with another from the panel who is then individually questioned. Once the requisite number of prospective jurors have filled the juror chairs and have been passed for cause, the lawyers exercise peremptory challenges.

Additionally, the court may require that attorneys only ask questions to those jurors seated in the box. When a juror in the box is excused and replaced by a new juror, the attorneys will stand up again and ask the new juror each of the previous questions. This can be a very inefficient process, but is sometimes used across the country.

Also, the court may decide to conduct individual questioning of a juror outside the presence of other jurors under circumstance when either the juror's answer might poison the rest of the panel or the inquiry may be about a sensitive subject. Individual voir dire may be used in cases that have been highly publicized, involve a sexual assault, or when the juror indicates a desire to discuss a matter privately.

I. Accepting the Panel

It is also important that you finish exercising your challenges in a potent way. When you have no further challenges that you want to exercise, rise, look over the jury one more time, look each juror in the eyes, and then confidently say, "Your Honor. We accept the jury as presently constituted." When you say this and look them in the eyes you can convey to them that you have a bond with them. It is your responsibility to be a seeker of truth and someone they can trust, and in turn, they are people you trust to well and truly try the case. Note that if your opponent exercises another peremptory challenge after you accept the panel, you can still exercise a peremptory against the replacement prospective juror.

J. Rules of Professional Conduct and Jury Selection

Pretrial and through the trial and even post-trial, trial counsel are obligated to ensure that trial by jury in this country means a trial by a fair and impartial jury. Trial lawyers must avoid even the appearance that they either improperly communicated with the prospective jurors or subjected them to any improper influence. Every jurisdiction has ethics rules to this effect. In almost every jurisdiction, those ethics rules are either identical to or a modified version of the Model Rules of Professional Conduct.

1. Rules for Jury Impartiality

Under Model Rule of Professional Conduct 3.5(b), counsel may not communicate with the jurors or prospective jurors during the proceedings unless authorized by court order or law.[57] The best practice is to avoid even the appearance that you have communicated with a prospective juror before or during trial. This includes indirect contact, such as through and investigator.

If the court has not already done so, attorneys can request that the judge inform the jurors that the attorneys have been told not to communicate to the jurors in any way, shape, or form. This instruction can help jurors understand that the attorney is not intending to be rude if an attorney sees them in the hallway, courthouse elevator or elsewhere and ignores them.

After a prospective juror has been discharged or the trial jury has been dismissed, rules and/or court practice in many jurisdictions allow the trial lawyers to speak with the jurors. When post-trial contact is permitted, some judges only allow the lawyers to speak with jurors after the verdict has come in, but before they leave the courthouse. Other judges allow lawyers to contact jurors in the days or weeks after a verdict has been delivered and jurors have been discharged. It is critical that counsel knows what the court permits. For example, Florida's federal district courts have local rules requiring that an attorney seek court approval prior to interviewing jurors and allow the court to limit the time, place, and manner under which the interview shall be conducted. Also, the rule requires that counsel avoid embarrassing any juror or influencing the juror's action in any subsequent jury service.[58]

No matter what the court's protocol and rules are for post-trial contact, a lawyer is prohibited from speaking to a juror who declines to communicate with the lawyer, and a lawyer may not harass, coerce or make misrepresentations to the discharged juror.[59] The reasoning is that the juror may be a juror on a future case.

Model Rule of Professional Conduct 3.5 provides that a lawyer must not:

---

57. Model Rules of Prof'l. Conduct r. 3.5(b).
58. S.D. Fla. Dist. Ct. R. 16(E).
59. Model Rules of Prof'l. Conduct r. 3.5(c).

(a) seek to influence a judge, juror, prospective juror or other official by means prohibited by law;

(b) communicate ex parte with such a person during the proceeding unless authorized to do so by law or court order;

(c) communicate with a juror or prospective juror after discharge of the jury if:

    (1) the communication is prohibited by law or court order;

    (2) the juror has made known to the lawyer a desire not to communicate; or

    (3) the communication involves misrepresentation, coercion, duress or harassment....

Attorney communication or contact with prospective jurors that violates the Rules of Professional Conduct includes communication through the Internet. When the New York Bar Association was queried about Internet communication with potential jurors, it issued an Ethics Opinion as follows:

> It is proper and ethical under MODEL RULES OF PROF'L. CONDUCT r. 3.5 for a lawyer to undertake a pretrial search of a prospective juror's social networking site, provided that there is no contact or communication with the prospective juror and the lawyer does not seek to "friend" jurors, subscribe to their Twitter accounts, send jurors tweets or otherwise contact them.[60]

It is important for lawyers to be aware of how social networking sites work. For example, some social networking sites send a message to users that someone has viewed their profile. Sometimes, specific information about who has viewed their profile is provided to them. LinkedIn is one example of a social networking site that contains such features. We discuss this further on page 94.

2. Rules Regarding Trial Publicity

Rules of Professional Conduct govern extrajudicial statements that a lawyer may and may not make about the case. Specifically, a lawyer should not make "an extrajudicial statement that the lawyer knows or reasonably should know will be disseminated by means of public communication and will have a substantial likelihood of materially prejudicing an adjudicative proceeding in the matter."[61] However, under the Model Rules, a lawyer may state:

---

60. N.Y. Cnty. Lawyers' Ass'n. on Ethics, Formal Op. 743 (May 18, 2011).

61. MODEL RULES OF PROF'L. CONDUCT r. 3.6(a).

(1) the claim, offense or defense involved and, except when prohibited by law, the identity of the persons involved;

(2) information contained in a public record;

(3) that an investigation of a matter is in progress;

(4) the scheduling or result of any step in litigation;

(5) a request for assistance in obtaining evidence and information necessary thereto;

(6) a warning of danger concerning the behavior of a person involved, when there is reason to believe that there exists the likelihood of substantial harm to an individual or to the public interest; and

(7) in a criminal case, in addition to subparagraphs (1) through (6):

   (i) the identity, residence, occupation and family status of the accused;

   (ii) if the accused has not been apprehended, information necessary to aid in apprehension of that person;

   (iii) the fact, time and place of arrest; and

   (iv) the identity of investigating and arresting officers or agencies and the length of the investigation.[62]

Model Rule 3.6(b)(7) authorizes prosecutors to release information in the interest of the public's right to know, such as the criminal charge and other matters of public record.

---

62. MODEL RULES OF PROF'L. CONDUCT r. 3.6(b).

Chapter 3

Challenges

"The decision today will not end the racial discrimination that peremptories inject into the jury selection process. That goal can be accomplished only by eliminating peremptory challenges entirely."

Thurgood Marshall,
Justice, United States Supreme Court
Batson v. Kentucky, 476 U.S. 79, 102–3 (1986)

"The State's new argument today does not dissuade us from the conclusion that its prosecutors were motivated in substantial part by race when they struck Garrett and Hood from the jury 30 years ago. Two peremptory strikes on the basis of race are two more than the Constitution allows."

John Roberts,
Chief Justice, United States Supreme Court
Foster v. Chatman, 136 S. Ct. 1737, 1755 (2016)

A. Challenges to Prospective Jurors

1. Three Types of Challenges

Challenges to prospective jurors fall into three categories:

1. Challenge to the pool;
2. Challenge for cause; and
3. Peremptory challenge.

In this chapter, we examine challenges for cause and peremptory challenges and how to exercise them. Also, we explain how to respond to the other side's challenges. Illustrative examples of how to challenge and respond are provided.

If you conclude that the jury pool was not properly selected, you can make a pretrial motion to challenge it. This is also referred to as a "challenge to the array." Ordinarily, challenges to the pool are made on the grounds that the jury pool fails to meet the constitutional requirement of a fair cross-section of the community, and it excludes a distinctive group in the community. In Chapter 14 on motions and responses regarding jury selection, we cover motions challenging the jury pool.

2. Have a Record

To be able to appeal any error made during jury selection, you must have a record of the error. You may wish to appeal the court's decision to refuse your challenge for cause. You may wish to appeal the judge's refusal to grant your *Batson* challenge to the exercise of opposing counsel's peremptory challenge. You may wish to appeal based upon uncovering after an adverse jury verdict that a juror failed to disclose something that you directly asked about during voir dire. You may want to appeal a judge's ruling on your offer of proof of a question that the judge prohibited you from asking a prospective juror. In each of these examples, you will need a transcript of the court's proceedings if you wish to appeal. Therefore, if the court you are in does not report jury selection, move to have it recorded including sidebars and in-chambers matters needed to preserve error for appellate review.

B. Challenges for Cause

A causal challenge asserts that a particular prospective juror is not qualified under the law to serve on the jury. No limit exists to the number of challenges for cause. When a person is removed due to a challenge for cause, another person from the panel replaces that person.

Challenges for cause fall into the following three subcategories:

1. Statutory qualifications;
2. Actual bias; and
3. Implied bias.

To be prepared for jury selection, you should be familiar with grounds for these challenges under your jurisdiction's statutes, rules and case law, and have that legal authority readily available if you need it. It is also helpful to be aware of the common standards used by your trial judge for determining whether or not to grant the challenge for cause. Some judges have strict standards that require potential jurors to explicitly state that they cannot follow the law in the case, while other judges require no such statements in order to determine that a potential juror is biased.

1. Statutory Qualifications

At pages 11–13, we discussed statutory qualifications to serve on a jury, such as having to be 18 years of age. Usually a court administrator, judge or court clerk has screened out these people before the panel reaches the courtroom. However, it can happen that a person not qualified by law to serve inadvertently ends up on the panel. If this occurs, and the unqualified prospective juror is discovered during the jury selection process, the person is subject to being removed when challenged for cause.

2. Bias and the Impartial Jury

The Fourteenth Amendment grants the parties to a civil suit the right to due process, which presupposes a fair and impartial jury, and the Sixth Amendment provides defendants in a criminal trial the right to an "impartial jury."[1]

A challenge for cause is based upon an assertion that the prospective juror is biased and cannot be fair and impartial. Challenges for cause at both the state and federal level are usually made when voir dire questioning or answers to juror questionnaire unearth information upon which a challenge can be founded. Under Federal Rule of Civil Procedure 47(c), "[d]uring trial or deliberation, the court may excuse a juror for good cause."

3. Actual Bias

While the parties are entitled to a trial by a fair and impartial jury, this does not mean that the sitting jurors cannot harbor any biases.[2] We all have some biases. Some prospective jurors think there are too many lawsuits. Others believe corporations are evil and deserve to be sued. In the criminal arena, some feel that if the defendant has been charged with a crime, he probably did it.

---

1. *See generally* U.S. CONST. amend. VI, XIV; *Morgan v. Illinois*, 504 U.S. 719 (1992).
2. *Morgan v. Illinois*, 504 U.S. 719 (1992).

While jurors are entitled to be biased, they should not serve on a jury if they have an actual bias, which is a bias that will keep them from rendering a fair and impartial decision. Actual bias has been statutorily defined as "a state of mind on the part of the juror in reference to the action, or to either party, which satisfies the court that the challenged person cannot try the issue impartially and without prejudice to the substantial rights of the party challenging ..."[3]

For the challenge for cause to be granted because the juror has an actual bias, the court must find that the prospective juror is incapable of setting aside the bias against the party or action and cannot try the case fairly and impartially. If a judge denies a challenge for cause when the prospective juror gives such an assurance, that is a sufficient record to affirm a denial of the challenge on appeal.[4] Naturally, the judge may grant the challenge for cause based upon actual bias even if the prospective juror states that the bias can be put aside. Notably, some research has shown that jurors may knowingly or unknowingly claim they can be fair and impartial when in fact, they cannot.

Bruner-McMahon v. Jameson[5] summarized the law regarding challenges for cause for actual bias and the appellate court's standard of review of a trial court's decision denying the challenge as follows:

> We review the district court's refusal to strike a juror for cause for an abuse of discretion, keeping in mind that the district court is in the best position to observe the juror and to make a first-hand evaluation of [her] ability to be fair.... A district court must grant a challenge for cause if a prospective juror shows actual prejudice or bias. *Id.* "Actual bias is a factual finding reviewed for clear error." ... We must review the issue based on "the transcript of *voir dire,* considered as a whole." ... Actual bias can be shown by the express admission of the juror.... To show a juror was biased, a [party] must show that the juror had such a fixed opinion that he or she could not judge impartially.... Thus, a juror is not shown to have been partial simply because he or she had a preconceived notion as to the guilt or innocence of the accused.... "It is sufficient if the juror can lay aside his impression or opinion and render a verdict based on the evidence presented in court." ...[6]

---

3. RCW 4.44.170(2).

4. *Mu'Min v. Virginia*, 500 U.S. 415 (1991).

5. *Bruner-McMahon v. Jameson*, 566 F. App'x. 628, 635–36 (10th Cir. 2014).

6. *Bruner-McMahon v. Jameson*, 566 F. App'x 628, 635–36 (10th Cir. 2014) (citations omitted).

Much of your jury selection questioning is intended to ferret out those who harbor actual bias. When you challenge a prospective juror for actual bias, the judge may step in to question the juror about whether the bias can be set aside. Also, the court usually will give opposing counsel an opportunity to respond to your challenge with further questioning of the prospective juror to show that the person could set aside the bias and decide the case fairly and impartially. After any further questioning and argument, the court rules on whether the challenge should be granted or denied. For this reason, it is important to obtain clear statements of bias from the potential juror in order to overcome attempts by the judge or opposing counsel to rehabilitate the individual in question.

If a prospective juror equivocates about being able to render a fair and impartial verdict when questioned, the challenge for cause should be granted.[7] Even if the prospective juror states that she can be impartial, the challenge for cause should be granted when the questioning of the juror has disclosed that the juror cannot render an impartial verdict.

4. Implied Bias

a. Federal Court

In federal court, challenges for cause may be based upon implied bias, also referred to as or "implicit bias." In *Rodriguez v. County of Los Angeles*, 96 F. Supp. 3d 990, 1010–11 (C.D. Cal. 2014), the District Court explained implied bias as follows:

> … A court may also presume bias "in those extreme circumstances where the relationship between a prospective juror and some aspect of the litigation is such that it is highly unlikely that the average person could remain impartial in his deliberations under the circumstances."

Courts have held that implied bias challenges should be reserved for extraordinary circumstances. For example, in *Seyler v. Burlington Northern Santa Fe Corporation,* the court held:

> The doctrine of implied or presumed bias is limited in application to those extreme situations where the relationship between a prospective juror and some aspect of the litigation is such that it is highly unlikely

7. *Miller v. Webb,* 385 F.3d 666, 672 (2004); *Wolfe v. Brigano,* 232 F.3d 499 (6th Cir. 2000), *McKeen v. Goins,* 605 F.2d 947, 953 (6th Cir. 1979).

that the average person could remain impartial in his or her deliberations under the circumstances.... Examples of such extraordinary situations include cases in which a prospective juror is a stockholder in or an employee of a corporation that is a party to the suit.... In these situations, the relationship between the prospective juror and a party to the lawsuit "point[s] so sharply to bias in [the] particular juror" that even the juror's own assertions of impartiality must be discounted in ruling on a challenge for cause.[8]

In *Smith v. Phillips*,[9] the Supreme Court provided other examples of situation where bias should be presumed as follows: "[E]xtreme situations that would warrant a finding of implied bias ... 'include a revelation that a juror is an actual employee of the prosecuting agency, that the juror is a close relative of one of the participants in the trial or the criminal transaction, or that the juror was a witness or somehow involved in the criminal transaction.'"[10]

When a party has made a challenge for cause based upon implied bias, the challenge may be denied if the juror has promised to be fair and impartial. For example, in *Allen v. Brown Clinic, P.L.L.P.*,[11] the court held:

> The factual basis for Edwin's claim of implied or presumptive juror bias falls well short of the showing necessary to support such a claim. Each juror pledged to be fair and impartial, and neither the long-past professional relationship with Brown Clinic or the relatively distant familial connections leads us to conclude the jurors were so closely associated with the defendants they could not be impartial. Accordingly, there was no abuse of discretion in the district court's decision to deny the challenges for cause.

b. State Court

States commonly have statutes that set out what are referred to as "implied biases," situations where bias is imputed to a person based upon a set of facts under which it is seemingly irrefutable that the person harbors a bias that would

---

8. *Seyler v. Burlington Northern Santa Fe Corp.*, 121 F. Supp. 2d 1352, 1362–63 (D. Kan. 2000) (citations omitted).

9. *Smith v. Phillips*, 455 U.S. 209, 222 (1982).

10. *See also Darbin v. Nourse*, 664 F.2d 1109, 1113 (9th Cir. 1981); *Board of Trustees of Johnson Cnty. Cmty. Coll. v. Nat'l. Gypsum Co.*, 733 F. Supp. 1412, 1416–17 (D. Kan. 1990).

11. *Allen v. Brown Clinic, P.L.L.P.*, 531 F.3d 568, 573 (8th Cir. 2008).

prevent the person from rendering a fair and impartial judgment. For example, if a lawyer for a party to the lawsuit is also the prospective juror's lawyer, the law establishes an undeniable presumption that the juror is biased. An example of such a state statute on implied bias is as follows:

> A challenge for implied bias may be taken for any or all of the following causes, and not otherwise:
> (1) Consanguinity or affinity within the fourth degree to either party.
> (2) Standing in the relation of guardian and ward, attorney and client, master and servant or landlord and tenant, to a party; or being a member of the family of, or a partner in business with, or in the employment for wages, of a party, or being surety or bail in the action called for trial, or otherwise, for a party.
> (3) Having served as a juror on a previous trial in the same action, or in another action between the same parties for the same cause of action, or in a criminal action by the state against either party, upon substantially the same facts or transaction.
> (4) Interest on the part of the juror in the event of the action, or the principal question involved therein, excepting always, the interest of the juror as a member or citizen of the county or municipal corporation.[12]

When it has been established that the prospective juror falls into one of the statutorily defined categories of implied bias, the judge should grant the challenge.

5. Exercising Challenges for Cause

When and how causal challenges are exercised, heard and ruled upon varies from jurisdiction to jurisdiction and court to court within each jurisdiction. Some courts allow counsel to make a challenge for cause when bias becomes apparent during the questioning of a prospective juror. In federal and some state courts, once the questioning of all prospective jurors is complete, the court hears challenges for cause before the parties exercise peremptory challenges. This is sometimes done outside the presence of the jurors. Other courts will entertain challenges for cause based on answers to questions on a juror questionnaire before voir dire commences.

---

12. RCW 4.44.180.

It is important to know how the court prefers to handle challenges for cause. It can be embarrassing for an attorney who makes the first causal challenge in open court to find out that cause challenges should be made outside the presence of the jury. This leaves the attorney in the position of being the only one to openly challenge a juror in front of the panel.

6. Challenging Attorney — Strategies and Techniques

a. Deciding to Challenge for Cause

Besides determining if you have grounds to challenge for cause, a couple other considerations should come into play when you are deciding whether to challenge for cause. The judge's propensity to deny challenges for cause may be a factor. Naturally, you do not want to irritate the judge by bringing a tenuous challenge for cause. Also, the type of case can cause the judge to be more likely to grant a challenge for cause. For example, in a death penalty case, the trial judge may be more likely to grant a defense challenge for cause in light of the nature of the case and the issues posed by the penalty phase.

b. In or Outside the Panel's Presence

When court practice is to have counsel challenge for cause in the presence of the panel, challenges for cause based upon actual bias should be exercised cautiously. When you challenge a potential juror for cause, you are essentially saying that the person cannot be fair and impartial, and this may well embarrass and alienate that person. Also, a challenge for cause can have spillover effect, alienating other members of the panel because one or more of them have befriended the challenged person or empathize with the challenged person. Further, the challenge could cause the other jurors to freeze up and stop the flow of information you are looking for from them. You can always delay making the challenge, continuing on with your conversation with the jurors. Later you can come back to the worrisome juror and exercise the challenge.

For these reasons, you want to make your challenges for cause outside the presence of the jury panel. Some judges regularly have challenges for cause exercised outside the jury's presence. Some judges have counsel exercise them during a recess; others have them done at sidebar and yet others have the counsel submit challenges for cause in writing.

If your judge does not routinely require that challenges for cause be made outside the jury's presence, you can argue that the court should because it will not only have an adverse effect on your client if your challenge is made in the jury's presence but also the other prospective jurors may learn what grounds can lead to being excused from jury service, such as financial hardship, and this may result in some of them adopting the same excuses.

To make a challenge for cause in the presence of the panel, do so with courtesy and make sure the grounds for the challenge are clear on the record. For example, a defense challenge to prospective juror Ellis could be stated this way: "Ms. Ellis, thank you so much for your candid answers. In light of the fact that as Ms. Ellis has told us that she is a tenant of the plaintiff, she may be better suited to serve on another case. Your Honor, we challenge Ms. Ellis for cause."

Once a juror has been excused for cause, it can be helpful to use it as an opportunity to encourage other jurors to be similarly open about their thoughts and feelings about the case. For example, the attorney might follow up with: "We really appreciate Ms. Ellis's candidness. That is exactly what we are looking for in this process. It doesn't mean you are a bad person if you say you cannot be fair. Some cases are just not good fits for people due to experiences they have had and it's important to the court and all of the parties to know this about you. So I encourage you to follow in Ms. Ellis's great example and be open and honest with us."

c. Defendant's Right to Be Present

In a criminal case, the defendant must be present, as is the defendant's right, and in both criminal and civil cases the public has a right to be present unless the requirements for courtroom closure, as discussed at pages 20 and 23, have been satisfied. In Chapter 2, we discuss both the defendant's right to be present at voir dire and the right to a public trial and exceptional circumstances that may justify courtroom closure.

d. Making a Record for the Challenge: Three-Concession Method

As the challenging attorney, before you make a challenge for cause, you must develop the best record you can that the potential juror harbors a bias and should be excused. You want to get the juror make three concessions: (1) that he has a bias; (2) that the bias prevents him from hearing the case fairly and impartially; and (3) that he should step aside. The perfect statement from a juror that you wish to challenge is that he cannot follow the law as instructed by the court as a result of his personal opinions or experiences. With that record, the court may well excuse the juror, saving you from having to challenge the person. If the court does not step in, you will have made a sufficient record upon which the court should grant your challenge and excuse the prospective juror.

i. Concession 1: Bias Exists

To make a good record, first get the person to concede that a significant bias exists. How do you get a prospective juror to do this? In Chapters 6 and 7, we describe how to get the prospective jurors to trust you and to provide you with useful information, such as these three concessions.

Bias Exists Example: A tactic that can be used to elicit the concession from the juror is to direct the juror's attention to the juror's oath that will be taken before the trial begins. For example, in Ohio, counsel might refer to Ohio Revised Code § 2945.28 and read it in part to the prospective juror as follows:

> ATTORNEY: Mr. Hines, if you are going to serve as a juror in this case, you will take an oath before the trial starts. Here, in Ohio that oath states that you "will diligently inquire into and carefully deliberate all matters between the State of Ohio and the defendant" and "you will do this to the best of your skill and understanding, without bias or prejudice."

After stating the oath, you can then ask whether the juror would be comfortable swearing or affirming under oath that they harbor no bias. Essentially you are appealing to the person's integrity and sense of fairness.

To lock the juror into an opinion that best supports a challenge, seek to get the person to say that the view has been held for a significant amount of time and that it is a strongly held opinion.

ii. Concession 2: Cannot Set Aside Bias

Second, after the juror has conceded harboring a bias, have the person admit that he cannot set the bias aside and decide the case fairly and impartially. As each concession is given, you can express your appreciation for the person's honesty.

iii. Concession 3: Best to Step Aside

Third, try to get the person to concede that it would be unfair for him to sit in judgment in your case and that he would be better suited to another case. Here, with your questions and statements, you are appealing to the juror's sense of fairness and decency. If this third concession is obtained, the prospective juror has disqualified himself from service. At this juncture, don't challenge for cause. Pause. Given the record that you have made, the court is likely to step in and politely excuse the person from service on your case. If the judge does not excuse the juror *sua sponte*, make your challenge for cause.

Making a Record Example: Even if you do not achieve the ideal situation where the prospective juror concedes both a bias that cannot be set aside and that she should not sit on the case, as the following example shows, you have made a sufficient record for the court to grant your challenge. The concession that the person has a bias that she doubts can be set aside should be sufficient.

In *Retractable Technologies, Inc. v. Becton, Dickinson and Company*, defense counsel made a record regarding the relationship between the prospective juror and opposing counsel:

> MR. BAXTER: ... Mr. Henderson?
>
> JUROR HENDERSON: Yes.
>
> MR. BAXTER: You are the Democratic Chairman in Smith County.
>
> JUROR HENDERSON: Smith County, yes.
>
> MR. BAXTER: And you followed Mr. Carroll (plaintiff's counsel)?
>
> JUROR HENDERSON: Not directly.
>
> MR. BAXTER: He is a former Chairman?
>
> JUROR HENDERSON: Yes.
>
> MR. BAXTER: Somebody had the good sense to get rid of him.
>
> JUROR HENDERSON: I think he got tired of it, and—
>
> MR. BAXTER: Well, that is a tough job over here, isn't it?
>
> JUROR HENDERSON: It is indeed.
>
> MR. BAXTER: Anything about that, Mr. Henderson, if you get on this jury and—you have known Otis how many years?
>
> JUROR HENDERSON: Oh, seven, I think.
>
> MR. BAXTER: And you don't know me from anybody. And you sit on that jury and he starts telling you something is X and I tell you it is not X, who are you going to believe?
>
> JUROR HENDERSON: I guess it depends on whether it looks like X or it looks like Y.
>
> MR. BAXTER: Okay. Anything about that I need to worry about having you on this jury?
>
> JUROR HENDERSON: I think I can be objective. But, you know, if you have a good friend arguing a case, it is difficult to be completely objective.
>
> MR. BAXTER: Okay. Would it be fair to say, Mr. Henderson, that as we sit here today, we are probably not on a level playing field? And I understand that, you know—

JUROR HENDERSON: Well, again, I think I am a rational person. A lot of people around here don't think so. And I would try to be objective; but I couldn't tell you, in all honesty, that I could be.

MR. BAXTER: All right. Thank you. We will take it up with the Judge, Mr. Henderson. Thank you very much.[13]

Later, when defense counsel challenged Mr. Henderson for cause, plaintiff's counsel did not object, and Mr. Henderson was excused.[14]

e. Reversing the Bias

When you have a person like Mr. Henderson in the previous example, who candidly admits a bias towards the other side, you may be able to take advantage of the prospective juror's sense of fairness. That juror may, with encouragement from you, express a desire to bend over backwards to be fair to your side of the case. When that happens, you may decide to not challenge for cause at that time, because not only has the juror given you that assurance, but also your opponent may ultimately decide to exercise a peremptory challenge against that very same person whom you originally contemplated challenging for cause.

f. Challenge Denied

Above all, don't challenge for cause if you don't have a peremptory challenge in reserve just in case the challenge is not granted. When your challenge for cause has been denied, ordinarily you will be inclined to exercise a peremptory challenge to remove the person from the jury. Further, to preserve error for appeal when the trial court denies a challenge for cause, the party challenging the prospective juror must use a peremptory challenge against the challenged juror, exhaust all remaining peremptory challenges and notify the judge that the challenged juror will remain on the on the list of jurors will remain on the jury. The stated rationale for these requirements is that "[t]his ensures that 'the court is made aware that the objectionable jurors will be chosen' while there is still time 'to determine if the party was in fact forced to take objectionable jurors.'"[15]

---

13. Transcript of Proceedings at 27–28, *Retractable Techs., Inc. v. Becton, Dickinson and Company,* 2:08cv16 E.D. (Tex. Sept. 3, 2013), App. 1.2.

14. *Id.* at 43.

15. Urista v. Bed, Bath & Beyond, Inc., 245 S.W.3d 591, 596 (2007) (quoting Cortez v. HCCI-San Antonio, Inc., 159 S.W.3d 87, 91 (Tex. 2005)); Cortez ex rel. Estate of Puentes v. HCCI-San Antonio, Inc., 159 S.W.3d 87, 90–91 (2005); McMillin v. State Farm Lloyds, 180 S.W.3d 183, 192–95 (2005).

7. Responding Attorney — Strategies and Techniques

a. To Join or Not to Join

As the attorney who is responding when opposing counsel has challenged a potential juror for cause, you need to decide whether you will oppose the challenge or join in it. If it is readily apparent to all in the courtroom that the person is so entrenched in their bias that they will not be able to set it aside and hear the matter fairly and impartially, your best course of action is to join in the challenge. This showing of reasonableness can boost your credibility with the judge and the other potential jurors.

In making your decision, consider whether or not you want the next person in line to fill the challenged person's seat if the challenge is granted. The next juror may be worse for you. Also, you should take into consideration the fact that if the challenge is denied, opposing counsel is likely to have to expend a peremptory challenge to remove the challenged person who was not excused.

Above all, consider the ramifications if the court agrees with you and denies the challenge. If that happens and you prevail at trial, your opponent will have a potential issue for appeal. You do not want to retry the case when it is reversed on appeal.

b. Rehabilitation of the Challenged Juror

Generally, once a prospective juror has been challenged, the judge may seek to rehabilitate the juror by having the juror express a willingness to set aside bias and try the case fairly and impartially. If the judge does not take the initiative to do this, you can ask the court to allow you to ask further questions. If the court permits you to question the challenged juror, this is your opportunity to rehabilitate the person. Your questions should be designed to show that the prospective juror can set aside their bias and decide the case fairly and impartially.

Rehabilitation questions probe into how strong the person's attitudes are, whether certain facts the person might not have considered would change the person's views, why the prospective juror can be fair and impartial, and, of course, whether the court's instruction that the person must set aside the bias would cause the person to comply with the court's directive. Your questions should be confined to matters relating to the challenge, if you have previously had an opportunity to question the prospective juror.

Rehabilitation Example: Questioning to rehabilitate the prospective juror can run along the same lines that the Judge used with prospective juror Mr. Thomas in *In re TFT-LCD (Flat-Panel)* as follows:

> THE COURT: ... And again, one of the things you'll have to promise me and take an oath to do is decide this case just based on the evidence in the case that you hear here in the courtroom. And not based on anything you learned or thought before you heard the case. Because it's important that the parties have a jury that's—all of whom are deciding the case based on the same evidence. Because otherwise, it doesn't make sense.
>
> So, do you think you can do that? Can you put aside your ideas about how things have been and just listen to the evidence in this case? Do you think you can do that?[16]

Alternatively, the rehabilitating attorney may appeal to reasonableness and human nature in order to leave the juror feeling that her bias is not strong enough to constitute the kind of bias that warrants a for cause challenge. For example, the rehabilitation question might go as follows:

> We all have opinions and feelings. That's what makes us human. No one in this courtroom is asking you to stop being a human being. It's perfectly fine to have feelings and opinions. So what we are asking is, in this case where you know almost nothing about the facts, can you listen to those facts as they come in with an open mind and apply the law that the court will instruct you on?

This kind of question can often lead jurors to reassess their alleged bias and embrace more socially-confirming conclusions, such as the one that they can listen with an open mind and apply the law, despite any personal feelings or opinions.

c. Coaxed Rehabilitation Disfavored

Some appellate courts have frowned upon the type of rehabilitation that puts a potential juror in the position where the person will not disagree with the court.[17] If the potential juror clearly states an actual bias against the sub-

---

16. Transcript of Proceedings at 38, *In re TFT-LCD (Flat-Panel)*, No. 07-MDL-1827 SI, 10-CV-4572, 10-CV-5452, 10-CV-4114 (N.D. Cal. July 22, 2013), App. 1.1.

17. *State v. Braunreiter*, 185 P.3d 1024 (2008).

stantial rights of a party, coaxed recantations by either the court or counsel in which a prospective juror states they will merely follow the law do not cure or remove the legitimate grounds for a challenge for cause.[18]

Coaxed Rehabilitation Example: In a driving under the influence case, the prospective juror was a member of Mothers Against Drunk Driving (MADD), who said, among other things, that he would not want a jury of people in his "frame of mind" and that he did not think he would get a fair trial in that circumstance. The judge denied a defense challenge for cause after rehabilitating the juror as follows:

> THE COURT: ... do you think you can put all that aside and give both parties here a fair trial?
> MR. BAUMAN: I do.
> THE COURT: ... Do you understand that it's not illegal to drink and drive?
> MR. BAUMAN: I do.
> THE COURT: Do you think that you can keep a fair and open mind throughout that entire trial?
> MR. BAUMAN: Yes.

The defendant's guilty verdict was overturned on appeal on the grounds that the juror's membership in MADD and his belief that his niece had been killed by an intoxicated driver, when combined with his answer that he would not want six jurors with his frame of mind on the jury if he were in the defendant's position, was sufficient to establish actual bias and justify his removal for cause.[19]

An approach that can forestall the judge from coaxing a recantation from a prospective juror is to make a pretrial motion for the court to refrain from attempting to rehabilitate potential jurors who express reservations about serving or who state that they cannot be fair and impartial. The argument is that this type of judicial questioning is coaxed rehabilitation that places undue pressures the prospective jurors.[20] A motion requesting the court not to rehabilitate prospective jurors can be found in the Appendix 3.1 on the companion online supplement http://caplaw.com/jury.

---

18. *State v. Robinson*, 177 P.3d 488, 493 (Mont. 2008); *State v. Freshment, 43 P.3d 968* (Mont. 2002).

19. *City of Cheney v. Gruneweld*, 55 Wash. App. 807, 810–11 (1989).

20. Appendix 3.1, Motion re Voir Dire Rehabilitation.

8. Challenging Based on Responses in a Juror Questionnaire

When the panel has completed supplemental questionnaires, the court may entertain challenges for cause before beginning jury selection. The following is an example of an exchange between the court and counsel based upon their readings of questionnaires and resulting challenges for cause.

Challenge for Cause Based on Questionnaire Example 1: In *In re TFT-LCD (Flat-Panel)*, the panel members completed a questionnaire. Before Judge Susan Illston brought the panel into the courtroom, she considered plaintiff's challenges for cause based upon responses to the questionnaire:

> MR. SILBERFELD: There are possible cause challenges.
> One of them we actually stipulated to, but the Court did not exclude that individual.
> THE COURT: Yes.
> MR. SILBERFELD: And that is Mr. Nemecek, No. 12.
> THE COURT: Yes.
> MR. SILBERFELD: I don't know if it was mentioned in what was submitted to the Court, but Mr. Nemecek knows a number of people who are involved in this. One is a paralegal, I think, for Toshiba; I can't—
> MR. FREITAS: For HannStar, Your Honor.
> THE COURT: In a social sense, or a Biblical sense?
> MR. FREITAS: Purely social, Your Honor.
> THE COURT: Okay. I mean, there are so many lawyers in this case, we wouldn't have any lawyers on this panel who didn't know some of them.
> So, what else?
> MR. SILBERFELD: This individual apparently dated one of my partner's wives.
> THE COURT: So we are getting close to Biblical now, aren't we?
> MR. SILBERFELD: I don't want to make a Federal Court record out of this. But the third thing is, you know, he is a lawyer. And he's written an article about the pass-on defense.
> THE COURT: Oh.
> MR. SILBERFELD: And he says that. So, you know, rather than spend a great deal of time on this, you know, I think we have a cause challenge as to him.

MR. TOTO: Not only that, Your Honor; he's tweeted and has written about this case in particular. He wrote about the AUO criminal verdict. He wrote about some things, some of your rulings in the Dell case, as well as the criminal case for AUO, including some somewhat-obscure rulings, showing that he's following the case pretty closely.

So, we think he brings non-record evidence to the case, and could really be an influence on the jury.

MR. SILBERFELD: I'm actually trying just to protect the virtue of my partner's wife.

THE COURT: You'd better not tell her what you did.

MR. SILBERFELD: I'm sure she'll hear about it.

THE COURT: Well, frankly, she does not move me, nor does your paralegal move me. But tweeting about the criminal trial and other things does.

I think it would be—it would be hard for him to set previously-developed opinions aside, and it would be impossible for the other jurors not to ask him what he thought.

So, I can see how that might be bad.

MR. SILBERFELD: That is Juror Number—

THE COURT: What number is he?

MR. SILBERFELD: No. 12, Mr. Nemecek.

THE COURT: Who does he work for?

MR. SILBERFELD: He has his own firm, Qian and Nemecek?

MR. TOTO: Qian and Nemecek.

MR. SILBERFELD: Here in the Bay area.

THE COURT: Okay, what else? I think, when he—you can—you can tell the jury folks to excuse him at this time.

THE CLERK: Okay.[21]

As previously mentioned, when a challenge for cause has been made, the judge may allow counsel on the other side to respond with further questioning. In addition to permitting opposing counsel an opportunity to question the prospective juror, the court may question the juror to determine whether the juror should be disqualified for actual bias. Note in the following example how the judge states the challenge and the grounds for it.

---

21. Transcript of Proceedings at 11–12, *In re TFT-LCD (Flat-Panel)*, No. 07-MDL-1827 SI, 10-CV-4572, 10-CV-5452, 10-CV-4114 (N.D. Cal. July 22, 2013) App. 1.1.

Challenge for Cause Based on Questionnaire Example 2: In *In re TFT-LCD (Flat-Panel)*, defense counsel challenged a prospective juror for cause based upon a response to a question in the supplemental questionnaire:

> MR. TOTO: Your Honor, we did have one more for-cause challenge that we would like to raise.
>
> THE COURT: Okay.
>
> MR. TOTO: No. 9, Raymond Thomas.
>
> THE COURT: Yes.
>
> MR. TOTO: Yes, Your Honor. This juror indicated that he thinks most products are priced too high because they are made overseas. That was response to Question 34(a) on Page 11. He also said prices are too high for products at issue, because they're made outside of the USA.
>
> And finally, he checked the box "No" for the question of whether he could set aside his own opinions and be impartial. 57(c). So, we believe he's shown bias here, and should be excused for cause.
>
> THE COURT: All right. Well, I'll inquire. We'll see....[22]

Rehabilitation Example: Later, Judge Illston did inquire of Mr. Thomas as follows:

> THE COURT: ... Mr. Thomas. Where's Mr. Thomas? Mr. Thomas, you indicated in your questionnaire a viewpoint about prices, and how products are priced. And again, one of the things you'll have to promise me and take an oath to do is decide this case just based on the evidence in the case that you hear here in the courtroom. And not based on anything you learned or thought before you heard the case. Because it's important that the parties have a jury that's—all of whom are deciding the case based on the same evidence. Because otherwise, it doesn't make sense.
>
> So, do you think you can do that? Can you put aside your ideas about how things have been and just listen to the evidence in this case? Do you think you can do that?
>
> PROSPECTIVE JUROR THOMAS: Yeah, I think I can do that.
>
> THE COURT: You've been introduced to who the parties in the case are. Do you think you can be fair to both sides in this case?
>
> PROSPECTIVE JUROR THOMAS: I think so.

---

22. *Id.* at 13–14.

THE COURT: Everybody has a level playing field when they start with you?

PROSPECTIVE JUROR THOMAS: Oh, yeah. Yeah.[23]

9. Ruling on a Challenge for Cause

a. Standard on Appeal

Once the questioning is completed, the judge will rule on the challenge. The trial judge's decision to deny a challenge for cause ordinarily will be reviewed under an abuse of discretion standard.[24] In reviewing the court's decision, the appellate court examines the prospective juror's responses as a whole.[25] The appellate court will reverse the trial court's ruling only if the court abused its discretion and the party who opposed the challenge exhausted peremptory challenges.[26]

b. The Equivocating Juror

If the court denies a challenge for cause against a prospective juror who will not give an unequivocal assurance to set aside bias and serve fairly and impartially in reaching a verdict, the verdict must be set aside.[27]

C. Death Penalty Qualification and Challenges for Cause

Jury selection in capital cases is carefully scrutinized on appeal and in post-conviction relief, and it is a common area for reversal.[28] An excellent resource for any judge or lawyer who is planning for jury selection in a capital case is Chapter 6 on Jury Selection in *Presiding Over a Capital Case: A Benchbook for*

---

23. *Id.* at 38–39.

24. *See State v. Falls Down*, 79 P.3d 797 (Mont. 2003).

25. *State v. Hausauer*, 149 P.3d 895 (Mont. 2006).

26. *See State v. Braunreiter*, 185 P.3d 1024 (2008); *State v. Robinson*, 177 P.3d 488 (Mont. 2008).

27. *Thompson v. Gray*, 248 F.3d 621 (7th Cir. 2001); *United States v. Gonzalez*, 214 F.3d 1109, 1113–14 (9th Cir. 2000); *United States v. Padilla-Mendoza*, 157 F.3d 730, 733–34 (9th Cir. 1998); *United States v. Salamone*, 800 F.2d 1216, 1226–27 (3d Cir. 1986).

28. V. Lee Sinclair, *Chapter 5, Jury Selection* of Presiding Over a Capital Case: A Benchbook for Judges, 106 (photo. reprint) *available at* http://www.judges.org/capital casesresources/book.html.

Judges, written by Judge V. Lee Sinclair of Ann Arbor, Michigan and published by The National Judicial College.[29]

1. Prosecutor Challenges for Cause

The major distinguishing feature of a death penalty jury selection is death qualifying the jury. In the seminal Supreme Court case on death qualification, *Witherspoon v. Illinois*, 391 U.S. 510 (1968), the prosecutor had successfully challenged for cause jurors who expressed general reservations about imposing the death penalty. The Supreme Court reversed, holding that the Sixth Amendment requirement of an impartial jury was violated when prospective jurors were excluded merely because they "voiced general objections to the death penalty or expressed conscientious or religious scruples against its infliction."[30]

However, based on footnote 21 in the *Witherspoon* opinion that states what the Court was not prohibiting in its decision, *Witherspoon* grew to stand for the situations where a challenge for cause to disqualify a juror is well founded. Based on footnote 21, a challenge for cause should be granted if either the juror made it unmistakenly clear that they would automatically vote against the death penalty despite the evidence or if the juror's attitude about the death penalty would keep the juror from "making an impartial decision as to the defendant's guilt."[31] Later, the Supreme Court in *Wainwright v. Witt*,[32] revisited footnote 21 and modified its position, deciding that the juror need not make it "unmistakenly clear" that they would automatically vote against the death penalty. To meet the requirements for a challenge for cause, the prosecution must only show "the juror's views would prevent or substantially impair the performance of his duties as a juror in accordance with his instructions and his oath."

2. Defense Challenges for Cause

Morgan v. Illinois[33] involved a reverse-*Witherspoon* challenge. Defense counsel had successfully challenged prospective jurors who would automatically vote for the death penalty. The Supreme Court applied the same standard in *Morgan*

---

29. *Id.*
30. *Witherspoon v. Illinois*, 391 U.S. 501, 522 (1986).
31. *Witherspoon*, 391 U.S. at 514 n. 21 (1992).
32. *Wainwright v. Witt*, 469 U.S, 412 (1985).
33. *Morgan v. Illinois*, 504 U.S. 719 (1992).

that it had in *Witherspoon-Witt.* The Court quoted the Fifth Circuit, as follows: "All veniremen are potentially biased. The process of voir dire is designed to cull from the venire persons who demonstrate that they cannot be fair to either side of the case. Clearly, the extremes must be eliminated, i.e., those who, in spite of the evidence, would automatically vote to convict or impose the death penalty or automatically vote to acquit or impose a life sentence."[34]

3. Guiding Principles

In *Uttecht v. Brown*,[35] Justice Kennedy reexamined the Supreme Court's decisions on death qualifying a jury and then laid out the following four principles governing jury selection in capital cases:

> These precedents establish at least four principles of relevance here. First, a criminal defendant has the right to an impartial jury drawn from a venire that has not been tilted in favor of capital punishment by selective prosecutorial challenges for cause.... Second, the State has a strong interest in having jurors who are able to apply capital punishment within the framework state law prescribes.... Third, to balance these interests, a juror who is substantially impaired in his or her ability to impose the death penalty under the state-law framework can be excused for cause; but if the juror is not substantially impaired, removal for cause is impermissible.... Fourth, in determining whether the removal of a potential juror would vindicate the State's interest without violating the defendant's right, the trial court makes a judgment based in part on the demeanor of the juror, a judgment owed deference by reviewing courts (citations omitted).

D. Peremptory Challenges

Court rules and statutes afford each side a number of peremptory challenges, also referred as a "strikes" in some courts. A party may freely exercise a peremptory challenge against a prospective juror without having to state a reason for the challenge. Prior to the United States Supreme Court's decision in *Batson v. Kentucky*,[36] holding that peremptory challenges may not be used to remove

---

34. *Smith v. Balkcom,* 660 F.2d 573, 578 (1981) (emphasis in original), *modified,* 671 F.2d 858, *cert. denied,* 459 U.S. 882 (1982).

35. *Uttecht v. Brown,* 551 U.S. 1, 6 (2007).

36. *Batson v. Kentucky,* 476 U.S. 79 (1986).

people from the jury based upon race, the Supreme Court described the nature
of a peremptory challenge as follows:

> The essential nature of the peremptory challenge is that it is one ex-
> ercised without a reason stated, without inquiry, and without being
> subject to the court's control.... While challenges for cause permit re-
> jection of jurors on a narrowly specified, provable and legally cogniz-
> able basis of partiality, the peremptory permits rejection for a real or
> imagined partiality that is less easily designated or demonstrable....
> It is often exercised upon the "sudden impressions and unaccountable
> prejudices we are apt to conceive upon the bare looks and gestures of
> another," ... upon a juror's "habits and associations," ... or upon the
> feeling that "the bare questioning [a juror's] indifference may some-
> times provoke a resentment," ... It is no less frequently exercised on
> grounds normally thought irrelevant to legal proceedings or official
> action, namely, the race, religion, nationality, occupation or
> affiliations of people summoned for jury duty.[37]

Except for *Batson* and its progeny's prohibitions, the peremptory challenge
remains unfettered.

1. Number of Peremptory Challenges

a. History and Controversy

Originally, in America, the right to exercise peremptory challenges in a criminal case belonged only to the defendant. It was not until 1865 that federal law
granted the prosecution a couple peremptory challenges.[38] Up until 1986,
twenty states and the federal system used an asymmetrical scheme.[39] However,
the trend since *Batson v. Kentucky* has been to provide a symmetrical allocation
of peremptory challenges, with advocates for this approach asserting that no
reason exists to continue the practice of giving an advantage to the defense in
criminal cases.[40]

Some academics, commentators and judges argue that peremptory
challenges have proven to be a failure and should be eradicated. Justice Thur-

---

37. *Swain v. Alabama*, 80 U.S. 202, 220 (1965) (citations omitted).
38. *See* Roberts, *Asymmetry as Fairness: Reversing a Peremptory Trend*, 92 WASH. U. L.
REV. 1503, 1534 (2015).
39. *Id.* at 1504.
40. *Id.* at 1536.

good Marshall took this position in his concurring opinion in *Batson*.[41] The arguments against peremptories include: removing qualified jurors is anti-democratic; *Batson* is difficult to enforce; and peremptory challenges serve no real purpose.[42]

However, proponents of peremptory challenges would argue that judges often apply unreasonably high standards for granting cause challenges, and peremptory challenges provide the necessary relief to this problem. In fact, research has shown that jurors will often say they can be fair and impartial even when they cannot. The reasons vary. Some jurors feel pressure to say the socially acceptable thing in the courtroom (that they can be fair). Some jurors fail to appreciate the true extent of their bias. In rare instances, you may have stealth jurors who, for some reason, want to be a juror in the case and say whatever is necessary to accomplish this goal.

b. Federal Courts

Today, for federal civil cases, each party is entitled to three strikes. When several defendants or several plaintiffs are involved, they may be considered as a single party for the purposes of making challenges, or the court may allow additional peremptory challenges and permit them to be exercised separately or jointly.[43]

In a federal criminal case, the type of case determines the number of peremptory challenges allotted each side. In a death penalty case, each side has 20 peremptory challenges. In a felony case, the prosecutor has six peremptory challenges and the defendant or defendants jointly have ten peremptory challenges. In a misdemeanor case, each side has three peremptory challenges. The court may allow additional peremptory challenges to multiple defendants, and may allow the defendants to exercise those challenges separately or jointly.[44]

c. State Courts

At the state court level, a statute, court rule or both authorize the number of peremptory challenges allotted to the different parties, and the number varies from jurisdiction to jurisdiction. For example, the state statute codifying the number of peremptories in a civil case could provide that each party shall be entitled to three challenges, and that when there is more than one party on

---

41. *Batson*, 476 U.S. at 102–03.
42. Roberts, *supra*, at 1538.
43. 28 U.S.C. § 1870; FED. R. CIV. P. 47(b).
44. FED. R. CRIM. P. 24(b).

either side, they shall join in a peremptory challenge before it can be made. Additionally, the statute may provide that if the court finds that a conflict of interest between parties on the same side exists, the court may allow each conflicting party up to three peremptory challenges.[45] State court rules or statute may also provide an additional peremptory for an alternate juror.[46]

For criminal cases, a state court rule setting the number of peremptory challenges could use a symmetrical scheme allotting each side an equal number of challenges. For instance the rule could provide that in a prosecution for a capital offense the defense and the state may peremptorily challenge 12 each; in a prosecution for a felony offense six jurors each; and in any other prosecution, three jurors each. When several defendants are on trial together, the state court rule could provide that each defendant be entitled to one challenge in addition to the number of challenges provided for one defendant, with discretion in the trial judge to afford the prosecution such additional challenges as circumstances warrant.[47]

2. In Front of the Jury Panel or Not

Peremptory challenges ordinarily are exercised after challenges for cause. How peremptory challenges are exercised differs from court to court. In one court, they are taken openly with the panel observing the process, but in another court, they are exercised out of the panel's hearing, either at the side bar, in chambers, when the panel is out of the courtroom for a recess, or in writing.

As we discussed at pages 48–49 regarding challenges for cause, it is preferable that you exercise your challenges outside the jury's presence. You may make the same arguments we discussed there for the court to follow this approach for peremptories. Again, it is critical that you determine how the court will proceed before jury selection commences.

If it is your turn to exercise a peremptory challenge, and you are doing so in front of the panel, you should do so as politely as possible. During jury selection questioning, either the court, you or opposing counsel should have softened the blow by explaining to the panel that if a person is excused, it should not be taken personally and that many reasons exist for why an attorney would excuse a juror.

To exercise a challenge, you should rise and state, "We would respectfully excuse juror number 8, Mr. Dunham, and we thank you, Mr. Dunham." When

---

45. RCW 4.44.130.

46. *See, e.g.,* WASH. SUPERIOR COURT CIV. R. 47(b).

47. WASH. SUPERIOR CT. CRIM. R. 6.4(e)(1).

you have reached that point when you do not wish to exercise any further peremptories, rise from your chair, look confidently at the seated jurors and inform the court, "Your Honor, we accept the jury as presently constituted."

3. Procedure for Exercising Peremptory Challenges

Either statute or court rule may require that a particular method of jury selection and exercising challenges be followed in your courtroom. This may be augmented by the court's standing order or the judge's online advisory to trial counsel. If the trial court fails to adhere to a statutorily required method for jury selection, it can result in a reversal on appeal. For example, in *State v. Crabb*,[48] the Kansas Court of Appeals reversed a conviction, holding that the defendant was entitled to a new trial because the trial judge had utilized the "jury-box" method of jury selection, discussed in the next section, rather than the method statutorily required in Kansas.

The two methods that are most often utilized are the jury-box method and the struck method.

a. Jury-Box Method

The jury-box method has also been referred to as the "traditional," "sequential," "hot-box" or "strike and replace" method. *United States v. Severino*[49] describes the method as follows:

> In empaneling the jury in this case, Judge Lowe employed the "jury box" system, which is the traditional method of jury selection, *see* Sand, *Jury Selection and Race Discrimination,* N.Y.L.J., June 10, 1986, at 3, col. 1. In this system, 12 prospective jurors are seated in the jury box and questioned to determine whether they should be excused for cause. Any prospective juror who is excused for cause is immediately replaced. After 12 prospective jurors have been seated and have survived all challenges for cause, the defendant and the prosecutor proceed to exercise their allotted peremptory challenges, in some prescribed pattern of alternation, against the currently seated prospective jurors.

The jury-box method is employed in some federal courts, and it is not an abuse of discretion for a trial judge to use it provided it does not prevent the defendant from exercising all peremptories.[50]

---

48. *State v. Crabb*, 51 Kan. App. 2d 159, 343 P.3d 539 (2015).
49. *United States v. Severino*, 800 F.2d 42, 47 (2d Cir. 1986).
50. *United States v. Thompson*, 76 F.3d 442, 451–52 (2d Cir. 1996).

b. The Struck Method

Another common method of exercising peremptory challenges is the struck jury method. Under this method, the full panel is questioned. Challenges for cause are made as they arise or after questioning is completed. Then, the parties strike prospective jurors from the panel until the requisite number of jurors is left. Depending on the judge's practice, the strikes can be exercised by either alternating back and forth between the parties or instead the parties each submit written strikes. This method is used in both state and federal courts. The following are federal and state examples of this method.

i. Federal Court Struck Method Example

Judge Ronnie Abrams of the United States District Court, Southern District of New York describes her struck method on a website as follows:

> RULES FOR JURY SELECTION: STRUCK PANEL METHOD
> RONNIE ABRAMS, UNITED STATES DISTRICT JUDGE
> [April 3, 2013]

> The following is a description of the struck panel method by which juries will be selected in trials before Judge Abrams.
> The Court will conduct a voir dire of a number of panelists computed by totaling: the number of jurors to be selected (8 in most civil cases and 12 in criminal cases); the number of alternates (none in civil cases and usually 2 in criminal cases); and the number of peremptory challenges. Thus, in a civil case with an 8-person jury and 3 peremptory challenges per side, the Court will voir dire 14 panelists. See Fed. R. Civ. P. 47, 48; 28 U.S.C. § 1870. In a single defendant criminal case in which the defendant has 10 and the Government has 6 peremptory challenges, plus 1 each with respect to alternates, see Fed. R. Crim. P. 24, the Court will voir dire 32 panelists (12 jurors + 2 alternates + 10 peremptories for defendant + 6 peremptories for the Government + 1 peremptory for defendant for the alternates + 1 peremptory for the Government for the alternates). In trials expected to last for substantially more than a week, the Court will consider increasing the number of jurors in a civil case and the number of alternates in a criminal case.
> The panelists will be voir dired in the Courtroom. If issues are raised that are better discussed outside the presence of the entire panel (e.g., sensitive issues, requests to be excused), Judge Abrams will follow up with the individual jurors either at sidebar or in the robing room.

After the follow-up voir dire, the Court will entertain challenges for cause. Each panelist excused for cause will be replaced, so that there is a full panel before any peremptory challenges are exercised.

Once all challenges for cause have been heard and decided, the Court will conduct the final voir dire in the Courtroom, asking each panelist individual questions relating to county of residence, education, occupation, prior jury service, etc.

The parties will then exercise their peremptory challenges against the panelists who compose the potential members of the regular jury (in the ordinary civil case, against all 14 panelists; in the ordinary criminal case, against the first 28 panelists). Peremptory challenges will be exercised simultaneously, with each party submitting a written list of the panelists it wishes to excuse. The panelists on these lists will then be excused without knowing which party challenged them. Any overlap among the lists of challenges will not result in parties receiving additional challenges. The jurors will be selected starting with the un-challenged juror with the lowest number. For example, in an ordinary civil case, if there was an overlap of 1 peremptory challenge, the 5 challenged panelists would be excused and the first 8 of the remaining 9 panelists would be seated as the jury. In an ordinary criminal case, if there was an overlap of 1 peremptory challenge, the 15 challenged panelists would be excused and the first 12 of the remaining 13 would be seated as the jury.

Finally, where applicable, the parties will exercise their peremptory challenges against the panelists who compose the potential alternate jurors (in the ordinary criminal case, against panelists 29 through 32). Again, peremptory challenges will be exercised simultaneously. In the event of an overlap in challenges, the jurors will be selected from those with the lowest numbers.[51]

ii. State Court Struck Method Example

In Alabama, the statutory scheme for the struck method provides that in a criminal case after the jurors have been questioned and challenges for cause have been taken, if any, the prosecutor strikes one juror's name from a list of qualified jurors and the defendant then strikes one, and they continue to strike off names alternately until only 12 jurors remain on the strike list and that is

---

51. Ronnie Abrams, *Rules for Jury Selection: Struck Panel Method* (Apr. 3, 2013), http://www.nysd.uscourts.gov/cases/show.php?db=judge_info&id=726 (Jan. 9, 2017).

the jury for the case. If the defendant refuses to strike, the judge exercises the strike for the defendant. The number of names on the strike list at the start is not less than 36 if it is a capital case, not less than 24 if it is a felony case and not less than 18 if it is a misdemeanor. The parties can agree to fewer names.[52]

4. Strategically Exercising Peremptory Challenges

a. Don't Run Out of Peremptories

Strategically, the bottom line for exercising peremptory challenges when counsel are alternating back and forth in exercising challenges is that you do not want to run out of peremptory challenges and have the next person seated in the jury box be worse than the ones who have been excused. Therefore, you have to learn as much as you can about those in the panel who may move into the jury box as a result of other prospective jurors being excused. You need to question those members of the panel who are seated in the spectator section of the courtroom who may sit on the jury. If you have a sizable panel, you may be able to conserve questioning time by ignoring those in the panel who are seated so far in the back of the room that they likely will never be seated in the box.

Even though you have accepted the panel, if opposing counsel removes other jurors and you have preserved peremptory challenge(s), you can continue to exercise a challenge against any replacement jurors until your peremptories are exhausted.[53] This is particularly important when you believe that those who are presently on the jury are better than what you will get to replace anyone who is excused. For example, if you are down to your last peremptory challenge and the next person who will be seated in the box is worse than anyone currently on the jury, save your peremptory and accept the jury as it is. If the other side exercises a peremptory, you still have a peremptory to use against the replacement juror. However, it is critical that you confirm with the court in advance that a peremptory strike is not lost when you pass or accept the panel as is. While rare, some courts consider a pass as a conceded peremptory, which can place you in a difficult situation.

Alternatively, you may ask the court in advance if you are allowed to strike jurors outside of the box. Some judges leave it up to attorneys as to how they use their strikes and allow them to strike outside of the box. Consequently, it is important to know if this is an option available to you.

---

52. *See, e.g.,* Ala. Code § 12-16-100 (1981).
53. *See, e.g., Portch v. Sommerville,* 113 Wash. App. 807, 55 P.3d 661 (2002).

As part of this, it is important for you to remain aware of which jurors are "in play," meaning they could realistically make it on to the jury. For example, if there are going to be 12 jurors and each side has 3 strikes, jurors 19 and on up are not in play. Jury selection can be chaotic, and it is easy to get lost in all of the information that is circulating. There have been times when attorneys have attempted to strike a juror outside the box and struck someone who was not actually in play. This results in a wasted strike. Peremptory strikes are limited in number enough the way it is; attorneys should not waste them.

b. Wait and See

Later, in Chapter 13, we discuss the assessment of prospective jurors to determine whether or not to exercise peremptory challenges against them. Now, we want to mention an important strategy to use when exercising peremptory challenges. The tactic is to let counsel on the other side exercise a peremptory challenge against a prospective juror whom you want off the jury. As you assess each juror to decide whether you want to excuse them, you should step into opposing counsel's shoes to see whether counsel may want to remove that same person.

As we mentioned earlier in the discussion of challenges for cause, you may be able to nudge opposing counsel into removing a person you do not want on the jury even when the person makes a statement of bias against your client and/or case. Sometimes, the juror in question makes statements that are troubling for both parties, and a game of chicken ensues with peremptory strikes. You may also be able to lead the prospective juror to understand that it is critical that that bias be set aside and that the juror hear the case impartially. During that dialogue with the juror, you may be able to get the person to commit to being fair to your client. This may well cause opposing counsel to think that the juror may have changed and now be biased in your client's favor. If you conclude that your opponent may remove the person, postpone exercising a challenge against the person as long as possible in the hopes that the other side will remove that juror.

c. Juror Placement in the Panel

As previously noted, many state courts will seat alternate jurors on the panel. In most courts, the judge will not tell the jury who the alternates are, because they want each juror to actively listen as if they were going to participate in deliberations. There are a variety of methods used by courts to determine who the alternate jurors will be. Some courts randomly pick seat numbers at the conclusion of trial before deliberations begin. However, many courts are increasingly identifying the seat numbers of the alternate positions before jury selection begins. This provides additional information to the attorneys as to how they might exercise their peremptory strikes, particularly in situations where an attorney feels that she does not have a sufficient number of peremptories to remove all of the jurors she is concerned about. In this situation, the attorney may determine that she is less concerned about jurors in the alternate positions and instead focus her peremptory strikes on the jurors who will actually deliberate in the case. While it is certainly possible that the alternate juror could eventually replace a dismissed juror, the attorney may determine that it is better to use her last strike on a non-alternate and run the risk that an alternate could be required.

d. The Importance of Assessing Leadership Potential

It is not unusual for an attorney to find himself in the position of not having enough peremptories to remove all of the venire members he is concerned about. This situation calls for difficult decisions and forces the attorney to find ways to distinguish between various bad jurors. When this situation arises, you should focus on opinion leadership as a determining factor for how you are going to prioritize your peremptory strikes. In other words, if you are going to have a bad juror on the jury, you at least want it to be someone who is not going to be an opinion leader. These individuals will exert the least amount of influence on deliberations and may ultimately hold weaker positions in the case that can be challenged by other jurors who are more vocal and forceful during the discussion in deliberations.

There are several things to look for when trying to identify opinion leaders on the jury, so let's take a look at the most common indicators:

1. *Prior jury service.* Research has consistently shown that prior jury service is a strong indicator of who will serve as the foreperson on the jury. This makes sense, as a common ice-breaking question at the start of deliberations is, "who has done this before." Other jurors often perceive prior experience as a juror as an indication of expertise on what is supposed to happen, which makes that individual a more attractive candidate for foreperson. Serving as a foreperson is not a guarantee of opinion leadership, but it does position the individual to exert a lot of influence over deliberations if he or she desires. For example, one study found that forepersons account for as much as 25% of the comments made during deliberations.

2. *Prior foreperson.* If the juror has previously served as a foreperson, this means that previously jurors have felt they possessed the nec-

essary skills to serve in this role. Consequently, this individual is more likely to serve as a foreperson again.

3. *Management position in the workplace.* Someone who holds a management position at her workplace has experience managing groups of people and, consequently, may be more comfortable serving in a leadership role. This is a person who is used to stepping in and resolving arguments and disagreements between individuals, which may position her to do so during deliberations.

4. *Higher education.* Research shows that greater education can be an indicator of opinion leadership. These are individuals who often enjoy challenges and are comfortable working through complex and competing information in order to resolve a problem. These characteristics position them to exert considerable leadership in deliberations.

5. *Strong moral convictions.* Research shows that jurors who express strong moral convictions exert more influence during deliberations. In other words, if a juror makes strong appeals to core values or principles during voir dire, he may be motivated to argue aggressively in deliberations due to the personal connection via the value or principle he has with the case.

6. *Case-related expertise.* Lawsuits typically involve lots of complex information that jurors make great efforts to understand. When a juror has case-related expertise, due to their education or job, they may be able to exert considerable influence on the other jurors. If other jurors perceive this expertise, they may defer to this juror as they attempt to make sense of issues in the case. This can be extremely dangerous, as this non-testifying expert on the jury may be tempted to fill information gaps in the case with their own personal experiences and beliefs about how things happen in the real world.

7. *Strong communication skills.* Jurors who appear comfortable and confident speaking during voir dire are strong candidates for opinion leaders in deliberations. In many respects, voir dire is a form of public speaking. When a juror speaks, she is speaking in front of a large group of individuals in what is often perceived as an intimidating environment. A juror who is comfortable and confident speaking in the courtroom will also be comfortable and confident playing an active role in deliberations. Similarly, jurors who are articulate in addition to their comfort and confidence are more likely to influence other jurors during deliberations.

8. *Socially active.* The final indicator to look for is the socially active juror. This social activeness may occur inside of the courtroom. For

example, if the juror is a frequent volunteer for different organizations, this suggests he or she is comfortable being in new and different social situations. Inside the courtroom, it may be apparent that the juror likes to strike up conversations with those around him during downtime or breaks, which indicates that he is very comfortable taking the lead in forming relationships with the strangers around him. This can be a strong indicator of influence within jury deliberations.

In Chapter 13, we discuss opinion leaders in more depth and also examine other categories of jurors and whether they can help or hurt your case.

5. *Batson* and Its Offspring

It is critical that you have a working knowledge of *Batson v. Kentucky*[54] and related case law for you to be able to make a *Batson* challenge to prevent your opponent from improperly exercising a peremptory challenge based on the prospective juror's membership in a cognizable group. Conversely, you may need to respond to a *Batson* challenge to your exercise of a peremptory challenge. *Batson* held that a state prosecutor could not exercise a peremptory challenge based on race because it violated the Equal Protection Clause rights of both the defendant and the jurors. Later, the United States Supreme Court extended the *Batson* doctrine to civil cases.[55] Defendants in criminal cases are also subject to *Batson* and may not improperly exercise peremptory challenges.[56]

The party making the *Batson* challenge need not be a member of the cognizable group in order to make it. In *Powers v. Ohio*,[57] a white defendant objected under *Batson* to the prosecution's exercise of peremptory challenges against seven black prospective jurors, but the trial judge disallowed the *Batson* challenges. The Supreme Court held that it was not required that the juror and the party raising the *Batson* challenge share the same race. Rather, the Court held that "race is irrelevant to a defendant's standing to object to the discriminatory use of peremptory challenges."[58]

---

54. *Batson v. Kentucky*, 476 U.S. 79 (1986).
55. *Edmonson v. Leesville Concrete Co.*, 500 U.S. 614 (1991); *J.E.B. v. Ala. ex rel. T.B.*, 511 U.S. 127 (1994).
56. *Georgia v. McCollum*, 505 U.S. 42 (1992).
57. *Powers v. Ohio*, 499 U.S. 400 (1991).
58. *Powers v. Ohio*, 499 U.S. 400, 416 (1991).

a. Cognizable Groups

Since the *Batson* decision, its cognizable groups have been expanded to include ethnicity.[59] Other cognizable groups falling under the *Batson* doctrine include: white males;[60] Native Americans;[61] homosexuals;[62] and individuals with a particular sexual orientation.[63]

Batson has not been extended to these groups: unemployed persons;[64] people who harbor reservations about the death penalty.[65] and ex-felons.[66]

b. Other Groups — Religion, National Origin and Economic Status

An argument exists that under 28 U.S.C. § 1862 three other protected groups exist—those with a particular religion, national origin or economic status, and that prospective jurors cannot be deselected on those grounds. 28 U.S.C. § 1862 provides:

> No citizen shall be excluded from service as a grand or petit juror in the district courts of the United States or in the Court of International Trade on account of race, color, *religion*, sex, *national origin, or economic status*.

United States v. Dejesus[67] skirted the issue of whether the exercise of peremptories on the basis of religion is unconstitutional. In *Dejesus*, the United States Court of Appeals affirmed the District Court's findings that the "government's strikes were based on the jurors' heightened religious involvement rather than their religious affiliation," and did not reach the question of "whether a peremptory strike based solely on religious affiliation would be unconstitutional."[68]

---

59. *Hernandez v. New York*, 500 U.S. 352 (1991) (also including gender); *J.E.B. v. Ala. ex rel T.B.*, 511 U.S. 127 (1994).

60. *People v. Willis*, 27 Cal. 4th 811, 813 (2002).

61. *State v. Locklear*, 505 S.E.2d 277 (N.C. 1998).

62. *People v. Garcia*, 77 Cal. App. 4th 1279 (2000).

63. *SmithKline Beecham Corporation v. Abbott Labs.*, 740 F.3d 471 (9th Cir. 2014).

64. *People v. Johnson*, 47 Cal. 3d 1194 (1989).

65. *People v. Pinholster*, 1 Cal. 4th 865, 913 (1992).

66. *People v. Karis*, 46 Cal. 3d 612, 631 (1988).

67. *United States v. Dejesus*, 347 F.3d 500 (3d Cir. 2003).

68. *Dejesus*, 347 F.3d at 510.

c. Three-Step Process

Batson announced a three-step process for a trial judge's decision-making when a *Batson* challenge has been made. First, the party making the *Batson* challenge must establish a prima facie showing that the opposing party's peremptory challenge was exercised on the basis of race, gender or ethnicity. Second, if the showing has been made, then the burden shifts to the party who exercised the challenge to offer a race-neutral (or gender-neutral or ethnicity-neutral) explanation for challenging the prospective juror. Third, if a neutral explanation is presented, then based upon what the parties have offered, the judge will decide whether the side that made the *Batson* challenge has proved purposeful discrimination.[69]

i. Step One: The Batson *Challenger*— *Prima Facie Showing*

Counsel may make the *Batson* challenge or the court may sua sponte raise the challenge. For instance, if the judge observes that counsel has exercised a peremptory challenge against a member of a cognizable group, the judge may ask counsel to state a non-discriminatory reason for exercising the peremptory.

To make a prima facie case that the peremptory challenge was based on race, gender or ethnicity, the party bringing the *Batson* challenge need raise only an inference that the other party has excluded a member of a cognizable group.[70] To establish this, counsel should make a record that opposing counsel has exercised a peremptory against a prospective juror who belongs to a cognizable group and that grounds exist for the inference that the peremptory was exercised for discriminatory purposes.

You should watch and listen closely for evidence that opposing counsel is acting in a discriminatory way by treating members of a cognizable group differently. You are looking for a pattern of exclusion of a cognizable group. This is critical because, as will be seen in the discussion of step three, the trial court will do a comparative analysis to determine whether the treatment of a member of the cognizable group was different from that of the rest of the panel. Further, if the *Batson* challenge fails and the issue is raised on appeal, the appellate court likewise should do a comparative analysis.

---

69. *Batson v. Kentucky*, 476 U.S. 79, 96–98 (1986); *Johnson v. California*, 545 U.S. 162, 168 (2005); *Foster v. Chatman*, 136 S. Ct. 1737 (2016).

70. *Batson v. Kentucky*, 476 U.S. 79, 96 (1986).

The strongest evidence of discriminatory use of peremptory challenges is that opposing counsel has exercised peremptory challenges to excuse multiple members of a minority group. Other evidence of discrimination can be that the questions addressed to members of a cognizable group differ from those asked or not asked at all of other prospective jurors. In sum, similarly situated jurors should be treated the same.

The *Batson* challenger should make the challenge not only before the jury is sworn but also before the venire is dismissed. A timely challenge both provides the trial judge an opportunity to remedy any discriminatory act and forestalls any claim that the challenge was untimely and thus waived. Although federal circuits that have considered the timeliness issue have not arrived at a set rule, some have held that the challenge should be raised before voir dire is completed or the jury sworn.[71] While the United States Supreme Court has not ruled on the timeliness question, in *Ford v. Georgia*,[72] it considered the Georgia Supreme Court's rule requiring that any *Batson* claim should be "raised prior to the time the jurors selected to try the case are sworn" and observed "any *Batson* claim [to] be raised not only before trial, but in the period between the selection of the jurors and the administration of their oaths, is a sensible rule."

On the state court level, *State v. Ford*[73] held that a *Batson* challenge is not timely if the jury has been sworn and the venire dismissed, and observed that "[s]everal jurisdictions have closely analyzed *Batson*'s language and concluded that the U.S. Supreme Court envisioned that a *Batson* challenge must be made before the jury is sworn," and cited several state appellate decisions barring *Batson* objections after the jury is sworn and the venire is dismissed).

ii. Step One: Avoiding or Responding to a Batson *Challenge*

The best way to avoid a *Batson* challenge is to do the right thing, not discriminate either in exercising peremptories or in conducting voir dire. All prospective jurors should be treated equally unless a neutral reason exists for doing otherwise.

Counsel should be aware of and keep a record of the race, gender, and ethnicity of every prospective juror who belongs to a cognizable group and against

---

71. *United States v. Cashwell*, 950 F.2d 699, 704 (11th Cir. 1992); *Government of Virgin Islands v. Forte*, 806 F.2d 73, 75–76 (3d Cir. 1986); *United States v. Contreras-Contreras*, 83 F.3d 1103, 1104 (9th Cir. 1996).

72. *Ford v. Georgia*, 498 U.S. 411, 422 (1991).

73. *State v. Ford*, 306 Mont. 517, 39 P.3d 108, 112 (2001).

whom a peremptory challenge is exercised, along with detailed notes of the race-neutral reasons for the challenge. For each challenged person who fits within a cognizable group, counsel should be ready to provide the judge with that neutral justification for the peremptory challenge.

At this juncture, the burden is with the party making the *Batson* challenge to make a prima facie showing of discrimination. The responding party should refrain from explaining why the peremptory was exercised.

iii. Step Two: The Batson Challenger

If the court rules that a prima facie case has been made that the peremptory was exercised as a result of prohibited discrimination, the burden shifts to the party exercising it to provide a neutral justification.

iv. Step Two: The Responder — Neutral Justification for the Challenge

The second step requires the responding attorney to offer nondiscriminatory grounds for the exercising the peremptory. The process does not require that the response to the *Batson* challenge provide an explanation for the peremptory challenge that is either persuasive or even plausible. Rather, the issue is the facial validity of the explanation. Unless the discriminatory intent is inherent in the attorney's explanation, it will be assumed neutral.[74]

At this point, the explanation may be based on the challenging attorney's personal observation. Neutral grounds found legitimate under *Batson* include:

- the juror appeared to fall asleep during voir dire;[75]
- the juror had an angry look and appeared not to want to be there;[76]
- the juror had a strong personality;[77]
- the juror did not have experience being employed;[78]
- the juror fidgeted;[79]
- the jurors who were disinterested or inattentive or could not work with other jurors;[80]

---

74. *Purkett v. Elem*, 514 U.S. 765, 767 (1995).
75. *United States v. White*, 552 F.3d 240, 251–52 (2d Cir. 2009).
76. *White*, 552 F.3d at 251.
77. *United States v. Fields*, 378 F. Supp. 2d 1329, 1331 (E.D. Okla. 2005).
78. *Stubbs v. Gomez*, 189 F.3d 1099 (9th Cir. 1999).
79. *United States v. Power*, 881 F.2d 733 (9th Cir. 1989).
80. *United States v. Changco*, 1 F.3d 837, 840 (9th Cir. 1993).

- the juror "wore a beret one day and a sequined cap the next";[81]
- the juror had a dental abscess;[82]
- the juror lacked outside hobbies and interests;[83] and
- the juror served on a jury that previously acquitted a criminal defendant.[84]

After examining such explanations, commentators have observed:

> Many of the above explanations had a tenuous connection, at best, to the trial; in one case, the prosecutor even admitted that the explanation was "rather a stretch." However, the courts approving these explanations often cited the Supreme Court's rule that a trial judge must accept even "silly or superstitious" explanations at step two so long as the explanations are facially race and gender neutral; moreover, the Court further dictates that lower courts can reject those reasons at step three only if they find that the attorney is lying.[85]

v. Step Three: The Batson Challenger — Trial Court Determination

During the third step, the party raising the *Batson* challenge has the burden of proving purposeful discrimination. At this third step, the persuasiveness of the responding lawyer's explanation becomes relevant. The court may find that the lawyer's explanation for exercising the peremptory challenge was a mere pretext.[86]

The trial court must determine on the record whether there is a legitimate factual basis underpinning the neutral justification offered by the party wanting to exercise the peremptory challenge and whether there was purposeful discrimination.[87] During this step, the trial court will decide whether the party challenging the prospective juror had discriminatory intent. The trial court's decision calls for an evaluation of the challenging attorney's credibility and whether the basis offered is a legitimately neutral justification or a pretext. On

---

81. *Smulls v. Roper*, 535 F.3d 853, 856 (8th Cir. 2008) (en banc).
82. *United States v. Walley*, 567 F.3d 354, 357 (8th Cir. 2009).
83. *Lewis v. Bennett*, 435 F. Supp. 2d 184, 191 (W.D.N.Y. 2006).
84. United *States v. Douglas*, 525 F.3d 225, 241 (2d Cir. 2008).
85. Jeffrey Bellin & Junichi P. Semitsu, *Widening Batson's Net to Ensnare More Than the Unapologetically Bigoted or Painfully Unimaginative Attorney*, 96 CORNELL L.R. 1075, 1097 (2011).
86. *People v. Reynoso*, 74 P.3d 852, 860 (2003).
87. *Snyder v. Louisiana*, 552 U.S. 472 (2008).

this issue, the best evidence is the demeanor of the attorney who exercised the peremptory challenge.[88] The Supreme Court has held that the trial court's ruling on this issue will not be overturned on appeal unless it is clearly erroneous, holding that the trial court's role is pivotal, because the trial judge must evaluate the demeanor of the attorney exercising the challenge.[89]

At this stage, the *Batson* attorney exercising the peremptory challenge attempts to establish the discriminatory intent of the *Batson* challenger and establish that the explanation was a mere pretext. This is where a comparative analysis comes into play. The United States Supreme Court did a comparative analysis in *Miller-El v. Dretke*[90] and held: "If a prosecutor's proffered reason for striking a black panelist applies just as well to an otherwise-similar nonblack who is permitted to serve, that is evidence tending to prove purposeful discrimination to be considered *Batson*'s third step."

Comparative Analysis Example: *Foster v. Chatman*[91] serves as an example of the comparative analysis and the fact-finding process conducted in step three. In *Foster*, the Supreme Court reversed and remanded a case in which the defendant had 30 years before been convicted of capital murder and sentenced to death. The Court's decision focused only upon *Batson*'s third step and whether the prosecution purposefully discriminated in exercising peremptories against prospective jurors Garrett and Hood.

The Court noted that on their face, the eleven justifications offered for striking black prospective juror Garrett "seem[ed] reasonable enough."[92] However, the Supreme Court found that, based on the evidence, that the prosecutor's assertion that striking Garrett was a last minute decision was false ("In short, contrary to the prosecutions submissions, the State's resolve to strike Garrett was never in doubt.").[93]

While the prosecution offered eight reasons for striking another prospective juror Hood, the Supreme Court held, "An examination of the record, however, convinces us that many of these justifications cannot be credited."[94] The Court noted that, pretrial, the prosecutor stated that the only reason he was concerned about Hood was that he had an 18-year-old son who was about the same age as the defendant, but later in a motion for new trial, the pros-

---

88. *Hernandez v. New York*, 500 U.S. 352, 365 (1991).
89. *Snyder v. Louisiana*, 552 U.S. 472 (2008).
90. *Miller-El v. Dretke*, 545 U.S. 231, 241 (2005).
91. *Foster v. Chatman*, 136 S. Ct. 1737 (2016).
92. *Id.* at 1749.
93. *Id.* at 1750.
94. *Id.* at 1751.

ecution pointed to Hood's church affiliation and a belief that the affiliation would prevent him from imposing the death penalty. The Supreme Court examined both reasons and discredited each. First, the Court noted that another white juror, who had a 17-year-old son, was accepted and that this justification was pretextual. Second, the Supreme Court pointed out that Hood asserted four times that he could impose the death penalty, and held that the record persuaded the Court that race, not religious affiliation, was the prosecutor's true motivation. In addition to the comparative analysis, the Supreme Court relied on notations in the prosecution's file, stating: "The contents of the prosecution's file, however, plainly belie the State's claim that it exercised its strikes in a 'color-blind' manner."[95]

vi. Step Three: The Responder— Meeting the Batson Challenge

It bears repeating that the best way to avoid or meet a *Batson* challenge is to do the right thing—treat all prospective jurors the same unless you have a non-discriminatory reason for doing otherwise. But, counsel needs to do more. Whenever counsel exercises a peremptory challenge against a member of a cognizable group, counsel should be ready to refute any contention that the challenged juror was treated differently. This requires that counsel be able both to identify others on the panel who are similarly situated and to distinguish the situation of the challenged juror from that of the unchallenged jurors.

In *Foster*, the prosecution claimed that notes in the State's file were made in an effort ensure that the State was "thoughtful and non-discriminatory in [its] consideration of black prospective jurors [and] to develop and maintain detailed information on those prospective jurors in order to properly defend against any suggestion that decisions regarding [its] selections were pretextual."[96] The Supreme Court found the claim reeked of an afterthought and that "the focus on race in the prosecution's file plainly demonstrates a concerted effort to keep black prospective jurors off the jury."[97]

If the court denies the *Batson* challenge and excuses the juror, counsel should present findings of fact to the court that support the trial court's ruling that a neutral basis existed for exercising the peremptory challenge and that the party bringing the *Batson* challenge has not proven purposeful discrimination.

---

95. *Id.* at 1755
96. *Id.*
97. *Id.* at 1742.

Batson **Challenge Example:** In *People v. Harmon*, a domestic violence assault case, the defense made a *Batson* challenge (referred to in California as a *Batson-Wheeler* motion), the prosecution responded, and the judge ruled:

(The following proceedings were held at the sidebar)

THE COURT: We are at sidebar. Go ahead.

MR. WILLIAMS: Yes, Your Honor. There's very few people of color on this venier (sic.) as it is. Already one person of color was excused before, Juror No. 5, and I don't remember this witness saying anything, that I can see—I can only see him being excused as to race. I don't think he was in any way even inquired of regarding any question.

THE COURT: So the first issue you believe is a challenge due to group association?

MR. WILLIAMS: That's correct.

THE COURT: Okay. So the issue is regarding a prima facie case of discrimination.

MR. WILLIAMS: Yes.

THE COURT: Do you want to make a record of your strong likelihood that the person is excused because of his group association? And let me grab my notes relating to that juror.

(Brief pause in the proceedings.)

THE COURT: Okay. Go ahead.

MR. WILLIAMS: Yes, Your Honor.

I just don't see any other reason for him being excused other than race. He is not—I don't think either one of the defense counsel or prosecution inquired of him personally or he has posed any opinions whatsoever to either side that would make him excludable or to get rid of him other than race.

That's the only thing I can see. I didn't see him make any comments about police officers. He didn't make any comments regarding anything in his background. That he had been arrested. That he favors one side or the other.

So the only thing that I can see is he's being excluded or excused because of race.

THE COURT: Okay. I would find he's within a recognized group, that being black.

People want to respond?

MS. CORSA: Yes, Your Honor.

First, I don't believe the defense has made a prima facie case. However, I do have reasons for that peremptory.

First of all, this is a male and he appeared to be late 40's, early 50's, still single, no kids, no family, seems to lead a very isolated life. I don't know that he has the relationship experience to relate to the relationship dynamics in this domestic violence case.

He works as a custodian and lives in downtown Los Angeles, which seems to add to that somewhat isolated life. His occupation by its nature is one that does not involve group activities and teamwork, and I'm not sure that he could work as a team, in a team setting, to reach a group decision in this case.

Furthermore, his body language throughout the proceedings, from my observations, he had his arms folded, he looked annoyed to be here, he didn't respond to questions I asked, he did not volunteer information, and every time I looked at him, he looked away and had a look that appeared to be very unhappy to be here, and based on that I exercised that peremptory.

THE COURT: Anything else you want to add?

MR. WILLIAMS: No, Your Honor.

THE COURT: I find, based on the explanation of the People, that in fact the peremptory was not exercised based on or predicated by group bias, but rather the People have valid reasons for excusing the juror, so the Wheeler motion is respectfully denied.[98]

d. Implicit Bias, *Batson*'s Third Step and Potential Change

In *State v. Saintcalle*,[99] the Washington State Supreme Court decided that the trial court's finding that there was no purposeful discrimination by the prosecutor in exercising a peremptory strike against a black prospective juror was not clearly erroneous, and therefore, the conviction was affirmed. But, the majority opinion questioned whether, given the nature of implicit bias, *Batson* was sufficient to eliminate racial discrimination in jury selection. The majority opinion stated:

> However, we also take this opportunity to examine whether our *Batson* procedures are robust enough to effectively combat race discrimination in the selection of juries. We conclude that they are not. Twenty-six

98. Transcript of Proceedings at 189–90, *People v. Harmon*, 2007 WL 5181456, 188–192 (2007), App. 3.2

99. *State v. Saintcalle*, 305 P.3d 326, 329, 178 Wash. 2d 34 (2013).

years after *Batson,* a growing body of evidence shows that racial discrimination remains rampant in jury selection. In part, this is because
Batson recognizes only "purposeful discrimination," whereas racism
is often unintentional, institutional, or unconscious. We conclude that
our *Batson* procedures must change and that we must strengthen *Batson* to recognize these more prevalent forms of discrimination.

The Court went on to observe that *Batson's* third step is inadequate to
address implicit bias as follows:

> Unconscious stereotyping upends the *Batson* framework. *Batson* is
> only equipped to root out *"purposeful"* discrimination, which many
> trial courts probably understand to mean conscious discrimination....
> But discrimination in this day and age is frequently unconscious and
> less often consciously purposeful. That does not make it any less per-
> nicious. Problematically, people are rarely aware of the actual reasons
> for their discrimination and will genuinely believe the race-neutral
> reason they create to mask it.... Since *Batson's* third step hinges on
> credibility, this makes it very difficult to sustain a *Batson* challenge
> even in situations where race has in fact affected decision-making....
>
> More troubling for *Batson* is research showing that people will act
> on unconscious bias far more often if reasons exist giving plausible
> deniability (e.g., an opportunity to present a race-neutral reason).[100]

Both a concurring justice in *Saintcalle,* who called for the immediate elim-
ination of peremptory strikes, and the majority of the court held that it had
the "authority to pioneer new procedures within existing Fourteenth Amendment frameworks" and that the change should be considered through a rule-
making process, rather than in the specific case.[101]

In the wake of the *Saintcalle* decision, the American Civil Liberties Union
of Washington proposed the following court rule for the Washington State
Supreme Court's adoption:

RULE 36. JURY SELECTION

(a) **Scope of rule.** This procedure is to be followed in all jury trials.
(b) A party may object to an adverse party's use of a peremptory chal-
    lenge on the grounds that the race or ethnicity of the prospective
    juror could be viewed as a factor in the use of the challenge, or the

---

100. *Id.* at 336 (citations omitted).
101. *Id.* at 337–38.

court may raise this objection sua sponte. When such an objection is made, the party exercising the peremptory challenge must articulate on the record the reasons for the peremptory challenge.

(c) Using an objective observer standard, the court shall evaluate the reasons proffered for the challenge. If the court determines that an objective observer could view race or ethnicity as a factor for the peremptory challenge, the challenge shall be denied.

The comments to the proposed rule explain that it is intended to remove the requirement that the trial court find purposeful discrimination. The comments, in part, state:

[1] The purpose of this rule is to eliminate the unfair exclusion of potential jurors based on race. This rule responds to problems with the *Batson* test described in *State v. Saintcalle*, 178 Wn.2d 34 (2013), and provides a different standard for determining whether a peremptory challenge is invalid than that provided for in *Batson v. Kentucky*, 476 U.S. 79 (1986). For purposes of this rule it is irrelevant whether it can be proved that a prospective juror's race or ethnicity actually played a motivating role in the exercise of a peremptory challenge.

[2] An objective observer is one who is aware that purposeful discrimination and implicit, institutional, or unconscious bias have resulted in the unfair exclusion of potential jurors based on race in Washington....[102]

---

102. https://www.courts.wa.gov/court_rules/?fa=court_rules.proposedRuleDisplay&ruleId=537.

Chapter 4

Preparation for Jury Selection

"I feel that luck is preparation meeting opportunity."

Oprah Winfrey,
Media proprietor, talk show host, actress

"Well, I will outwork the other side every single time. At the start of every trial, the other side starts out working as hard as I do. But at some point, they say, 'I'm going to go out with my girlfriend,' or spouse, go to the opera, go see the latest movie. And at every trial I've ever had, the other side stops working as hard as me—if they ever did, sometimes they never do."

David Boies,
Preeminent trial lawyer
Lawdragon, 198 (2012)

A. Preparing for a Successful Jury Selection: Five Goals

1. The Primary Goal: Deselection

Your preparation for jury selection should be guided by what you want to accomplish during that phase of trial. It is important to begin with a clear understanding of what you actually have control over versus what you may not have control over. Despite the fact that procedures vary from venue to venue and judge to judge, there is a single goal that will always be within your control: collecting information about prospective jurors that will enable you to deselect problematic prospective jurors from the panel. This is the most important task of jury selection and should guide your decisions.

At least four reasons exist for making deselection your chief goal for jury selection. First, jury selection is not like a draft in professional sports. The only thing you have control over during jury selection is the removal of jurors. Consequently, it does no good to focus on identifying the good jurors. Second, focusing on good jurors is actually counterproductive, because it outs those jurors to the other side. In other words, if you are asking questions designed to identify your good jurors, the answers they give will help the other side understand that those same jurors are not good for them. This is an unfortunate result if the other side would have otherwise not noticed the good jurors in question.

Third, negative attitudes and experiences are much more predictive of human behavior than positive experiences and attitudes. For example, if you look at the comments section of any online publication, the bulk of the comments rarely consist of praise. Instead, they tend to consist of criticism. In other words, the critical viewpoints, not the positive ones, are the ones that motivated the people to comment.

This phenomenon of negative attitudes and experiences driving behavior is particularly true in jury deliberations. The old adage in the jury consulting industry is that a verdict is a product of what jurors choose to focus on and talk about most during deliberations. Over time, focus naturally becomes critical. In other words, if jurors are going to spend hours or days talking about the defendant in deliberations, it is not going to consist of hours or days of praising the defendant. There is only so much praise that can be given, in part because praise does not evolve over the course of jury deliberations in the way that criticism does. Praise is one-dimensional and lacks all of the dramatic narrative elements that pull jurors into the issue. Conversely, criticism can evolve over the course of a long discussion. Jurors can talk about motives and they can theorize about what led a particular party to make a particular decision. This gossip style of discussion is often more self-sustaining in deliberation than praise. Consequently, if deliberations are going to be driven by critical focus, it is important for attorneys to identify what kind of criticism the jurors commonly embrace, whether it be beliefs that corporations put profits above all else or that plaintiffs abuse the legal system to obtain undeserved windfalls.

Fourth and finally, the case for deselection boils down to risk management. The risks of being wrong about a bad juror are so much greater than the risks of being wrong about a good juror. In the former scenario, you are now stuck with someone on the jury whom you thought was good, but is in fact bad.

That is a pretty severe consequence. In the latter scenario, it is unfortunate to eliminate a juror from the panel because you erroneously thought he was bad, but that does not have as much of an impact on the jury as the first scenario.

2. Four Other Goals

Four other goals can be sought, but those should never be sought at the expense of successfully accomplishing your primary task of deselection. It makes no sense to cede your actual control over these items in exchange for trying to accomplish less measurable and less reliable goals. The other goals that may be desirable, but involve a great deal of uncertainty as to whether they can actually be accomplished, are these:

1. Leaving a favorable impression of yourself;
2. Dealing with case weaknesses and juror misconceptions;
3. Gathering material from the jurors for use at trial, such as a promise to follow a particular law; and
4. Advancing your legal position, case story and theme in order to determine whether or not the prospective jurors are receptive to them.

Considerable debate exists concerning whether the last goal of introducing your legal position, case narrative and theme is effective and sensible, and we discuss the pros and cons throughout this book.

In this chapter, we explore the preparation that is necessary to effectively accomplish all five goals. Specifically, we examine the following: scouting both the judge and prospective jurors; assembling both your voir dire tools and team; planning to make and meet objections; preparing the trial team and the client; and developing an agenda for jury selection.

B. Scouting the Court — Know Your Judge's Proclivities

Because the ways individual judges conduct jury selection differ from each other, it is critical that you learn what your judge expects of you during jury selection. You want to be prepared to effectively engage in jury selection, as your judge will conduct it. Moreover, you want the judge to neither interrupt you, nor correct you and/or reprimand you during jury selection. The lack of preparation not only hurts you and your client but also impacts all trial lawyers. Some judges across the country have adopted strict jury selection procedures that place significant limits on attorneys due to perceptions that attorneys do not wisely and effectively use the time they are given. A common victim in this scenario is attorney-conducted voir dire. Some judges, particularly in the Northeast, simply do not allow it. Some have openly stated that they believe it is a waste of time, citing anecdotes of questionable strategies deployed by various attorneys.

If you have had an opportunity to observe your judge conduct jury selection or have had a jury trial before the judge, then you are familiar with the judge's expectations of counsel. If you have not had the luxury of watching the judge conduct jury selection before, you can ask colleagues, court personnel or the judge for guidance. Judges often appreciate such inquiries in advance of trial, and they send the message to the court that you are organized and prepared. Also, as we will discuss later, you can search online for the judge's guidelines for jury selection.

1. Questions about the Court's Procedures

The following is a checklist of questions and follow-up questions about the court's procedures that you will need to have answered before commencing jury selection:

- Are attorneys' preliminary statements to the panel allowed? (Any limitations?)
- Where to stand? (Free to walk around? Behind a lectern?)
- What types of questions are impermissible?
- Can attorneys ask questions to the entire jury venire or only those seated in the box?
- How much attorney-conducted voir dire time will each side receive?
- How are challenges for cause to be exercised? (In front of the panel? At side bar? Other?)
- If more than one party is on a side, how may peremptory challenges per party? Or, are they joined in a challenge?
- Are any of the peremptories designated only for alternate spots?
- How will the alternate jurors be selected?
- How are peremptory challenges to be exercised? (In front of the panel? Side bar? Other?)
- How much time per side for questioning? (More than one round of questioning?)
- Will the prospective jurors fill out customized questionnaires?
- How will jurors who are struck from the box be replaced? (Numerically or random?)

- Any other instructions on how the court would like jury selection conducted?
- If one side passes when it is their turn to exercise a peremptory, do they lose that peremptory challenge or are they simply limited to peremptory challenges to only new jurors into the box?
- How does the jury select its presiding juror? (Some venues have statutes or rules in place that designate a particular seat number, such as seat number one, as the presiding juror.)

2. Court Rules and Statutes

You should familiarize yourself with your jurisdiction's court rules and statutes governing jury selection. For a federal trial, you will need to know Federal Rules of Civil Procedure 47 and 48, any district court local rules, and the individual judge's rules, standing order or directives.

a. Federal Civil Rules on Jury Selection

Federal Rule of Civil Procedure 47 Selecting Jurors states:

(a) EXAMINING JURORS. The court may permit the parties or their attorneys to examine prospective jurors or may itself do so. If the court examines the jurors, it must permit the parties or their attorneys to make any further inquiry it considers proper, or must itself ask any of their additional questions it considers proper.

(b) PEREMPTORY CHALLENGES. The court must allow the number of peremptory challenges provided by 28 U.S.C. § 1870.

(c) EXCUSING A JUROR. During trial or deliberation, the court may excuse a juror for good cause.

Federal Rule of Civil Procedure 48 Number of Jurors; Verdict; Polling provides:

(a) NUMBER OF JURORS. A jury must begin with at least 6 and no more than 12 members, and each juror must participate in the verdict unless excused under Rule 47(c).

(b) VERDICT. Unless the parties stipulate otherwise, the verdict must be unanimous and must be returned by a jury of at least 6 members.

(c) POLLING. After a verdict is returned but before the jury is discharged, the court must on a party's request, or may on its own, poll the jurors individually. If the poll reveals a lack of unanimity or lack of assent by the number of jurors that the parties stipulated to, the court may direct the jury to deliberate further or may order a new trial.

b. Federal Criminal Rules on Jury Selection

Federal Rule of Criminal Procedure 24 Number of Jurors; Verdict; Polling provides:

(a) EXAMINATION.
    (1) *In General.* The court may examine prospective jurors or may permit the attorneys for the parties to do so.
    (2) *Court Examination.* If the court examines the jurors, it must permit the attorneys for the parties to:
        (A) ask further questions that the court considers proper; or
        (B) submit further questions that the court may ask if it considers them proper.

(b) PEREMPTORY CHALLENGES. Each side is entitled to the number of peremptory challenges to prospective jurors specified below. The court may allow additional peremptory challenges to multiple defendants, and may allow the defendants to exercise those challenges separately or jointly.
    (1) *Capital Case.* Each side has 20 peremptory challenges when the government seeks the death penalty.
    (2) *Other Felony Case.* The government has 6 peremptory challenges and the defendant or defendants jointly have 10 peremptory challenges when the defendant is charged with a crime punishable by imprisonment of more than one year.
    (3) *Misdemeanor Case.* Each side has 3 peremptory challenges when the defendant is charged with a crime punishable by fine, imprisonment of one year or less, or both.

(c) ALTERNATE JURORS.
    (1) *In General.* The court may impanel up to 6 alternate jurors to replace any jurors who are unable to perform or who are disqualified from performing their duties.
    (2) *Procedure.*
        (A) Alternate jurors must have the same qualifications and be selected and sworn in the same manner as any other juror.
        (B) Alternate jurors replace jurors in the same sequence in which the alternates were selected. An alternate juror who replaces a juror has the same authority as the other jurors.

(3) *Retaining Alternate Jurors.* The court may retain alternate jurors after the jury retires to deliberate. The court must ensure that a retained alternate does not discuss the case with anyone until that alternate replaces a juror or is discharged. If an alternate replaces a juror after deliberations have begun, the court must instruct the jury to begin its deliberations anew.

(4) *Peremptory Challenges.* Each side is entitled to the number of additional peremptory challenges to prospective alternate jurors specified below. These additional challenges may be used only to remove alternate jurors.

   (A) *One or Two Alternates.* One additional peremptory challenge is permitted when one or two alternates are impaneled.

   (B) *Three or Four Alternates.* Two additional peremptory challenges are permitted when three or four alternates are impaneled.

   (C) *Five or Six Alternates.* Three additional peremptory challenges are permitted when five or six alternates are impaneled.

3. Court's Published Guidelines

The trial judge may have published guidelines for jury selection. The first stop in researching the judge is the judge's website. The following are examples of a federal judge's instructions to trial counsel and a state trial court judge's instructions. These examples illustrate the contrasting approaches between the federal and state court levels and the difference in the amount of information that judges can provide online:

Federal Court Judicial Guidelines Example:

United States District Court
Western District of Washington
Honorable Marsha J. Pechman

Voir Dire

Judge Pechman uses the "struck jury" system of juror selection. The entire panel is assigned numbers and seated in order.

The parties are requested to submit questions which they would like addressed to the entire juror panel. The questions must be submitted in advance of the day of jury selection and should be questions which can be answered with a "yes" or "no;" open-ended questions are not appropriate for this phase of voir dire. Judge Pechman asks the questions to the panel as a whole. Once Judge Pechman has questioned the panel, they are turned over to counsel for the parties for their portion of voir dire.

Time limits for voir dire are established at the pretrial conference, depending on the type of case and the issues presented; for example, each side may be given an initial round of 20 minutes with a follow-up round of 10 minutes (if needed). Questions may be addressed to the panel as a whole or to individual jurors. Challenges for cause are made at the time they arise.

Following the conclusion of counsel's voir dire, peremptory challenges are made against those seated in the jury box, then the juror with the next highest assigned number outside the box is seated. Peremptory challenges continue until both sides are satisfied with the jurors seated, or until those challenges are exhausted.[1]

State Court Judicial Guidelines Example:

JURY SELECTION OVERVIEW
Honorable Timothy A. Bradshaw
King County Superior Court

Voir dire is conducted under the direction of the Court. The Court has the responsibility to ensure a fair trial and to remind the jurors of the fundamental principles that govern trials. Counsel may be interrupted without objection. Counsel will act with respect for jurors and their service. The parties must have an accurate estimate of trial length.

The following types of questions are generally improper:

1. Repetitive or embarrassing questions
2. Questions meant to establish a personal rapport with a juror
3. Questions that ask a jury to speculate on a verdict if certain facts are proved
4. Questions that 'push' the evidence as opposed to gleaning information from a juror

---

1. Hon. Marsha J. Pechman, *Voir Dire*, United States District Court, Western District of Washington, http://www.wawd.uscourts.gov/sites/wawd/files/PechmanVoirDire.pdf (Jan. 9, 2017).

5. Questions that are irrelevant to a juror's qualifications
6. Questions that ask a juror to define legal terms

Logistically please note:

1. Counsel will advise jurors of potential witnesses.
2. Peremptory challenges are to be made only against jurors 'seated' in the jury box.
3. Alternate jurors are advised that they are alternates and are seated in chair(s) 13–15.
4. For cause challenges are to be made timely and in open court.

On the following pages is a list of general questions the Court will usually ask. They are subject to supplementation or change depending on the circumstances of the case.

If counsel intends to inquire into matters not usually pursued during voir dire, counsel must notify the Court ahead of time.

Your cooperation will ensure a thorough and prompt selection of the jury.

Thank you.[2]

An example of a court's general questions, like the ones mentioned here by Judge Bradshaw, can be found at pages 32–33.

C. Scouting the Prospective Jurors

1. Investigation of Prospective Jurors

If, prior to trial, your jurisdiction allows you access to a list of prospective jurors in the jury pool along with contact information, you, your jury consultant or other members of your trial team can investigate them. Background research on jurors can be conducted in a variety of ways, including conducting criminal background checks or reviewing other relevant databases. An assistant or investigator may be able to gather information about a prospec-

---

2. Timothy A. Bradshaw, *Judge Directory*, KING COUNTY SUPERIOR COURT, http://www.kingcounty.gov/~/media/courts/superior-court/docs/judges/bradshaw-jury-selection-overview.ashx?la=en ; *see also,* J. Susan J. Craighead, *Judge Directory*, KING COUNTY SUPERIOR COURT, http://www.kingcounty.gov/courts/SuperiorCourt/judges/craighead.aspx.

tive juror's occupation, age, family size, neighborhood and other personal background information.

a. Jury Tampering

It is worth mentioning that under 18 U.S.C. § 1503, jury tampering is prohibited at the federal court level, and every state has a similar criminal statute prohibiting jury tampering.[3] Generally, to be guilty of the crime of jury tampering, the perpetrator must attempt to influence the outcome of the case by communicating with a juror.

b. Internet Searches

A wealth of background information about potential jurors exists on the Internet, particularly in social media, such as Facebook, Twitter, and LinkedIn. Online investigation of prospective jurors is so prevalent that it has even been said: "Anyone who does not make use of [Internet searches] is bordering on malpractice."[4] However, this kind of claim is likely borne out of the belief that "more information is always better." As previously noted, this may not be the case. Attorneys need to determine whether or not Internet searches are worth the time and attention. If so, search websites that can be used to acquire background information about prospective jurors abound, and they range from Google (http://www.google.com) to a search engine designed to provide background information on people, such as pipl (http://www.pipl.com) and court electronic records, such as pacer (http://www.pacer.gov/).

c. Ex Parte Communication and the Internet

Under Model Rule of Professional Conduct 3.5 and the comment to the rule, a lawyer may not communicate ex parte with a prospective juror during the proceeding unless authorized to do so by law or court order.

The American Bar Association issued this Formal Opinion addressing Internet investigations of prospective and selected jurors as follows:

> Unless limited by law or court order, a lawyer may review a juror's or potential juror's Internet presence, which may include postings by the juror or potential juror in advance of and during a trial, but a

---

3. *See, e.g.,* N.M. STAT. §38-5-5.

4. Carol J. Williams, *Jury Duty? May Want to Edit Online Profile,* L.A. TIMES (Sept. 29, 2008), http://articles.latimes.com/print/2008/sep/29/nation/na-jury29 (Jan. 9, 2017).

lawyer may not communicate directly or through another with a juror or potential juror.

A lawyer may not, either personally or through another, send an access request to a juror's electronic social media. An access request is a communication to a juror asking the juror for information that the juror has not made public and that would be the type of ex parte communication prohibited by Model Rule 3.5(b).

The fact that a juror or a potential juror may become aware that a lawyer is reviewing his Internet presence when a network setting notifies the juror of such does not constitute a communication from the lawyer in violation of Rule 3.5(b).

In the course of reviewing a juror's or potential juror's Internet presence, if a lawyer discovers evidence of juror or potential juror misconduct that is criminal or fraudulent, the lawyer must take reasonable remedial measures including, if necessary, disclosure to the tribunal.[5]

The reasoning behind this Formal Opinion was stated in the ABA Committee's conclusion:

In sum, a lawyer may passively review a juror's public presence on the Internet, but may not communicate with a juror. Requesting access to a private area on a juror's ESM (electronic social media) is communication within this framework.

The fact that a juror or a potential juror may become aware that the lawyer is reviewing his Internet presence when an ESM network setting notifies the juror of such review does not constitute a communication from the lawyer in violation of Rule 3.5(b).

If a lawyer discovers criminal or fraudulent conduct by a juror related to the proceeding, the lawyer must take reasonable remedial measures including, if necessary, disclosure to the tribunal.

Internet research during jury selection is common practice. For example, when a New Jersey trial judge ordered plaintiff's counsel to close his laptop because he had not informed opposing counsel of intent to use the courtroom Internet during jury selection, plaintiff on appeal claimed that he had been denied the use of the Internet. The New Jersey Appellate Court did not overturn

---

5. ABA, Formal Op. 466 (2014) (Lawyer Reviewing Jurors' Internet Presence); full opinion can be found in Appendix 4.1.

the trial court, because the plaintiff could not point to a single juror whom he would have dismissed based on the Internet research. However, the Appellate Court observed:

> That [plaintiff's counsel] had the foresight to bring his laptop computer to court, and defense counsel did not, simply cannot serve as a basis for judicial intervention in the name of "fairness" or maintaining "a level playing field." The "playing field" was, in fact, already "level" because [I]nternet access was open to both counsel, even if only one of them chose to utilize it.[6]

The Missouri Supreme Court has gone so far as to hold that counsel must perform a pretrial Internet search with Case.net, Missouri's automated case record service, to preserve the issue of a potential juror's non-disclosure for appeal.[7]

d. Your Jurisdiction's Restrictions

Your jurisdiction may have restrictions regarding online research, and it is critical for the attorneys and jury consultant to be aware of any local rules associated with such research. For example, some jurisdictions do not allow attorneys to conduct social media searches on potential jurors. Even when courts allow these online searches, problems can still arise. For example, some social media sites, such as LinkedIn, allow users to see who has viewed their social media page. Potential jurors may be sensitive to these searches and express concern to the judge. This can sometimes place attorneys in a precarious situation with the court. Finally, attorneys risk backlash from jurors who discover that the attorneys or someone associated with the attorneys searched their social media websites.

e. Value of the Information

The distinction between interesting versus meaningful information obtained from background searches is most important when considering the time and cost that is required. For larger venires, it is time-consuming to search every potential jurors' social media sites. Attorneys may determine that the expense

---

6. *Carino v. Muenzen*, No. L-0028-07, 2010 WL 3448071, 10 (N.J. Super. Ct. App. Div. Aug. 30, 2010).

7. *Johnson v. McCullough*, 306 S.W.3d 551, 559 (Mo. 2010).

and time spent are simply not worth it in light of the lack of meaningful information that is typically obtained from these searches. Other attorneys may determine that any additional information about prospective jurors is worth the time and cost to obtain the information.

Internet searches sometimes produce meaningful background information that is helpful in identifying jurors who have biases. Usually, these situations are case-specific. For example, the search may reveal that a prospective juror owns stock in a company that is a party to the case. And, it may provide you with insight into the candor of a prospective juror when the person claims not to know anything about that corporate party. Failure to disclose such information can serve as grounds for a challenge for cause.

More often, however, social media searches provide interesting information about prospective jurors, but that interesting information usually is neither important nor meaningful information. Before conducting such an investigation, it is important to have a clear idea of what kinds of information you are looking for in your investigation. Otherwise, the investigation becomes an open-ended and rather arbitrary attempt to connect unrelated or, at best, peripherally related findings to how you believe the jurors in question might decide the case. More information is not always better and can often serve as a distraction.

For example, during an Internet search, you may discover that one juror is an active volunteer at her Catholic parish. Upon discovering such information, you may feel as if you discovered something about the juror. The need to feel as if you have greater control over a process that intimidates most attorneys may lead you to want to ascribe some sort of meaning to the fact that this juror is an active volunteer in her Catholic church. But the question is: What does this information actually tell you about the juror within the context of jury selection of your case? It is too easy to make broad assumptions. For example, you may assume that this means they are devoutly religious, when in fact, the only reason they volunteer is because it is a family requirement for their child who they desired to attend private school. Maybe, in reality, religion is not an important part of their life, and instead, this is just a requirement they need to meet. Moreover, this information may be largely irrelevant depending on the type of litigation. A juror's particular belief about the existence of God tells us very little about how she might decide a patent infringement case.

Then, again, the information mined through the investigations of prospective jurors' personal histories must be screened to ensure that it does not constitute a discriminatory reason for exercising a challenge. In the forgoing example, to prevent the person who is a Catholic from sitting on a jury just because of that affiliation would be to discriminate against that person in violation of 28 U.S.C. § 1862, which provides:

> No citizen shall be excluded from service as a grand or petit juror in the district courts of the United States or in the Court of International Trade on account of race, color, *religion*, sex, national origin, or economic status.

Regarding using involvement in religious activities versus religious affiliation as a basis for exercising a peremptory, see the discussion on page 73.

The key in any investigation is to know what you are looking for and not get distracted by anything else, which can be tempting to do.

Attorneys often conduct background searches simply to fill the information void. For example, in venues where the court provides the jury pool list in advance of the actual jury selection, attorneys may feel it is useful to attempt to learn something about prospective jurors rather than simply wait until the day of jury selection. In other instances, attorneys may feel they likely will not receive sufficient information during voir dire, and therefore, they use the Internet and social media as an alternative source of information.

Opinions about the value of background searches vary within the community of jury consultants. Some believe background searches provide important information. Others contend that, setting aside case-specific nuances, background searches rarely provide meaningful information.

2. Jury Service Track Records

Some organizations that engage in a significant amount of trial work, such as defense attorneys for insurance companies, prosecutors and plaintiffs' lawyers, maintain records of juror performance. The track record can include information such as the verdict and the amount of an award.

3. Community Attitude Research

When the magnitude of the case and the budget permits, you may decide to use a jury consultant to research a sample of the population in the community from which the jury pool will be drawn. Based on the study, the consultant can formulate profiles of people who would be sympathetic to your client's claims or defenses and those who would be resistant. A consultant can also gather a focus group to assess your case, and provide you with feedback about your case and juror receptivity to it. All of this information can be valuable to jury selection.

4. Standard Juror Information Form

Having the prospective jurors complete a questionnaire is another method of gathering information about them. Two types of questionnaires exist: (1) the basic juror information form and (2) a customized questionnaire designed for particular case.

Some courts have a juror information form ("short form"), which is a standard questionnaire. In some jurisdictions, this type of standard juror information form is regularly mailed out to members of the jury pool along with the juror summonses.[8] Another approach is to have the pool write out answers on the form when they arrive for jury duty.

More technologically advanced courts have online questionnaires for potential jurors to fill out before they arrive at the courthouse for jury service. In either instance, the information collected from potential jurors is usually limited to basic information, such as demographics, job, whether or not the individual has been party to a lawsuit, and whether or not the person has previously served as a juror.

a. Accessing the Information

Once the juror standard information form has been filled out and returned to the court, a copy is distributed to counsel for use during jury selection. It is important that you know when the information form is available to you. It could be that it will only be available on the day of trial, meaning that you will have to go through the forms on the day of trial and organize information in whatever method you use during jury selection, such as on paper or a computer tablet. Some courts have this information available to counsel days in advance of trial, and you may be able to go to the courthouse and review the information. If you can get the information in advance, it is a great advantage, because you can study the juror information in advance of the trial's start date.

b. Utilizing the Information

It is also important that you know what type of information the court will routinely gather on the standard form because that information not only will aid you in assessing the potential jurors but also help you plan your questioning to avoid asking about matters already revealed in the standard form. You do not want to waste the court's or anyone else's time asking questions that have

---

8. MINN. STAT. § 593.40 (2016).

already been asked and answered. Also, when a questionnaire indicates that inquiring in open court might cause embarrassment to the prospective juror or contaminate the rest of the panel, you can request that inquiry on the sensitive subject be conducted outside the presence of the rest of the panel. Finally, as you will see from the example of the short form below, the prospective jurors are asked why they think they should not be required to serve, such as because of a physical disability or a grounds for being excused. This may provide you with grounds to challenge for cause.

Juror Information Form Example: The following is a list of questions contained in a federal district court's mailed out questionnaire along with the court's explanations for asking each question:

(Question #1) **Are you a citizen of the United States?**—You must be a U.S. Citizen to be eligible to serve.

(Question #2) **Are you 18 years of age or older?**—You must be at least 18 years or older to serve.

(Question #3) **Has your primary residence for the past year been in the same county and state?**—If your answer is no to either or both questions, indicate on the back of the form names and dates of other primary residences.

(Question #4) **Do you read, write, speak, and understand the English Language?**—If another person helps fill out the form for you, please explain why and indicate the name of the person on the back of the form.

(Question #5) **Are any charges now pending against you for a violation of state or federal law punishable by imprisonment for more than one year?**—If so, please explain on the back of the form: The date and nature of the offense, the potential sentence imposed if convicted, and the name of the court. A person is disqualified from jury service only for criminal offenses punishable for more than one year, but it is the maximum *penalty*, and not the actual sentence, which is the determining factor.

(Question #6) **Have you ever been convicted of a state or federal crime for which punishment could have been more than one year in prison?**—If so, please explain on the back of the form: The date and nature of the offense, the sentence imposed, and the name of the court. Unless your civil rights have since been restored, a person is disqualified from jury service for criminal offenses punishable for more than one year, but it is the maximum *penalty*, and not the actual sentence, which is the determining factor.

(Question #7) **Were your civil rights restored?**—If you indicate yes, the court requires official documentation, such as a discharge order. You may find either of these PDF brochures for those convicted in Washington State—**Restoring Your Right to Vote in Washington** and **How Ex-Felons Can Restore Their Right to Vote in Washington**. Otherwise, if your answer to question #6 was "no," you do not have to answer this question.

(Question #8) **Do you have a physical or mental disability that would interfere with or prevent you from serving as a juror?**—Please explain on the back of the form why you are unable to serve and provide medical documentation, if easily attainable. Do not ask the court to contact your doctor for verification.

- Since you may be called over the course of a two-year period, it is important that the court know whether your medical condition is permanent or temporary. Therefore, any information you can provide would be helpful to the court.
- If you wish to serve, but require some sort of accommodation by the court, please indicate the accommodation required on the back of the form.

(Question #9) **Exempt Occupations**—Only the following three full-time occupational categories are considered exemptions from serving:

- Public official of the United States, state, or local government who is elected to public office or directly appointed by one elected to office;
- Member of any governmental police or regular fire department;
- Member in active service of the armed forces of the United States.

If you have a question on whether you fall under one of these three categories, it is best to make a note of your concerns in the "Remarks" section on the back of the questionnaire.

(Question #10) **Race/Ethnicity**—Your answer to this question is required solely to avoid discrimination in juror selection and has absolutely no bearing on qualifications for jury service. In this way, the federal court can fulfill the policy of the United States, which is to provide jurors who are randomly selected from a fair cross section of the community.

(Question #11) **Sex**—Your answer to this question has no bearing on qualification for jury service. However, this information is helpful to the court for statistical reporting purposes and your response is appreciated.

(Question #12) **Occupation**—Federal law requires that you answer this question about your occupation so that we may determine whether you fall within an exemption category.

(Question #13) **Education**—Your answer to this question has no bearing on qualification for jury service. However, your response is appreciated.

(Question #14) **Grounds for requesting excuse**—If one of the following categories applies to you and you wish to be excused for that reason, fill in completely the circle for your category at question 14 on the form:

- A person having served as grand or petit juror in federal court within the last two years;
- A person who serves without compensation as a volunteer firefighter or member of a rescue squad or ambulance crew for a federal, state, or local government agency.

(Question #15) **Marital Status**—Your answer to this question has no bearing on qualification for jury service. However, your response is appreciated.

(Question #16) **Signature**—Be sure that you sign the form. If another person had to fill out the questionnaire for you, that person must indicate his or her name, and the reason why under the "Remarks" section on the back of the form.[9]

5. Customized Juror Questionnaires

Both state and federal courts sometimes have prospective jurors complete a customized juror questionnaire that will help the court and parties learn more about the jurors. Even in instances where the court has potential jurors fill out the short juror information form, the judge may determine that a customized questionnaire is also necessary. The customized questionnaire may supplement the standard juror information form, or the customized one may incorporate the questions from the standard form.

The most common reason for utilizing a customized questionnaire is the nature of the case. Some cases involve highly sensitive issues, and the court believes potential jurors are more likely to be candid in their responses if the potential jurors provide the answers in a questionnaire rather than in open court. A common example is a case involving sensitive personal issues

---

9. Juror Qualification Questionnaire, http://www.wawd.uscourts.gov/jurors/qualification-form#Q8 (Jan. 9, 2017).

(allegation of sexual abuse, sexual harassment) or social issues (attitudes on race, police activities). Many courts have determined that a customized questionnaire is essential in this type of case, and some courts have even developed standard questionnaires for these types of cases. Other cases warranting the use of customized questionnaires are complex trials, trials involving high publicity or death penalty trials.

Some judges have developed or adopted customized questionnaires for types of cases that routinely make it to trial in their courtroom. For example, in King County in Washington State, some judges have developed customized questionnaires for asbestos cases that routinely make it to trial within that venue.

Another reason for a court to authorize a customized juror questionnaire is that their use will make the process of jury selection more efficient. The premise is that a questionnaire, agreed upon by the parties, helps the court and counsel more quickly and efficiently gather information about the prospective jurors than through the ordinary voir dire process. Another rationale is that less time will need to be spent during voir dire and that more information can be gathered with the customized questionnaires.

a. Requesting a Customized Questionnaire

If you want the trial judge to have prospective jurors complete a customized questionnaire, you may make your request in your trial brief, in a motion or, if situation permits, with an informal request. At pages 307–313, we discuss such requests for and responses opposing customized questionnaires. Attorneys requesting the use of a customized questionnaire are most likely to receive approval from the court when both sides jointly make the request in advance of the day of jury selection and when the parties have agreed upon a mutual questionnaire before submitting it to the court for approval. Judges are unlikely to allow such questionnaires when they are proposed to the court for the first time when jury selection is supposed to begin.

b. Problems with Customized Questionnaires

The court may decide not to allow customized questionnaires, because they present logistical and time consumption problems for the court. First, the court may not have the time or resources to create a sufficient number of copies of the questionnaires for the potential jurors on the morning of jury selection. Second, the court may not have the time or resources to make copies of the completed questionnaires in order that all parties have access to them before the jury selection process begins. For this reason, it is helpful to have provided the court the necessary number of copies of the questionnaire for jury selection and offer to make copies for opposing counsel. Some judges are more willing to allow a questionnaire when doing so does not significantly increase the workload for the court staff. It is also helpful to limit the length of the questionnaire. Generally speaking, judges are more likely to approve a one- or two-page questionnaire than a questionnaire that is eight or more pages in length.

Questionnaires may also pose problems for attorneys. A common problem is that attorneys do not have sufficient time to review the completed questionnaires before jury selection begins. This is often the case with larger venires. Most judges want to keep the jury selection process moving and do not like to take long breaks to allow attorneys to spend time reviewing the completed questionnaires. This time problem can be avoided in the rare situation where the court decides to have the potential jurors complete questionnaires prior to the day of jury selection, such as on the Friday before the Monday when jury selection will take place. Finally, while questionnaires can provide attorneys with a lot of useful information, they can also be distracting and unnecessary.

c. Jury Consultant Assistance with Preparation

An attorney can employ a jury consultant in developing a customized juror questionnaire in four ways. First, a jury consultant can help attorneys determine whether or not a customized questionnaire is appropriate for the case. Second, a jury consultant can help attorneys pick the most appropriate areas of exploration for a customized questionnaire. Third, a consultant can help attorneys craft the questions. The wording of a question is very important, because the wording can influence a potential juror's willingness to be open and honest in disclosing personal information. Fourth, a jury consultant can assist with the review of the questionnaires during jury selection. Some consultants have developed effective systems for managing this data in a way that allows for meaningful review within short timeframes.

d. Templates

We provide several examples of juror questionnaires in Appendices that can be found on the online supplement http://caplaw.com/jury, which is a companion to this book. You can use these questionnaires as templates for drafting your customized juror questionnaire. In the Appendix you will find questionnaires from the following:

- *In re TFT-LCD (Flat-Panel)* trial—App. 4.2;
- O.J. Simpson robbery trial—App. 4.3;
- Boston Marathon bomber trial—App. 4.4;
- Juror Questionnaire asbestos trial—App. 4.7; and

- People of California vs. Michael Jackson child molestation trial— App. 4.8.

Customized Questionnaire Example: Another example is Appendix 4.5, which is a 21-page questionnaire tailored for a high profile capital murder case. In addition to questions found in a standard juror information form, such as those pertaining to hardship and eliciting juror background information, the questionnaire delves into these subjects, among many others:

- what the juror may have heard or read about the case;
- opinions that the person may have formed about the case;
- what the person may know about the cost associated with the trial of a capital case;
- any opinion the person may have formed about the fact that the governor had announced a moratorium on the death penalty which suspended executions for the balance of his term as governor;
- the person's beliefs about the death penalty;
- the strength of the person's view of the death penalty;
- whether the person's view on the death penalty is influenced by the person's religious, spiritual, political, or philosophical beliefs;
- the person's views on and life imprisonment without parole; and
- the prospective juror's views on the insanity defense.

D. Assembling Your Tools for Jury Selection

1. Jury Selection Tools

In order for you to carry out jury selection in a confident, conversational manner, you should have your jury selection trial tools readily available. We recommend that you consolidate these tools into as few places as possible and have them at counsel table. You can have a separate jury selection trial notebook, file folder or a computer folder with the necessary tools in it. You may also have a computer tablet for keeping track of juror information. Your essential jury selection tools include the following:

- The law regarding jury selection, such as challenges for cause, peremptory challenges and *Batson* challenges;
- A list of potential objections;
- Your motions that apply to jury selection;
- A place to record where the members of the panel are sitting and your notes about them;

- A place to record challenges for cause and the rulings;
- A place to record peremptory challenges;
- Information, if any, gathered pretrial about the jury panel members;
- Juror profiles of the best and worst jurors;
- A list of witnesses so that the panel can be asked whether they are acquainted with them;
- Planned questions; and
- An agenda of topics and questions for voir dire.

2. Law and Objections

In trial, you will need to have the law on jury selection at hand if an issue arises. This can include statutes and rules regarding jury selection, as well as at least summaries of case law on *Batson* issues. A list of common objections applicable to jury selection and responses to those objections is also a valuable tool. You can review the objections list before questioning commences to get yourself ready. Such an objections list can be found on page 112. From trial to trial, both the materials on the law of jury selection and the list of objections will be useful, and they can be stored in a jury selection binder or in a computer file for easy access.

3. Your Judge's Rules and Procedures

As we discussed at pages 87–93, some judges post their jury selection procedures online, and they expect counsel to adhere to them in their courts. Other judges will have written procedures that they distribute to trial counsel. These procedures should guide your conduct during jury selection, and those procedures belong in your trial binder or in a computer folder.

4. Jury Panel Seating and Challenges Chart

a. Paper Juror Seating Chart

You will need a seating chart, like the one that follows, where you can insert the jurors' names and take your notes. Jurors usually will be seated in the jury box and in the courtroom's spectator section. This sample chart can be altered to suit your court's seating arrangement. Some courts provide numbered cards to members of the panel. When the juror is referred to, it is by number, such as "juror number six," instead of or in addition to the juror's name.

Because the jury selection process normally moves quickly, you need a system that fits your note-taking and organization style. You should also have

***** **PANEL** *****

38	39	40	41	42	43	44	45
30	31	32	33	34	35	36	37
22	23	24	25	26	27	28	29
14	15	16	17	18	19	20	21

***** **JURY BOX** *****

1	2	3	4	5	6	Alternate 1
7	8	9	10	11	12	Alternate 2

note-taking shortcuts and abbreviations for common words. A time worn technique for note taking is to use little yellow sticky notes that fit in the boxes of your seating chart. When a juror is removed from a seat, you need only replace it with another sticky note on which you can write notes about the replacement juror. When you write the name of someone with a difficult name to pronounce, it helps to write it phonetically. You can also develop abbreviations for answers to common questions. For example, "P" could indicate that the person had been or is a party to a lawsuit or "JC" stands for prior jury service on a civil case. Most of all you will want a code for recording your assessment and rating of the person for deselection, and it could be a numerical system with 1 being the absolute worst possible juror on a scale of 1 to 10.

As part of this process, it is also important to keep track of who is in play and who is not. A chart such as the example provided here tells you who is in the box, but it does not tell you where the cutoff is if each side exercises all of their peremptory strikes. For example, if there are 12 jurors and 3 peremptory challenges for each side, that means 18 jurors are in play. You may want to add a few more jurors and go up to 24, for example, in order to account for potential cause challenges. With this approach, you know that juror 25 and on up are unlikely to make it on to the jury, so you do not need to waste time and resources on them. In some situations where attorneys failed to track who was in play, they wasted valuable strikes on venire members who had no chance of making it into the jury box.

b. Paper Challenges Chart

Besides the seating chart, you need a chart to keep track of peremptory challenges and challenges for cause and the court's rulings on the challenges for cause. You do not want to be in the situation where you have lost count of the number of peremptory challenges you and opposing counsel have exercised.

Challenges for Cause / Excused by Judge

Excused by Judge	Exercised by Plaintiff		Exercised by Defendant	
	Granted	Denied	Granted	Denied

Peremptory Challenges

Exercised by Plaintiff	Exercised by Defendant

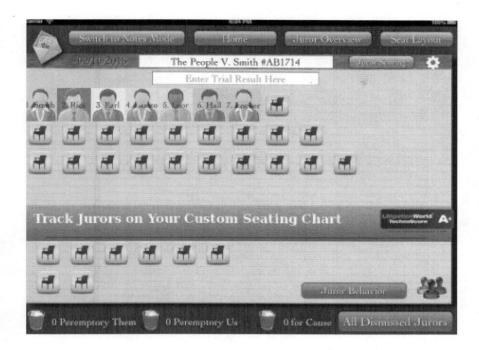

c. Electronic Jury Panel Seating and Challenges Charts

Eventually keeping a record of jurors on paper will become totally obsolete; it will be replaced by tablets with software applications that will facilitate the tasks. For example, the iJuror app, which is relatively inexpensive, eases the tasks of recording information about the jurors, the challenges, and much more.[10] iJuror can be used on an iPad, Android or Windows tablet.

iJuror allows you to do the following: configure the juror seats in the court-room with up to 96 seats; add fundamental information about the juror by merely rotating a dial; rate the jurors with a color-coded rating system; keep a record of both peremptory and for cause challenges; store prepared questions and then enter answers to the set questions by each of the prospective jurors; and share information through Dropbox.

If your courtroom has a mobile hot spot and you use iJuror, you can have an assistant assist you by observing voir dire and providing you with comments

---

10. *See* iJuror, https://itunes.apple.com/us/app/ijuror/id372486285?mt=8; JuryPad, https://itunes.apple.com/us/app/jurypad/id580845085?mt=8; JuryTracker, https://itunes .apple.com/us/app/jurytracker/id408560814?mt=8; Jury Duty, https://itunes.apple.com/us/ app/jury-duty/id414359607?mt=8.

on your computer tablet in real time as you question the prospective jurors. Most importantly, it relieves you for the most part from taking notes, which distracts your attention from conversing with the jurors.

It is good practice to have a failsafe system in place in case you have a technology failure. For instance, if you are using iJuror, it is a good idea to have an assistant keep a paper jury selection chart going just in case.

E. Profiles of the Best and Worst Jurors

1. Reasons for Developing Juror Profiles

The practice of identifying the characteristics of the hypothetical *best* and *worst* jurors can be beneficial to you for at least two reasons. First, the process can aid you in your preparation for jury selection. The activity of thinking about who would be favorable and unfavorable jurors forces you to step into the jurors' shoes and to look at your case theory, theme and evidence from their perspectives. You are compelled to ask who would be sympathetic to your client and your case narrative. Your ideal juror would have something in common with your client and/or your case narrative. Alternatively, you will think about the traits of people who would disapprove of your client or your case. With insights gained through this profiling exercise, you can develop better questions for the jury because you know what you are looking for. For instance, if your client is a corporation, and your hypothetical worst juror profile is someone who harbors animosity against corporations, you can develop questions focused on identifying people on the panel with similar attitudes.

Second, pretrial preparation of the *best* juror and *worst* juror profiles can assist you during jury selection. When you are selecting a jury, you are fully engaged in assessing the prospective jurors in a fast-paced process, calling for quick decisions. Therefore, it is valuable to have thought through beforehand what you are looking for or looking to avoid in a juror. At a minimum, the profiles give you a starting point for assessing potential jurors.

Obviously, under *Batson v. Kentucky* and its progeny, profiling based on race, ethnicity, gender or membership in any cognizable group is prohibited under the Equal Protection Clause.[11]

Developing juror profiles ensures that you have a plan going into jury selection. The process of jury selection is simply too chaotic and fast-paced to go into it without a clear understanding of who you do and do not want on

---

11. *Batson v. Kentucky*, 476 U.S. 79 (1986).

the jury. Many scholars debate whether or not a case can be won in jury selection, and there are arguments for each side. However, regardless of whether or not the case can be won in jury selection, it is very clear that the case can be lost in jury selection.

2. Jury Consultant

If your financial resources permit and the magnitude of the case calls for it, you may employ a jury consultant to assist you with your preparation for jury selection. Jury consultants can assist with jury selection in a variety of ways and can often work with attorneys to provide valuable advice within a limited budget. One way a consultant may assist is by developing the jury profiles. See Chapter 5 for a discussion of jury consultants and how you can get the most out of utilizing a consultant.

F. Making and Meeting Objections

1. Making Objections

a. The Judge's Rules

Of paramount importance in developing your trial plan concerning objections you may make during voir dire are the judge's rules regarding what is impermissible during jury selection questioning. Judge's preferences vary greatly, so it is important to understand those of the judge in your case. If you know whom your trial judge will be prior to trial, you can investigate to determine what the court does not permit by watching the judge during jury selection, going to the court's website, speaking to colleagues who are familiar with the court's practices, and so on. It is also helpful to join the listserves of your local bar organizations. For example, most states have a plaintiff's bar association and a defense bar association. Becoming part of these associations and joining their listserves allows you to reach out to others who have previously represented plaintiffs or defendants in front of your judge.

If you do not know whom your trial judge will be prior to the trial date, you can have a list of common jury selection objections. When you are assigned out to trial, you can question the judge about what is impermissible and modify your list.

Besides scouting the court, you also should scout opposing counsel in order to learn what to expect from counsel during jury selection. You want to determine what opposing counsel may do during jury selection that is objectionable.

The best way to learn is to watch opposing counsel in trial, but if that is not possible, consult with colleagues, court personnel and attorneys who have been in trial with the lawyer.

b. Objections List

Just as it is useful to construct juror profiles because of the rapid pace of jury selection and the need to make quick decisions on who to deselect, it is likewise helpful to have thought about what objections you may make during jury selection and how you might respond to objections. If, as part of your pretrial preparation, you have created an objections list for jury selection, you will be better prepared to act on the spot during trial. You can utilize the list provided here or create your own list. Just before voir dire begins, review your objection list. With this last minute refresher, you will be ready to object.

The following is a list of objections to jury selection questions based upon a judge's list of improper questions, which he published online (see pages 92–93):

Objection. The question:
- has already been asked;
- is unfair and embarrassing to the juror;
- is meant to establish a personal rapport with the juror;
- asks the juror to speculate on a verdict if certain facts are proved;
- doesn't seek information from the juror but is anticipating the evidence;
- is irrelevant to the juror's qualifications; or
- asks the juror for the definition of a legal term.[12]

Additional possible objections include:

Objection. The question:
- anticipates instructions on the law;
- misstates the law;
- misstates what the evidence will be;
- is argument;
- poses an improper hypothetical question;
- asks for a verdict from a previous trial;
- seeks to indoctrinate the jurors; or
- contains inadmissible evidence.

---

12. Timothy A. Bradshaw, *Judge Directory*, KING COUNTY SUPERIOR COURT, http://www.kingcounty.gov/~/media/courts/superior-court/docs/judges/bradshaw-jury-selection-overview.ashx?la=en.

Objecting is for naught if you don't have a record for appeal should the court rule against you. If you are in a jurisdiction that does not routinely report voir dire, move to have it recorded. This includes recording sidebars and in-chamber's matters necessary to preserve error for appeal.

c. Motion in Limine

Regarding the last potential objection on the objection list—objecting because opposing counsel's question or statement contains inadmissible evidence—you may have a particular evidentiary issue that concerns you. For instance, assume you, as plaintiff's counsel, are concerned that opposing counsel may mention insurance during voir dire. When opposing counsel references insurance, the jurors may well conclude that the defendant in your case has insurance coverage that will cover the loss. The law on what, if anything at all, can be mentioned about insurance during jury selection differs from jurisdiction to jurisdiction. For example, *Harris v. Alessi*[13] describes how, in Idaho, references to insurance are acceptable under limited circumstances but not in others, as follows:

> It is entirely proper for counsel to ask the jurors such questions as may reasonably be necessary to ascertain whether they are free from a bias or interest that may affect their verdict. To this end it is proper for counsel, in good faith, to ask of each juror whether he is interested as an agent or stockholder or otherwise in a specified casualty company. Or he may be asked the broad question whether he is interested in any insurance company insuring against liability for negligence. But counsel must take pains to propound such questions in such a manner as not unnecessarily to convey the impression that the defendant is in fact so insured. It is misconduct on the part of counsel for plaintiff in such actions so to frame his question that it goes beyond what is reasonably necessary to serve the legitimate purpose of eliciting the facts he is entitled to adduce in order to secure a jury free from bias or prejudice, if it is also apparent that the question may fairly be said to have the effect of serving the illegitimate purpose of prejudicing the jury by fixing in their minds the idea that the defendant is protected by insurance against liability for negligence.[14]

If you expect that opposing counsel may do something objectionable during voir dire, such as improperly referencing insurance, you can file a motion in

---

13. *Harris v. Alessi*, 120 P.3d 289 (Idaho 2005).
14. *Harris v. Alessi*, 120 P.3d 289 (Idaho 2005).

limine requesting that the court prohibit opposing counsel from doing so. See pages 313–319 for a discussion of a motion in limine to prohibit opposing counsel from asking improper questions.

2. Avoiding and Meeting Objections

Ideally, opposing counsel will not object to any of the questions you ask during jury selection. To avoid objections to your questions, you should prepare your questions with a clear understanding of the judge's parameters concerning what is not permissible questioning. Then, with the help of your objections list and whatever else you can think of as possible objections, try to anticipate what opposing counsel might object to and plan to avoid any objection by, for instance, rephrasing or dropping a question. For every question that you ask, be ready to explain why the information you are seeking will aid you in deciding whether to exercise a challenge and why the question or line of questions you are asking is proper.

G. Assembling Your Team

As we have mentioned, jury selection moves rapidly along, and you will be engrossed in conversing with the prospective jurors. Under these circumstances, you do not want to hinder your communication with them by stopping to take many notes and losing eye contact. Further, if you are taking extensive notes, it is likely you will overlook significant nonverbal behavior of jurors other than the one you are questioning. For example, you may not see another prospective juror shake her head. For these reasons, it is advantageous to have another person or persons with you to take notes and observe the jurors while you question the prospective jurors. The other person(s) can also offer opinions about the suitability of the potential jurors to your case.

Your teammate could be co-counsel, your client, a legal assistant, an investigator, a jury consultant or, if you are a prosecutor, a detective. If you intend to have several team members attend trial, it is important to communicate to everyone exactly what their role is. While feedback is important, there is also the risk of having "too many cooks in the kitchen," which only adds to an already chaotic process. Sometimes, attorneys are only given a few minutes after the end of voir dire to identify against whom they want to exercise peremptory strikes on. In this scenario, it is not helpful to have three different people trying to tell you whom they do and do not like. At a minimum, you should figure out a process in advance for receiving this feedback. For example, you may ask those on your team to simply write down their top three favorite and least favorite jurors on a piece of paper.

H. Preparing Your Client

When you prepare your client for trial, pay particular attention to jury selection because this is when the jurors get their first impressions of the players in the courtroom. From the moment the jurors walk through the door to the courtroom, the trial is underway and the jurors collectively perceive every little thing that is going on in the courtroom, and they start assessing you and your client. It is important that you educate your client along these lines and about the importance of making a positive first impression.

As part of this, it is important for your client to understand that he should be conscious of his behavior outside of the courthouse. Some attorneys tell their client to be on their best behavior within a half-mile of the courthouse. A rude act in the parking lot, such as cutting someone off, could turn out to be an unfortunate encounter with one of the jurors that comes back to haunt the client.

1. Familiarize

Familiarize your client with the voir dire process. If possible, take your client to the courtroom where the case will be tried, or one like it, in order to inform the client about the courtroom, where the different players are in the courtroom and the roles they have in the trial. If you do not do a courtroom visit, at least draw a sketch of the courtroom layout and use that to explain where the judge, clerk, court reporter, bailiff, jurors, and counsel are located. Provide your client with an outline of how jury selection works, including: how challenges are exercised, how you decide on who to deselect including the prohibition against discriminatory challenges, and the role the client plays in the decision-making regarding who to challenge.

2. Dos and Don'ts

Things you should tell your client *to do* include: (1) *do* dress properly for the court appearance because jurors will judge the client on appearance; (2) *do* have good posture; (3) *do* pay close attention to what is happening because you want the client's input; (4) *do* communicate with you only in the proper way during trial (if you are engaged in an activity and the client wants to communicate with you at that time, the client should write notes that you will look at before concluding what you are doing) because otherwise you cannot concentrate on your trial work; and (5) *do* remember that this is serious and behave accordingly.

Things that you want the client *to refrain from doing* include: (1) *don't* make facial expressions that show whether the client likes or doesn't like something (the best face is a poker face) because jurors may react unfavorably if they think the client's behavior is offensive; (2) *don't* slouch; (3) *don't* chew gum; (4) *don't* communicate with opposing counsel or an opposing party, including doing so in a friendly manner because you do not wish to leave the impression with the jury that the trial is just a game; and (5) *don't* over-communicate with you in such a way as to give jurors the impression that the client is panicked over something that has happened.

3. Jury Selection Involvement

Of course, the degree to which you want your client's participation in jury selection depends on several variables, such as the ability of your client to productively assist, the nature of your relationship with your client, and your obligations under the Rules of Professional Conduct. Here we assume that you want your client involved.

You can tell your client how important a role they can play during jury selection. Tell the client to pay close attention to all of the prospective jurors, particularly the ones to whom you are not talking because your attention will be focused on the individual with whom you are conversing. That is when you need the client's extra eyes and ears. Your client should look for any nonverbal signals that the prospective jurors should be deselected. Tell the client to also pay close attention when opposing counsel is questioning the jury because that is a good time to see how jurors react to opposing counsel and what is being said.

Involve your client in the deselection decision-making. Ask the client if they think there is someone they don't want on the jury and why. As mentioned, you have explained to your client that only nondiscriminatory reasons are acceptable. Consultation with the client is in accord with the Model Rules of Professional Conduct. Rule 1.4 that calls for reasonable consultation with the client regarding the means for achieving the client's objectives. Rule 1.2 provides, "A lawyer may take such action on behalf of the client as is impliedly authorized to carry out the representation."

What if you and your client disagree over whether to exercise a challenge? In such a situation, your decision should prevail. This position that you make the ultimate decision regarding the challenge is supported by the comment to Rule 1.2 that states:

> On occasion, however, a lawyer and a client may disagree about the means to be used to accomplish the client's objectives. Clients normally defer to the special knowledge and skill of their lawyer with respect to the means to be used to accomplish their objectives, particularly with respect to technical, legal and tactical matters.

You should discuss the possibility of a disagreement with your client during pretrial preparation, and have an understanding that you will make the final decision regarding deselection of jurors.

I. Agenda for Voir Dire

1. Topics for Discussion

Pretrial, you should prepare an agenda for what you intend to cover during voir dire. Your agenda should contain the following:

- Preliminary remarks that you will make at the outset of your part of jury selection (provided that the court will permit you to make preliminary remarks) (see page 33 regarding preliminary remarks);
- General questions aimed at determining who should be excused or may not be qualified to serve under the law, such as hardship or prior jury service (see pages 30–33 and 35 for these general questions) provided they have not been asked before you either by the judge or opposing counsel; and
- Specific questions designed to identify prospective jurors who should be deselected because they match a bad juror profile and/or harbor biases regarding your legal position (see pages 239–246) and/or your case narrative (see pages 246–267).

Once you have formulated your ideal agenda, prioritize the topics you want to cover and pare back on your list because you will not have time to discuss them all with the prospective jurors. Be sure that your questions will cover your worst suspicions. While some lawyers prefer to cover the general questions first before launching into questions aimed at uncovering the jurors who match the bad juror profile or case specific questions, as you will see in later chapters, you may want to jump right into the case specific questions because you know that what you cover first is more likely to be retained by the jurors. Ultimately, however, the order of your agenda should be guided by what you are comfortable with and what you think will best engage the jury in a conversation with you.

Also, it is critical to keep in mind that you should remain flexible and vary from your agenda if your dialogue with the jurors carries you to other fruitful areas of discussion.

The following are attorney agendas for jury selection in criminal and civil trials. The full transcript of the voir dire can be found in the Appendices on the online supplement http://caplaw.com/jury.

2. Criminal Case Illustration

Defense Agenda Example: *People v. Harmon* was a domestic violence case. The defense attorney's agenda included the following topics:

- Brief preliminary remarks designed to make the prospective jurors comfortable and willing to disclose ("... MR. WILLIAMS: As the judge said, I know this is a very formal setting, but try to pretend we're all in the living room and speak as freely as possible because what we want is your honest answers, and there's no wrong answers, but we want you to be honest.");
- Presumption of innocence;
- Defense has no burden;
- False accusations;
- Defendant has no obligation to testify;
- Proof beyond a reasonable doubt;
- Defendant does not have to testify;
- Whether any prospective juror has been the victim of domestic violence;
- Whether a man can be the victim of domestic violence;
- Motives for a person to lie or exaggerate about domestic violence; and
- Gruesome photographs.

Prosecution Agenda Example: The prosecution's agenda in *People v. Harmon* included covering the following topics:

- Presumption of innocence;
- One-witness case;
- Whether any juror had been accused of domestic violence;
- Whether any juror had been the victim of domestic violence;
- Use of force against a loved one;

- A man's use of physical force against a woman who was screaming and yelling;
- A man's use of physical force against a woman who kicked;
- A victim of domestic violence who stays in a relationship;
- Following a law even if you disagree with it;
- Jurors are not involved in punishment;
- Injuring a person with a preexisting injury;
- Testimony about medical treatment;
- Circumstantial evidence; and
- The CSI effect.

3. Civil Case Illustration

Plaintiff's Agenda Example: *Brown v. Davis and Davis* was a wrongful death suit in which Kenneth Brown Jr. was driving across a bridge in Missouri when a truck driven by the defendant was also crossing the bridge. A log skidder loaded on the trailer hit the bridge, became dislodged and landed on Brown's vehicle, killing him. Mr. Brown's wife bought suit on her own behalf and that of her two children. The truck driver, Kenneth Davis, Jr., admitted his negligence and that it caused Brown's death but denied being reckless. Defendant William Davis, who was present, denied liability, as did William Davis Logging, Inc., which was alleged to be negligent and reckless in how it shipped the log skidder.

Plaintiff's agenda explored the following subjects during voir dire:

- Whether any juror had a family member killed through negligence or recklessness;
- Familiarity with the scene of the collision;
- Whether any juror had encountered a tractor trailer at the scene;
- A monetary award for loss of life;
- Whether the jurors could award a large dollar amount;
- Whether any juror had a connection with the insurance business;
- Following a law even if you disagree with it; and
- The value of parental guidance and support.

Defense Agenda Example: Defense counsel who represented truck driver Kenneth Davis, Jr. had these topics on the agenda for the defense voir dire:

- Setting aside sympathy for the plaintiff;
- Prejudice against truck drivers;
- Whether any juror had never driven negligently or in violation of the rules of the road;

- Aggravated damages;
- Whether any juror had been in a car accident;
- No need to call a witness twice;
- Whether the jurors could not hold it against counsel if counsel's questions got into sensitive areas;
- Defending on damages when liability has been admitted; and
- Understanding the client's reaction to the process.

J. Voir Dire Scripts

As an alternative to an agenda for voir dire, you may want to actually script out the questions that you intend to ask. As we will discuss in chapter 8, the wording of your voir dire questions has an important impact on jurors' willingness to respond or, more important, respond truthfully. For example, questions that suggest right and wrong answers are more likely to result in jurors offering the right or more socially acceptable answer rather than the honest answer. Consequently, it is often valuable for attorneys to work out the precise wording of their voir dire questions in advance so that their on-the-fly wording does not undermine their ability to obtain honest and accurate responses from jurors.

K. Practice, Practice, Practice

While trial lawyers are accustomed to practicing their opening statements and closing arguments, they tend to neglect practicing jury selection. Practice is fundamental to a good performance no matter what you do in trial. Know your agenda down pat. Know the topics that you will cover. Practice both your opening remarks and your questions until they come naturally to you. Practice with regular folks, not lawyers. Think about the responses that your questions will provoke and where the conversation may lead. If you can, participate in a mock voir dire. This will also help you determine which questions are helpful and which ones are not. For example, a session of mock voir dire may help you realize that the question that you thought would be extremely helpful is actually confusing to the average person, preventing you from getting any meaningful responses.

Chapter 5

Getting the Most Out of a Jury Consultant

> *"Many trials are won and lost during jury selection ... But it's not because jury consultants are trying to stack the deck. It's because jury consultants and lawyers are successful or unsuccessful in figuring out which jurors are unreceptive to their message and getting rid of them."*
>
> "Judging Juries"
> *Dallas Morning News*, June 2002

A. Getting the Most Out of a Jury Consultant

You may decide to employ a jury consultant, an expert, to assist you both pretrial when you gather information about the jury panel and prepare for jury selection, during jury selection and sometimes throughout trial. The work of a jury consultant falls under the work product doctrine.[1]

V. Hale Starr, Ph.D. and Mark McCormick, LL.B. in *Jury Selection*, 4th Edition, summarize what a consultant can provide a trial lawyer:

> What the consultant *can* do is help attorneys understand their cases from the juror's perspective—to see the case through the "juror lenses." These lenses are founded in juror life experiences. And once the case facts are viewed through the jurors' lenses, the jurors' translation of facts becomes more visible and clear. As a result, once some level of juror explicability is attained, the consultant can help adapt and cus-

---

1. *In re Cendant Corp. Sec. Litig.*, 343 F.3d 658 (3d Cir. 2003).

tomize case themes to bolster one case face detract from another. But the key factor is that the consultant's familiarity with and ability to analyze juror life experiences and behavior can help the attorney or trial team to expose potential road blocks before jury selection begins and a potentially tortuous trial begins. Consultants also help improve presentations, whether in style, tone, mannerisms, or the message itself. And most importantly, consultants help to reveal hidden juror biases against (or in favor of) the client. Ultimately, consultants help attorneys focus on how their message will come across to the jurors.[2]

The decision concerning whether or not to employ a jury consultant can be driven by the size of your case and whether your client can afford the consultant's fee. For large cases, the fees of consulting firms may range from $10,000 to $400,000.[3] However, for a smaller fee, a solo consultant can perform a limited number of tasks, such as run a focus group for you.

Specifically, jury consultants can provide the following nine services:

1. Perform a study to gauge the community attitudes towards the case;
2. Assist in designing juror profiles;
3. Conduct a focus group or mock trial;
4. Hold a mock jury selection;
5. Work on the formulation of questions for jury selection;
6. Sit in during trial and evaluate the prospective jurors;
7. Help construct a specialized juror questionnaire (pages 102–105);
8. Do background research on the prospective jurors (pages 93–98); and
9. Aid in the selection of a case theme (pages 190–192).

Throughout the rest of this chapter, we examine the first six listed services that a consultant can provide. The other three services, seven through nine, are described at the specified pages.

B. Performing a Community Attitude Assessment

If you are trying the case in your hometown, you may believe that input from a jury consultant about community attitudes is superfluous. However,

---

2. V. HALE STARR, PH.D. & MARK McCORMICK, LL.B., JURY SELECTION 6-8 to 6-9 (4th ed. 2012).

3. Elizabeth D. Bottman, *Jury Consultants: No Case Is Too Big or Too Small*, KING COUNTY BAR BULLETIN (Aug. 2014), available at https://www.kcba.org/newsevents/barbulletin/BView.aspx?Month=08&Year=2014&AID=article9.htm.

if you are considering whether to file or try the case in a venue foreign to you, you may decide to employ a jury consultant to assess the foreign venue's community attitudes about matters pertinent to your case. To assess those community attitudes the consultant would conduct a poll or a survey. Polling the community is similar to taking a political poll or spot-checking work. A community attitude assessment is typically conducted over the telephone, but other techniques, such as internet-based polling or in-person surveys, are sometimes employed. To conduct the community attitude survey, the consultant randomly selects a significant sample of the community from which the prospective jurors will be summoned. These members of the community are asked to answer a limited number of questions designed to have the respondent select between positions. Then, the answers are tabulated to reflect the attitudes in the community towards the salient facts of the case.

1. Snapshot of Community Attitudes

A community attitude survey provides the attorney and client with a snapshot of case-specific attitudes and experiences that are most prominent within the trial venue. This can help the attorney and client understand and assess the risk of proceeding to trial with the case. In some instances, where a plaintiff has a choice over where to file a lawsuit, a plaintiff may actually conduct a community attitude survey before filing that lawsuit in order to determine which trial venue is the most favorable for the plaintiff.

Finally, community attitude surveys sometimes serve as a substitute for a mock trial or focus group and are intended to root out attitudes about aspects of the case. The assessment is used to mold profiles of the worst and best juror, which the trial lawyer can use in jury selection to evaluate the prospective jurors and decide whom to challenge.

Rather than having a jury consultant conduct a survey to determine community attitudes, another, and some would argue better, approach is to associate counsel who lives in the other community and understands her neighbor's attitudes.

2. Change of Venue Motion

If the court concludes that the jury selection process, by itself, will not effectively remove jurors with strong biases due to the existence of widespread bias throughout the community, it can order a change of venue. When this occurs, usually the case will be moved to a different trial venue or, in rare instances, jurors from a different venue will be brought into the home venue to try the case.

The most common use of a community attitude assessment is to support a change of venue motion. While change of venue motions are normally brought in criminal cases, they are also used in civil cases. Some cases receive significant media attention or are otherwise widely known about in their trial venues, and in these situations, jury selection sometimes is unable to produce a fair and impartial jury. Consequently, an attorney may wish to change venue and rely upon a community attitude survey to support a motion for change of venue. The American Society of Trial Consultants Professional Code explains:

> Surveys have been accepted as evidence by courts for more than 40 years. For example in *Zippo Manufacturing Co. v. Rogers Imports*,[4] the courts have stated, "The weight of case authority, the consensus of legal writers, and reasoned policy considerations all indicate that the hearsay rule should not bar the admission of properly conducted public opinion surveys."[5]

3. Research-Based Profiles

Community attitudes surveys, due to their large sample size, can assist counsel with the development of their good and bad juror profiles. While a mock trial or focus group has little predictive value due to its small sample size (usually 10 to 40 mock jurors), a community attitude survey usually involves hundreds of jury-eligible people within the trial venue. This large sample size creates the opportunity to identify statistically significant relationships between juror characteristics and their general leanings on issues in the case.

This kind of research is particularly helpful in trial venues where the judge allows very little attorney voir dire questioning. For example, many federal judges, particularly those in the Northeastern region of the United States, do not allow any attorney-conducted voir dire at all. If the judge does not allow a juror questionnaire, does not allow attorney-conducted voir dire, and conducts limited or less meaningful judge voir dire, this research can serve as a valuable substitute for identifying candidates for your peremptory challenges.

---

4. *Zippo Mgf. Co., v. Rogers Imports*, 216 F. Supp. 670 (1963).
5. Am. Soc'y. of Trial Consultants Prof'l Code, http://www.astcweb.org/Resources/Pictures/Venue%2010-08.pdf, p. 19.

C. Design Juror Profiles

In advance of trial, an attorney with the assistance of a jury consultant can design juror profiles. Juror profiles, as we discussed at pages 110–111, are a tool intended to help attorneys determine during voir dire which jurors are good or bad for the case. Jury consultants tend to focus on attitudes and experiences because they believe they are more accurate predictors of juror behavior, and therefore are reliable for the deselection process. While demographics are sometimes relevant, they tend to be less helpful for picking a jury. Many jury consultants argue that demographics are only helpful because we tend to assume individuals with similar demographics tend to have similar attitudes and life experiences. Given the reasoning process behind such assumptions, it makes sense to focus directly on attitudes and experiences rather than make potentially erroneous assumptions based on the temptation to assume everyone of a particular demographic thinks the same way or has had the same life experiences.

A typical jury profile consists of lists of what the jury consultant considers high-risk attitudes and experiences. The term "high risk" is important, because it suggests that certain attitudes and experiences create a higher risk of jurors adopting adverse views of the case, rather than being determinative of those views. Consequently, it is rare for jury consultants to look at only one factor in order to determine whether a juror is good or bad. Instead, jury consultants look at a variety of factors in relationship to each other in order to judge the risk level.

High-risk attitudes and experiences are strong attitudes that a juror may hold or prominent experiences the juror may have had that are going to influence the manner in which the evidence and testimony will be perceived and considered. For example, a person who has had an experience of being hospitalized for a medical emergency and felt forced to wait too long before she was cared for by a doctor, might be considered high risk for a defendant in a medical malpractice case. The concern is that this juror's personal experience may serve to fill in evidentiary gaps in the trial narrative with what the juror wants to believe. This juror might be predisposed to conclude the doctor was negligent based on a belief derived from the personal experience, which has led them to believe that doctors are often negligent in addressing patients' needs in a timely manner.

It is important for attorneys to consider the extraordinary influence that attitudes and experiences exert on people's perceptions of events and issues. One of the commonly cited theories of human decision-making in jury consultant literature is motivated reasoning. Motivated reasoning refers to how people tend to focus on and accept evidence and arguments that reinforce what they want to believe about the world, while rejecting evidence and arguments that go against what they want to believe.

Researchers at Emory University in Atlanta, Georgia have conducted fMRI brain-imagining studies that reveal the extent of motivated reasoning. In 2004, these researchers conducted a study in which participants viewed footage of George Bush and John Kerry, the presidential candidates from that year's election. The researchers divided the participants up by their political orientation and placed them in fMRI machines that examined what was going on in their brains as they were exposed to various stimuli. Democrats were shown video clips of John Kerry contradicting himself, and Republicans were shown clips of George Bush contradicting himself. The imaging showed that these contradictions flung the brains of their supporters into total chaos. However, as soon as those same participants were able to "explain away" or discount the alleged contradiction, the imaging revealed that their brains released dopamine, which is known as the brain's pleasure drug. The researchers described it as participants essentially giving themselves a neurological pat on the back for eliminating a threat to what they wanted to believe.[6]

This study and many others demonstrate the power of attitudes. Experiences operate in the same way. Arguments and evidence at trial that resonate with jurors' own personal life experiences will seem more likely to be true to those jurors and, consequently, take on greater salience as jurors attempt to make sense of the case and reach a verdict.

Juror profiles may also include personality characteristics, such as whether or not the person is quick to make a decision or tends to be detail-oriented. These factors can be revealing of the style of decision-making used by jurors, which can influence their perceptions of a case. For example, a juror who is quick to make up his mind about an issue may be less favorable for a defendant who has to wait until after the plaintiff's case-in-chief to present its theory of the case. Anything attorneys believe might make a potential juror resistant to their case theory should be included on the list.

D. Conduct a Focus Group or Mock Trial

1. Focus Group vs. Mock Trial

Attorneys often hire jury consultants to conduct a focus group or a mock trial for a case. A focus group or a mock trial is a popular way to learn about

---

6. Drew Westen, Pavel S. Blagov, Keith Harenski, Clint Kilts & Stephan Hamann, *Neural Bases of Motivated Reasoning: An fMRI Study of Emotional Constraints on Partisan Political Judgment in the 2004 U.S. Presidential Election*, JOURNAL OF COGNITIVE NEUROSCIENCE, Vol 18, Issue 11, 1947–1958 (Nov. 2006).

how prospective jurors might react to the case. Some people use the terms "focus group" and "mock trial" interchangeably, but they refer to two different types of jury research. A focus group is designed to be an exploratory exercise. The presentations are typically segmented and followed by open-ended discussion by the participants. A goal of a focus group is to provide guidance to the attorneys for discovery.

On the other hand, a mock trial involves a detailed case presentation with a verdict form and jury instructions, followed by deliberations. The goal of a mock trial is to test the case presentation and make adjustments for trial. While focus groups are typically conducted early in discovery, mock trials are typically conducted closer to trial.

2. Jury Selection Strategy

While jury selection strategy is not often the primary reason for conducting a focus group or mock trial, they can help attorneys learn about how various juror attitudes and experiences influence the way in which the case will be decided. Sometimes, they reveal high-risk attitudes or experiences that might not have otherwise been considered. The shortcoming associated with the use of focus groups or mock trials to guide jury selection is the small sample size. The typical focus group or mock trial involves twenty to thirty participants and is conducted somewhere within the city or county within which the trial will take place. The small sample size means any findings from the project are not predictable, at least from a statistical standpoint. However, many attorneys find the data obtained from focus groups and mock trials to be valuable for jury selection purposes even if it is not statistically predictive. For example, while not statistically predictive, it is still an important finding if a demographically diverse group of people is arriving at the same conclusions.

When used to guide jury selection strategy, jury consultants typically rely on extensive background questionnaires completed by the focus group or mock trial participants. These questionnaires go well beyond the typical court questionnaire and tend to explore a variety of case-related attitudes and experiences. For example, a questionnaire in a mock trial involving a product liability claim might explore participants' beliefs about corporations, balancing safety and profit, and the adequacy of product warnings. This data, along with qualitative data obtained from the group discussions or deliberations is compared to the final leanings of the participants. Any factors identified in this analysis are incorporated into the juror profiles.

3. Mechanics of a Focus Group

While no universal procedure for conducting a focus group exists, generally, the jury consultant recruits a focus group from the community where the trial will take place. Ideally the group is comprised of a representative cross-section of the community. The number could be up to 12 if one focus group will be used. Alternatively it could be a larger group that would be divided into three or more focus groups that will deliberate separately. The group assembles in a location where their actions can be videoed and observed through closed circuit monitoring or a one-way mirror.

At the outset of the presentation of the case, the group members may be given a statement of the case, much like the one that a judge would deliver before beginning jury selection.

Next, the focus group receives presentations of both sides of the case with the plaintiff's presentation going first, followed by defense. The goal is to have the opposing party's case presented as effectively as possible in order to produce meaningful results. The presentations are a combination of the case narrative that would be delivered in opening statement together with some argument of the application of the law to the facts, giving the focus group the essence of the case theories and themes. How long the lawyer presentations take depends upon the complexity of the case, how much the party can afford, and who is running the program. They could take as little as a half hour a side.

The group may be given an abbreviated statement of the law. Another option is to present the case in written form. Following the presentations of the law and the cases, the consultant may have the group complete a questionnaire to determine their early impressions about the case.

The focus group next deliberates as a jury would. The consultant and trial teams observe the deliberations. After deliberations, the consultant facilitates a discussion of the case to flesh out matters discussed during deliberations and to explore those aspects of the case that have not been discussed. The consultant may submit a written report of findings and conclusions to the trial team.

4. Do It Yourself

If your budget permits you to hire a reputable jury consultant to conduct the focus groups for you, it is likely that the focus groups will be correctly conducted and produce reliable results. Alternatively, if your case is too small to warrant the expense of hiring a consultant, you can conduct your own focus groups. Consultant David Ball Ph.D. in his book entitled *How to Do Your Own Focus Groups* offers step-by-step guidance on how to orchestrate focus groups. This book contains sample letters, forms, and questionnaires.[7]

The two most important issues to consider with the DIY method are: (1) the source of the sample and (2) the quality of the opposing side's presentation. The source of the sample refers to where you get your focus group or mock trial participants. It is best to find a diverse group of people that you do not know. Attorneys sometimes use friends or family members with the DIY approach, and this can be problematic because friends and family members are often less willing to offer the critical feedback that you need the most. It is also important to get a diverse group of people in order to avoid any bias with your sample. For example, if your focus group is a bunch of people from your law firm's office, such as paralegals or assistants, these are all people who have specialized knowledge of the law and may not be representative of the kinds of people who will actually show up on the jury at trial.

It is also important to ensure that you have as strong of a presentation as possible for the other side in order to avoid false positives with your results. For this reason, if there is any imbalance in the presentations, it is better to have that imbalanced favor the other side. While you would never engineer a mock trial to purposely lose, you will learn a lot more from losing than you will from winning.

E. Hold a Mock Jury Selection

Jury consultants sometimes assist attorneys with jury selection by conducting a mock jury selection project. Mock jury selection is a useful training tool for attorneys. Designs of mock jury selection projects vary among jury consultants. However, these projects generally have two common goals. First, they provide attorneys insight about juror characteristics, such as attitudes and experiences, and how they relate to the case. In this respect, it is similar to a focus group or a mock trial. The two key differences between a mock trial and a mock jury selection are the format and the depth of the information received from the mock jurors. A mock jury selection utilizes a voir dire format to collect information about the jurors, followed by a post-voir dire case discussion to determine how effective the voir dire strategy was at uncovering bias. This feedback is typically less in-depth than a mock trial, where mock jurors spend hours de-

---

7. *See generally* DAVID BALL PH.D., HOW TO DO YOUR OWN FOCUS GROUPS: A GUIDE FOR TRIAL ATTORNEYS (2001).

liberating in great detail with the verdict form and jury instructions. In some situations, a mock trial may be preceded by a mock jury selection, but this is not typically the case within the jury consulting industry.

The second goal of a mock jury selection is to train and prepare the attorney. Voir dire is a difficult process. There are a variety of factors that can limit an attorney's effectiveness, ranging from possible communication apprehension to time constraints posed by the court. These factors can undermine an effective jury selection strategy if not properly addressed. A mock jury selection allows the attorney to identify hurdles that may arise in voir dire and make adjustments before the actual trial.

An example of a common hurdle is time constraints imposed by the court. The amount of voir dire time often seems like a lot of time to ask questions. For example, if the court provides each side with thirty minutes of voir dire time, the attorneys may think this is plenty of time to ask all of the needed questions. Some attorneys may wonder how they will fill an entire thirty minutes. In reality, thirty minutes will go faster than anticipated, and the attorneys may realize that their strategy attempts to accomplish too much in light of the limited voir dire time.

Jury selection is essentially a public speaking event, and this can be another hurdle for the trial attorney. While the best public speakers practice their speeches before giving them, attorneys rarely practice voir dire beforehand, which is unfortunate. A mock jury selection provides this critical practice and allows the attorney to get a feel for the voir dire questions and how they need to be asked as well as how the jurors may react to and respond to the questions. The comfort and familiarity that comes with this practice allows attorneys to avoid common missteps in voir dire, such as a rapid-fire pace or a disruptive discomfort with silence. The lack of practice often shows with even the most experienced trial attorneys. The attorney may speak too quickly or show a level of nervousness that is distracting. This is often the case in the first five minutes of voir dire. It is not unusual for an experienced attorney to have a choppy first five minutes of voir dire before becoming comfortable with the process and able to effectively execute the voir dire strategy.

F. Work on the Formulation of Questions

Jury consultants are particularly good at helping attorneys with the crafting of voir dire questions that get to the essence of a case. Once the juror profiles are created, which outline the characteristics that make a prospective juror good or bad for the case, the questions for eliciting information about these characteristics need to be developed. This is no easy task. In some respects, drafting voir dire questions is an art. A myriad of factors influence prospective jurors' willingness or ability to provide an honest response to the question. For example, some questions may touch on sensitive areas that prospective jurors simply are not comfortable discussing. In other instances, the wording of a question may imply a socially desirable or undesirable response. Prospective jurors are conscious of how their answers may sound, just as any person considers how their comments impact their social standing. No one wants to be seen as a sexist or racist, even though that person may have strong sexist or racist attitudes.

Sometimes, the voir dire question simply does not make sense to the jurors despite the attorney's best efforts to craft a meaningful question on an important issue.

Because jury selection primarily focuses on deselection, the process involves getting prospective jurors to disclose attitudes or beliefs that may not be socially desirable or are not generally comfortable views to express. While not a cure-all, this is where the wording of the question can make a significant difference. Questions may be drafted in a way that the wording of the question makes prospective jurors more comfortable disclosing their beliefs and experiences.

In addition to the wording of the question, jury consultants may also provide input on the order or style of questions as well as how to draft questions in a manner that allows the important ones to be asked and answered within the sometimes limited timeframe of jury selection, which is an important consideration, since some venues may only allow ten minutes of attorney voir dire per side while other trial venues allow attorneys to conduct extensive voir dire.

G. Participate in Jury Selection

One of the most important services that jury consultants can provide is in-court assistance during the jury selection process. A strategy is only as good as the execution, and a critical component of execution in court is information management. During jury selection, there is a seemingly infinite amount of information about prospective jurors to effectively track. With a large panel, this information can be extremely difficult to effectively track. Trial attorneys have to balance the duties of conducting voir dire while also tracking and analyzing the information that comes out of voir dire, which is a very complex task. In addition to assessing the responses from prospective jurors, it involves being aware of which prospective jurors currently make up the jury, which prospective jurors are/would be the alternates (if such information is available during jury selection), and which prospective jurors will become part of the jury when a cause challenge is granted or a peremptory challenge is exercised.

Most jury consultants who regularly assist with jury selection have developed systems for tracking and managing all of this information that allow them to provide quick evaluations of prospective jurors and determine how the overall dynamic of the jury is impacted if a challenge for cause is granted or a peremptory challenge is exercised. This is a critical component of an effective jury selection strategy.

Chapter 6

Favorable Impression of You

"And what a jury is looking for is authenticity, someone who is real. A jury is like 12 people who you lock in a boat in a storm and they have no idea how to get out. And then two people come along and one says I know the way, and the other says no, I know the way. If you understand your job is to be the one that the 12 jurors follow, then you can win your case."

David Boies,
Preeminent trial lawyer
Lawdragon, 198 (2012)

"There are facts," he said, *"and the jurors listen to them, but even more, they watch you. They watch to see what happens to your face, how it changes when witnesses speak. For them, at bottom, the answer is how you appear in the courtroom, what you look like, how you act."*

Nels Gudmondsson,
Fictional defense lawyer
Snow Falling on Cedars
David Guterson

A. Favorable Impression of You

This and the following six chapters explore strategies, techniques, and patterns of questioning that you can employ in an effort to achieve the five goals for jury selection: (1) elicit information that will enable you to intelligently exercise challenges to deselect high risk jurors; (2) make a favorable impression of yourself on the jurors; (3) question them to determine whether they will be receptive to your client, legal position, and case story; (4) handle case weaknesses and juror misconceptions; and (5) gather material from the jurors for use in closing argument, such as a promise to follow a particular law.

In this chapter, we concentrate on techniques and strategies that you can employ during jury selection to make a good impression on the panel members and cause them to feel that you are trustworthy and someone to whom they can freely reveal their opinions and biases.

B. Presence

In order to picture how you want to be perceived by the prospective jurors, put yourself in their place and ask yourself, "If I were on the jury, what characteristics would I look for in a lawyer I could trust?" Your presence, your ability to convey your character to the prospective jurors, is critical. You don't want to come across as the stereotypical trial lawyer who is the subject of fiction and lawyer jokes. Your presence should project, as David Boies puts it, "authenticity, someone who is real," someone whom they will trust and follow.

1. Projecting Sincerity

Above all, the trait that jurors look for in a trial lawyer is sincerity. A lawyer who projects sincerity, confidence in self and in the rightness of their case, conveys a favorable impression to the jury. A sincere lawyer is someone jurors believe is a seeker of truth. A sincere lawyer gives the impression of being fully prepared, having examined the case from all sides. A sincere lawyer is a person who would not mislead or hide information. Although you cannot express personal opinions about the credibility of witnesses or about the justness of a cause, you can project sincerity.[1]

To project sincerity to the jury and thus, make a positive impression, you must believe in your case (unless you are an exceptionally good actor). Some trial lawyers talk themselves into believing in an improbable case, thus, are capable of projecting sincerity. If you believe in yourself and what you are championing, it will be reflected in your demeanor. If you do not believe in your case and yourself, your body language will betray you to the jury.[2]

---

1. MODEL RULES OF PROF'L CONDUCT r. 3.4.
2. ALLEN & BARBARA PEASE, THE DEFINITIVE BOOK OF BODY LANGUAGE: THE HIDDEN MEANING BEHIND PEOPLE'S GESTURES AND EXPRESSIONS 27 (2004).

2. Being Yourself and Being Human

While it is an excellent practice to watch talented trial lawyers and borrow what you can, take away only what fits you. If you admire the hard-hitting manner of another lawyer, but that is not your style, do not try to be something that you aren't. It is critical that you be yourself, because jurors can detect a fraud. The best public speakers are those who adapt the core principles of effective public speaking and persuasion to their own personal style.

3. Friendly

You want to be open and friendly with the prospective jurors. Show them both in your voice and manner that you want to engage them in a conversation. Again, picture yourself talking to your good friend over a cup of coffee—coffee chat—or whatever vision makes you feel comfortable when you and your friend share your thoughts. Avoid in any way being imposing or threatening.

Dale Carnegie, lecturer, trainer and author of *How to Win Friends and Influence People,* taught the following: "Remember that a person's name is to that person the sweetest and most important sound in any language."[3] While the court may have issued numbered cards to the prospective jurors and you are required to state a juror's number for the court record, remember Carnegie's point and call the juror by name. Say, "Juror number 5, Mr. Swan, ..." You can always refer to your notes for a juror's name. Out of courtesy and because you are in a formal setting, use the juror's surname, not the person's first name. If you are one of the gifted people who can remember a significant number of names, memorize the jurors' names. If you, like most of us, can't retain many names, memorize a few of their names and call on them by their names.

If you are not certain how to pronounce a juror's name, just ask them. This will show them that you care enough to get it right.

4. Humor

It is a good practice to refrain from attempting humor. If are ever tempted, recall when defense counsel made history by telling a knock-knock joke in opening statement to an unamused jury in the 2013 trial of George Zimmerman for the murder of Trayvon Martin.

---

3. DALE CARNEGIE, HOW TO WIN FRIENDS AND INFLUENCE PEOPLE 88 (1936).

Humor is a unique genre of entertainment because it is so subjective. For example, horror movies often make a lot of money worldwide, because horror is not necessarily culture-dependent. The same is not true for humor. Your venire is diverse, even if it doesn't look diverse. Humor can quickly offend some folks. Some jurors may conclude humor is entirely inappropriate in the courtroom, particularly if the case involves serious issues such as a death or a tragic injury. Attempts at humor may send the signal to jurors that you do not take the process seriously.

Generally, let the judge and the jurors make the jokes, and then you can respond appropriately. The exceptions to this rule are if you are extraordinarily funny (a rare quality, but if you have it, self-deprecating humor is the best), and your position in the case permits humor (also, a rare situation).

5. Communicating Nonverbally

Your appearance and body behavior determine how the prospective jurors perceive you, and they are visual media through which you communicate. Indeed, 60 to 80 percent of communication is nonverbal.[4] This point is sometimes lost on attorneys. In fact, some research shows that jurors are much more likely to be visual learners than attorneys. Consequently, an attorney who is not a visual learner may be more likely to discount the influence of nonverbal behavior. In fact, some stubborn attorneys insist that what they say is more important than what they look like while they are saying it, which is simply not the case. Decades of marital research and therapy have established that how you say something is more important that what you actually say.

a. Your Countenance

The foremost ways of communicating in a nonverbal way are the two we have already mentioned: (1) being sincere and (2) being yourself. When you are sincere and yourself, your countenance will show it. Your face will be open, unaffected, earnest, and friendly. Smile when the occasion calls for it.

b. Interaction with Opposing Counsel

Opposing counsel could be your law school classmate and one of your closest friends. But, when you are in trial, it is time for you to treat it as serious business and not engage in friendly interactions with opposing counsel. The

---

4. Allen & Barbara Pease, The Definitive Book of Body Language: The Hidden Meaning Behind People's Gestures and Expressions 10 (2004).

last thing you want to communicate to the jury is that this is just a game you and opposing counsel are playing. If opposing counsel attempts to leave an impression that you two are engaged in a friendly exchange, do not participate. Of course, you should be courteous. Just not chummy.

c. Your Dress and Accessories

The conventional wisdom is to have a professional appearance and to not wear anything that will distract the jurors from what you are trying to communicate. Traditional conservative attire for men is the trial uniform of a dark suit of either navy blue, charcoal grey or black with both a pale blue or white shirt and a bland necktie of red or blue and with a modest pattern. Women's ware is not so simple. However, a woman's trial uniform can also be the conservative dark dress or slacks, depending on the local practice regarding slacks, blouse and comfortable shoes without spiked heels that will click clack across the courtroom floor.

While these trial uniforms are certainly important because they can project professionalism, sincerity and a degree of authority, the bottom line remains the same. That bottom line is that you want to be perceived as authentic. You want to wear what is comfortable for you, what will make the jury receptive to you, and, of course, what the court will find acceptable.

Some very successful trial lawyers eschew the trial uniform for what works for them. For examples, Gloria Allred wears what she feels suits her to trial, which could be a red dress, and Rusty Hardin another successful trial lawyer wears lighter colored suits in trial. Consult Hale Starr and Mark McCormick's *Jury Selection* for an extensive discussion of appropriate courtroom attire.[5]

Just as you want to avoid clothing that will distract the jurors from your message, you also want to avoid accessories that distract.

d. Personal Appearance

Just as clothing and accessories are important, personal appearance and grooming matter. A trial lawyer should be presentable and, thus, not sidetrack the prospective jurors with some idiosyncrasy in appearance. For instance, male trial lawyers should consider whether a beard or facial hair could influence how prospective jurors' perceive them. Male and female trial lawyers alike should consider whether piercings and tattoos will off put some jurors.

---

5. HALE STARR & MARK MCCORMICK, JURY SELECTION 432–33 (3d ed. 2001).

e. Meaningful Eye Contact

Through eye contact, we make a personal connection. Looking a person in the eye conveys that you are speaking honestly and that you are trustworthy. Your goal is to make eye contact with all of the potential jurors. You want to make meaningful eye contact, not just a fleeting glance and not a stare. When you are speaking to an individual juror, it is easy to focus just on that person. When you are speaking to the panel, a technique for making eye contact is to speak to a particular juror and look that person in the eyes until you finish a statement. Then, shift your gaze to another prospective juror in another part of the jury box or spectator section and do the same. Repeat the process in your ongoing effort to make eye contact with as many of the prospective jurors as possible.

However, it is important to avoid a situation where you repeatedly focus your eye contact on the same few jurors. This is an easy situation to fall into, because it is natural for public speakers to focus their eye contact on those in the audience who seemed to be most engaged. However, this can make jurors feel uncomfortable, resulting in negative perceptions of you and/or your client.

f. Body Behavior

Your body behavior communicates your thoughts. Through your body behavior you want to communicate to the prospective jurors that you are sincere, candid, interested in what they have to say, and real.

i. Gesturing

Studies have repeatedly shown that gestures enhance a speaker's credibility. To project both confidence, openness, receptiveness and to employ your hands in gestures as part of your communication, you can do two things. First, you can begin by steepling—bend your elbows, with your upper arms at your side, hold your hands out in front of you and touch the tips of the fingers of each hand to the corresponding fingers on the other hand. Fingers should be pointing away from the body. This shows that you have confidence and are thinking about something (even if it's only steepling). Besides instilling confidence in you and displaying it to the jurors, this position for the hands makes sure they are neither in your pockets, behind you nor in the fig-leaf position. Also, when you move your hands out of the steepling position (a position which you should only maintain for a short time), they will be out in front of and to the sides of your body (envision yourself as ready to hug someone with your arms) and ready to gesture.

Second, gesture naturally in ways that emphasize what you are saying. If you make a point, don't point. Rather than pointing with an extended finger, you can effectively point with fingers of a downturned hand. To show that you are open and trustworthy, gesture with your palms up. This palm-up gesture is best when it accompanies a question.

ii. Nodding

Use your head. When you want to support something that a juror has said, nod your head up and down to show your assent. If the juror condemns something, shake your head in agreement.

iii. Lean In

When speaking to a juror, show your interest by leaning in towards the juror and if the court permits, move closer.

g. Courtroom Position

Courtroom practice dictates where you stand for jury selection. Federal and some state and local courts require that you stand behind a podium. Others will allow you to move around the courtroom. If you can, do not stand behind a podium. Stand where the jurors can see you, which is what they are accustomed to during a conversation. Movement makes your communication more dynamic and engaging. If the court requires you to use a podium, you may be allowed to step to the side of the podium, enabling the jurors to see all of you.

You may need to move behind counsel table so that you can address not only those in the jury box but also those in the spectator section. Stand in one place for the most part but you may wish to move in closer to a juror to improve communication. If you do, do not enter the space of the jury. Stand back from and do not lean on the jury rail.

h. More on Nonverbal Communication

For a further discussion of nonverbal communication, see pages 281–285 where we discuss using body behavior to evaluate the prospective jurors.

6. Be Comfortable—Converting Nervousness to Energy

During jury selection, you are in front of a courtroom full of strangers, and they are all concentrating on you. Nervous? Of course you are, but that can be a good thing.

a. What Is Important and What Isn't

Converting nervousness into positive energy is a matter of knowing what is important and focusing on that. When you get absorbed in yourself and how you are being perceived by others in the courtroom—the prospective jurors, spectators, courtroom personnel and so on—that can make you nervous and interfere with your conversation with the jurors. In the scheme of things, you are not really that important. The prospective jurors are for the most part thinking about themselves and what they will say when questioned, not you. That's right, you are not that important. Understanding that, you can shift your attention away from yourself to what is important: the task at hand—a conversation with your audience, the prospective jurors.

b. Effectively Managing Your Mistakes

You will make some sort of mistake during jury selection. It may be something simple, such as screwing up the wording of a voir dire question. It may be something a little more embarrassing, such as spilling your cup of water all over yourself (hopefully, this is not the case, but it does happen). The key to effectively managing your mistakes is to acknowledge them, maybe make light of them (self-deprecating humor can humanize you), and then correct them. For example, it is not unusual for an attorney to screw up the wording of a question, get flustered, and simply move onto the next question in order to escape the awkward moment. The problem is that you have now skipped over what was potentially an important voir dire question. Instead, if this happens to you, stop and back up. A simple statement such as, "boy, I really messed that one up; let me give it another try" can humanize you with the jurors and enhance your credibility. In short, you don't have to be perfect. Don't let small mistakes disrupt your overarching goal.

c. Preparation and Practice

Your concentration during jury selection should be on any preliminary remarks that you are permitted to make, your questions, and the responses that you get from the jurors. Be passionate about delivering your remarks, asking good questions, generating a good conversation with the jurors and evaluating them. Performing these tasks smoothly and enjoyably comes only thorough preparation and practice. With that preparation and practice, you will gain confidence and be able to convert any nervousness into energy and enthusiasm to conduct an effective jury selection. In Chapter 4, we cover how to prepare; in Chapter 7, we offer you preliminary remarks; and in Chapters 9–11, we provide jury selection questions that you can convert to your own.

C. Professionalism

Besides learning what the judge's protocols are for jury selection, a trial lawyer must to know the judge's preferences for how counsel should professionally behave in the courtroom. Noncompliance with what the court expects of counsel can result in a judicial reprimand that can harm counsel's standing with the jurors. Jurors are aware of everything that goes on in the courtroom. You want to appear professional and prepared at all times in and around the courthouse—on the elevator, in the courthouse coffee shop, in the hall outside the courtroom and in the courtroom. Everywhere you can be seen and heard by the prospective jurors.

Courts demand certain professional behavior, and there are at least four standards of professional conduct that you and your trial team must comply with in any courtroom. First, do not waste the court's time. Don't be late. Courts expect you to be on time, and it is good practice to give yourself plenty of time and arrive early. Second, stand when you address the court or the jurors unless your jurisdiction has a different practice requiring you to remain seated. Third, never make facial expressions that mock or show displeasure with a prospective juror, opposing counsel, court personnel or the judge. Fourth, do not bring any of the following into a courtroom: food; beverages; gum; or a phone, unless it is either on vibrate or off.

D. Civility

As we have mentioned before, jurors are extremely observant, seeing virtually everything that happens in a courtroom. If they see that courtroom personnel and others in the courtroom treat you with respect and courtesy, that makes a favorable impression. Civility goes beyond what is required by rules of professional responsibility, which are minimal ethical standards. Civility means being courteous to and respectful of others.

Civility begets civility. Therefore, how you treat others is important. Lawyers naturally behave respectfully towards the judge, but some neglect the lower bench—the court reporter, court clerk, and bailiff. Being friendly and courteous towards the lower bench is not only good practice for its own sake, it can result in them returning the favor, and the jurors can see that. No matter how you may feel about opposing counsel, be civil. Granted this will be difficult at times, and on those unfortunate occasions when opposing counsel misbehaves, rise above it and be civil.

The American Board of Trial Advocates promulgated *Principles of Civility, Integrity, and Professionalism,* which govern courtroom conduct as follows:

When in Court I Will:
1. Always uphold the dignity of the court and never be disrespectful.
2. Never publicly criticize a judge for his or her rulings or a jury for the court's verdict. Criticism should be reserved for appellate court briefs.
3. Be punctual and prepared for all court appearances, and, if unavoidably delayed, notify the court and counsel as soon as possible.
4. Never engage in conduct that brings disorder or disruption to the courtroom.
5. Advise clients and witnesses of the proper courtroom conduct expected and required.
6. Never misrepresent or misquote facts or authorities.
7. Verify the availability of clients and witnesses, if possible, before dates for hearings or trials are scheduled, or immediately thereafter. Promptly notify the court and counsel if their attendance cannot be assured.
8. Be respectful and courteous to court marshals or bailiffs, clerks, reporters, secretaries, and law clerks.[6]

---

6. To encourage civility, many state and local bar associations have also embraced creeds of civility, such as the Washington State Bar Association's Creed of Professionalism adopted in 2001, available at http://www.wsba.org/Legal-Community/Committees-Boards-and-Other-Groups/Professionalism-Committee (Jan. 9 2017). However, the creed does not supplant or modify the Washington Rules of Professional Conduct.

Chapter 7

Mining Useful Information

"When people talk, listen completely. Most people never listen."

Ernest Hemingway

"Voir dire is interactive. It is the 'hello, nice to meet you, are you the right person to sit in judgment' part of the case. Yet, for many attorneys voir dire is torture. There is a reason it is not taught if at all in law school. We need to think like a lawyer but communicate like a good neighbor to a large group of people we know almost nothing about. The approach is wholly different from any other type of legal proceedings ... It is no wonder many of us dread voir dire. Compounding our distress, judges generally do not allow adequate time for voir dire."

Karen Koehler,
Trial lawyer and author
Voir Dire, 49 (December 2010)

"Everyone has an invisible sign hanging from their neck saying, 'Make me feel important.' Never forget this message when working with people."

Mary Kay Ash,
Businesswoman

A. Mining Useful Information

In order to gather information from the prospective jurors that will help you decide whether to exercise a challenge, you want to stimulate a good, open conversation. However, because jury selection is a foreign situation for the jury panel members, most will be reluctant to speak out, at least at first. Public speaking is not easy for most people, and the formal courtroom setting can be intimidating. Under the circumstances, if you do the vast amount of the talking, you are gaining little if anything. Instead, you want to remove barriers to communication, and get them talking. You want to mine for useful information, and in particular, you want to drill down and unearth the prospective jurors' biases and preconceived notions that are harmful to your case.

In the preceding chapter, we covered the primary method for generating a good exchange with the jury, and that is by making a favorable impression and developing a rapport with the prospective jurors. The prospective jurors will be more likely to carry on a freewheeling discussion with you if they trust you. Now, in this chapter, we explore additional strategies and techniques for removing barriers to open communication between you and the jurors and generating a fruitful discussion.

B. Preliminary Remarks

The trial judge may allow you to make opening remarks at the outset of your exchange with the panel. These remarks resemble a mini opening statement. If the court allows you to make opening remarks, take it as an opportunity to break down barriers to communication and to introduce your legal position, case narrative and case theme. In preparing your preliminary remarks, once again put yourself in the jurors' situation, but this time ask what you would like an attorney to say that would put you at ease. Ask yourself what the attorney could say that would allay fears that you may have as a juror, such as of being embarrassed.

1. Matters to Cover

In your preliminary remarks, stress how important an open discussion is to achieving a fair and impartial trial. Both at the outset and when introducing a new subject for discussion, make sure you explain why the information sought is relevant to the selection process, because once they understand the purpose, it is more likely to prompt responses and make your questioning reasonable.

Some of the matters to discuss in your preliminary remarks include the following:

- An introduction of yourself and your client if you have not yet been introduced or it has been some time since you were initially introduced to the panel;
- A statement of the case theme;

- A statement of your legal position;
- A summary of your case narrative;
- An explanation of the importance of an open exchange between the prospective jurors and you;
- An explanation of the importance of revealing reasons why this may not be the right case for some of the prospective jurors; and
- To the extent possible, a statement that will alleviate any concerns that they may have that you will embarrass or otherwise make them uncomfortable.

2. Illustrations of Preliminary Remarks

Now, let's examine the next best thing to co-chairing a trial with a veteran trial lawyer, which is to review transcripts of skilled trial lawyers. The following are illustrations of preliminary remarks.

Preliminary Remarks Example 1: The following prefatory remarks by plaintiff's counsel in a patent case demonstrate how to introduce a corporate client, discuss the opportunity for an exchange between counsel and the prospective jurors, and explain the case theory and theme (doing the right thing) in terms that are clear and understandable:

> THE COURT: ... All right. At this time, I'll allow counsel for the Plaintiff to voir dire the jury.
>
> MR. CAWLEY: Thank you, Your Honor.
>
> As I recall from Your Honor's order, it's 40 minutes?
>
> THE COURT: Yes, sir, that's correct.
>
> MR. CAWLEY: Good morning, Ladies and Gentlemen.
>
> You know, I have to say, this is my favorite part of the trial, because as this case goes on, as you've heard for several days, you will hear witnesses talk and lawyers talk; but this is the only opportunity that we have to get to meet and hear from the citizens who have done their important civic duty and agreed to serve as jurors.
>
> The United States of America is just about the only company—excuse me—the only country left in the world that decides cases like this by juries. And we do that because we trust you. We trust your common sense.
>
> And even though cases like this one may involve some complex things that people are not very familiar with, we know that you have the ability to learn about them and to make the right decision.

As Judge Davis has told you, this is when we get a chance to learn a little bit about you and to ask you some questions.

To be able to do that, I'd like you to understand that during the course of this trial, you will be hearing about some people at a company called Ericsson who did the right thing. They and their company chose to let other companies use their ideas to help people communicate.

Now, they didn't have to make that choice. They could have chosen to keep their ideas secret. Because their ideas were patented and protected by United States patents, they could have chosen to be the only ones who use those ideas and to prohibit anyone else from using their patented ideas.

But they didn't do that. Instead, they committed to let other companies use the ideas that they had developed to develop products and to make a profit.

What they asked in return is that if another company used Ericsson's patented inventions to make a profit, that they pay a reasonable royalty to Ericsson for using the patent.

You'll hear, during the course of this case, that many companies around the world agreed to do that. They did the right thing, too. And they've paid millions of dollars to Ericsson for the right to use Ericsson's patents in their products.

But you'll also hear that the Defendants in this case, even though they use Ericsson's patents, have refused to pay fair value, and that's why we're here.

We're here because this is a very important case. This is a case that asks whether a company like Ericsson should be entitled to recover fair value for someone's use of their property, their patented inventions.

Now, at the very outset, let me just ask you, how many of you have heard of the company Ericsson?[1]

Preliminary Remarks Example 2: The following introductory remarks by counsel in a breach of contract case illustrate how to encourage the prospective jurors to disclose bias and to alleviate any concerns they may have about having to disclose something they do not wish to discuss in open court:

---

1. Transcript of Proceedings at 21–23, *Ericson, Inc. v. D-Link Corporation, et al.,* 6:10cv473E.D. (Tex. June 3, 2013), App. 7.1.

MR. HARRIGAN: Thank you, your Honor. First of all, I know that both parties, and the lawyers, all appreciate the time that you folks are willing to take to help us resolve this case, and also, obviously, the forthright manner in which everybody has responded to questions. I will have some questions, some general, and they may lead to more specific questions to individual people.

The court has asked some questions that clearly anyone would want to know about prospective jurors. But there may be things that—experiences you have had with either one of the two companies here. Motorola is now owned by Google. And by the way, one of the questions I would like to know is whether anybody owns stock in Google, which I'm not sure whether that question related to Motorola or Google, so we wanted to clarify that.

But, at any rate, there may be things that have occurred in your lives, somebody's lives here, that affect whether you can be fair to either Motorola or Microsoft that we haven't been smart enough to ask a question about. So one general question that I will have is, if any of you, as you go through this, if it occurs to you that you have some experience that would affect your ability to be impartial to these two parties, just raise your hand and let's talk about it.

And another thing is, it may be that something has occurred that you don't particularly want to talk about in open court, in which case just say that, and then we can—the court will tell us how to approach that issue.[2]

3. Objectionable Remarks

If you are concerned that opposing counsel may cross the boundary line between making introductory remarks and delivering an opening statement or that counsel may introduce objectionable information, suggest to opposing counsel that you and opposing counsel exchange the preliminary remarks for review. If opposing counsel declines, ask the court to require that counsel exchange their remarks with you. If you find any part of opposing counsel's remarks improper, ask counsel to remove them. If counsel does not remove those statements, you can make a motion in limine to the trial court to have counsel prohibited from making them. Ultimately, an exchange of remarks can prevent

---

2. Transcript of Proceedings at 46–47, *Microsoft Corp. v. Motorola, Inc.*, C10-1823-JLR (W.D. Wash. Aug. 26, 2013), App. 7.2.

both the introduction of objectionable information and forestall objections during your delivery of counsel's remarks.

C. Make a Personal Connection

1. Something in Common

Seek to make a personal connection with the prospective jurors through self-disclosure. We all communicate better with people with whom we have something in common. You can make a personal connection by revealing something you have in common with the jurors. When you disclose something about yourself that you have something in common with them, you become more than just a lawyer.

Sharing begets sharing. Humanize yourself and show the jurors that you are vulnerable, and it is more likely that they will share their personal information with you. As legendary trial lawyer Gerry Spence put it, "I tell the jury when I'm nervous, when I screw up and when I'm afraid."[3] To share your vulnerabilities shows that you are both human and honest.

Sharing Example: In *Retractable Technologies, Inc. v. Becton, Dickinson and Co.*, defense counsel wanted to have the prospective jurors reveal their experiences either giving or getting needle shots:

> MR. BAXTER: ... Okay. Is there anyone that is—besides our juror up here that is a diabetic like I am and has to give themselves insulin shots every day?
> You don't use the pen—
> JUROR HUDSON: I use the pen.
> MR. BAXTER: You use the pen.
> JUROR HUDSON: Put the needle on it.
> MR. BAXTER: Yes, ma'am. Do you use the Nano needle like I do?
> JUROR HUDSON: (Nods head.) Yes.
> MR. BAXTER: Okay. Is that made by BD; do you remember?
> JUROR HUDSON: Yes, it is.
> MR. BAXTER: Do you like those needles?
> JUROR HUDSON: Yes, I do.
> MR. BAXTER: They are great, aren't they?

---

3. Cheryl McCall, *For Country Lawyer Gerry Spence, It's Open Season on Big Corporations*, PEOPLE (Aug. 24, 1981).

JUROR HUDSON: Yes, you can't hardly feel it.

MR. BAXTER: Right. And you screw it on and give yourself the injection, screw it off, and it is in that safety cap, and you throw it in the jug?

JUROR HUDSON: True.

MR. BAXTER: Okay. And that works pretty well?

JUROR HUDSON: Yes.

MR. BAXTER: Okay. Thank you, ma'am.

Anybody else give themselves shots on a daily basis for diabetes or anything of that sort?[4]

If you go too far and obviously try to ingratiate yourself with the jurors, it may not only undermine your efforts to make a favorable impression but also your comments may be both objectionable as irrelevant and in violation of the court's rules regarding proper questioning.

2. Sharing Your Life

a. Talking about Yourself

Counsel may want to lay out some of their personal history during voir dire either in preliminary remarks or questioning. While counsel cannot lay out a personal history in depth, counsel may include some personal information. Counsel might begin voir dire with a elevator-ride self-introduction along these lines: "I'm going to be asking you some personal questions, and it seems only right that you should know a little about me. I am with a local law firm here in town. I'm married and have three children ..."

Another time that a trial lawyer may interject personal information occurs when the court asks the jurors to introduce themselves by answering a series of questions. When that happens counsel may do the same, as occurred in the following example:

Sharing Your Life Example: The judge in a patent infringement case had members of the jury panel introduce themselves by answering nine questions projected on a screen in the courtroom. When it came time for plaintiff's counsel to address the jurors, she did what the jurors had done.

MS. DERIEUX: Good morning. I hope I can keep close enough to this microphone and still see everyone.

---

4. Transcript of Proceedings at 35–36, *Retractable Techs., Inc. v. Becton, Dickinson and Co.*, 2:08cv16 E.D. (Tex. Sept. 3, 2013), App. 1.2.

First, I want to thank each and every one of you for being here this morning. We recognize that jury service disrupts your lives and interferes with your other obligations. And I want to say first we appreciate everyone being here this morning.

Just so we're kind of even, I'll start with the information that y'all started with. My name is Elizabeth DeRieux. I'm an attorney. I work with a firm in Gladewater, Texas, Capshaw DeRieux. I have an English degree, and I started out my career teaching English in high school with a degree from Lamar University of Beaumont. Later I went to the University of Houston and got a law degree.

I am married. My husband is Pete Adams. He is a retired attorney, and we own Gladewater Books. And so his full-time job now is running a bookstore. We have four children. They're all grown now, and I've never been selected to serve on a jury.[5]

Another time that counsel may mention some of counsel's own personal background arises during jury questioning when a juror mentions something that the juror and counsel have in common. For instance, counsel might say, "Mr. Snider, like you, my father drove a tractor-trailer. What kind of rig do you drive?"

b. Opposing the Introduction of Counsel's Background Information

On the other hand, statements by counsel that introduce personal background information can be viewed as violative of both the rules of evidence and the rules of professional responsibility, and you may wish to object or make a motion in limine to preclude opposing counsel from making them.

Counsel's personal background does not qualify as relevant evidence under Federal Rule of Evidence 401, because it does not have "any tendency to make a fact more or less probable than it would be without the evidence," and the counsel's background is not of consequence in determining the action. No plausible argument can be made that it has any bearing on the case. Because it is not relevant evidence, it is inadmissible during the trial.[6] Voir dire is part of the trial.[7] Further, FRE 103(d) states, "to the extent practicable, the court must conduct a jury trial so that inadmissible evidence is not suggested to the jury by any means." Referring to irrelevant personal background information is not only a

---

5. Transcript of Proceedings at 38, *Simpleair, Inc. v. Google*, Case 2:13cv587 (E.D. Tex. Mar. 17, 2014), App. 7.3.

6. Fed. R. Evid. 402.

7. *Gomez v. United States*, 490 U.S. 858, 873 (1989).

violation of the rules of evidence but also arguably unethical. Model Rule of Professional Conduct 3.4 "Fairness to Opposing Party and Counsel" provides, "[a] lawyer shall not: ... (e) in trial, allude to any matter that the lawyer does not reasonably believe is relevant or that will not be supported by admissible evidence ..."

For these reasons, if you make the motion to prohibit counsel from mentioning any personal background information during voir dire or, for that matter, during any other part of the trial, the trial court should grant it. A motion in limine is preferable to objecting, because if you object to opposing counsel trying to tell the jury a little bit about himself, opposing counsel may just give a shoulder shrug and shake of the head, indicating that you are just trying to hide something from the jurors.

The key lesson from this is to keep it short if you choose to disclose any personal background information. You do not want to have an objection sustained against you in the first few moments of your voir dire, particularly if the judge might add his or her own commentary about the inappropriateness of your comments. Furthermore, jurors do not like to have their time wasted. They like efficient and organized attorneys. If your comments about your own personal background drag on, it could lead jurors to conclude that you are wasteful of their time and, consequently, dislike you.

D. Nonjudgmental

1. Nonjudgmental and the Deselection Approach

It is critical to remain nonjudgmental throughout your questioning, particularly when you encounter troublesome comments from prospective jurors. It is only natural to want to be an advocate for your position when a prospective juror says something that you disagree with. You may be concerned that the juror's statement will poison the panel against your case. You will have an urge to refute what the prospective juror has said and to show that person and the other jurors the light. However, if you display a negative reaction and engage in any refutation, it is likely to cause not only that particular juror to withhold further information but also others to not speak freely. If they don't speak freely, you won't get the information you need to exercise challenges.

As unpleasant as it may be for you to hear a juror make negative comments, this is exactly what a deselection strategy requires. You need jurors to feel comfortable making such comments. If you demonstrate negative verbal or nonverbal reactions, it may discourage other jurors who agree with the comment from informing you of their agreement, which undermines your efforts to deselect.

Another major reason for you to remain nonjudgmental throughout voir dire is that you do not want to give clues to your opposing counsel about whom you like and do not like in the jury panel. Sometimes, this may be obvious regardless of your verbal or nonverbal reactions. Other times, your opposing counsel may not pick up on whom you do not want, particularly if a juror has made comments that cut both ways. If the opposing counsel does not know whom you dislike, it could lead him to strike jurors that you actually want to remove from the panel, which functionally provides you with additional peremptory strikes.

a. Hug the Expression of the Negative

If a prospective juror expresses a view that is harmful to you or your case, rather than seeing it as a contaminant that may spread to other members of the panel, seize upon it as an opportunity to show your willingness to listen and not pass judgment. You want jurors to reveal how they feel about issues in the case, because otherwise you will not be able to determine whether or not to deselect them. Therefore, no matter how damaging the juror's response might be to your case, do not let it show either in your body behavior or voice. Make it pleasant and safe to talk to you. You get more with honey than vinegar. Indeed, you ought to praise the person for being open and forthright — "Ms. Riley, thank you, that's exactly what we want to hear. Thanks for speaking up and being straightforward with us."

Unless the prospective juror were to offer inadmissible evidence, such as stating what was in the evening news about the case, the juror's open disclosure of a belief is not going to pollute the rest of the panel. If the juror expresses a view that is harmful to your case, that disclosure is unlikely to cause other jurors to abandon their views and to adopt that prospective juror's opinion.

b. Tainting the Pool

As noted in the previous two sections, attorneys often express concern that a juror's comments could do what is known as "taint the pool." In other words, these attorneys are concerned that a negative comment by a juror could somehow cause other jurors to focus on the negative issue or even adopt similar beliefs.

This should not be a worry for you. First, if a juror holds a negative attitude about you or your client, you need to know. There are two opportunities over the course of trial for a juror to make such comments: (1) in voir dire when you can do something about it or (2) in jury deliberations when you have no control at all. Obviously, you want to find out that a juror holds a negative attitude when you can do something about it.

Second, other jurors are not going to be persuaded by a random comment made by another stranger during jury selection. As previously noted, despite the popular belief to the contrary, there is no research that supports the argument that jurors are persuaded during jury selection. However, even if this were the case, the juror who changes his mind based on some random comment made by another venire member is probably going to change his mind a few times over the course of the trial because, evidently, it takes very little to influence such a juror. He is certainly not going to serve as an opinion leader during deliberations if he is so easily influenced.

c. Generate a Group Discussion

When you have a juror who expresses an opinion, albeit not in your favor, you should ask the panel if anyone else has similar views — "Does anyone have a similar feelings about ...?" If this does not provoke a response, address the question to a particular juror, "Ms. Gordon, how do you feel about ...?" Hopefully, others with similar views will speak up and this will lead to a group discussion among the jurors. When you have generated a group discussion, you can more readily identify how the jurors view issues in the case, which is what you are looking for.

There may be a temptation to seek out jurors who hold opposite viewpoints. For example, you may find yourself so troubled by the negative view expressed by one juror that you want to counter it with opposing views from other jurors. However, you should resist this temptation. Seeking out jurors who hold opposite viewpoints only reveals your good jurors to the other side. As we have previously mentioned, you want your good jurors to remain as quiet as possible and hopefully go undetected by the other side.

2. Accentuate the Positive

When you get a response, especially one that supports the proposition that the parties are entitled to a fair and impartial trial, it is another chance to show your gratitude and support. In this way, you encourage that juror and others to give your client a fair and impartial trial. Further, if the juror says something favorable to your case, you can give the person a nod of appreciation.

Praising Example: Plaintiff's counsel's response in *In re TFT-LCD (Flat-Panel)* illustrates this:

MR. SILBERFELD: Anything about that fact cause you to have any feelings one way or the other about whether companies ought to be sued or not?

PROSPECTIVE JUROR HARPER: No.

MR. SILBERFELD: Okay. Or whether the fact that your employer may be sued sometimes causes you to have feelings about whether you would have a tendency to side with either the plaintiff on this case or the defense on this case?

PROSPECTIVE JUROR HARPER: No.

MR. SILBERFELD: Okay. So right now as you sit here, if this were a race and we were at the starting line, Best Buy, HannStar, Toshiba, we're all equal?

PROSPECTIVE JUROR HARPER: All even.

MR. SILBERFELD: Okay. Great. Thank you.[8]

E. Conversational

Hallmarks of a good conversation are paying attention to the other person, actively listening, and having something to say. You want to remove any obstructions and carry on a conversation as though you were having that coffee chat.

1. Removing Obstructions

a. Your Notes

The first and biggest obstruction that will prevent a good conversation is the notes you have prepared for jury selection. Notes are like eye magnets, attracting your eyes to them. This will cause you to look away from the person or people with whom you want to communicate. It is unnatural to converse with a person who frequently refers to notes. Also, when you look at your notes, you will lose your focus on what the other person in the conversation is saying or how the other person is behaving.

When you are in the planning stage, write out your voir dire questions. Then, rehearse your questions, just as you rehearse your opening statement and closing argument. Practice them until they are natural and conversational. If you have to have notes, they should be idea notes in large print that you can glance at and prompt your memory. If you have to refer to your notes, glance

8. Transcript of Proceedings at 55, *In re TFT-LCD* (*Flat-Panel*), No. 07-MDL-1827 SI, 10-CV-4572, 10-CV-5452, 10-CV-4114 (N.D. Cal. July 22, 2013), App. 1.1.

down at the couple words, then look up and at the person or persons with whom you are conversing.

Regarding taking notes on what the prospective jurors say, if possible, leave the note taking to a member of your trial team. If you do not have a note taker, restrict your notes to major things and use abbreviations. At pages 108–110, we cover ways to record information gathered during jury selection.

b. The Podium

The second biggest obstruction to a natural conversation is a lectern. As we have previously mentioned, if the court permits, do not stand (hide) behind a podium. It is unnatural for a conversation. It gives you the appearance of being a lecturer who is speaking to the jurors rather than someone who expects to have an exchange of ideas. Stand where all the prospective jurors can see you. Your body language should be casual, again as though you were having the coffee chat with your friend.

c. Talking Too Much

According to the dictionary, a "conversation" "is an informal talk involving two people or a small group of people: the act of talking in an informal way."[9] Unfortunately, trial lawyers have a tendency to talk and talk. They tell stories, and they make speeches. They lecture. A lecture is not a conversation. A lecture does not stimulate much of a back-and-forth conversation. The more you talk during jury selection, the less time the prospective jurors will talk, and consequently you will draw out less information from the jurors. Remove this barrier by talking less, provoking the jurors to speak out. You will have plenty of time to talk during opening statement and closing argument. Now, talk little, ask questions, encourage the prospective jurors to talk, and actively listen to them.

2. Principles of Carrying on a Good Conversation

Besides removing hindrances, apply the following principles for carrying on a good conversation: actively listen; use plain English; have a conversational tone and manner; and have something interesting to say.

a. Listen Actively

Above all else, the most important skill possessed by a good conversationalist is active listening. Nothing will let the jurors know that you are attentive and

---

9. *Conversation*, MERRIAM-WEBSTER'S DICTIONARY (New ed. 2016).

engaged more than listening to their responses and asking good follow-up questions. Thinking ahead to the next question you want to ask will interfere with your ability to listen. After you have asked a question, do not shift your attention to the next question for you to ask. Instead, listen. Listen to what the prospective jurors have to say so you can learn about them and make informed decisions when the time comes to exercise your peremptory strikes. Do not rush on to another question; rather, give the person your full attention and time to respond.

When a prospective juror is speaking, lean in a little, make eye contact, cock your head a bit, nod if you approve of what is being said, don't interrupt except with short words of support, such as "that's good," and, most of all, be interested in the person and what is being said. In your mind, you should be thinking that the only other person in the room is the juror to whom you are speaking.

If you are interested, you will instinctively have follow-up questions to ask. The best follow-up questions that you can ask a prospective juror is: "What else?" and "Tell us more about that." Use them over and over. They never grow stale.

b. Speak Clearly, Simply, and in Plain English

In framing your questions, use easily understood language and simple-sentence questions. You want your questions to be clear to everyone in the panel. Use plain English, avoiding any legal jargon and technical terms. Rather than referring to what you are doing as "voir dire," an expression that you and the other trial lawyers are accustomed to but the prospective jurors are not, call it "jury selection." Rather than a "previous altercation," say "fight." Rather than talking about a "pulmonary edema," call it "fluid in the lungs." Using legalese or technical terms may impress a few, but the words may either be misunderstood or not understood by the jurors.

c. Use a Conversational Tone and Manner

Speak in a conversational tone; you are not there to lecture or in any way speak down to the prospective jurors. Also, your nonverbal behavior should be appropriate to the situation, smiling when the situation calls for it. Act as though you were talking to a friend about something important.

d. Have Something Interesting to Say

Finally, to take part in a good conversation, have something interesting to say. Jury selection can be particularly boring if the questions asked are not, or at least appear not, to be pertinent to jury selection. For instance, a question about what news programs the prospective juror watches on television seems remote and not very thought provoking. We will get to types of interesting questions you may ask in the next chapter.

3. The Overly Talkative and the Quiet Ones

a. Cut Off the Overly Talkative Ones

Sometimes, during jury selection, one or more people try to dominate the discussion, and this can prevent you from hearing from and being able to evaluate other jurors. These dominators also can irk the other prospective jurors. Additionally, the other jurors can blame counsel for not cutting off the talkers.

When you encounter this, like the talk show host, you must manage the conversation and give others an opportunity to speak. A technique for accomplishing this is called the "bouncing-ball" technique. If juror Mr. Norman has been co-opting the conversation, you politely take the ball from Mr. Norman and bounce it over to another juror, saying, "Thank you, Mr. Norman. What do you think, Ms. Wickstrand?" as you turn to face Ms. Wickstrand.

Sometimes, however, the bouncing-ball strategy does not effectively quiet a talkative juror. She may continue to raise her hand throughout voir dire or throw her answers out. If this occurs, you should politely tell her that you appreciate her openness, but you have heard a lot from her and would really like to learn more about some of the other jurors.

b. Involving the Quiet Ones

While you may have generated a nice exchange with most of the panel, there are always the silent prospective jurors who will say nothing unless you directly speak to them. One research study revealed that in both civil and criminal cases, 28 percent of the prospective jurors did not respond affirmatively to questions asked in open court. However, when questioned individually, 10 percent of them in civil cases and 17.5 percent in criminal cases later disclosed biases that led to a challenge for cause.[10] Therefore, make sure that you talk with the silent ones. They may have something pertinent to your case that they are not saying. You don't want to leave them out of the conversation.

---

10. Laurie R. Kuslansky, Ph.D., *Jury Selection and Voir Dire: Don't Ask, Don't Know*, WASH. BAR BULLETIN 23 (Oct. 2014).

Chapter 8

Questioning Strategies & Techniques

"There's no harm in asking."

Anonymous

"I never learn anything talking. I only learn things when I ask questions."

Lou Holtz,
Football coach and television
college football analyst

A. Questioning Strategies and Techniques

In this chapter, we suggest methods for asking questions that will generate a dialogue with the jury panel. Also, we offer strategies and techniques that you can use in questioning the prospective jurors in ways that will expose their biases and gain commitments from them.

B. Breaking the Ice Strategies

The court's practice may allow you to ask both general questions of the panel and questions directed at individual jurors. Because most people are reluctant to speak in a strange setting, in this case the courtroom, a question to the whole panel that asks for some individual to speak up often is met with a deathly silence. You will need to break the ice and warm them up for a good conversation.

1. Conversation with an Individual Juror

An approach that can get a good conversation going and engage the jury is to have a conversation with an individual juror. Identify a juror whom you think will not be intimidated. Someone who is likely to be talkative. Make sure that you put the person at ease and give the person a feeling of not being singled out and put on the hot seat. Then, address your interesting initial question to that person. Once you have the conversation going with that person, then redirect your questions to the panel.

Once you have broken the ice, your goal is to hear from as many prospective jurors as you can get involved in the conversation in order to produce information pertinent to issues in the case and juror biases. It is their disclosures that will aid you in deciding whom you will deselect from the jury. Think of yourself as a talk show host who is facilitating a discussion in the audience. When someone expresses an opinion, ask the panel if anyone agrees or has a different view.

The following is an example of how to both break the ice, introduce your case theory through questioning and use visuals during voir dire. While what follows is a somewhat lengthy excerpt from a jury-selection transcript, it illustrates how to break the ice and generate and manage a good conversation.

Individual Juror Icebreaker Example: In *Retractable Technologies, Inc. v. Becton, Dickinson and Company,* plaintiff's counsel, at the outset of voir dire, selected a venireperson, Ms. Moreland, and engrossingly questioned her about the threat to personal health and safety presented by a needle shot, and then turned the questioning to the panel:

> MR. CARROLL: Ms. Moreland?
> JUROR MORELAND: Yes, sir.
> MR. CARROLL: Are you afraid of shot needles?
> JUROR MORELAND: No, sir.
> MR. CARROLL: Not a bit?
> JUROR MORELAND: Not at all.
> MR. CARROLL: This case is about what can happen to somebody if that somebody is unlucky enough to get stuck with a dirty shot needle.
> Have you ever heard anything—you are a reader, right?
> JUROR MORELAND: Yes, sir.
> MR. CARROLL: Have you ever read anything about the health dangers associated with being stuck with a dirty needle?
> JUROR MORELAND: Well, I have not particularly read anything, but I have seen it on the news.

MR. CARROLL: Okay. One of the things that you and the seven of you—seven other of you who are going to hear about in this case is two words called "needle stick." Is that what you read about?

JUROR MORELAND: Yes, sir.

MR. CARROLL: Okay. One of the things that you are going to learn if you are on this jury, is that needle stick can kill people. Is that what you have read?

JUROR MORELAND: Well, I have seen it on the news. I didn't particularly read it, yes.

MR. CARROLL: Right. You can get one of 30 different diseases, viruses, bugs from problems with a dirty needle.

JUROR MORELAND: Yes, sir.

MR. CARROLL: Okay. So here is my question to you: Have you ever given anybody a shot?

JUROR MORELAND: Yes, sir.

MR. CARROLL: And who would that person be?

JUROR MORELAND: That would have been my mother.

MR. CARROLL: Do you know whether when you were giving your mom shots that you ever used a product that was supposed to be a safety needle?

JUROR MORELAND: Well, it was the needles given to us by the Hospice, and we had disposable things to put them in after they were used.

MR. CARROLL: You had a box to drop them in?

JUROR MORELAND: Yes, sir.

MR. CARROLL: Now, you understand, Ms. Moreland—and by the way, I hope you don't think I am picking on you.

JUROR MORELAND: Oh, no, sir.

MR. CARROLL: Okay. Good.

You understand that one of the things that happens in hospitals is that sometimes people get in a rush and the pace of the activity is a lot more frantic than maybe at your house when you were dealing with your mom?

JUROR MORELAND: Yes, sir.

MR. CARROLL: And did you ever have any problems with needle sticks at your house?

JUROR MORELAND: No, sir.

MR. CARROLL: And you understand—and, again, I apologize if this sounds too personal, that needle sticks aren't a problem for the person who gets stuck, by design? You see what I am saying?

JUROR MORELAND: Yes, sir.

MR. CARROLL: My bugs are my bugs. Mr. Baxter (defense counsel) don't want my bugs.

JUROR MORELAND: That's correct.

MR. CARROLL: But if I got stuck and then if, unfortunately, Mr. Baxter got stuck, that would be a needle stick.

JUROR MORELAND: Yes, sir.

MR. CARROLL: Okay. Now, and—

Your Honor, may I ask Ms. Ferguson to turn on the ELMO?

THE COURT: Okay. Sure.

MR. CARROLL: And she tells me I am going to have to go right over there—

THE COURT: That's fine.

MR. CARROLL:—if that is okay, Your Honor?

THE COURT: You bet.

MR. CARROLL: Thank you, sir.

Ms. Moreland, don't sit down.

JUROR MORELAND: Okay.

MR. CARROLL: Okay. Now, can you see me over here?

JUROR MORELAND: Yes, sir.

MR. CARROLL: Okay. I'm going to try to deal with the ELMO (document camera that projects the item on a screen).

You got any idea—

May I have an ELMO helper?

Pete, will you be my ELMO helper? Thank you. Thank you. Great. Thank you. Is that it? Thank you. Okay.

Now, everybody—now, y'all can see up here, right? Everybody can see?

Okay. Ms. Moreland, bear with me. Shot needle, right, can you see it?

JUROR MORELAND: Yes, sir.

MR. CARROLL: Okay. Now, obviously when that needle goes into my arm and comes out, nobody else in the world would want it stuck into her or him, correct?

JUROR MORELAND: Correct.

MR. CARROLL: So one of the ways that I guess you might protect this needle from ever sticking anybody else is to somehow cover it again just like it is covered before.

JUROR MORELAND: Yes, sir.

MR. CARROLL: Did you try that at home ever?

JUROR MORELAND: Yes, sir.

MR. CARROLL: Okay. You are going to hear in this case that is a no-no.

JUROR MORELAND: Okay.

MR. CARROLL: Okay. And nobody is going to take you to jail or anything. But can you see why that would be a no-no?

JUROR MORELAND: Yes.

MR. CARROLL: Watch what happens to my finger. See how close it is to the point? (Demonstrating.)

JUROR MORELAND: Yes, sir.

MR. CARROLL: And one of the things that you and your juror members are going to hear from Ms. Duesman over here, who has been doing this stuff a long time, is you don't want to get your fingers too close to the point. And they even teach people to keep your fingers away from the sharp.

And that kind of makes sense, does it not?

JUROR MORELAND: Yes, sir.

MR. CARROLL: So if you have a device that you have to manipulate to cover the needle, you've got to be extra careful, correct?

JUROR MORELAND: Yes, sir.

MR. CARROLL: Suppose though—suppose though—and I want everybody to watch this, please. Suppose you have a needle—and you see this now? (Indicating.)

JUROR MORELAND: Yes, sir.

MR. CARROLL: I have got it drawn back, right?

JUROR MORELAND: Yes, sir.

MR. CARROLL: It is full of medicine, and it is going into my arm. Now, I want everybody to watch the needle. I'm going to put my finger right under it. (Demonstrating) There goes the medicine. I get a little ouch. What happened to the needle?

JUROR MORELAND: It disappeared.

MR. CARROLL: It disappeared. That is what Tom Shaw spent nine years of his life developing. He developed it so that nobody ever again would have to get stuck with a dirty needle.

And our lawsuit is because we say that the folks at this table don't want our innovation on the market because they don't control it, and they are big and they control the market and we are little and we don't. That is what our lawsuit is about.

Thank you, Ms. Moreland.

MR. CARROLL: Has anybody, in addition to Ms. Moreland, given a shot?

All right. Now, let me tell you how I want to do this. I want you to keep your hands up, if you will, so we can write your names down. And then I want to ask you a question generally to everybody on the panel who has got a hand up.

If I don't ask you specifically, it is not because I am not interested in what you have to say, but I have got a very limited amount of time to talk with you, and this is important.

Those of you who have given shots, have you had any experience different from Ms. Moreland; that is, you are giving shots to somebody in your family like Ms. Moreland was giving her Mama a shot?

Okay. Hold on just one second. Okay. Don't give up on me. Ms. Hudson.

JUROR HUDSON: Yes.

MR. CARROLL: Do you mind standing up, please, ma'am? And you are from Beckville; is that right?

JUROR HUDSON: That's correct.

MR. CARROLL: Tell me about your shot-giving experience?[1]

2. Interesting, Nonthreatening Question to the Panel

A variation on the ice-breaking technique just discussed and illustrated is to begin your conversation with the panel members by posing an interesting question to the whole panel. It should be one to which a good number will respond in the affirmative and want to discuss. You want a good number of the prospective jurors to agree by raising their hands or cards, as the court's procedure requires. Get them to say "yes." For instance, in the *Retractable Technologies, Inc. v. Becton, Dickinson and Co.* case, plaintiff's counsel, rather than starting with only Ms. Moreland, could have begun the questioning by asking the panel if anyone had experience giving shots to someone. This would have caused several in the panel to raise their hands. Then, counsel could inquire of those who responded.

C. Open-Ended Questions

The most important principle to remember if you want to get the panel members talking is that you must frame your questions to be open-ended, not

---

1. Transcript of Proceedings at 9–13, *Retractable Techs., Inc. v. Becton, Dickinson and Co.*, 2:08cv16 E.D. (Tex. Sept. 3, 2013), App. 1.2.

close-ended, Closed-ended questions produce 85 percent less information than open-ended questions.[2] Closed-ended questions, such as "Have you ever served on a jury?" can be answered in a word. On the other hand, an open-ended question, such as "How do you feel about lawsuits against doctors?" requires thought and more than a one- or two-word response. When you pose an open-ended question to a prospective juror, you are encouraging the person to talk, and the answer gives you an opportunity to listen and assess the person. An open-ended question produces more information about the person or about the person's views on a topic. Also, when a juror speaks up, it is more likely that other jurors will join in the exchange.

To craft an open-ended question, use language along these lines:

- What do you think about this proposition ...?
- Why do you feel that way about ...?
- Tell us about ...
- How can ...?
- The evidence may show ... What is your reaction to that?

Open-Ended Question Example: Tell me about your shot-giving experience?[3]

When you have asked an open-ended question, listen carefully to the response, because the answer is likely to cause you to have a follow-up question. Asking a follow-up question is likely to not only provide you with deeper information but also leave the impression on the panel that you are listening and care about their responses.

Of course, we are not at all suggesting that you should not also ask closed-ended questions. Such questions can be extremely valuable, particularly if the judge has placed significant limitations on your time to question the prospective jurors. The best approach is one that utilizes both kinds of questions.

D. Forced-Choice Questions

A technique for generating a meaningful exchange with the jurors is to employ what is referred to as a "forced-choice" question style where the attorney presents two opinions and asks prospective jurors which side they tend to agree with. For example, a common, generic attitude that defendants in a

---

2. Laurie R. Kuslansky, Ph.D., *Jury Selection and Voir Dire: Don't Ask, Don't Know*, WASH. BAR BULLETIN 23 (Oct. 2014).

3. Transcript of Proceedings at 13, *Retractable Techs., Inc. v. Becton, Dickinson and Co.*, 2:08cv16 E.D. (Tex. Sept. 3, 2013), App. 1.2.

case might be concerned about is the belief that, if a case makes it all the way to trial, it must have considerable merit. This is a belief many people have that derives from an assumption that the justice system weeds out meritless claims.

Forced-Choice Question Example: The forced-choice version of a question goes something like this:

> ATTORNEY: I have some friends who believe that, if a case makes it all the way to trial, there must be merit to the claims brought by the plaintiffs. I have other friends who would disagree and argue that cases make it to trial for all sorts of different reasons that do not necessarily have anything to do with the merit of the case. By a show of hands, how many of you are more like the first group of friends and tend to be believe that, if a case makes it all the way to trial, there must be merit to the claims?

Another Forced-Choice Question Example: In a patent infringement trial held in federal district court, plaintiff's counsel propounded a forced-choice proposition and solicited the prospective jurors' views as follows:

> MS. DERIEUX: All right. Thank you very much.
> It has been said—I think maybe those of you who have heard the media reports regarding patent litigation, you might have heard that some people have divided the patent attitude sort of into two groups. Group 1 folks think that patents are great; they promote innovation and that innovation is necessary for us to maintain a spot in the world market. Without intellectual property, you might not have as much research, because people would be reluctant to invest and justify the expenditures.
> What I'm going to call Group 2 are people that believe patents should not be protected by the Constitution and congressional law. Instead of protecting patents we should have unlimited competition. If someone can manufacture a good product and sell it, it shouldn't matter whether someone else already had the idea and got a patent on it.
> I'm going to start with Mr. Calhoun on this one. Mr. Calhoun, would you say that you fell into Group 1 or Group 2 or somewhere else?
> JUROR CALHOUN: Group 2.
> MS. DERIEUX: All right.
> JUROR CALHOUN: I believe they should be protected. Was that 2 or 1?
> MS. DERIEUX: That was actually Group 1.

JUROR CALHOUN: How about Group 1.

MS. DERIEUX: Tell me just briefly how—why you believe that's the right answer.

JUROR CALHOUN: I'm not an inventor, but I wish I was. I wish I could come up with something, and I would just try to put myself— I would want it protected, if I came up with something great that's going to change the world.[4]

A few aspects of this questioning technique make it effective. First, the attorney asking the question is presenting both sides of the question and presenting each as a reasonable opinion to have. The additional references to friends who hold each view helps remove any suggestions of judgment associated with one side of the opinion or the other. This helps prospective jurors feel more comfortable agreeing with one side of the opinion. The attorney should also raise his hand towards the end, to physically encourage responses from prospective jurors. Finally, this question only asks about the high-risk side of the opinion for the defense. In other words, attorneys want to design questions that provide useful information about high-risk attitudes and experiences that do not assist the other side with identifying who their high-risk jurors are. By asking only about those prospective jurors who believe there is merit to a case that makes it all the way to trial, the defense attorney is not doing any work for the plaintiff's attorney.

Another Forced-Choice Example: Here is another example of forced-choice questioning from *Costco Wholesale Corp. v. AU Optronics Corp.*, the antitrust case discussed at page 251. Plaintiff's counsel seeks the jurors' views on whether the laws of the United States should be applied to foreign businesses.

MR. BURMAN: Now, as you already know, some of the parties in this case are foreign companies. They also have domestic United States subsidiaries. You probably already noticed that the two defendant families have both an overseas component and an American or U.S. component. But there are people who think that the U.S. should stay out of other countries' business, that U.S. and U.S. laws should stay out of the way of businesses in other countries, even if those businesses produce products that are going to end up in the United States.

And then there's another camp that thinks that those companies ought to play by U.S. rules, if they want their products to be sold here,

---

4. Transcript of Proceedings at 45–46, *Simpleair, Inc. v. Google*, Case 2:13cv587 (E.D. Tex. Mar. 17, 2014), App. 7.3.

they should be willing to accept abiding by U.S. law. And, again, I would like to ask you to—you know, your views may fall somewhat in the middle, or a little bit to one side or the other. But to the extent you can, how many people feel that their views fall into that first category, that the U.S. laws ought to stay away from those foreign businesses and what they do overseas?

And as to the rest of you, if you could raise your hand if you believe that U.S. laws should apply if they are going to have their products end up in the United States. All right. Thank you.[5]

Forced-choice questions are particularly helpful when the judge has placed significant limits on the amount of time that you can ask questions to the jury panel. This is often the case in federal court, where judges may only allow 10–15 minutes of attorney-conducted voir dire if they allow any at all. Forced-choice questions allow you to quickly collect a lot of data about the venire. You can ask six to eight forced-choice questions in a ten-minute period. As the jurors raise their hand, you can put an "X" next to their name. At the end of your brief voir dire, you can look down and see which jurors have the most "X's" next to their name.

E. Scaled Questions

To keep your questions interesting and gather the jurors' views quickly on an issue in the case, you may wish to ask a scaled question. A scaled question asks for a response to be chosen from a range of values. You can pose the question to the whole panel and then ask each juror to give you a one-word response, explaining that you would stop and go into each person's answer and reason behind it but time would not allow for such lengthy discussions.

Scaled-Question Example: If counsel wanted to quickly determine the jurors' views on frivolous lawsuits, the following scaled question might be asked.

ATTORNEY: In general, how likely do you think it is that a frivolous lawsuit would make it to trial? Very likely? Likely? Unlikely? Highly unlikely?

Another example involves a numerical scale:

---

5. Transcript of Proceedings at 236–37, *Costco Wholesale Corp. v. AU Optronics Corp.,* No. cv13-1207RAJ (W.D. Wash. 2014), App. 8.1.

ATTORNEY: On a scale of one to ten, with one being very unlikely and ten being very likely, how likely do you think it is that a defective product could seriously injure you in your lifetime?

F. Hypothetical Questions

One strategy you can use to introduce your case theory and determine whether jurors will be open to it is to ask a hypothetical question. The hypothetical should pose a set of facts that are different from the case on trial and be fashioned to gather the potential jurors' views on an aspect of the case. Favorable attributes of a hypothetical question are that it be interesting and contain an easily understood fact pattern that the jury panel can relate to.

Judges usually will sustain an objection to a question that asks the prospective jurors to suppose that certain facts will be proven at trial and whether they will render a specific verdict if they are. The judge will view this as an effort to advocate, indoctrinate and get the jurors to prejudge the facts. The difference between acceptable and prohibited hypotheticals was described as follows in *Williams v. State:*[6]

> ... While it is certainly well settled that attorneys "may not have jurors indicate, in advance, what their decision will be under a certain state of evidence or upon a certain state of facts," ... the State's hypotheticals in this case did not attempt to elicit any such responses. Rather, the State's questions were geared towards eliciting whether the jurors would find reasonable doubt based upon an extreme set of unrelated hypothetical facts or sympathy. The jurors were not presented with the facts of this case, nor asked to offer their decisions during voir dire. These hypotheticals, designed to determine whether the jurors could correctly apply the law, are permissible.[7]

Hypothetical Question Example: In *United States v. Trinity Industries, Inc.,* the plaintiff, a private person (called a relator), prosecuted the action against the defendant under False Claims Act alleging that the defendant fraudulently enticed the United States to pay for what are called an "ET-Plus end terminal systems" that were materially different in dimension and geometry from the end terminal system that had been previously crash-tested and accepted for

---

6. *Williams v. State,* 931 So. 2d 999 (Fla. 2006).
7. *Williams,* 931 So. 2d at 999 (citation omitted).

use by the Federal Highway Administration. By law, the plaintiff is entitled to 25 to 30 percent of any jury award. Plaintiff's counsel explored how the jury would respond to the plaintiff's damages argument by posing a hypothetical. He then went on to discuss the award that the plaintiff was going to ask for and whether the jurors would be willing to make such an award.

Note that defense counsel did not object when counsel shifted from the hypothetical set of facts to those in the case to be tried.

> MR. BAXTER: Thank you, Your Honor.
> ... All right. I want to talk to you just a moment about damages because as we've told you, at the end of this trial, we're going to ask that you award damages to the United States of America, which I told you are going to get split basically 70—or 70 percent to the taxpayers and the rest to Mr. Harman.
> But here's the—the issue I want to talk to you about, damages. I want you to assume just a moment that this land is your land, and these trees are yours. Is there anybody, by the way, that's got some timber property or lives out in the country and you got some pine trees planted? All right. Good. You—you got these trees or your pine trees and you decide to take a two-week vacation and you come back and here's what you find. They're gone. You didn't tell anybody to cut them. And somebody came on your property and took them, and they took them wrongfully. And so now you go to—you find out who that is and you go to them and they say, oh, gosh, sorry, I made a mistake. Our map must have been wrong. Yeah, we took them, we cut them all up, and we sold them. And you say, well, you know, I was kind of attached to my forest, but at minimum, you're going to have to pay me for my trees. And they say, tell you what I'll do, I'll pay you for every other tree, how about that?
> Who's going to say, okay, that's a deal, you only have to pay me for half the trees you took? Anybody going to say that?
> What about if they were to pay you for 75 percent of the trees and they keep a quarter of them? Anybody think that's right?
> My point is this, is that when it comes to damages, the jury's going to have to consider it, but they have to consider whether or not they will give full damages.
> Now, in this case, we think the evidence is going to be that the Defendants have filed false claims in excess of $200 million with the federal government and been paid when they should not have been paid because the claims they filed were false.

Now, if we prove that, if that's true, is there anybody that would hesitate to write that number down, 218, 219, 220, whatever it is? Hundreds of millions of dollars if, in fact, that's the evidence, or is there anybody that's going to say, well, that's a lot of money, maybe I'll cut it in half and pay them for every other tree? Anybody going to say that? Can I count on everybody, if you find that the Plaintiff's right and the Defendants' wrong and the Judge asks you a damage question to give full damages for that, is there anybody that can't do it? Anybody just says that's too much money?[8]

G. Techniques for Designing Questions

The questions you ask in voir dire should be carefully crafted to gather the information you need in order to identify the prospective jurors you will deselect with challenges. Here we cover the topics that you can explore as well as provide examples of how to frame questions that may be employed to reveal biases relating to those topics. As you can see from these questions, most of them are aimed at either alleviating concerns that you have about how jurors may receive certain aspects of your case or confirming your worst fears, thereby allowing you to deselect the juror. In essence, questions are formulated to uncover what the jurors think about issues in the case. In later chapters on advancing your case theory, legal position, and case narrative, we provide more in-depth discussions of effective questions along with more illustrations.

1. Your Bad Juror Profile

A starting point for crafting questions to get prospective jurors to reveal information that will help you in deciding who to deselect is the high-risk or bad juror profile that you have developed. That juror profile is comprised of characteristics of people who have adverse reactions to your case. For instance, if you represent a landlord in a landlord-tenant case and a characteristic of the profiled bad juror is a person who had a dispute with their landlord that ended badly, you would want to inquire about the prospective jurors' experiences in renting and attitudes towards landlords.

---

8. Transcript of Proceedings at 85–86, *United States v. Trinity Indus., Inc.*, No. 2:12CV89-JRG E.D. (Tex. Oct. 13, 2014), App. 8.2.

For the experience-based items on the high-risk juror profile, you can simply ask "yes" or "no" questions. For example, you can just ask, "Has anyone here ever had an experience with their landlord that ended badly?"

For the attitudes listed on your high-risk juror profile, you should consider the forced-choice question format previously discussed in this chapter and add follow-up questions that allow you to more fully explore the strength and extent of those negative attitudes.

2. Your Legal Position

You need to fashion questions that hopefully will reveal any biases the jurors harbor against your legal position and the applicable law of the case that is favorable to your client. For example, a defense counsel in a criminal case who does not intend to call the defendant to testify would question the prospective jurors to determine if they could follow the law and not hold the fact that the defendant did not testify against the defendant.

3. Your Case Narrative

The main source for your questions that are intended to reveal juror bias is your case narrative. Your case story has central facts upon which your case rests, and a venireperson who views these matters with disfavor is likely to be someone that you do not want on the jury. For example, if your client were a corporation, you would want to inquire about any biases the potential jurors have against corporations.

A list of potential topics that usually emerge from an analysis of the story of your case includes these:

- The type of dispute;
- The nature of the incident that led to the law suit;
- The type of witnesses;
- The organizations involved in the case;
- The weaknesses in the case narrative;
- The location of the incident; and
- The evidence involved in the case, such as expert testimony.

4. Embarrassing or Personal Matters

Asking questions that pry into matters that might embarrass or distress a prospective juror can have unfortunate repercussions. Besides embarrassing the person being questioned, it can result in other members of the panel being offended that the lawyer made such an inquiry. Should you wish to probe into sensitive matters, you can request the court to have the panel fill out a customized questionnaire with those questions on it. Based on the responses, some jurors can be questioned apart from the rest of the panel so as to avoid any embarrassment. Alternatively, you can indicate in your initial remarks to the jurors that if their responses to any question might prove to be too personal for open discussion that they should indicate that they want to speak in private with the court and counsel.

H. Questioning to Get a Commitment

Not all of the questions you ask will be aimed at getting jurors to reveal information. You also will want to get the jurors to give you assurances. The commitment can be a promise to do any one of a variety of things, including: follow the law as given to the jury in the court's instructions; set aside a bias that the juror has revealed; or consider a particular piece of evidence. It is a legitimate inquiry to ask whether the juror will follow the law or consider certain evidence. However, efforts to argue the case through the use of commitment questions, such as asking a juror to commit to rendering a favorable verdict if certain facts are proven, will usually result in the court cutting counsel off. This is because the question is arguing the case and not seeking information that may be used by counsel to determine whether to exercise a challenge.

Assurances that trial lawyers can seek with commitment questioning are innumerable. For instance, defense counsel in a criminal case could ask the jurors to promise:

- That they will hold the prosecution to the burden of proof, requiring proof beyond a reasonable doubt as to each and every element of the charged crime;
- That they will decide the case based solely upon the evidence or lack of evidence produced in trial in the courtroom and not consider anything else;
- That as the defendant sits before them at the outset of trial, she is innocent and that the presumption of innocence continues throughout the trial unless it is overcome by proof beyond a reasonable doubt;
- That they will not in any way hold it against the defendant if she decides not to testify; and

- That they will not give more weight to a law enforcement officer's testimony than to any other witness's.

When you are crafting questions designed to elicit commitments from the jurors, you are not trying to stimulate a conversation. You are not trying to get them to open up and reveal information. Rather, you want a commitment. Therefore, contrary to the open-ended questions that you ask to generate a conversation, you ask close-ended questions. You normally want a "yes" answer to your question. For instance, you may ask, "Mr. Dekle, regarding the burden of proof, do you believe that you understand the burden of proof as it's been explained, and do you believe that you can follow those instructions from the Judge?" Commitment questions are designed to get the jurors nodding their heads in agreement.

In Chapter 12, which focuses on how to discuss case weaknesses and misconceptions with the jury, you will see that it is standard practice to ask closed-ended questions that commit jurors to setting aside their biases or misconceptions and follow the law.

1. Interlinked with Closing Argument

As you will recall, the fifth goal of jury selection is to gather material from the jurors for use in closing argument. Specifically, the commitment questioning style is intended to set up an argument during summation that collects on the jurors' promise made during jury selection. For example, counsel argues, "Ladies and gentlemen, you will remember that during jury selection you promised that you would follow the court's instructions on ... When you are back in that jury room, if anyone suggests otherwise, speak up and remind that person of that promise made under oath in this courtroom."

2. Case Story

With a well-structured series of questions, counsel can lay out the case narrative and identify whom the witnesses will be, and secure an agreement to a proposition from the prospective jurors. That is what defense counsel sought to do in the following example.

Case-Story Commitment Question Example: In *Retractable Technologies, Inc. v. Becton, Dickinson and Company*, defense counsel laid out his contention and then committed the prospective jurors to the premise of the client's case story:

MR. BAXTER: Okay. Does everybody agree with that; that doctors and nurses listen to their own experience, as opposed to what a salesman or ad might say?

Anybody disagree with that?

All right. Now, this case, as I told you, is about contracts. The allegation is going to be that hospitals somehow can't buy the products they want to buy, that is, they can't buy the RTI product, that they are somehow prohibited or kept from doing it; or as Mr. Carroll said, they are blocked from doing it?

Now—and that needle sticks are going on all across America because they are using unsafe products. Now, that is the allegation. That is really what he told you ...

Mr. Seat, let me ask you, if that were true, sir, and you were doing an investigation to see if that were true, who would you go ask to find out if that really were true?

JUROR SEAT: I would ask the personnel, ask the nurses.

MR. BAXTER: At the hospitals?

JUROR SEAT: Yes.

MR. BAXTER: So if it were true, you would expect that you would go and ask hospital administrators? Can you buy what you want to buy?

JUROR SEAT: Yes.

MR. BAXTER: Would you ask a nurse and a doctor, can you use the products you want to use?

JUROR SEAT: Yes.

MR. BAXTER: Would you ask them, if you don't have what you want, can you get somebody to get it for you?

JUROR SEAT: I would ask that.

MR. BAXTER: Is that who you would expect—if that is the allegation in this case, is that who you are going to expect to see get up here on this witness stand and testify that that is what is happening?

JUROR SEAT: I don't know who is going to get up there.

MR. BAXTER: I know, but is that what you would expect?

JUROR SEAT: I guess so.

MR. BAXTER: Okay. Thank you, sir.

Anybody disagree with what Mr. Seat says that if that is true, who you would expect to see climb on this witness stand are administrators and doctors and nurses and say, oh, my goodness get me some help, I am being blocked from getting the RTI product, help me out? Would everybody agree that is who you would expect to see testify? Raise your hand if you agree that is right.

Okay …[9]

3. Questioning about the Jurors' Duties

Part of your questioning of the prospective jurors to gain commitments should focus on explaining to them what their responsibilities are as jurors, because their understanding and acceptance of those duties are essential to having them embrace those that underpin your case. To formulate this type of question, review the juror's obligations with an eye towards those that help your client. For example, if the other side has the burden of proof, your questioning can focus on whether the prospective juror would follow the law and require the other side to meet their burden.

Jury Duty Commitment Question Example: The following pattern of questioning by defense counsel is designed to get the jurors committed to the proposition that in this patent case, each of them will strictly follow the court's jury instructions that benefit the defense:

> MR. JONES: … Now, in this particular case, you've already seen the film of the federal judiciary about patent cases.
>
> And in that film, they told you that patents had claims, and those claims described what was invented. Those claims described what the patent owner owned. Those claims described what the patent owner could exclude others from doing.
>
> Now, I believe Judge Davis will instruct you, if you are chosen as a juror, at the end of this case, that in order to infringe, a product must practice each and every element of a claim that describes the invention.
>
> I think he will instruct you, it has to be—every element of the claim must be practiced or must be done by the product. Nine out of ten isn't good enough; 99 percent isn't good enough. It has to be—100 percent of the elements must be practiced.
>
> Now, does anyone disagree with that concept? If he instructs you and if I'm right and he gives you that instruction, does anybody say: You know, I would disagree with that; 99 percent, that ought to be good enough? Anybody feel that way?

---

9. Transcript of Proceedings at 38–39, *Retractable Techs., Inc. v. Becton, Dickinson and Co.*, 2:08cv16 E.D. (Tex. Sept. 3, 2013), App. 1.2.

MR. JONES: Anybody feel like that's nitpicking to require every element of the claim to be practiced? Anybody feel like that?

I mean, going back—the reason for this is pretty simple. Going back to my analogy here, the reason you do that is because you're encouraging innovation. Even if you improve just one element, it improves the innovation of the particular device. So that's why we have it.

But does anybody have a problem with that?

Can anybody—and let my (sic) address this just in one other way and bring it more down to the specifics of our case.

In this particular case, the patents that are involved have some claim elements that are so basic, everybody does them. There's going to be no question about it.

We're going to admit that some of the elements, sure, we do those. Those are basic elements in the industry. Everybody does them.

There are other elements, though, that we're going to say, no, we don't do. We are different.

Now, does anyone think, because we say, yeah, we do some of the elements, that, therefore, we must infringe? Anybody?

Thank you so much.

Will each of you—can every one of you promise me that you'll require each and every element to be proven before you find a product infringing? Anybody can't?

Yes, sir. I appreciate it.

Mr. Vandenburg? Thank you, sir.

JUROR VANDENBURG: My experience has been that companies will go beyond their way to take the patent right and alter it just enough to make it to where it benefits them and not the party involved with the patent.

MR. JONES: Okay. So could you follow Judge Davis's instructions in that regard—

JUROR VANDENBURG: Absolutely.

MR. JONES:—if some element was changed?

JUROR VANDENBURG: Yes, sir.

MR. JONES: Okay. Okay. So you would require every element to be practiced by the product?

JUROR VANDENBURG: No. I would follow the Judge's direction.

MR. JONES: Okay. Thank you, sir. I sure do appreciate it.[10]

---

10. Transcript of Proceedings at 74–77, *Ericson, Inc. v. D-Link Corp.*, 6:10cv473E.D. (Tex. June 3, 2013), App. 7.1.

It is likely that the court will inquire of the panel as to whether they can fulfill their obligations as jurors. If the judge has thoroughly covered this subject, you may decide not to inquire about juror duties, particularly if your time to question the panel is limited.

I. Keep-Them-Focused Strategy

Most cases boil down to a few crucial factual and legal matters, and therefore, your jury selection conversations with the panel should be confined to only a few points. Beyond that, you will gain little, and you will surely sidetrack them. Don't waste their time. Strategically, you will profit from a focused inquiry because you will keep the prospective jurors on point, and you will not alienate them by overly prolonging the process.

J. Concluding — That Critical Catch-All Question

Address your last question to the whole panel. It is your most important question. It is your catch-all question aimed at bringing to the surface anything harmful to your case that any prospective juror might have been harboring but so far has not revealed. If anyone responds, then you can ask follow-up questions.

Catch-All Question Example: Defense counsel asked such a catch-all question in the *Retractable* case:

> MR. BAXTER: Is there anyone else that knows any reason besides what we have asked, why you in this case might not be a fair and impartial juror? Some other case maybe, but not this one. Anybody at all?
>
> Ladies and Gentlemen, on behalf of Becton Dickinson, we thank you very much for your attention; and we really look forward to bringing this case to you. Thank you very much.
>
> Thank you, Your Honor.[11]

Note the silence following defense counsel Mr. Baxter's last question when he asked the panel, "Is there anyone else that knows any reason besides what

---

11. Transcript of Proceedings at 43, *Retractable Techs., Inc. v. Becton, Dickinson and Co.*, 2:08cv16 E.D. (Tex. Sept. 3, 2013), App. 1.2.

we have asked, why you in this case might not be a fair and impartial juror? Some other case maybe, but not this one. Anybody at all?" More than a few trial lawyers have been surprised when a question along this line was not met by silence but instead by a juror's statement that indeed revealed important information. That is what happened in the following example.

Another Catch-All Question Example: In the patent infringement case mentioned earlier, plaintiff's counsel was winding up her voir dire when her last question provoked a response. Because her question elicited an answer, she made note of it for future use.

> ... I want to ask one more thing. And this is the—the—the question that if that lawyer had just asked me X, she would not want me on her jury. And so she just hasn't thought of it and I don't want to say anything because it might not be appropriate, but if she knew this and it—or I'm just waiting for her to ask this one question and then I'm going to stand up and tell her. Anything? Anyone?
>
> Yes, sir? Wait a minute. I have to write this down so the next time I do this, I'll ask this question.
>
> JUROR SHIRLEY: I own two patents. You never asked anybody if they owned a patent.
>
> MS. DERIEUX: Thank you.
>
> JUROR SHIRLEY: And it has been infringed against, but I didn't have enough money to take it to court.
>
> MS. DERIEUX: Are they—are they expired now or are they still—
>
> JUROR SHIRLEY: They are expired. I had them in '93 and '94. It was actually a patent on the same device and I'm making improvements. I had to get another patent for that, and so it's a fishing device. It's not something that's Internet—
>
> MS. DERIEUX: A patent is a patent.
>
> JUROR SHIRLEY: Yeah.
>
> MS. DERIEUX: Thank you very much.
>
> Is there anyone else on the panel that—that has that she should have asked me this question?
>
> JUROR SHELTON: No, but in regards to No. 8's question about monetary value of one company settling—
>
> MS. DERIEUX: Yes, sir.
>
> JUROR SHELTON:—I do not think it's justifiable if you accept a certain amount from one and ask more from the other.
>
> MS. DERIEUX: And thank you for raising your hand and following up. I appreciate that.

Is there anyone else?

Thank you very much for your time.[12]

Another way to phrase your concluding question is: "My last question is an important one for each of you. We've talked a good bit and covered several topics. As has been explained, it is critical that the parties receive a fair and impartial trial. So, is there anything that you feel we've missed? Anything at all—no matter how small it may seem? Something you feel you should have mentioned? Now is the time to let us know."

After asking the catch-all question, you want to end powerfully. If your last words follow the exercise your peremptories, then rise from your chair, look confidently at the seated jurors and inform the court, "Your Honor, we accept the jury as presently constituted."

If rather than finishing with your peremptories, the court is going to take challenges after you finish questioning the jurors, you may have an opportunity to finish with remarks like those in the next example.

Powerful Ending Example: In *Simpleair, Inc. v. Google*, defense counsel Ms. Ainsworth finished her questioning with these positive comments:

> THE COURT: You have one minute, Counsel.
>
> MS. AINSWORTH: Thank you, Your Honor.
>
> Ladies and gentlemen, I know that's a lot to cover, and you've heard a good bit from both sides in a short period of time. But I want to thank you again for your attention and for telling us some about your experiences and what you feel. And we look forward to presenting our case to all the people that are chosen on this jury. Thank you very much.[13]

Whenever the court's procedures allow you to make a parting comment, make it positive, friendly and leave the impression that you are looking forward to delivering your case to the jurors.

---

12. Transcript of Proceedings at 58–60, *Simpleair, Inc. v. Google*, Case 2:13cv587 E.D. (Tex. Mar. 17, 2014), App. 7.3.

13. Transcript of Proceedings at 84–85, *Simpleair, Inc. v. Google*, Case 2:13cv587 E.D. (Tex. Mar. 17, 2014), App. 7.3.

Chapter 9

Favorable Impression of Your Case

"To produce a mighty book, you must choose a mighty theme. No great and enduring volume can ever be written on the flea, though many there be who have tried it."

Herman Melville, *Moby Dick*
Ch. 104: The Fossil Whale (1851)

"And that's the great thing about the world of ideas—any of us with the right insight and the right message, can make an idea stick."

Chip and Dan Heath,
Made to Stick: Why Some Ideas Survive and Others Die, 252 (Random House 2007)

A. Favorable Impression of Your Case

As we discussed in Chapter 6, by the end of voir dire, you want the jurors to have a favorable impression of you. They should view you as a trustworthy person who is a seeker of truth. Equally important is the impression of your case that the jurors come away with at the end of jury selection. By then, ideally, you would like them to be so convinced that they will have a predisposition for your case, but to expect that you can persuade the jurors to that degree during voir dire is an unrealistic goal. Rather, your goal regarding advancing your case should be that they have enough of a favorable impression of your case that they will be receptive to it during the rest of the trial.

Leaving a favorable impression of your case through jury selection is predicated upon your pretrial work in crafting a case theory that you can introduce during jury selection. In this chapter, first we discuss how to assess the strengths and weaknesses of your case and how to fashion the three essentials of a case: (1) your legal position; (2) a persuasive case narrative; and (3) a case theme.

Next, we turn to strategies and techniques for advancing the three essentials during jury selection. By advancing these essentials, we are not recommending that you attempt to try your case during voir dire. Rather, we use the term "advance" in two ways. First, we mean that you should put them forward in such a way as to leave a favorable impression so the jurors will be open to it. Second, you should advance them in order to gain the jurors' views and learn whether they either can be fair and impartial or harbor a bias against your case and, therefore, should be deselected.

The two key questions that can guide you in crafting your inquires of the prospective jurors are: "What is it about your case weaknesses that might trouble them?" and "What are their likely preconceptions and biases against your case?" You want to learn who will be receptive to your case in spite of or occasionally because of those troubling aspects, and more important, who will not.

Lastly in this chapter, we discuss how to introduce your case theme. In the next two chapters, we discuss how to converse with the prospective jurors about your legal position and case story. Along the way, we offer trial transcripts of jury selections—the next best thing after being co-counsel with a skilled trial lawyer—to illustrate of how to discuss the three essentials with the panel. You may be able to modify the preliminary statements and patterns of questions in these transcripts to fit your case.

B. The Court's Boundaries

The extent to which trial judges will permit you to converse with prospective jurors about your legal theory, case story and theme varies widely from court to court. As we have explained, in some state and local courts and in federal courts, the judge conducts voir dire with limited attorney participation. In courts where attorney participation in jury selection is permitted, some judges will prohibit counsel from attempting to delve into how jurors view the law and facts of the case. These courts prohibit any efforts to indoctrinate and educate jurors during voir dire. At the other end of the spectrum are judges who permit counsel to try the case during jury selection, allowing them to roam widely during questioning to educate, indoctrinate and get commitments from the prospective jurors. Other judges fall somewhere in between the two extremes.

As we pointed out earlier, it is fundamental that you try to find out what latitude your trial judge will give you and plan your questioning accordingly. If you will learn who your judge will be on the day of trial, you may want to plan to try your case during jury selection. If the judge allows counsel to educate and indoctrinate during jury selection, opposing counsel may take full advantage of the opportunity. Then, you may need to engage in retaliatory maintenance of position (counter opposing counsel's advocacy) or you may well be defeated before the jury is sworn to try the case. If the judge does not permit counsel to attempt to try their cases during voir dire, you can always modify your planned approach.

Let's take a look at how a plaintiff's attorney attempted to try the case on damages during voir dire and what the repercussions were. As you read the transcript, you may think that defense counsel allowed plaintiff's counsel to go on too long before objecting. On the other hand, you may conclude that if you were defense counsel, you would be delighted with plaintiff's counsel's questioning because he exposed bad (high risk) prospective jurors for the defense whom you could deselect.

In any event, it is worthwhile to examine this example of how counsel can attempt to indoctrinate the panel during voir dire by using prospective jurors as surrogates and understand the ramifications of the indoctrination strategy. (See pages 217–221 regarding the use of surrogates.)

Indoctrination Example: *Brown v. Davis and Davis* was a wrongful death suit in which Kenneth Brown Jr. was driving across a bridge in Missouri when a truck driven by the defendant was also crossing the bridge. A log skidder loaded on the trailer hit the bridge, became dislodged and landed on plaintiff's vehicle, killing him. Mr. Brown's wife bought suit on her own behalf and that of her two children. The following is plaintiff's counsel's interchange with the jury panel:

> MR. WITZEL: ... Also as part of this case you're going to be asked to consider those elements of damage for wrongful death that the law of the state of Missouri allows and to consider whether or not there should be an award for those. And those items are comfort, companionship, instruction, counsel, training. Now, those aren't things that an economist puts a number on. Is there anyone here that feels since there isn't a hard and fast number to be put on those, those things shouldn't be compensated with money? ...
>
> This case is also going to involve the relationship between the boys and their father. I'd like to ask you this: Is there anyone here who feels that their relationship with their parents was an important concept in

development of you being the people you are today? Anybody who feels that parent input is to you an important element of development? Ms. Weber?

MS. WEBER: Yes.

MR. WITZEL: You raised your hand.

MS. WEBER: Uh-huh.

MR. WITZEL: You think it's an important part of development?

MS. WEBER: I do.

MR. WITZEL: Believe there's a certain role parents play?

MS. WEBER: Yes.

MR. WITZEL: Could you tell us what that role is?

MS. WEBER: I think they teach you your morals, they push you to be the best person you can be, whatever that is, but they support you but also don't let you act ridiculous without giving the right direction. At least that's what my parents did for me.

MR. WITZEL: Do you think that's an important function?

MS. WEBER: I do and I think you're lucky if you have it.

MR. WITZEL: And you think it's a loss if you don't.

MS. WEBER: Yes.

MR. WITZEL: Who else? Juror No. 4, Ms. Knickmeyer?

MS. KNICKMEYER: Knickmeyer.

MR. WITZEL: You raised your hand.

MS. KNICKMEYER: Yeah. I agree with her statements, yes, that it's important to have your parents there for you. Life can be difficult at any age, so I believe that, yes, it's important.

MR. WITZEL: Maybe more important in the teenage years.

MS. KNICKMEYER: Sometimes it is.

MR. WITZEL: Ms. Ferguson, and that was—you raised your hand?

MS. FERGUSON: Yes, I agree. I feel that the presence and involvement of a parent is certainly a significant impact on anyone's life at any age.

MR. WITZEL: Anyone else? Number 12, Mr. Mueller, you raised your hand.

MR. MUELLER: Yes. I do feel it's the responsibility of parents to do their best to raise their children as they see fit.

MR. WITZEL: Do you think it's a loss to a child not to have one of those parents participate in the development?

MR. MUELLER: Depends on the situation.

MR. WITZEL: Relationship between the kids and how that was, is that what you mean by the situation?

MR. MUELLER: Every situation, every family is different. But I do believe the parents have a role in the responsibility of raising of those children.

MR. WITZEL: Juror No. 14, Mr. Clarke?

MR. CLARKE: It's a huge responsibility as a parent to be—help raise your children and all that to become a better citizen, to learn how to follow the rules, stay with those rules, hold them responsible, guide them.

MR. WITZEL: Do you think that a parent that's fulfilling those obligations is performing an important function for that child?

MR. CLARKE: Most definitely.

MR. WITZEL: And if that type of relationship is taken away, it's a major loss to a child?

MR. CLARKE: It is a major loss to the children.

MR. WITZEL: Mr. Rozen?

MR. ROZEN: Yes. I think it's extremely important. I think it's a huge loss, especially with fathers and sons.

MR. WITZEL: Particularly in the teenage years?

MR. ROZEN: Absolutely, yes.

MR. WITZEL: And Mr. Bowers?

MR. BOWERS: I'd have to agree with every statement made. From a personal perspective I think once I decided to become a father that was the biggest job I had.

MR. WITZEL: That's the kind of relationship you developed with your kids?

MR. BOWERS: Yeah, as well as my father so.

MR. WITZEL: Being a father doesn't stop when you get older, is that your—in other words, being a father is a lifelong type of job?

MR. BOWERS: The way I see it, yes.

MR. WITZEL: Yes, sir. Juror No. 2?

MR. POWERS: I agree with all the statements that have been made. I think it's very important to have two parents. It's good to have that relationship and that support to get through life.

MR. WITZEL: You think it's important during the development years, particularly the teenage years?

MR. POWERS: Yeah, definitely.

THE COURT: Anyone else? Ms. Evans?

MS. EVANS: I feel it's very important because it helps to mold the child into adulthood, and especially as a teenager. And today with everything that's going on, I think it's very important.

MR. WITZEL: Ms. Labruyere.

MS. LABRUYERE: Yes. I feel it's very important not only in my own experiences, my parents have made me what I am. My dad and I have a very close relationship. I'm also a retired teacher and have witnessed the absence of one parent or another. And not only in the early years when I taught first grade, but as they grow and they consider what they're going to make of their lives and the education that they're going to be needing to pursue.

MR. WITZEL: Thank you. Mr. Byrd?

MR. BYRD: I agree with every statement that's been said so far with the jurors. I think parents are very important to a child's development, so I agree with everything that's been said.

MR. WITZEL: Thank you. Ms. Zurweller?

MS. ZURWELLER: I agree with all the statements, too. I think the loss of a father or any parent is devastating and really just beyond to put it into words. So I think it's a real important thing to be there for your kids, especially teenagers.

MR. WITZEL: Yes, ma'am.

MS. GOULD: I'm fortunate to have both of my parents still living and still married. My husband and his sister were—their mother was killed just before I knew them. She was killed in an accident—a bad car seat—when he was four and his sister was seven, and their father was absent. I've seen and I've heard the anecdotal stories for both of them about how hard it was being raised by an elderly grandmother.

MR. WITZEL: Thank you. Ms. Gildehaus.

MS. GILDEHAUS: Yes. I'm a teacher, retired teacher also and I've seen the effect that it has on little guys when they don't have one of their parents there and it affects them for the rest of their lives, so I agree with what everybody has said.

MR. WITZEL: Is there anyone here who thinks that seeing how the kids are doing, performing now and have while a parent was there is an indication of what kind of job the parent was doing before death? I guess I didn't state that very well. What I'm saying is this: Do you think a gauge, one of the gauges or one of the ways that you can gauge how well a parent was performing is to take a look at the kids?

MR. DEFRANCO: Your Honor, may I approach the bench?

THE COURT: You may.

(A BENCH CONFERENCE WAS HELD ON THE RECORD AND OUTSIDE OF THE HEARING OF THE JURY PANEL AS FOLLOWS:)

MR. DEFRANCO: Your Honor, we've given counsel great leeway, but this is just blatant indoctrination at this point. He's trying to produce evidence to the jury through each other about his claim for damages.

MR. HALVACHS: Not only is he indoctrinating the jury, he's also basically trying his case and he's getting evidence from teachers and other witnesses about what's happened in other situations, how those kids did. It's totally improper, Your Honor.

MR. WITZEL: Judge, I think these questions are totally proper. If one of those questions is going to be determining what type of parent he was, is to understand what type of gauge they use in making those decisions. In other words, is it fair game to look at how the kids are doing, how they did do. That's certainly an indication of how a parent was performing during the period of time he was here.

THE COURT: Mr. Witzel, I think you've really crossed the line over into arguing your case and I am not going to permit you to continue along this line. These are all things that you can argue in closing. Now, if you have some questions that are better geared toward determining whether these jurors have some real problems with issues or the type of evidence that may come in here in this trial, I'll allow you to explore that. But I will not allow you to pick up each way you plan to prove your damages and make a little mini-argument to the jurors and make sure that they all agree with you at this stage of the case. That is not going to happen anymore.[1]

C. Case Analysis — Strengths and Weaknesses

To craft a case theory to present during voir dire requires that you first identify your case's strengths and weaknesses. During voir dire, you should accentuate the positive aspects of your case. Even more important, you should question the jurors about weaknesses that will become evident during trial to determine whether the jurors can be fair and impartial in spite of them. In Chapter 12, we cover how to deal with case weaknesses and juror misconceptions.

The commonly accepted methodology for identifying case strengths and weaknesses is to have a brainstorming session. Simply draw a line down the middle of a piece of paper and list strengths on the left side of the page and weaknesses on the other side. Then, brainstorm and list all the strengths and

---

1. Transcript of Proceedings at 61–70, *Brown v. Davis and Davis*, No. 4:12 CV649-AGF (E.D Mo. 2014), App. 4.6.

weaknesses that come to mind. Regarding case strengths, consider the attributes of a good case story, asking whether your case narrative is about a good person or company that has been deprived of something or threatened with deprivation, whether the story can be proven through credible evidence and whether the story is about values that the jurors share. Regarding weaknesses in your case, ask whether the jurors might find something about your case troublesome or whether they could have any biases against your case.

+ STRENGTHS	− WEAKNESSES

The more people in your trial team whom you can involve in the brainstorming session the better. You want as many perspectives as you can get. During the brainstorming session, the participants should suspend passing judgment on any strength or weakness that is recognized, because that will only impede the process of gathering as many ideas as possible. Also, if an offering is criticized, people may be sidetracked discussing that one idea or be reluctant to share their other ideas. Note that some ideas will fit on both sides of the chart, being viewed as both strengths and weaknesses.

The brainstorming exercise should be performed as soon as possible after you enter the case, because that is when the matter is the freshest. As the case develops over time, other brainstorming sessions can be held because new developments may result in new strengths and weaknesses.

D. Case Theme

A well-crafted theme will not only guide you in planning for trial but also will grab the jurors' attention and guide them in reaching a verdict for your client. Jury selection is the earliest time the jurors will hear from you. Therefore, you should introduce your theme during voir dire. Later, you can integrate the case theme into the rest of the trial, particularly opening statement and closing argument. Ideally, years after one of your trials, if one of your jurors were to be asked what the case they sat on was about, they should respond with your theme, such as: "It was a case about personal responsibility."

A persuasive case theme is a short, clear statement of the core idea of your case. Attorneys commonly introduce their theme with the phrase, "This case is about ..."

While you may have more than one theme, it is best to have a single pre-dominant theme for your case. When you have multiple themes, you run the risk of weakening your main theme by distracting the jurors, particularly if the themes conflict.

Good case themes don't come easy. To find the right theme requires that you have a developed your legal position and a persuasive case story. Also, it requires imagination and arduous work.

1. Criteria for a Compelling Theme

For a theme to be compelling and stick with the jurors, it should meet the following three criteria: (1) be the central idea of your case and a moral imperative; (2) evoke emotion in the jurors; and (3) be memorable.

a. Central Idea — Moral Imperative

A good theme is a moral imperative — a strongly felt principle that compels action. A case theme encapsulates your case story of deprivation or threatened deprivation and moves the jury to right that wrong or threatened wrong with a verdict on your client's behalf. A good theme makes your case story about principles (not just a case about money) and channels what the jurors talk about during deliberations. The moral imperative usually involves your client, the opposing party, or another actor in your case and syllogistic reasoning. For instance, if you represent the plaintiff in a breach of contract case, the theme could be framed in terms of the principle that "a promise is a promise." The syllogism here is that people should be bound by their word, the defendant made a promise in the contract, and therefore the defendant should held to the promise. When the defendant broke the promise made in the contract, it is left to the jurors to take action and right the wrong with their verdict for the plaintiff.

b. Emotional

The theme should evoke emotion, and that emotion normally is the desire to correct a wrong or to bring justice to the case. Often, it points to the other side as having done something wrong or threatening to do something wrong. For example, if you represent the defendant in a multi-defendant case, the theme could be that your client is a "scapegoat," a Biblical reference to the practice of sending a goat out into the wilderness after the chief priest had symbolically placed the sins of the people upon it. No one likes to be wrongfully blamed, and this theme evokes the emotion of wanting to protect your client from being mistreated by a verdict for the plaintiff.

c. Memorable

Your theme should be short and catchy. By short, we mean a word or a phrase that will stick with the jurors. For instance, this case is about "greed." To be catchy, it should be interesting. Often the theme can be interesting because it is unexpected ("This case is about power and control.") or so apropos to the situation ("If it doesn't fit, you must acquit."). To be memorable, the shorter the better. Lengthy themes are hard to remember. No matter how complex your case is, you can condense it down to a short memorable phrase. The exception where the theme may be a little longer is when it is a line of poetry, which is memorable. (As Mahatma Gandhi put it, "Even if you are a minority of one, truth is the truth.")

Always bear in mind that the theme is not designed for lawyers and should not be phrased in legal terms. It is not "a case about negligence." The theme is intended for regular people—the prospective jurors—and should be plain English.

2. Finding Your Case Theme

Your search for a case theme should start soon after you enter the case and have formulated your first tentative legal position and case narrative. Just as you can involve your trial team in assessing your case for strengths and weaknesses, you can include them in this endeavor too. Also, you can involve colleagues, family and friends. Ask them for their impressions of the case and ask them to provide those impressions in a word or a phrase. If you have a focus group or conduct a mock trial, listen carefully to these decision makers, because they can be a valuable resource for a theme. They will see and describe your case, not as lawyers, but as neutrals who heard the case and served as decision makers. What motivated them? How did they express what they thought of the case? You are seeking just the right words for your theme, and they may give them to you.

It is always a good practice to borrow from successful trial lawyers. You can take a theme employed by another successful trial lawyer and adapt that theme to your case. Later in this chapter, you can read the themes developed by the lawyers in the antitrust cases we are using to illustrate different aspects of jury selection.

Here we offer you a list of trial themes that trial lawyers have crafted and that have been proven effective. Note that they meet the three criteria for a good case theme.

Examples: This case is about:

- "personal responsibility";
- "trust and betrayal of trust";
- "a deal is a deal";
- "power and control";
- "an erratic lane change led to a disastrous life change";
- "having a scapegoat";
- "accountability";
- "difficulty admitting a mistake";
- "real people being deprived of the truth";
- "ignoring the consequences";
- "inattention to detail";
- "profits over people";
- "misplaced blame";
- "a lapse of attention"; or
- "right sizing the company."

Look for quotes that the jurors can relate to, such as memorable quotes from movies, television, the media and other popular sources. Trial lawyer Lisa Marchese discusses one plaintiff's movie theme that is commonly used against corporations as follows:

> As someone who spends a lot of time defending corporations at trial, I wish I had a dollar for every time I heard, "Ladies and Gentlemen, do you remember in the movie *Wall Street* when Gordon Gekko said, 'every dream has its price'?" That statement along with the imagery of the evil Mr. Gekko provides the plaintiff with some powerful ammunition. (I was really hoping Wall Street II would give us defense types some rebuttal fodder … but evidently "greed" is still "good" in Hollywood.)[2]

In the *Enron* case, prosecutor Sean Berkowitz's statement in rebuttal argument drew on a theme from the movie *A Few Good Men*:

> Senior management had been lying to the public for years … *Enron could not handle the truth.*

You can also borrow from pop culture media stories, particularly those about trials. For example, perhaps the most popular case that jurors like to talk about during jury selection is the so-called "McDonald's coffee case." The

---

2. Lisa M. Marchese, *Choosing a Theme for Trial: In a Courtroom, the Facts Don't Speak for Themselves*, Wash. St. Bar Litig. Newsletter 3 (Winter 2010–2011).

inaccurate media portrayals of this case, to the effect that a woman spilled coffee all over herself and then sued for a million dollars, have made this case a symbol for the abuse of the legal system.

Contrary to the inaccurate media reports, the plaintiff in the McDonald's case was 79-year-old Stella Liebeck, and she did not contribute to her injuries. She was putting cream and sugar in her coffee cup, which she had between her legs, when it spilled. She suffered grievous injuries to her genitals, thighs and buttock. The coffee was abnormally scorching hot at 190 degrees, and the McDonald employees knew it. The original jury award was eventually reduced by 80 percent, and the plaintiff settled for an undisclosed amount. Later, the full story about the McDonald's case was revealed in a documentary film entitled, "Hot Coffee."

Another example is Bill Clinton who famously questioned the meaning of the word "is." This is a great example for cases, such as contract cases, where there are disputes over the meaning of certain language.

When will you have found just the right theme for your case? The answer is that you will know it when your find it. You will say to yourself, "Now that's what this case is all about."

E. Preliminary Remarks to Advance the Case Theme

Your case theme is the heart of your case. It encapsulates both your legal position and your case narrative. Ideally it is a moral imperative that will compel the jury to want to deliver the verdict you are seeking. At some juncture during voir dire you should either introduce your theme or at least lay a foundation for stating your theme in opening statement.

Case Theme Example: In *Retractable Technologies, Inc. v. Becton, Dickinson and Co.,* plaintiff's counsel stated the case theme in preliminary remarks as follows:

> PLAINTIFF'S COUNSEL: This case is about what can happen to somebody if that somebody is *unlucky enough to get stuck with a dirty shot needle.*[3]

---

3. Transcript of Proceedings at 9, *Retractable Techs., Inc. v. Becton*, Dickinson and Co., 2:08cv16 E.D. (Tex. Sept. 3, 2013), App. 1.2.

F. Questioning Strategies to Advance the Case Theme

A way to introduce your theme is to ask questions about the factual underpinnings for the theme. This approach lays the foundation for not only unrolling your theme in opening statement but also gives the jury a glimpse at your case narrative.

Case Story Question Example: A prosecutor in a date-rape case might question the prospective jurors about the circumstances of secrecy that commonly surround such crimes, and the secretive nature of the crime making the victim vulnerable to the sexual assault and a claim that it did not happen. For instance, the prosecutor could say to the prospective jurors, "You understand that rapes normally don't happen in a courtroom like this with over 40 people watching. They happen behind closed doors, in alleys, in places where there are no witnesses other than the two people involved. My question of you is, by a show of hands, would anyone require that we produce more than the victim—more than one witness—in this case before you could reach a guilty verdict? Would you require that we call multiple witnesses in order for you to find the defendant guilty?" The prosecutor would then ask follow-up questions of any jurors who raised their hands. With this series of questions, the prosecutor prepares the jurors for a case where only the victim will testify that the defendant raped her. Further, with these questions the prosecutor lays the groundwork for opening statement when the first words out of the prosecutor's mouth is the case theme: "Rape is a secretive crime."

Chapter 10

Advancing Your Legal Position

> *"We are bound by the law, so that we may be free."*
>
> Marcus Tullius Cicero,
> Jan. 3 103 BC–7 Dec. 43 BC
> Roman orator and lawyer

> *"Commitment to the rule of law provides a basic assurance that people can know what to expect whether what they do is popular or unpopular at the time."*
>
> Sandra Day O'Connor,
> Supreme Court Justice

A. Legal Position

During jury selection, you want to leave the jurors with a favorable impression of your legal theory, and you want to determine whether they harbor any biases against it. In fact, the best strategies simultaneously accomplish both. You can state your legal theory either during your initial comments to the jury, through your questions or both. However, as the illustrations in this chapter show, you should frame your questions on the law to probe for bias and not overstep into the court's prerogative as the instructor on the law of the case.

You want to educate the jurors about the law and probe for jurors who may have difficulty following that law. Therefore, no matter which side you represent, you should strive to describe your legal position in such a way that all the prospective jurors can understand it. It should be a clear, simple and sensible explanation. In this chapter, we offer strategies and techniques for doing this along with illustrative transcripts.

Naturally, the legal position component of the case depends on the side you represent and whether the case is civil or criminal. The prosecutor's allegations in the criminal charge or the civil plaintiff's claims and relief in the complaint are the legal positions that they will mold into voir dire questions. In describing this legal position during voir dire, plaintiff's counsel or the prosecutor should stress the threat or harm done to the plaintiff or victim in plain language the jurors can understand.

Generally, the defense's legal position is either that the plaintiff or prosecution cannot prove its case, that there is an affirmative or partial defense to the allegation, or a combination of these legal positions. In terms that the jurors will understand, the defense counsel in a civil case can explain that either the defendant did nothing wrong or the plaintiff can't prove it, or if the defendant did it, the plaintiff also contributed to the harm. In a criminal case, defense counsel describes what happened as either the government can't prove the crime beyond a reasonable doubt, or if the defendant did it, there is a defense, such as insanity or self-defense.

Commonly, the plaintiff or prosecutor must meet its burden, proving the elements of the charge or claim to prevail. Therefore, during jury selection, the defense will stress the importance of the burden of proof and the jury's role in requiring that the plaintiff meet its burden. In those situations where the defense has a burden of proof, as with an affirmative defense, the plaintiff will seek to have the jurors understand that their role is to hold the defense to its burden.

B. Initial Remarks Introducing the Legal Position

When the court allows counsel to make a preliminary statement to the jury about the case, you may lay out your legal theory.

Plaintiff's Initial Remarks Example: In *In re TFT-LCD (Flat-Panel),* three parties were involved when the case came to trial—plaintiff Best Buy and defendants HannStarr and Toshiba. Counsel were given an opportunity to address the jury with summaries of their cases, and each stated their legal positions in their preliminary remarks:

> PLAINTIFF'S COUNSEL: So, Best Buy has two kinds of claims. One is based on Minnesota state law, the Court will instruct you more about this at the end of the case. Best Buy is a Minnesota company, and it has a particular kind of claim based on state law. And it also has a second kind of claim based on federal law. And we'll talk more

about that as we get into the evidence. But in both kinds of claims, it's about the increased price of these glass panels being passed along to Best Buy as an overcharge.

Now, the overcharge itself was relatively small, but the damages involved are very, very large, because of the hundreds of millions of products over that eight-year period that Best Buy bought that contained these glass panels. The overcharges were passed on to Best Buy ...[1]

Defense Initial Remarks Examples:

DEFENDANT HANNSTAR'S COUNSEL: Counsel conceded that HannStar participated in the price-fixing meetings and stated that the overcharge was nothing like what Best Buy was claiming and that the overcharge was passed on to customers.[2]

DEFENDANT TOSHIBA'S COUNSEL: Counsel said that Toshiba did not participate in the meetings and otherwise did nothing wrong.[3]

C. Questioning That Introduces the Legal Position

1. Court's Province

It is the judge's prerogative to instruct the jury on the law. Courts usually prohibit counsel from either asking potential jurors to define legal terms, such as a preponderance of evidence, or in any fashion instructing them on the law. If you do, you may have the same experience that plaintiff's counsel had in the following example.

Judge's Prerogative Example: In *In re TFT-LCD (Flat-Panel)*, plaintiff Best Buy's counsel asked a prospective juror for an example of what would be illegal in terms of gathering competitive information, and at that juncture the judge stepped in as follows:

Just so you know, ladies and gentlemen, and I don't mean to interrupt, but the questions that are being asked are to help illuminate

---

1. Transcript of Proceedings at 34, *In re TFT-LCD (Flat-Panel)*, No. 07-MDL-1827 SI, 10-CV-4572, 10-CV-5452, 10-CV-4114 (N.D. Cal. July 22, 2013), App. 1.1.

2. *Id.* at 34–35.

3. *Id.*

really all of you to know who's suitable to be on the jury and who's not. And the legal questions that are being asked are being asked for that purpose. But I have to jump in and say: In this trial, in this case, I am the law. So in terms of what is legal and what is illegal, you will get instructions from me at the beginning of the case, and then more detailed instructions at the end, and that will tell you what the legal rules are that you're to apply.

So, as I say, I don't mean to interrupt, but the, what's legal, what's not legal, what you can do, what you can't do, to the extent that has to be decided by you in this case, that will be based on instructions that I will later give you at the end of the trial, just to be clear.

Thank you.[4]

2. Inquiring to Determine Possible Bias

As we have mentioned before, the essential question that can guide you in crafting your inquires of the prospective jurors is: What is it about your case that might trouble them—their preconceptions and biases? Regarding your legal position, you want to identify those prospective jurors who won't be able follow the law that is your legal position.

Additionally, you will want to leave the jurors with a positive impression of your legal theory. Two strategies can be employed to achieve that end. First, you can steer the conversation with the prospective jurors to express views favorable to your legal position. However, you should be careful with this approach. You do not want too much disclosure of a juror's favorable view of your case, because this only helps the other side identify who on the jury may be a problem for them.

A second strategy is to elicit the view that although the bias against the law or lawsuits may be justified for other cases, it does not apply to your case. For the case that the jurors will decide, the jurors can be fair and impartial.

a. Frivolous Lawsuits and the Litigation Lottery

Plaintiff's counsel in a civil case probably will want to inquire concerning whether the prospective jurors hold the view that there are too many frivolous lawsuits, and that most plaintiffs use lawsuits to win the so-called "litigation

---

4. Transcript of Proceedings at 56–57, *In re TFT-LCD (Flat-Panel)*, No. 07-MDL-1827 SI, 10-CV-4572, 10-CV-5452, 10-CV-4114 (N.D. Cal. July 22, 2013), App. 1.1.

lottery" and make a quick buck. Essentially, there are two key elements to this tort reformer bias: (1) that too many people are quick to blame others for their own poor decisions and (2) that too much money is awarded in lawsuits. These are very popular and perhaps the most consistent beliefs across the country that are detrimental to a plaintiff's case. In some plaintiff's cases, these topics may yield the most important information plaintiff's counsel may obtain about the jury. With open-ended questions and forced-choice questions (see pages 164–168), plaintiff's counsel can attempt to determine who holds these beliefs. Plaintiff's counsel's response to replies from jurors that there are frivolous suits should be neutral or positive because that will foster a further open discussion. Conversely, adverse reactions from plaintiff's counsel may discourage other jurors for disclosing their honest views of these issues, which prevents plaintiff's counsel from really understanding where the bias lies in the venire.

Plaintiff's counsel may be able to orchestrate the ensuing discussion in such a way that other views emerge that will support the proposition that the jury should give the plaintiff's case a fair and impartial trial. To accomplish this, plaintiff's counsel can use the two strategies. First, counsel can seek to elicit contrary views from other prospective jurors. A second approach is for counsel to embrace the idea that there are frivolous lawsuits. Then, counsel can guide the conversation to the point where even jurors who believe that there are frivolous lawsuits can set that aside that belief because the plaintiff's case should not be presumptively viewed as one of them.

Frivolous Lawsuits Example: *Jane Doe v. Robert Higgins* was a civil case in which the plaintiff claimed that the defendant gave her Vicodin when she was 15 years old and sexually abused her. During voir dire, plaintiff's counsel addressed the issue of frivolous lawsuits.

> MR. RECK (Plaintiff's lawyer): ... There is a lot of talk today about frivolous lawsuits. There's a lot of talk about litigation. There's a lot of talk about people filing lawsuits just trying to make money. And I'm sure that everybody has probably heard of a frivolous lawsuit or somebody has had an experience with it. The stories are in the newspaper. They're on TV. Some of you may even have had an experience with it.
>
> Is there anybody who's had an experience, is there anybody who's been a victim of what they think is a frivolous lawsuit?
>
> Yes ma'am. Can you tell me about that?
>
> PROSPECTIVE JUROR: When I first moved to Los Angeles, I got into a car accident and the other person sued me for a million dollars.
>
> MR. RECK: A million dollars?

PROSPECTIVE JUROR: Uh-huh.

MR. RECK: And I assume it was not a—not a very big car accident?

PROSPECTIVE JUROR: I think my car cost $12,000 at the time and I was paying it off. I didn't have anything. But my insurance company just dealt with it. Eventually went away.

MR. RECK: Did that make you upset?

PROSPECTIVE JUROR: Yes. Lost a lot of sleep.

MR. RECK: Did that case actually—was that a trial in that case?

PROSPECTIVE JUROR: No eventually. Went away. The insurance company took care of it.

MR. RECK: And in the course of that, did you have to fill out paperwork probably and send things back and forth to the attorney?

PROSPECTIVE JUROR: (No audible response.)

MR. RECK: Anybody else have an experience similar to that?

PROSPECTIVE JUROR: Through business.

MR. RECK: Pardon?

PROSPECTIVE JUROR: Through business.

MR. RECK: Through your business?

PROSPECTIVE JUROR: Also my wife got hit and even though she got hit, she got sued.

MR. RECK: So she was driving the car, she got hit and somebody found a lawyer and sued her, right?

PROSPECTIVE JUROR: That's correct.

MR. RECK: Did you guys end up—I mean, did the insurance company settle that case for you?

PROSPECTIVE JUROR: Yes.

MR. RECK: Probably a little bit of a hassle, you had do a bunch of paperwork, things like that?

PROSPECTIVE JUROR: I had strong feelings about the appropriateness of the whole process.

MR. RECK: Meaning you felt that the plaintiff, the person in the other car, probably should not have brought the lawsuit?

PROSPECTIVE JUROR: Correct.

MR. RECK: And in your opinion the accident was probably the other person's fault?

PROSPECTIVE JUROR: So the police report said.

MR. RECK: Really? Are you aware if that person ever recovered any money or any settlement amount?

PROSPECTIVE JUROR: I think a small amount of money.

MR. RECK: And did that seem wrong to you?

PROSPECTIVE JUROR: Yes.

MR. RECK: What about the business? What was your business again?

PROSPECTIVE JUROR: I have been in health care for over 20 years.

MR. RECK: You're manufacturing products in health care?

PROSPECTIVE JUROR: Yes, now.

MR. RECK: Okay. And is that the type of business you were in at the time this other lawsuit occurred?

PROSPECTIVE JUROR: Same kind of service, sometimes product.

MR. RECK: Okay. And I assume someone sued your business then?

PROSPECTIVE JUROR: Or sued some lawyers representing the business one time.

MR. RECK: Everybody found a lawyer and they just started suing, right?

PROSPECTIVE JUROR: Yes

MR. RECK: And did that lawsuit make you upset?

PROSPECTIVE JUROR: I thought it was frivolous and it turned out that the jury thought so also.

MR. RECK: So there was—there was an actual trial in that case?

PROSPECTIVE JUROR: Yes.

MR. RECK: And it was found that there wasn't liability?

PROSPECTIVE JUROR: No. The lawyers got off.

MR. RECK: Now, you guys have heard these stories and I'm sure that you've heard other things. There is a lot of talk and if anybody reads the paper about tort reform. There is things that are going up through government that are in Sacramento through even some governments that are in Washington D.C. talking about curtailing frivolous lawsuits.

And I'm—I'll be the first one to agree with you. I think there's too many lawsuits out there. Does anybody here think there's too many lawsuits out there? Just show of hands. It ...

It's totally okay. I'm not going to get upset with you.

Okay. Almost every single one of you did that and that's okay to have that opinion.

What is important to recognize, though and it's something that's important for all of us here to know is that you understand amidst this sea that's out there of frivolous lawsuits, of, you know, auto accidents where somebody runs into somebody else and then sues, there are still righteous cases.

Does anybody believe that there are simply no righteous lawsuits out there?

So everybody believes that, you know, there are still righteous lawsuits, right? Everybody believes that there can be a good lawsuit?

Okay. And everybody believes that courts are important, right?

Anybody here think courts are not important? It's okay. The judge won't come after you. At least I hope not.

And your role here is important, so it's important that we understand that we can do that.

Now, with that said, assuming we can get past the seal of frivolous lawsuits, we get down to a lawsuit that's actually here, what we're going to ask you do again is listen to that testimony, listen to it fairly and then come with a decision.

And doing that is going to require you to set aside those preconceived notions about frivolous lawsuits, that people are out there and people suing for no reason. Is there anybody who feels they can't set that part aside?

Thank you. I appreciate that.[5]

b. The McDonald's Case

Inevitably, whenever frivolous lawsuits are discussed, the notorious McDonald's case involving a woman who was burned by McDonald's coffee and was awarded what was believed to be an astronomical three million dollars in punitive damages may come up. If and when it does come up and you are plaintiff's counsel, you should know the facts of the case, which are discussed on pages 191–192, in order to be able to debunk any false assertions by prospective jurors and ask them to set aside what they have read or heard about the McDonald's case. However, in doing so, it is critical that you not alienate the juror who referenced the case. This will discourage other jurors from speaking up, potentially out of fear of sounding stupid.

c. Explaining the Law and Gaining a Commitment to Follow It

Asking a venireperson to explain what is meant by the "preponderance of evidence" or misstating the law is likely to prompt the judge to interrupt you even without the other side objecting. Whenever you plan to discuss the law with the prospective jurors, it must be remembered that the judge is the only one who instructs the jury on the law and that the judge guards this right.

---

5. Transcript of Proceedings at 72–77, *Jane Doe v. Robert Higgins*, Cal. Super. Ct., No. YC052780, 2007 WL-5417657, 72–77 (2007), App. 10.1.

Rather than asking a juror to explain the law or directly telling the jury what the law is, you can succinctly and accurately state a legal principle and ask the prospective juror whether they have any quarrel with it. You can justify your question as one probing for actual bias against a law. The jurors' responses will better enable you to properly exercise your challenges.

As we have stated before, the extent to which you may go into questioning about the law varies from courtroom to courtroom, and some judges may give you more latitude to discuss the law than others.

Introducing the Legal Theory Example: In *Retractable Technologies, Inc. v. Becton, Dickinson and Company,* plaintiff's counsel's questioning both introduced the legal theory and did it in a way the jury could understand:

> MR. CARROLL: One of the concepts that Judge Davis will talk to you about is something called market power. Market power. I am not going to tell you what it means because Judge Davis is the Judge of the law. He will tell you what it means.
>
> But one of the applications of this term "market power" is that it is applied differently to different companies depending on whether they do or don't have market power.
>
> Now, that sounds confusing. Let me tell you what I mean by that.
>
> Mr. Seat, may I talk with you just a second, please, sir? Now, do I get it right you work with Little Mexico down in Palestine?
>
> JUROR SEAT: Yes.
>
> MR. CARROLL: I figured y'all would have closed your doors when Tate McCain died.
>
> JUROR SEAT: We should have.
>
> MR. CARROLL: He was a good customer, wasn't he?
>
> JUROR SEAT: Yes.
>
> MR. CARROLL: Now, here is the question I have for you: Do you have dogs at your house down there in Palestine?
>
> JUROR SEAT: We do.
>
> MR. CARROLL: Big ones, little ones, or both?
>
> JUROR SEAT: Medium.
>
> MR. CARROLL: Medium. At my house we have got little tiny dogs, we have got two- and three-pound dogs, and we have got great big dogs, 80- and 90-pound dogs.
>
> We have a rule at the Carroll house for dogs; and that is, little dogs can get on laps, big dogs can't get on laps.
>
> Now, that kind of makes sense, does it not?
>
> JUROR SEAT: That's a good rule.

MR. CARROLL: That's a good rule.

And the little dogs may feel like they are special and get treated different because they get to get on laps. And the big dogs may feel like they are discriminated against because they are—because nobody wants a 90-pound Golden Retriever that has been in the lake, sitting on his or her lap.

The law I think that Judge Davis is going to give the eight of you who are the jury in this case, is similar to my big-dog, little-dog example. And that is, big dogs which have market power can't do some of the same things that little dogs which have no market power can do under the law.

I didn't make it up. We didn't make it up. The law made it up.

So my question to you, Mr. Seat, is: If that is the law and if you are a big dog, there are certain things you can't do that a little dog can do because you are a big dog, can you apply that law?

JUROR SEAT: (Pause in proceedings.) I think you lost me somewhere.

MR. CARROLL: Sorry. Mr. Seat, I'm going to tell you it won't be the first time.

Let me tell you what I mean. If the law says that you are a big dog and you have market power, you may not do certain things.

JUROR SEAT: Okay.

MR. CARROLL: But at the same time if you are a little dog, that restriction doesn't apply to you because you are a little dog. That is a different standard of applying conduct.

Do you see what I am saying? You with me? You see?

JUROR SEAT: I do, I do.

MR. CARROLL: So the question to you is, that may not sound fair to some people. Are you one of those people?

JUROR SEAT: It—

MR. CARROLL: Yes?

JUROR SEAT: I guess I am.

MR. CARROLL: You guess you are. So my question is, if you have—you have a restaurant in Palestine, Texas.

JUROR SEAT: Yes.

MR. CARROLL: And your restaurant is a good restaurant and a big deal in Palestine, Texas. But if you are competing with a chain restaurant, an El Chico, say—you don't have one of those down there, I don't think?

JUROR SEAT: We do not.

MR. CARROLL: You do not. It may be if El Chico qualifies as a big dog, they can't do things that affect consumers, that affect the public, that don't apply to you. Do you see what I am saying? Because of the size.

JUROR SEAT: Okay.

MR. CARROLL: Do you see what I am saying?

Well, if that is the rule, would that make sense to you that you wouldn't want a bigger competitor doing certain things even though you as a smaller competitor may be free to do them?

JUROR SEAT: Okay. Yes.

MR. CARROLL: Does that make sense to you?

JUROR SEAT: Yes, it does.

MR. CARROLL: Understanding that, can you apply the law if that is, in fact, what Judge Davis tells you the law is?

JUROR SEAT: I can.

MR. CARROLL: You can. Good. Thank you, Mr. Seat.

Now, that is a tough concept. Is there anybody—and I am sure it could have been asked a lot better than I asked it. I bet Mr. Baxter will give it a whirl. But is there anybody, in addition to Mr. Seat, who thinks that, while that may not be right, that may not be fair, that may not be the American way, everybody ought to be treated different whether you are a big dog or you are a little dog even though the antitrust law may say different, anybody just think, well, that is not right; I don't want to be a part of anything where big dogs are treated different from little dogs?

Anybody on the front row?

Anybody on the second row?

Anybody beginning with Mr. Sturrock?

Mr. Sturrock, how does that strike you?

JUROR STURROCK: It's fair.

MR. CARROLL: It's fair.[6]

Other Law and Commitment Examples: We provide several other examples of jury questioning that sets out the law and then asks the jury whether they can follow that law. These other examples include:

- Self-defense (see pages 239–240);
- Burden of proof (see pages 240–246);

---

6. Transcript of Proceedings at 17–19, *Retractable Techs., Inc. v. Becton, Dickinson and Co.*, 2:08cv16 E.D. (Tex. Sept. 3, 2013), App. 1.2.

- Presumption of innocence (see pages 253–254);
- Circumstantial evidence (see pages 263–265), and
- Sympathy (see pages 267–268).

In sum, the court will normally allow your questions that explore whether the prospective jurors would follow the law that expresses your legal theory or harbor any biases against a particular law. But, your questioning should not invade the court's domain as the lawgiver.

Chapter 11

Advancing Your Case Story

"Well when I was an attorney, a long time ago, young man, I err ... I realized after much trial and error, that in the courtroom, whoever tells the best story wins. In unlawyer-like fashion, I give you that scrap of wisdom free of charge."

John Quincy Adams,
Amistad movie (1997)

"The story's power is twofold: It provides simulation (knowledge about how to act) and inspiration (motivation to act). Note that both benefits, simulation and inspiration, are geared to generating action ... [A] credible idea makes people believe. An emotional idea makes people care ... [T]he right stories make people act."

Chip and Dan Heath,
Made to Stick: Why Some Ideas Survive and Others Die, 206 (Random House 2007)

A. Case Story

Jurors are wired for a good story. We all are. Pretrial, you have ideally crafted a credible, compelling story. During trial, you will be storytelling because, as the saying goes, "Whoever tells the best story wins." The jury will utilize a story to organize and understand the evidence or lack of evidence and the case as a whole. Fail to provide the jurors with a believable, persuasive story, and either the other side will provide a storyline for the jurors or the jurors may construct their own narrative in an effort to comprehend the case.

Sociologists have conducted studies of jury decision-making in criminal cases and concluded that jurors assembled evidence produced in fragments throughout the trial into a story, and then in deliberations, evaluated the story to determine whether it made sense.[1] Other researchers of juror decision-making found that jurors use stories to sort the information presented at trial and compare their personal stories with those offered at trial.[2]

As we have previously stressed when we use the word "advance" in the phrase "advancing your case story," we are not suggesting that you attempt to try your case in jury selection. Rather, in this chapter, we examine how your discussion with the prospective jurors can not only begin to tell your case story in such a way that they will be receptive to it but also uncover whether they have any biases against it.

Construction of a compelling story, like baking a good cake, requires that you, the chef, include all of the right ingredients. The recipe for a compelling case story calls for these three ingredients: (1) a good person or company (think your client); (2) a story of deprivation or threatened deprivation; and (3) believable evidence. With the required ingredients in mind, you can analyze your case to identify the ingredients that will satisfy the recipe. Then, you can blend them into preliminary remarks and questions that communicate your case story to the jurors.

No matter how complex the case, your story for trial must be simple, clear and plausible. It should resonate with jurors' own personal experiences and attitudes. The more familiar the story is to your audience, the better. Conversely, stories that contradict jurors' personal experiences are more likely to get rejected, discounted, or explained away. You should also edit out all unnecessary information, stripping the story down to the three essentials with just enough detail to bring the story to life.

Jury selection is not the time to lay out your complete case narrative for at least three reasons. First, laying out your story in voir dire potentially exposes your good jurors to the other side while wasting limited and valuable time to unveil biases in the jury pool. Second, because of time constraints, you would not be able to tell the full story even if you wanted to. Third, you want to tease out the story only in as much detail as you need to determine whether the jurors will be receptive to it, and make them want to hear the full story in opening statement and through the rest of the trial. Once again, the essential

---

1. *See generally* LANCE BENNETT & MARTHA FELDMAN, RECONSTRUCTING REALITY IN THE COURTROOM (1981).

2. Nancy Pennington & Reid Hastie, *A Cognitive Theory in Juror Decision Making: The Story Model*, 13 CARDOZO L. REV. 519, 520 (1991).

question for you to ask as you plan for jury selection is: What is it about your case that might trouble them—their preconceptions and biases? Now, concerning your case story, you want to identify those prospective jurors who won't be able to accept your story. More specifically, you can focus on the three components of the story.

B. Good Person or Company

Ideally, the jurors will have a positive impression of the person or company you represent. You should humanize the client and convey the best possible impression of that person to the jury. How you behave towards your client in front of the jury will have an effect on the jurors. Putting your hand on your client's shoulder and referring to the client by first name can give the impression that the client is a decent person. Mentioning your client's favorable background information (mother or father of three children) likewise can leave a positive impression.

If you represent a corporation, you probably can cast the company in a favorable light. It may be a corporation that is well thought of in the community or may produce a product that the public likes. Also, you can seek to have a selected corporate representative with whom the jurors can identify. You can have the representative seated at counsel table, introduce that representative to the prospective jurors and refer to the person during voir dire.

On the other hand, your client may not be sympathetic, attractive or have any redeeming qualities that you can discern. When your client is vulnerable to attack, it is best to candidly concede the weakness and own it. Normally, this concession will enhance your credibility with the jurors. Generally, you can take the position that all of us deserve protection under the law.

It is ideal if the narrative relayed to the jury is about a human being. To the greatest extent possible, you want to humanize the protagonist, usually your client, with your narrative. If your client is a corporation, you can still put forward a human face as representing the corporation, and introduce that person during jury selection.

Good Person Example: In *Retractable Technologies, Inc. v. Becton, Dickinson and Company,* when counsel's turn came to introduce himself and his client, he said:

> COUNSEL: At counsel table—and I will get you to stand up—I have got my Becton Dickinson corporate rep. This is Mr. John Ledek.

John is an Air Force Academy graduate, flew planes in the Gulf War.
And we are lucky enough to have him at Becton Dickinson.[3]

The protagonist in the narrative need not be a human being. Rather, the
narrative can be about a corporation that provides goods or services. A compelling narrative can be crafted to tell about the business entity's success, and
how it has been wrongfully blamed or oppressed. During voir dire, counsel
can emphasize this through questions to the jury.

Preliminary Remarks Good Corporation Example: Defense counsel in *Retractable Technologies, Inc. v. Becton, Dickinson and Co.* in a preliminary
statement to the jury before beginning the defense round of questioning, talked
about a good corporation.

> MR. BAXTER: Thank you, Your Honor. May it please the Court.
> Ladies and Gentlemen, as I told you, my name is Sam Baxter. It is
> my privilege to represent Becton Dickinson in this case ...
> And it is important. And the eight of you that get to hear it are
> going to get to make a monumental decision. It is not about who has
> the cleverest needle. It is not about who developed it for nine years
> because BD was the first in the market with safety products.
> We were there earliest. We are the one that forged ahead. We are
> the one that developed the very first safety product. And we have been
> at the forefront of that fight to reduce needle sticks and reduce injuries
> in the hospitals and to reduce deaths.
> As a matter of fact, when you look at the statistics, the number of
> confirmed AID deaths since 1999 from a needle stick from an injection
> is zero, thanks in large part to the work that BD has done to get safety
> syringes and safety catheters into the hospital.
> Now, those are the facts. That is what you are going to hear about.[4]

Good Corporation Questions Example: *In Re TFT-LCD (FLAT-PANEL)*
provides an illustration of how counsel through questioning the jurors can
paint a picture of the corporation that counsel represents as an entity that does
good and should be valued. Plaintiff's counsel used the specialized
questionnaire that the panel members had completed as a source for identifying
and questioning several prospective jurors. This is one example of this type of
questions:

---

3. Transcript of Proceedings at 8, *Retractable Techs., Inc. v. Becton, Dickinson and Co.*,
2:08cv16 E.D. (Tex. Sept. 3, 2013), App. 1.2.
    4. *Id.* at 25.

MR. SILBERFELD: All right. You told us in the questionnaire that you shop at Best Buy all the time.

PROSPECTIVE JUROR VOLPE: All the time.

MR. SILBERFELD: Good experience? Bad experience?

PROSPECTIVE JUROR VOLPE: Well, it's very convenient to where I live, and they have everything from microwaves to DVDs to printers, ink cartridges. Everything. One-stop shopping.

MR. SILBERFELD: You're satisfied with your experiences there?

PROSPECTIVE JUROR VOLPE: Yes, I am.

MR. SILBERFELD: All right. Great.[5]

C. Deprivation

Stories that move us are about good versus evil and deprivation or threatened deprivation. From the story of David and Goliath with the potential loss of David's life to today's good-versus-evil stories told in today's books and movies (think Harry Potter versus Voldemort) and television shows, we have been programmed to cheer for good to triumph over evil and right the wrong or prevent the wrong from happening. This storyline stirs our emotions and compels us to want good to win out. At the end of the trial, your case story should call upon the jurors to pick up a rock, put it in the sling, and act for the good. The jurors should want to finish the story with a verdict for your client. By rendering the verdict, the jurors are doing something meaningful, doing the right thing, doing justice.

Virtually any lawsuit can be framed to tell a story about both good versus evil and deprivation or threatened deprivation. Patent infringement can be told as a story of theft. The plaintiff was deprived of what was rightfully hers, and therefore, the jury should provide recompense. In a criminal case, the defense story can be that the evidence does not prove beyond a reasonable doubt that the defendant committed the crime, and, therefore, the jurors should prevent the defendant from being wrongfully convicted. In a civil case, the defense narrative may suggest that the plaintiff is asking others to pay money for injuries that were caused by the plaintiff's own poor decision-making. This tort reformer narrative casts the plaintiff as the villain who represents all that is wrong with the lawsuits these days.

---

5. Transcript of Proceedings at 57, *In re TFT-LCD (Flat-Panel)*, No. 07-MDL-1827 SI, 10-CV-4572, 10-CV-5452, 10-CV-4114 (N.D. Cal. July 22, 2013), App. 1.1.

1. Preliminary Remarks

If the court permits counsel to deliver preliminary remarks to the jury, that is an opportunity to succinctly tell a story of deprivation of threatened deprivation.

Stories of Deprivation Example: *In re TFT-LCD (Flat-Panel)*, counsel on both sides made opening remarks to the jury that appealed to the prospective jurors' values and contained stories of good versus evil involving deprivation or threatened deprivation.

Plaintiff's Counsel: In preliminary remarks during jury selection, plaintiff's counsel told a story of the defendant's misconduct and the resulting harm.

> PLAINTIFF'S COUNSEL: This case is brought by Best Buy against HannStar, and Toshiba. And it involves claims of a price-fixing conspiracy that lasted eight years.
>
> The claim is that the Defendants who are here conspired with other firms who are not a part of this case, now, to fix prices of an electronic component that's used in things like the glass on this Black-Berry (Indicating), televisions, computer monitors, laptops, the screens that are here in the courtroom (Indicating). And, these are called TFT-LCD panels. And they're incorporated into what we call finished products. And this glass is what makes these electronic products work.
>
> The price-fixing conspiracy that lasted eight years between 1996— pardon me, 1998 and 2006 caused the prices of finished products to be higher than they should have been had the prices been fair ones. And, that difference between a fair market price and the actual price is what we refer to as an "overcharge." And that overcharge is what the damages in this case are about that was imposed on Best Buy and others by not only these Defendants (Indicating), but the conspirators who are not here.
>
> Now, in society today we all buy products of various kinds like cell phones, computer monitors, televisions and so forth. They're a basic necessity of modern life. And typically there are many consumers that are involved in bringing these products out. So, at our level, we buy products, all of us, and we buy them either online or we buy them from a retailer.[6]

---

6. *Id.* at 33.

Defendant Toshiba's Counsel: Defense counsel's story in essence was that the defendant was wrongfully accused. In preliminary comments, Defense counsel told the jurors that the defendant was innocent of any wrongdoing.

> DEFENDANT TOSHIBA'S COUNSEL: In the course of this trial, I, with my colleagues, will show you—will prove to you—that those other interactions that Toshiba people had with their competitors were perfectly proper, and were not hidden from their customers. And in fact, often, the customers wanted Toshiba to interact with its competitors in order to find out what the competitors were charging, in the hopes that Toshiba would price lower.
>
> So, bottom line, Toshiba didn't participate in any of the meetings. Toshiba was not prosecuted, charged, or convicted of anything. And we'll prove that Toshiba didn't do anything wrong in the course of this trial.[7]

2. Questions-about-the-Story Method

A method of communicating the story of your case during jury selection is to integrate it into your questions. Your questions tell the story. Specifically, you want to cover the components of your case narrative that the jurors can relate to: a good person or company being deprived or threatened with deprivation. Frame your questions about the case story to be aimed at determining how the prospective jurors will relate to your story and whether they harbor any biases that will prevent them from fairly and impartially considering it.

While judges usually frown upon any questions that ask the prospective juror to prejudge the case, you can phrase your questions in such a way as to avoid or meet any objection along that line.

Plaintiff's Story Example: Plaintiff's counsel in *In re TFT-LCD (Flat-Panel)* sought to advance the plaintiff's price-fixing case narrative, stress the impact of price fixing on consumers through questions about price matching and a competitive marketplace and to determine how the jury would respond to the case story. The following illustrates how to work the case story into questioning with the human story being about the juror-consumer who benefits from competition. This example also illustrates the reality that sometimes you do not

---

7. *Id.* at 36.

always get anywhere on your first try and that you may not get the responses you want from the prospective jurors:

> MR. SILBERFELD: ... You had some experience at Bed, Bath & Beyond?
>
> PROSPECTIVE JUROR ERWIN: For a short time, like six months.
>
> MR. SILBERFELD: Did they have a price match policy when you were there?
>
> PROSPECTIVE JUROR ERWIN: Not that I recall.
>
> MR. SILBERFELD: So you never had any particular experience with it?
>
> PROSPECTIVE JUROR ERWIN: No.
>
> MR. SILBERFELD: As a consumer, have you ever had any experience at any store, Bed, Bath & Beyond, Best Buy or anyplace, where you go in and you say, I saw this at another store for a lower price?
>
> PROSPECTIVE JUROR ERWIN: No, I haven't.
>
> MR. SILBERFELD: Okay. And do you know whether you shopped at Best Buy.
>
> PROSPECTIVE JUROR ERWIN: Yes.
>
> MR. SILBERFELD: What kind of experience have you had there?
>
> PROSPECTIVE JUROR ERWIN: My experience was fine there.
>
> MR. SILBERFELD: Fine.
>
> PROSPECTIVE JUROR ERWIN: It was good. No bad experience.
>
> MR. SILBERFELD: Great. Thank you.

Miss Hanson, good morning. Now it is afternoon. Good afternoon. You have a daughter who works at Target, I think?

> PROSPECTIVE JUROR HANSON: Yes, I do.
>
> MR. SILBERFELD: And does she have any experience that she's ever shared with you about matching prices with competitor's prices? Has that ever come up?
>
> PROSPECTIVE JUROR HANSON: No.
>
> MR. SILBERFELD: What does she do there?
>
> PROSPECTIVE JUROR HANSON: She is the person who answers the phone when you call the store, and those duties include finding replacements for employees who call in last minute, can't work that day, and she has to find someone to fill their place. The operator.
>
> MR. SILBERFELD: All right. Do you have any thoughts about whether it's a good thing, a bad thing or a neutral thing when businesses compete against each other for your consumer dollars or any of our consumer dollars.

PROSPECTIVE JUROR HANSON: No, that's normal.

MR. SILBERFELD: Okay. Great, thank you.[8]

But, do not be deterred if you don't get the answers you want right away. Persevere in your efforts to spin out your case narrative if at first you do not succeed. Plaintiff's counsel persisted in the effort to stress the benefits of competition in the market place. Plaintiff's counsel later moved to another juror with the same strategy, and this time it proved successful and ended on a humorous note:

MR. SILBERFELD: You bought a television, and there was something about the cables weren't included or something like that?

PROSPECTIVE JUROR LIN: Oh. I think overall, when you buy a TV, the cables should be included.

MR. SILBERFELD: Okay. I agree with you. You wouldn't characterize that as a bad experience at Best Buy?

PROSPECTIVE JUROR LIN: No, no, no. I had a good experience because they price-matched everything for me.

MR. SILBERFELD: And tell me about that interchange over the television and the price matching. How did that work for you?

PROSPECTIVE JUROR LIN: I brought my nephew with me who had an iPhone, and every time—I started out with the TV, but then we ended up—because I had to buy a new receiver, I had to buy a blue ray player, because everything has to be upgraded from my 20-year-old TV. I ended up spending a whole lot more money. So for every new item that was added on to my purchase, of which I initially went just for a TV, my nephew said, Oh, Auntie Karen, you can get this at Amazon for this much, this much, this much. So the salesperson at Best Buy just matched everything for us.

MR. SILBERFELD: Overall?

PROSPECTIVE JUROR LIN: Overall.

MR. SILBERFELD: Okay experience?

PROSPECTIVE JUROR LIN: Yeah.

MR. SILBERFELD: Happy with the TV?

PROSPECTIVE JUROR LIN: It's going to be installed on Thursday. But it depends on if I have to—

MR. SILBERFELD: And you may not be there. Okay.

(General laughter)[9]

---

8. *Id.* at 61.

9. *Id.* at 62–63.

There are also questioning styles for this strategy that do not require as much back-and-forth with jurors, which can be valuable when judges allow very little time for attorney voir dire questioning. For example, a plaintiff's attorney in an employment retaliation case might use a question such as: "In this case, my client claims that he was retaliated against by the City because of some complaints he made against his boss related to inappropriate behavior in the workplace. My client repeatedly told his boss that he found those comments offensive and derogatory, but his boss just didn't care, so he reported him, and was fired as a result of those complaints. By a show of hands, is there anyone here who would just find it hard to believe the City would do something like this?"

When asked to the entire panel in this fashion, the attorney can quickly learn about where potential bias exists in the jury and conduct individual follow-up as necessary.

Defendant Story Example: In *Retractable Technologies, Inc. v. Becton, Dickinson and Co.*, the defense case narrative was that Becton Dickinson was fairly competing in the market place by giving discounts for its needles and that plaintiff Retractable was not willing to lower its prices to compete. To lay out this narrative, defense counsel put the prospective jurors in a position similar to the hospitals in searching for discounts on needles:

MR. BAXTER: Okay. Thank you, ma'am.

Who all thinks that when you buy something, price is important? Let me put it to you differently. Does anybody think price isn't important? Anybody at all?

Who goes to yard sales or garage sales or estate sales? Anybody on the jury panel? One over here. Raise your hand. I am just going to take the numbers down. Okay.

Is there anybody here that buys on volume?

Yes, ma'am, No. 17.

Anybody else?

Who shops at Sam's or Costco, hold your hand up?

All right. Who is familiar with any sort of loyalty card or discount so that if you give a company or store repeat business, they will either give you a discount or they will give you something free at the end of the promotion or things of that sort? Anybody taken advantage of that?

Anybody see anything wrong with that? Hold your hand up if you think that is somehow wrong; that they shouldn't do that?

If you buy in volume, do you think you ought to get a discount? Is there anybody that thinks that is somehow wrong if you get a discount if you buy in volume, anybody at all?[10]

This question is effective because it accomplishes two simultaneous goals. First, it draws a point of comparison between the defendant's actions and similar actions of others whom jurors may view in a more favorable light. Second, the actual question focuses on those who disagree with or dislike such behavior. In other words, this question establishes a theme while ultimately remaining focused on identifying potential bias.

3. Surrogate Method

A complementary method to folding your narrative into questions is to identify and take advantage of a juror who can serve as a surrogate to educate the other jurors about the story of your case. Finding a prospective juror who has had an experience similar to the one in your case does this. While you probe for bias, you can have the person tell what happened to her that is like what happened in your case. As we have previously discussed, the downside of this strategy is that it can highlight your good jurors and the other side may well exercise a causal or peremptory challenge to remove the surrogate juror.

Surrogate Example: In the *Brown v. Davis and* Davis, the wrongful death case discussed at pages 183–187, plaintiff's counsel utilized the surrogate technique to tell the story of the case. Recall that Kenneth Brown Jr. was driving across a bridge in Missouri when a truck driven by the defendant was also crossing the bridge. The load on the trailer came loose and landed on plaintiff's vehicle, killing him. Mr. Brown's wife sued on her own behalf and that of her two children. The truck driver Kenneth Davis, Jr. admitted his negligence and that it caused Brown's death but denied being reckless. Defendant William Davis, who was present, denied liability, as did William Davis Logging, Inc., which was alleged to have been reckless and negligent in how it shipped the log skidder.

Through his questioning, plaintiff's counsel related the plaintiff's story and simultaneously sought out prospective jurors who had lost family members due to negligence or recklessness of another person. Those prospective jurors, who like the plaintiff had lost a family member due to negligence, could speak about their reaction to what happened. Thus, the jurors became surrogates for the plaintiff and told part of the story.

---

10. Transcript of Proceedings at 37–38, *Retractable Techs., Inc. v. Becton, Dickinson and Co.*, 2:08cv16 E.D. (Tex. Sept. 3, 2013), App. 1.2.

MR. WITZEL: Thank you, Your Honor.

Ladies and gentlemen, at this point the lawyers each get a chance to ask some additional questions, try to follow up so that we can find out if there are parts of your life that might have a particular impact on your decisions. And along those lines, I'd like to ask you as a panel, first of all, with regard to those sitting in the jury box. You heard that this is an action for wrongful death. Is there anyone here who has had any close member of their family that was killed as a result of someone's negligence or recklessness?

THE COURT: Let us identify who you are for the record.

MS. WEEDEN: Robbie Weeden.

THE COURT: And that's Juror No. 8. Thank you, ma'am.

MR. WITZEL: Ms. Weeden, it was a close family member?

MS. WEEDEN: It was a close family that caused the accident, so I didn't know with the question. It wasn't an actual family member that had a death, but it was a family member that caused the death.

MR. WITZEL: This lawsuit involves claims by Kristen and the boys that their father/husband was killed as a result of negligence and recklessness. Does the fact that you had a family member that was involved in that type of a situation, would that influence your decision in deciding this case?

MS. WEEDEN: No.

MR. WITZEL: You think you could be fair?

MS. WEEDEN: Yes.

MR. WITZEL: Yes, ma'am.

MS. GILDEHAUS: I had a daughter that was killed in a car accident. It never went to court or anything, so never no tickets or anything, so I can't say who was negligent.

MR. WITZEL: Could you tell me how long ago that occurred?

MS. GILDEHAUS: It was 19 years.

MR. WITZEL: Was that an automobile collision?

MS. GILDEHAUS: It was an automobile and a truck, yes.

MR. WITZEL: Where did that occur, do you know?

MS. GILDEHAUS: In Franklin County.

MR. WITZEL: Do you think that that experience would affect your judgment in deciding this case?

MS. GILDEHAUS: It's a pretty emotional thing. It will.

MR. WITZEL: Thank you. Anyone else? Yes, sir.

MR. HARRISON: I had a grandmother that died of a heart attack and it was a result of negligence on the hospital's part because they didn't have a machine close enough to restart her heart, so that was negligence in the hospital.

MR. WITZEL: Was there any lawsuit filed over that?

MR. HARRISON: No, nobody did anything about it.

MR. WITZEL: You feel that because of that experience that that would influence your ability to deliberate in this case?

MR. HARRISON: I mean, just negligence in general after that happened kind of irks me, you know, negligence on anybody's part. So I can't say for sure whether it would or not, but negligence on anybody's part is a pet peeve, I guess you could say.

THE COURT: And just for the record that's Juror No. 6.

MR. WITZEL: Thank you, Your Honor.[11]

Surrogate Example Continued: Having elicited reactions from the prospective jurors concerning the effect of the loss of a family member due to someone else's fault, plaintiff's counsel in the wrongful death case voir dire turned to telling the story about the defendant truck driver with a wide load on a narrow bridge being a threat to the safety of others on the bridge. Again, he asked for the first-hand experiences of the jurors, who like the deceased driver Kenneth Brown, Jr. had encountered a truck with a wide load on a bridge. Because the bridge where the collision took place was a distance away from where the case was being tried, plaintiff's counsel used a nearby bridge as a surrogate bridge in his questioning.

MR. WITZEL: Anyone else? This case involves a collision which took place on the Champ Clark Bridge. It's a two-lane wide bridge that goes from Louisiana, Missouri over to the State of Illinois. Is there anyone here that's familiar with that bridge or who has ever driven across it?

See if I can bring something a little closer to home. There used to be a bridge out in St. Charles, the old St. Charles Bridge. Anybody ever drive across that old two-lane St. Charles Bridge? We've got a number of hands here. Ms. Knickmeyer, and you're familiar with that old bridge?

MS. KNICKMEYER: Yes.

MR. WITZEL: It's not there anymore.

MS. KNICKMEYER: No.

MR. WITZEL: Did you have occasion to drive across that often?

MS. KNICKMEYER: Yes.

MR. WITZEL: Did it cause you any anxiety when you were driving across that bridge?

---

11. Transcript of Proceedings at 53–55, *Brown v. Davis and Davis*, No. 4:12 CV649-AGF (E.D Mo. 2014), App. 4-6.

MS. KNICKMEYER: Yeah, I would say so. It was a very old bridge, very, I don't know, just old and very narrow.

MR. WITZEL: Did you ever encounter any tractor trailer coming across with a flatbed carrying a wide load?

MS. KNICKMEYER: Can't say I did, no.

MR. WITZEL: Who else? Juror No. 5, Ms. Ferguson. You also are familiar with the old St. Charles Bridge?

MS. FERGUSON: Yes.

MR. WITZEL: Did you have occasion to go across that often?

MS. FERGUSON: Yes.

MR. WITZEL: When you went across that, did you have any anxiety about it?

MS. FERGUSON: Some, yes.

MR. WITZEL: And I'll ask you the same question. In the course of going across that bridge, did you ever encounter any flatbed truck carrying a wide load?

MS. FERGUSON: I remember trucks, but nothing specific, whether they were flatbed or a box van, but I do remember passing large vehicles.

MR. WITZEL: Did that cause you any anxiety?

MS. FERGUSON: Yes.

MR. WITZEL: Thank you. And Mr. Mueller.

MR. MUELLER: Yes.

MR. WITZEL: And you are familiar with that same bridge?

MR. MUELLER: Yes, and others like it.

MR. WITZEL: Two-lane bridge, twenty feet wide?

MR. MUELLER: Whatever. It was two lanes, yes.

MR. WITZEL: When you went across that bridge, was that something you did frequently?

MR. MUELLER: Pretty often. I've been over it a number of times.

MR. WITZEL: There's some other ones, the old bridge out along the Missouri River. Some of those are the old two-lane bridges. When you went across those two-lane bridges like that, did you have any anxiety that caused you any concern?

MR. MUELLER: Because they're narrow and a curve in the middle.

MR. WITZEL: What about with the—did you ever have an occasion to be confronted with an oversized load?

MR. MUELLER: I can't remember if it was oversized, but I did in a similar bridge in Cape Girardeau had two trucks slap mirrors together.

MR. WITZEL: You weren't involved in any type of collision with that, though.

MR. MUELLER: No. Glass went over my head, but no.

MR. WITZEL: And there was some other hands. Yes, sir, Mr. Bowers.

MR. BOWERS: Actually, in my college days I used to drive a dump truck out of St. Charles Sand Company and we went over that bridge all the time.

MR. WITZEL: How wide of a truck were you driving?

MR. BOWERS: Tandem dump truck. I have slapped mirrors with another truck so it was that much.

MR. WITZEL: Did you ever carry oversized loads across that bridge?

MR. BOWERS: No.

MR. WITZEL: I guess I would have to ask the question the other way, though. You were in the truck, so as far as anxiety about—

MR. BOWERS: I was scared to death all the time.

MR. WITZEL: Yes, ma'am. That would be Ms. Labruyere.

MS. LABRUYERE: Labruyere.

MR. WITZEL: Which bridge, St. Charles?

MS. LABRUYERE: Yes, and as well the Cape bridge and yes, I have encountered tractor trailer size vehicles and feeling very uncomfortable and slowing down and being very cautious.

MR. WITZEL: Anyone else? Yes, ma'am.

MS. ZURWELLER: The St. Charles Bridge

MR. WITZEL: Ever encountered an oversized load?

MS. ZURWELLER: Not that I remember. And it's been a while since I've been there, so I don't remember anything in particular.

MR. WITZEL: I think they took that bridge away a while ago.

MS. ZURWELLER: Yeah.[12]

Another Surrogate Example: For another example, see pages 160–164.

4. Believable Evidence

For your case story to be persuasive, the jurors must believe that your witnesses and exhibits are credible. During voir dire, you want to determine the jurors' receptivity to the evidence in your case. Do they have a belief that cir-

---

12. *Id.* at 55–59.

cumstantial evidence is insufficient to prove a case? Will they require more than one witness to prove an essential fact? Will they consider the testimony of expert witnesses? These are just a few of the issues that you may want to cover in jury selection.

In Chapter 12, we discuss the evidence that you may produce at trial and how to assess whether the jurors are biased against it. Specifically, Chapter 12 examines the following:

- Problematic witnesses;
- Defendants in a criminal case;
- Expert witnesses;
- One-witness cases;
- Forensic science evidence;
- Circumstantial evidence; and
- Conflicting testimonies.

D. Damages

1. Plaintiff Voir Dire on Damages

The amount of money awarded by juries in lawsuits is a divisive topic. According to one nationwide survey, 63% of jury-eligible citizens believe there should be limits on the amount of money a jury can award in a lawsuit. Another study found that 79% of respondents believe too many people file lawsuits in an effort to get money they do not deserve. Numerous studies show similar results. These attitudes about damages can serve as powerful filters for the issues in the case. During voir dire in a civil case, you have an opportunity to discuss damages, and you should take advantage of it, regardless of whether you are the plaintiff or the defendant. If you are plaintiff's counsel, among other things, you can precondition the jurors against sticker shock and probe for those in the jury panel who might be quick to conclude that greed is the real motivation for the lawsuit. These are jurors who will not only exert downward pressure on damages in deliberations, but also may put up significant resistance to your theory of liability simply because they perceive questionable motivations behind the lawsuit.[13]

The first damages issue to examine is jurors' comfort with the amount of damages you plan on requesting. Some jurors have a threshold for damages

---

13. Unpublished studies conducted by Sound Jury Consulting for seminars and internal research.

and will not award any amount over that threshold, regardless of whether or not the evidence supports doing so.

Plaintiff's Damages Example 1: Plaintiff's counsel discussed damages during voir dire in *Retractable Technologies, Inc. v. Becton, Dickinson and Co.* as follows:

> COUNSEL: Okay. We are suing for loss of profits because we say that this company through a deliberate campaign of lying about our product and scaring off our customers and putting a lemon on the market that they knew was a defective product, that they have kept us down for all the years that we have been trying to break into the market; that they have kept their big hand on top of our head just enough where we can barely clear the river water.
>
> And because of that, we are suing for what our people are going to tell you is a calculation of the money we would have made if they had played by the rules. And that number is going to be around 300 million dollars, 300 million dollars; a ton of money.
>
> But I will tell you that the evidence is going to be that it is a drop in the bucket compared to what these people make.
>
> So the question I have for you is, is there anybody on the panel who simply couldn't ever give a little dog 300 million dollars even if the little dog proves to you that that was what the little dog didn't make because of this unfair conduct? Anybody?[14]

Plaintiff's Damages Example 2: In *In re TFT-LCD (Flat-Panel)*, plaintiff's counsel not only introduced the amount of the award that would be requested but also dealt with the concern that the potential jurors may believe that there are too many law suits and awards are too high, as follows:

> MR. SILBERFELD: Good afternoon, sir. Do you have any views about whether there ought to be limits on either the number of lawsuits or the kind of damages one can get in the lawsuit based on any experience you've had?
>
> PROSPECTIVE JUROR CHEN: Number of lawsuits and the …?
>
> MR. SILBERFELD: The amount of damages.
>
> PROSPECTIVE JUROR CHEN: I don't quite understand your question.

---

14. Transcript of Proceedings at 20, *Retractable Techs., Inc. v. Becton, Dickinson and Co.*, 2:08cv16 E.D. (Tex. Sept. 3, 2013), App. 1.2.

MR. SILBERFELD: Sure. In this case, if the evidence justifies it, the jury is going to be asked to award Best Buy hundreds of millions of dollars. I'll tell you that right now. That's what the claim is. It will be up to the jury following the Court's instructions to make that decision. But when I say to you a—"hundreds of millions of dollars," right here, right now, does that shock you in some way where you're saying to yourself: Boy, I don't think I could ever do that?

PROSPECTIVE JUROR CHEN: No. I have managed some projects where that's not an unusual amount of money. Involved some potential claim disputes, resolved some kind of change-orders—yeah. That's not out of the budget.

MR. SILBERFELD: So that's not an issue for you?

PROSPECTIVE JUROR CHEN: No.

MR. SILBERFELD: If it's justified, right?

PROSPECTIVE JUROR CHEN: Yes.

MR. SILBERFELD: Wonderful. Thank you.[15]

Plaintiff's Damages Example 3: *U.S. Ethernet Innovations v. Texas Instruments* was a patent case. Plaintiff's counsel employed a parking ticket analogy to both explain (argue) the damages sought and inquire about whether the jurors could consider returning a large award. All without an objection or the judge intervening.

MR. HILL: ... Now, I want to ask one last set of questions before I'm done here in a minute. I think I've got just a few more minutes left.

Is there anybody who came here today and parked at a parking meter out here on the square?

Well, that's good, because they only give you two hours on those meters, and if you did, you would have a ticket by now.

If you parked at a parking meter out here, it's a quarter an hour. That's what those parking meters charge. What would happen if— and we'll ask Mr. Hickey. He's our police expert here.

This isn't really police work, Mr. Hickey, but it's as close as I've got to it, okay? What would happen if you put a penny in that meter and park there for an hour?

JUROR HICKEY: It would definitely not take your money for the time that you would need.

MR. HILL: You think you might get a ticket?

---

15. Transcript of Proceedings at 67–68, *In re TFT-LCD* (*Flat-Panel*), No. 07-MDL-1827 SI, 10-CV-4572, 10-CV-5452, 10-CV-4114 (N.D. Cal. July 22, 2013), App. 1.1.

JUROR HICKEY: Yes, sir.

MR. HILL: All right. If you get that ticket, is it going to be more than the 25 cents that you should have paid for that hour?

JUROR HICKEY: Yes, sir.

MR. HILL: Might be $8, $10?

JUROR HICKEY: If you're lucky.

MR. HILL: If you're lucky? Might be more than that? Certainly more than a penny?

JUROR HICKEY: Yes, sir.

MR. HILL: All right. Now, let's say that you claim, once you find that ticket on your window, that that parking spot is only worth a penny, even though everybody else pays 25 cents for it for an hour, so you don't pay the ticket. What could happen to you then?

JUROR HICKEY: It could result in a warrant for your arrest.

MR. HILL: All right. They might put a boot on your car?

JUROR HICKEY: Or a boot, yes, sir.

MR. HILL: All right. And it's going to cost you some money to get that boot off, isn't it?

JUROR HICKEY: Yes, sir.

MR. HILL: Going to cost you more than a penny?

JUROR HICKEY: Yes, sir.

MR. HILL: More than a quarter too, right?

JUROR HICKEY: Quite a few quarters.

MR. HILL: Okay. And if you get arrested, they could do that. And then, of course, you could ask for a trial, if you wanted to, couldn't you?

JUROR HICKEY: Yes, sir.

MR. HILL: And let's say you have a trial and you admit that you either didn't put money in the meter or you think it was only worth a penny, and so you only put a penny in the meter. Is the city going to accept that, you think?

JUROR HICKEY: No.

MR. HILL: Think you'll get convicted?

JUROR HICKEY: More than likely, yes, sir.

MR. HILL: All right. And if you get convicted, what's it going to cost you for that parking spot?

JUROR HICKEY: Quite a bit more than the original penny or 25 cents, several hundred.

MR. HILL: Like $500?

JUROR HICKEY: Possibly.

MR. HILL: Okay. If you paid—if they tell you it's $500 at that point, and you say, well, I'll just pay my quarter now ...

JUROR HICKEY: Too late at that point.

MR. HILL: Too late at that point. Okay.

Let me tell you, once you've heard the evidence in this case, we're going to ask that you award us money damages, and the money damages that we're going to ask for are the royalties that TI owes for using our technology without a license.

That license is kind of like renting that parking space. We say that TI owes a royalty in this case of, on the low end, 25 cents per computer processor they sold that uses this technology. I think the evidence is going to reflect that TI says that they owe us a penny or less.

The reason I raise that is because TI has sold millions of these products. And so the damages that we seek could total several million dollars. It's going to be a substantial number.

Talking about lawsuits generally, is there anyone who feels like they could never consider a damage award of several million dollars in any type of case?

Is there anyone who just hears that and says, you know, you had me on this jury service thing up until you told me that I might have to award that kind of money damages against a party and that gives me a concern? No?[16]

Plaintiff's Example 4: For another example of how plaintiff's counsel can use a hypothetical question to gauge the jurors' reaction to a damages' argument see pages 170–171.

These examples primarily deal with concerns about the amount of money requested by the plaintiff, but plaintiff's attorneys should also ask questions about different kinds of damages and whether or not there are categories of damages that some jurors are unwilling to award. For example, it is not unusual for some prospective jurors to indicate that they do not believe in damages for pain and suffering. These are individuals who are perfectly comfortable determining the amount of economic damages or actual damages suffered by the plaintiff and awarding those, but are uncomfortable awarding what they believe to be an arbitrary number. This is particularly true when the case involves the loss of a loved one. Many jurors have difficulty with the idea of placing a value

---

16. Transcript of Proceedings at 55–58, *U.S. Ethernet Innovations v. Tex. Instruments*, No. 6:11cv491 (E.D. Tex. 2014), App. 11.1.

on a life and simply refuse to do it. It is important for the plaintiff to identify and remove these individuals from the venire.

Finally, plaintiff's attorneys want to address the motivational issue. In other words, it is important to identify jurors who are going to be quick to conclude that the plaintiff only filed the lawsuit because she is seeking a quick payday. These are people who are so fixated on the issue of damages that it will be difficult for them to listen to the liability evidence in a fair and unbiased manner.

2. Defense Voir Dire on Damages

While some defense counsel may not want to discuss damages and rather concentrate on plaintiff's inability to prove liability, there are many reasons to address this issue in jury selection. Some jurors have an unrealistic sense of money while others misunderstand the very purposes of damages, both of which can lead to exaggerated awards or runaway verdicts.

It is important for defense attorneys to probe jurors on these issues, particularly if the defendant is a corporation. Two common beliefs for corporate defendants to target are: (1) that large damage awards are a drop in the bucket for large corporations and (2) that large damage awards are the only way to send a message to a corporate defendant and force it to change the way it does business.

These two beliefs can tell defense attorneys a lot about prospective jurors. These help defense counsel understand jurors' general disposition towards large corporations and whether or not individual venire members are inclined to use this lawsuit as an opportunity to send a message to large corporations everywhere.

The desire to send a message is not only relevant in cases where jurors can actually award punitive damages. Despite instructions from the court that damages should not be designed to punish a defendant, this can occur. If jurors do not have a punitive damages option on the verdict form, they may simply shift this number into noneconomic damages.

Defense Damages Example: In *In re TFT-LCD (Flat-Panel)*, counsel for defendant HannStar in preliminary remarks during jury selection first conceded that HannStar had participated in price-fixing meetings and then stated that the damages claimed by Best Buy were exaggerated.[17] Later, when questioning

---

17. Transcript of Proceedings at 35, *In re TFT-LCD (Flat-Panel)*, No. 07-MDL-1827 SI, 10-CV-4572, 10-CV-5452, 10-CV-4114 (N.D. Cal. July 22, 2013), App. 1-1.

the prospective jurors, defense counsel returned to discussing damages in his questions:

> MR. FREITAS: Mr. Harper. You just heard something this morning about HannStar. I guess you hadn't heard of them before.
>
> You heard that the company pleaded guilty in the Department of Justice investigation to participating in the crystal meetings. What's your reaction to hearing that?
>
> PROSPECTIVE JUROR HARPER: I think I—I didn't really have a reaction. And, the fact that the Judge said to not consider that, (Inaudible).
>
> MR. FREITAS: Okay. Well, the issues that are going to be decided in this case are different from the issues, at least some of them, that were decided when HannStar accepted responsibility.
>
> Do you think that you could keep the things that were decided and the things that weren't decided separate?
>
> PROSPECTIVE JUROR HARPER: Yes.
>
> MR. FREITAS: One of the things that we will be arguing about is the extent to which Best Buy might have been harmed. And there weren't any decisions in the government case about whether Best Buy was harmed, whether anyone else was harmed, or what the extent of any harm was.
>
> Do you think you could approach the case giving us a clean slate on that?
>
> PROSPECTIVE JUROR HARPER: Yes.[18]

E. Utilizing Visuals to Advance Your Case Story

Visuals can play a principal role in your jury-selection presentation of your case story. First, visuals can be a powerful way of conveying your case narrative to the jury. Second, visuals can make the complicated simple to understand. Third, visuals foster juror retention. While people retain less than 15 percent of what they hear, they recall over 90 percent of what they hear and see. Fourth, visuals can capture the jurors' attention and dramatically convey your case theory in a way that words alone can't. Seeing is believing.

---

18. *Id.* at 72–73.

The trial court is vested with discretion regarding how jury selection is conducted, including what visual aids may be shown. Your visual may be a PowerPoint presentation, an enlarged photograph of the scene, a chart illustrating the burden of proof, or a scene diagram or photographs of a guardrail and damaged car as in the following example transcript. It could be a chart setting out the applicable law. For instance, in *Etheridge v. State*,[19] the trial court was held to have not abused its discretion when it allowed the prosecution to utilize a chart when exploring death penalty issues with the prospective jurors. On the other hand, appellate courts have held that it was not an abuse of discretion for a trial court to prevent defense counsel from displaying gruesome photographs during voir dire.[20]

If you plan to use visuals during jury selection, see if opposing counsel will stipulate to their use. If counsel won't stipulate, make a motion to use it or otherwise raise the issue with the judge. Generally, it is a good idea to gain the court's approval before showing them.

Visuals Example 1: In *United States v. Trinity Industries, Inc.* (pages 169–171), an action brought under the False Claims Act, plaintiff's counsel, during jury selection had pictures of a guardrail followed by a picture of a damaged car projected on a screen in the courtroom for the jurors to see during his preliminary remarks.

> MR. BAXTER: Okay. Now, the Judge has told us that we can give a very brief summary of what this lawsuit is about, and so I want to endeavor to do that in under three minutes. But here's what it's about.
>
> My client, Joshua Harman, has been working on the highway since he was 18 years of age, and he had a company that installed guardrails.
>
> And let me see a guardrail. Can I get on the—Ms. Schroeder, can I get that on for Mr. Diaz? Thank you, ma'am.
>
> We've got Plaintiff—maybe if you hit that button. There we go.
>
> And he installed guardrails like this all over the United States but primarily in Virginia and the Atlantic Seaboard. This happens to be the product that you're going to hear a lot about. And it is a terminal head on the end of a guardrail, and you're going to hear how that works. But suffice it to say, he's installed these. And as he's installing

---

19. *Etheridge v. State*, 903 S.W.2d 1, 8 (Tex. Crim. App. 1995).

20. *People v. Whisenhunt*, 186 P.3d 496, 513–14 (Cal. 2008); *Commonwealth v. Keohane*, 444 Mass. 563, 829 N.E.2d 1125 (2005).

these, he realizes that something has gone awry, because he starts seeing all over the highways and hears reports about accidents involving these guardrails that are horrific accidents.

And let me see if I can see one of the cars. Accidents like this where the guardrail, after the car hits it and the device that's supposed to protect the car from either hitting another obstacle or hitting going down the ditch or going down into the river, is actually being harpooned by the guardrail, much to the consternation, obviously, of anybody in that car.

And he starts seeing accidents like this all over America, and he conducts his own investigation—

MR. MANN: Your Honor, I'm going to object to that statement as totally outside of any evidence in this case about all over the country. I object to that. That's outside the evidence and not appropriate and certainly prejudicial by saying that.

THE COURT: All right. Well, your objection is overruled.

Let's proceed.

MR. BAXTER: Thank you, Your Honor.

THE COURT: Stay within your time, Mr. Baxter.

MR. BAXTER: Yes, Your Honor.

He then conducts his own investigation, and he realizes that the product that we saw before has not been approved by the federal government, and it has defects. And as a result of that, he has become what is known as a whistleblower. This is a whistleblower case, and it's part of the False Claims Act that encourages people that has information about companies that are defrauding the United States of America to come forward and to blow the whistle, and that's exactly what he's done in this case. And that's the sort of evidence you're going to hear over the next week or so.

Now—I'm through with that, Your Honor. Thank you.

THE COURT: Let's move along.

MR. BAXTER: Thank you.[21]

Visuals Example 2: Another example comes from a patent case in which defense counsel employed paperclips and Wi-Fi chips to grab the jurors' attention, pose an analogy, and simplify and explain the case.

---

21. Transcript of Proceedings at 52–54, *United States v. Trinity Indus., Inc.*, No. 2:12CV89-JRG E.D. (Tex. Oct. 13, 2014), App. 8.2.

MR. JONES: ... Now, with regard to patents, Mr. Cawley (plaintiff's counsel) talked about patents. I don't know, but I've been told that the first patent on this paperclip was in about 1896.

Can y'all see the paperclip? Everybody's familiar with a paperclip. And it puts paper together. I've also been told that there are at least 200, if not more, patents concerning paperclips after the one in 1896 that does this.

And the reason for that is pretty simple. This paperclip concerns one way to clip paper. But if you clip paper using another way, such as this clip (indicating), then that's a different patent and different patents issued.

Now, the principle is this, and I think it's a principle of patent law, and that is that you don't have a patent on clipping paper; you have a patent on a particular way to clip paper.

In this case, Ericsson claims that its patents concern a specific way to transfer data using Wi-Fi. They don't claim to have invented Wi-Fi, but they claim to have invented a certain narrow way to transmit data over Wi-Fi.

Now, these products of these Defendants, they transmit data over Wi-Fi, but they do it in a different way.

Does anybody think that just because we transmit data over Wi-Fi, that we must infringe these patents? Anybody think that? Anybody think that should be the case? Anybody at all?

Thank you.

Now, these—this particular case is going to concern Wi-Fi chips. And these are Wi-Fi chips right here (indicating) I'm holding in my hand, if you can see them.

And these Wi-Fi chips are made by Intel.

This Wi-Fi chip right here is the crane peak chip. You can buy it for about $2.50.

This particular Wi-Fi chip is made by Intel. It's the Taylor peak chip. It has different features. You can buy it for about $8.79.

Now, these whole things—you see the whole green thing I'm holding up? They're referred to as Wi-Fi cards or Wi-Fi chipsets. And the little black things you see in the middle of them, those are the actual chips.

Can everybody see that?

And there are different versions of these Wi-Fi cards, and this is the base version, and it costs about $2.50 right now. I think that the average price, when this lawsuit was filed, for all Wi-Fi chips across the industry in 2010 when this case was filed was about $2.41.

My question to you is: Before today, before I pointed these out to you, did anybody have any knowledge of Wi-Fi chips? Anybody? Had anybody ever seen these chips before?

Before I talked about it, did anybody know anything about the price of these chips?

Thank you.

Now, going back to my paperclip analogy, the contention of Ericsson is that for these products, such as the laptops like you see over here and routers, when they have these Wi-Fi chips, that they infringe these patents because they do data transmitting their particular way as set forth in their patents. In fact, the evidence is going to show you that we do data transmitting in a different way.

Does anybody have any knowledge, prior to today, about how data is transmitted wirelessly? Anybody know anything about that?

Yes, sir. And that's Mr. Henry, right?

JUROR HENRY: Yes, sir.

MR. JONES: And what knowledge do you have of that, sir?

JUROR HENRY: Not a lot, but I do some work in the secure transmission of data across wireless.

MR. JONES: Thank you, sir.

In doing that, have you ever purchased any of these Wi-Fi chips individually?

JUROR HENRY: No.[22]

Visuals Example 3: Plaintiff's counsel in *Retractable Technologies, Inc. v. Becton, Dickinson and Company* utilized a shot needle, shown with the aid of a document camera, during voir dire to advance his case narrative. (See pages 160–164.)

---

22. Transcript of Proceedings at 70–74, *Ericson, Inc. v. D-Link Corp., et al.*, 6:10cv473E.D. (Tex. June 3, 2013), App. 7.1.

Chapter 12

Case Weaknesses & Misconceptions

> *"You got to accentuate the positive,*
> *Eliminate the negative,*
> *And latch on to the affirmative.*
> *Don't mess with Mr. In Between."*

> Johnny Mercer

> *"Even though our study did not reveal a so-called 'CSI effect' at play in courtrooms, my fellow researchers and I believe that a broader 'tech effect' exists that influences juror expectations and demands."*

> Hon. Donald E. Shelton, Judge,
> *Michigan NIJ Journal* No. 259, March 2008

A. Case Weaknesses and Misconceptions

Every case has its weaknesses. It could be sympathy for the other side, a prior bad act of a chief witness, a community attitude that disfavors the client, or some other defect. In Chapter 9 at pages 187–188 we described the brainstorming exercise that can be utilized to identify your case weaknesses. Here we are concerned neither with a vulnerable aspect of the case that can be removed with a motion in limine to preclude the other side from offering the damaging evidence or mentioning it nor with a minor weakness that it will backfire on the other side if they try to exploit it. Rather, we are focusing on other weaknesses that the jury is bound to learn about either from you or your opponent.

The jury will be charged with the responsibilities of evaluating and weighing the evidence or lack of evidence. Therefore, it is axiomatic that your story should be supported by credible witnesses and exhibits. Beyond that, the jurors must accept your case story as a credible one. If the story is one that comports with what jurors understand to be common, real life experience, then it probably will be viewed as believable. However, if your evidence runs contrary to the common understanding of how the world operates or is outside the realm of what jurors have experienced, you will need to educate them during the trial. For example, some prospective jurors may have the preconceived notion that sexual assault victims make an immediate outcry that they have been assaulted. However, the evidence may show that the victim did not make an immediate outcry. To educate the jurors, a prosecutor may call an expert to disabuse those jurors of that misconception. Also, your evidence may contradict preconceptions that the jurors bring with them to the courtroom. For example, they may believe that doctors can do no wrong or that corporations can do nothing right. In this chapter we offer strategies and techniques for dealing with case weaknesses and misconceptions during voir dire in order to ensure that the jurors are willing to fairly and impartially consider and weigh your evidence and find it credible.

B. Case Weaknesses

1. Embracing Case Weaknesses

When the jurors will inevitably learn about your case weakness during the trial, it is critical that you take the initiative to reveal it to the jurors. If you do not, you increase the damage, because the jury will learn of the defect from your opponent, and it will appear that you concealed it.

When is the best time to raise a weakness? The answer is: During jury selection. This is the earliest opportunity to reveal the problem, and if you do it during jury selection, you may preempt the other side from revealing it first. Also, by bringing the matter up first, you inoculate the panel against being infected by a claim that your case is weak.

There are at least four advantages to be gained by disclosing your case weaknesses to the jury. First, it shows that you are candid about defects in your case and willing to concede them. This candor can build your credibility in the minds of the jurors. Second, you can couch the weakness in the best light possible. Third, through your apparent confidence when you disclose the weakness, you can convey the idea that when your case is inspected from all vantage points, including a critical one looking for vulnerabilities, it is still a strong case. Fourth, and perhaps most important in jury selection, when you question the prospective jurors about your case weaknesses, you may be able to identify those who will not be able to move beyond the problem and give your client a fair trial, and, thus, enable you to deselect them.

We have previously discussed the concern about tainting the pool. (See pages 152–153.) This common concern is born out of the belief that discussing one of your case weaknesses in jury selection primes jurors to focus on those weaknesses or potentially convinces some to view your case as weak when they otherwise would not have done so. As previously noted, there is simply no evidence to support this tainting the pool effect. Few jurors remember jury selection by the time they reach the deliberation room, because they have been overwhelmed with all sorts of complex information and confusing processes over the course of trial. Most important though is the fact that jurors have two opportunities to talk about your case weaknesses: (1) in voir dire when you can do something about it by exercising a challenge for cause or peremptory challenge or (2) in jury deliberations when there is nothing you can do it about it. Obviously, it is best to get jurors talking about these weaknesses when you can do something about it. Not only will this exercise help you identify candidates for peremptory strikes, but also it will help you understand how your jury panel thinks about key weaknesses in your case, which allows you to make important strategic adjustments in the opening statement and throughout trial.

It is critical to understand that you should not avoid a topic just because it poses a weakness. This creates a situation where you are failing to learn important information about your jurors. It may turn out that only two prospective jurors are strongly moved by your case weakness, but if you fail to ask, you will never discover those two and they may make it onto the jury, where they can wreak havoc during jury deliberations.

2. Questioning about Weaknesses

To frame questions about your case weakness, plan to be candid with the prospective jurors. However, you can put the weakness in its best light and the context of the case. Keep in mind that you considered this weakness in evaluating your case and concluded that, despite it, you deserve to prevail. After prefacing your question to prospective jurors with the disclosure of the problem, ask for their views. Follow up your initial questions, which reveal a negative, with questions about whether knowing that weakness, they could give your client a fair trial. Your goal is to get them committed to setting aside their biases and giving your client a fair trial based on the evidence and the law.

Questioning About Weakness Example: In *In re TFT-LCD (Flat-Panel)*, defendant HannStar had a major case weakness. HannStar had pled guilty to participating in the price-fixing meetings that were at the heart of the plaintiff's case. Counsel for HannStar frankly conceded the weakness and then attempted to shift the potential jurors' focus to damages. Questioning went as follows:

> MR. FREITAS: Mr. Silberfeld (plaintiff's counsel) made reference to a conspiracy that he described as lasting for eight years. Now, the evidence about the plea and the evidence about the activities by HannStar won't necessarily match up with that.
>
> Do you think if you are chosen for the jury you could keep separate what it was that was established by the plea regarding the timing and the nature of the activities, and anything else that Best Buy might try to prove regarding HannStar, or any other company?
>
> PROSPECTIVE JUROR LASH: Yes, I can.
>
> MR. FREITAS: Can you think of any reason why it would be difficult for you to do that?
>
> PROSPECTIVE JUROR LASH: No, I can't.
>
> MR. FREITAS: Ms. Hanson, sorry for moving around.
>
> PROSPECTIVE JUROR HANSON: Yes.
>
> MR. FREITAS: What was your reaction that HannStar was in a government case and accepted responsibility for participating in a crystal meeting where price was discussed, and sometimes agreed?
>
> PROSPECTIVE JUROR HANSON: It felt like a separate issue, wouldn't be regarded in this case.
>
> MR. FREITAS: All right. That is not something that would interfere with your ability to listen to Judge Illston's instructions, follow the law as she gives it to you?
>
> PROSPECTIVE JUROR HANSON: No.
>
> MR. FREITAS: Ms. Volpe, please. As the case goes forward, if you are on the jury, you will hear the Court provide instructions on the issues surrounding—well on all of the legal issues, specifically including what the government case established, what it means, and what it doesn't mean.
>
> Can you think of any reason why you would have a hard time following the Court's instructions, and deciding the case based on what the Court tells you the law is, and the facts as you find them?
>
> PROSPECTIVE JUROR VOLPE: No, I can't think of any reason I would have a hard time doing that.

MR. FREITAS: I think you mentioned that you have a relative who works at All-American—or was that Ms. Hanson? Is that—

PROSPECTIVE JUROR VOLPE: My son works at All-American Fence Company.

MR. FREITAS: All-American what, excuse me?

PROSPECTIVE JUROR VOLPE: Fence, Fence.

MR. FREITAS: Fence. Okay. I didn't get the full name. Thank you.

Ms. Irwin, please, Ms. Irwin, do you think that it's fair that after having participated in the government case and having accepted responsibility for participating in the crystal meetings, that HannStar has the right to come into this trial and challenge what Best Buy says about the harm that it supposedly suffered?

PROSPECTIVE JUROR ERWIN: Yeah, sure.

MR. FREITAS: There's no reason why you think we should lose the right to do that, simply because of what took place in the government case.

PROSPECTIVE JUROR ERWIN: No.

MR. FREITAS: Ms. Linkhorn, is there anything that you've heard about the case or specifically about HannStar that makes you doubt that you could be fair to HannStar and all of the other parties?

PROSPECTIVE JUROR LINKHORN: Not at all.

MR. FREITAS: No reason that you couldn't give us a clean slate, a fair start, on all of the issues that haven't been resolved by our participation in the government case.

PROSPECTIVE JUROR LINKHORN: No. No.

MR. FREITAS: Thank you. Mr. Sangal?

PROSPECTIVE JUROR SANGAL: Yeah.[1]

You can also use the forced-choice question style previously discussed in Chapter 8. This question format throws out both the weakness and the strength and then asks who tends to gravitate towards the weakness. For example, consider a product liability case where there is evidence that your corporate defendant rushed a product to market without adequate safety testing. An example of a forced-choice question for this issue might be as follows: "I know some people who would say that most companies try to put out safe products because the people at those companies who make those products have friends and family members who rely on those products being

---

1. Transcript of Proceedings at 73–74, *In re TFT-LCD (Flat-Panel)*, No. 07-MDL-1827 SI, 10-CV-4572, 10-CV-5452, 10-CV-4114 (N.D. Cal. July 22, 2013), App. 1.1.

safe. I know other people who would disagree and argue that most companies rush products to market without conducting adequate safety testing. By a show of hands, how many of you are more like that latter group and would argue that most companies rush products to market without conducting adequate safety testing?"

This question accomplishes a few things. First, it throws out two reasonable but opposing beliefs, and does so without suggesting one belief is right or wrong. This is an important balance to strike, because you want jurors to give open and honest answers rather than giving answers they think you want to hear or answers that seem more socially acceptable. Second, by throwing out two reasonable sides to the same issue, this question allows the attorney to address a key weakness without bringing undue attention to it. In other words, the presence of the counterargument helps create a more balanced sense of the issue. Finally, this question focuses on identifying those who are more likely to hold beliefs that are going to lead them to focus more on your particular case weaknesses.

C. Misconceptions

The media has shaped the thinking of some prospective jurors about how trials are conducted and how participants in the justice system behave. For instance, the *CSI* television series created the expectation, referred to as the "CSI effect," that forensic evidence recovered from the crime scene could be rapidly analyzed and provide conclusive proof.

It is incumbent upon counsel to identify current events, cultural beliefs, and other factors that may have caused jurors to bring particular biases into the courtroom. It is highly unlikely that counsel can disabuse potential jurors of their expectations and beliefs formed by outside sources. However, counsel can raise them in jury selection and distinguish what the juror believes from what will be learned during the trial and should be considered in deliberations.

In the remainder of this chapter, we focus on some common misconceptions that need to be addressed during jury selection. The strategies and techniques that are explained can be applied to other preconceived notions that prospective jurors may have in your cases. Also, the examples of patterns of jury-selection questions that are from actual jury-selection transcripts may be modified for your case.

D. The Law

1. Disagreement with a Particular Law

Some prospective jurors come to court with adamant biases against particular laws, and other jurors come with misconceptions about what the law is or with merely feelings that are not in harmony with the law. The death penalty is an example of the first type of disagreement with the law where some potential jurors irreversibly oppose it. We have discussed death qualification of jurors in capital cases where opposition to the death penalty law can result in exclusion from jury service at pages 59–61.

The second type of opposition to a law involves a situation where a juror has feelings that run contrary to the law but not so obstinately that they cannot be set aside. The techniques for overcoming this second type of bias are illustrated by the following example.

Anti-Law Example: *People v. Edwards* was a murder trial. The defendant Allen Edwards claimed he acted in self-defense in a street fight, and the prosecution's case theory was that the defendant exercised excessive force. The prosecutor was faced with a juror who thought that street fights had no rules, and her questions to the juror were designed to let the juror know that the law was different from the juror's understanding of it and to gain a commitment from that jury and the panel to follow the court's instruction on excessive force. Once having gained the juror's assurance, the prosecutor could refer back to it in closing argument: "You will recall during jury selection when we discussed excessive force and you all assured us you would follow the court's instructions on self-defense, which does not allow excessive force."

> MS. CHON (Prosecutor): Do you think—Do you have any personal feelings regarding street fights and what is allowed or isn't allowed or shouldn't be allowed?
>
> PROSPECTIVE JUROR SEAT NO. 11: Well, I think there has to be a limit, there has to be a point where it stops.
>
> MS. CHON: And Juror No. 12.
>
> PROSPECTIVE JUROR SEAT NO. 12: In a street fight, I don't see no rules.
>
> MS. CHON: If the court told you and gave you a definition for what is excessive force and asked you to apply it to the evidence that's been presented, do you think you can do that, or do you think because you believe that street fights, there are no rules, that you can't follow the judge's directions?

PROSPECTIVE JUROR SEAT NO. 12: I follow the rules.

MS. CHON: Okay.

So you'll put your personal feelings aside?

PROSPECTIVE JUROR SEAT NO. 12: Yes.

MS. CHON: And does anyone disagree with that, does anyone here sitting, 1 through 18, think they can't put away their personal feelings and apply the law as the court directs you to do so, does anyone have a problem with that?

And, I see no show of hands.

Thank you.[2]

2. Burden of Proof

a. Criminal Cases

High on the list of misconceptions that some jurors bring to a criminal trial are those regarding the burden of proof and the defendant's right to remain silent. They can confuse the burden of proof in a criminal case with that in a civil case. Some erroneously believe that it is the defendant's obligation to prove that a reasonable doubt exists rather than the prosecution's burden to prove the allegations beyond a reasonable doubt. Also, despite books, television and movies portraying the defendant being told that he has a Fifth Amendment right to remain silent, some jurors still believe that the defendant should testify and that if he doesn't, they can hold it against him.

Criminal Case Example: In *People v. Harmon*, after defense counsel discussed the fact that the defendant is to be presumed innocent, he, with the court's assistance, moved on to discuss the jurors' obligation to acquit if the prosecution failed to prove an element of the crime even if the defendant never testified.

MR. WILLIAMS: ... Does anybody else feel like that? Anybody disagree with that?

Juror No. 6, you disagree with that?

PROSPECTIVE JUROR NO. 6: He doesn't have to say a word.

MR. WILLIAMS: And why is that?

PROSPECTIVE JUROR NO. 6: Because the burden of proof is on the prosecution.

---

2. Transcript of Proceedings at 102–03, *People v. Edwards*, No. BA305749 (Cal. 2007), App. 12.1.

MR. WILLIAMS: And so you would be—you would be able to decide this case and hold the prosecution to their burden even if you didn't hear from Mr. Harmon?

PROSPECTIVE JUROR NO. 6: Yes.

MR. WILLIAMS: And what about you, Juror No. 4? You were shaking your head.

PROSPECTIVE JUROR NO. 4: I'm in agreement with that. I do have one question. Am I allowed to ask a question? How do you define beyond a reasonable doubt?

THE COURT: You'll get an instruction.

PROSPECTIVE JUROR NO. 4: I will?

MR. WILLIAMS: You'll get that instruction. You'll definitely hear a lot more about that from both sides and the judge.

So in this case, Juror No. 16, If Mr. Harmon wouldn't say, testify in this case, would you hold that against the defense or would you have a hard time even if they haven't met their burden finding Mr. Harmon not guilty? Do you think you could do that?

PROSPECTIVE JUROR NO. 16: I couldn't tell you unless I went through it and heard all the evidence.

MR. WILLIAMS: But I'm saying, hearing all the evidence, they haven't met that one element.

THE COURT: I think MR. WILLIAMS is saying that you've evaluated the case and you're saying to yourself, the People have not proven the case beyond a reasonable doubt. That's the hypothetical.

PROSPECTIVE JUROR NO. 16: Then it would be not guilty.[3]

Although the defense attorney in this example discussed the fact that the defendant may not testify, note that no mention was made of the defendant's right to remain silent. The prosecutor must avoid discussing this topic, because the defendant has sole discretion over whether to testify at trial, and the prosecutor commits error by commenting on the defendant remaining silent.[4]

The prosecution and defense may also explore the jurors' attitudes about the burden of proof. For example, there are many people who believe the standard for convicting criminals, particularly those accused of sexual or violent crimes, should be lower than it actually is. These individuals tend to believe that too many criminals walk due to technicalities. It is important for criminal

---

3. Transcript of Proceedings 130–31, *People v. Harmon*, 2007 WL 5181456, 131–32 (2007), App. 3.2.

4. *Griffin v. California*, 380 U.S. 609 (1965); *Harris v. New York*, 401 U.S. 222 (1971).

defense attorneys to probe for these beliefs about the burden of proof because they may influence the way prospective jurors perceive the evidence and testimony in the case. For example, prospective jurors who hold these beliefs may just adopt a lower bar for what constitutes proof beyond a reasonable doubt.

To a lesser extent, beliefs about the burden of proof may negatively impact the prosecution's case. For example, some prospective jurors may need proof beyond all doubt in order to convict. While jurors certainly do not determine the sentence and in their deliberations they are not to consider the fact that punishment may follow conviction except insofar as it may make them careful, they are certainly aware of the gravity of their decision-making. Consequently, these prospective jurors may be entirely dismissive of circumstantial evidence because they believe it is too ambiguous and does not reach their proof-to-a-certainty threshold.

b. Civil Cases

In civil cases also, counsel will want to explore whether the jurors can follow the law on the burden of proof to be applied, and the plaintiff's counsel will want to disabuse the jurors of any preconception that the burden is the same as in a criminal case. Also, plaintiff's counsel may want to make sure that the magnitude of the case, such as the high dollar award sought in the next example, will not cause the jurors to heighten the burden.

The defense may also want to address jurors' beliefs about the burden of proof in civil cases. For example, one of the most common ways in which confusion over the burden of proof can be harmful to the defense is when jurors conflate this burden on negligence and proximate cause. In other words, some jurors fail to appreciate that the plaintiff has an independent burden to prove negligence and then a separate, independent burden to prove that such negligence was the cause of damage to the plaintiff. These jurors often assume that proving negligence is the same as proving causation, which removes significant hurdles for the plaintiff.

Defense attorneys may also want to discuss how the defendant's status may influence jurors' beliefs about the applicable burden of proof. Some prospective jurors may have such strong reactions to the idea of corporate misconduct that they functionally hold the plaintiff to a lower burden of proof. It is important for defense attorneys to learn whether or not they hold these beliefs during jury selection.

Finally, defense attorneys may want to address an issue that often arises when plaintiff's attorneys raise the issue of burden of proof in voir dire. It is common for plaintiff attorneys to describe the preponderance of evidence at just having to prove the case 51%, just one percent more than an even 50/50. The problem is that this can often get conflated with other comments that the plaintiff and defense start off even. Ultimately, this can leave some jurors believing that the plaintiff and defendant start off at 50/50, and the plaintiff only needs to get to 51 percent. Instead, the defense should make it clear to jurors that, using this analogy of percentages, the plaintiff starts off at zero and needs to get to 51.

Instructing the jury on the law is the court's prerogative. Therefore, if you ask the prospective jurors what their understanding is of "a preponderance of evidence" or if a juror inquires about its meaning, as happened in the last example, it is likely that the judge will intervene and tell the jury panel that they will receive an instruction that defines the phrase, which the judge did in the last example. Alternatively, the judge then and there may instruct the jury panel on the burden.

If you are considering having a discussion with the prospective jurors about the burden of proof, find out in advance what your judge permits. Determine whether the judge will define the burden for the jury panel before you ask questions and how far, if at all, you can go in questioning them about the burden, because you do not want the judge to interrupt you. Also, make sure you do not misstate the law, because that is likely also to result in the judge's intervention even without an objection by opposing counsel.

The judge may preempt any attempt the lawyers may make to either define the burden or try to get the prospective jurors to provide their understanding of the burden by giving the jury panel a brief explanation of the burden or reading the jury instruction before attorneys begin their questioning. That is what was done in the following example.

Court's Explanation of the Burden Example: Before you get your opportunity to talk to the jury about the burden of proof, the judge may have already done so. For example, in *Simpleair, Inc. v. Google*, a patent infringement trial only on damages, Judge Rodney Gilstrap explained the burden of proof in his introductory remarks to the jury.

> COURT: One thing that I want to call your attention to, ladies and gentlemen, is about the question regarding the burden of proof that will be applied in this case, because this is a damages case in a patent suit. The jury that's chosen and selected to hear the evidence will be required to apply a burden of proof, which is called a preponderance of the evidence.
>
> When responding to the lawyers' questions about the burden of proof, I need to instruct you that the party who has the burden of

proof on any claim or affirmative defense by a preponderance of the evidence means that the jury must be persuaded by the credible and believable evidence that the claim or defense is more probably true than not true. I'll say that again. More probably true than not true.

Sometimes this is talked about as being the greater weight and degree of credible testimony. Let me give you an illustration in this regard.

I think all of you can see the statue to my left, of the goddess of justice, Lady Justicia, she's called. You'll notice that she holds the sword of justice in her right hand. You'll notice that she's blindfolded, and you'll notice that in her left hand she holds the raised scales of justice.

I call your attention to the fact that those scales are exactly balanced, exactly equal. And you should consider that during the trial of this case, the jury selected, as you hear the evidence, that evidence will be placed on those scales of justice. And when the evidence is complete and the jury is asked to answer the questions in the verdict form, you will consider whether the party who has the burden of proof has met that burden of proof by a preponderance of the evidence.

And you can simply think about placing all the evidence on those scales of justice. And if, after all the evidence is placed on those balanced scales, if those scales tip in favor of the party who has the burden of proof by a preponderance of the evidence, even if they tip ever so slightly, that party has met the burden of proof by a preponderance of the evidence.

Now, none of this is to be confused with what you probably have heard about on TV and in the media called the burden of proof of beyond a reasonable doubt. That's a burden of proof that applies in a criminal case. It has absolutely no application in a civil case such as this one. I give you these instructions because it is possible that during the questioning, some of the lawyers may ask the panel if they are able and willing to apply the burden of proof in this case fairly, and that burden of proof is by a preponderance of the evidence.[5]

Plaintiff Explanation of the Burden Example: When the judge has provided the jurors with an explanation of the preponderance-of-evidence burden of proof and differentiated it from the burden in criminal cases, you can reference the judge's remarks and adapt your questions to the situation. That is what

5. Transcript of Proceedings at 23–25, *Simpleair, Inc. v. Google*, No. 2:13cv587 (E.D. Tex. 2014), App. 7.3.

plaintiff's counsel did in the *Simpleair, Inc. v. Google* case that was used in the previous example, as follows:

> MS. DERIEUX: All right. The Judge talked to you briefly about the burden of proof, and you'll recall that he told you that the burden of proof—and we use the example of the lady of justice with the scales being even—and the preponderance of the evidence, which is the burden of proof that SimpleAir has to meet in this case.
>
> If it's one tiny bit one way or the other is—what we perhaps call it a peppercorn—just a little bit heavier on one side, SimpleAir has met its burden of proof. Ms. Horace, I just need you to talk to me.
>
> JUROR HORACE: Yes, ma'am.
>
> MS. DERIEUX: On the burden of proof, do you believe that you understand the burden of proof as it's been explained, and do you believe that you can follow those instructions from the Judge?
>
> JUROR HORACE: I believe so.
>
> THE COURT: Hold that microphone a little closer, Ms. Horace, please.
>
> JUROR HORACE: I believe so. Yes, ma'am.
>
> MS. DERIEUX: Well, let me just ask you. Do you believe that a company bringing a really big lawsuit—and I will tell you that there will be over a million dollars at issue in this lawsuit—do you believe that that changes your attitude toward the burden of proof and you can still follow the Judge's instruction regarding the preponderance of the evidence burden of proof?
>
> JUROR HORACE: Yes, ma'am. I believe I—I would. I don't think the monetary figure would make a difference.
>
> MS. DERIEUX: All right. Anybody disagree with Ms. Horace?[6]

Defense Explanation of the Burden Example: Defense counsel will want to make sure that the jurors understand the burden of proof and are willing to follow the law, holding the plaintiff to meeting the burden. In the *Simpleair, Inc. v. Google* case, defense counsel also referenced the judge's remarks, and asked whether they understood it and whether they would hold plaintiff to that requirement for the proof of damages even though the plaintiff had already proven a patent infringement.

> MS. AINSWORTH: The—Judge Gilstrap mentioned to you the issue of burden of proof, and I think that you'll hear more about that

---

6. *Id.* at 52–53.

in the case, but as the Plaintiff, SimpleAir, they bear the burden of proof to show you by a preponderance of the evidence that they're entitled to a certain amount of damages that they're seeking. But because we have an unusual situation that there was already a finding of infringement, does any—does anybody feel like, well, you know, they met their burden of proof once on that issue, they shouldn't have to meet a burden of proof again in this case? Does anyone feel like that success in the first case just transfers over and they shouldn't have to prove something to you by a preponderance of the evidence? Nobody feels that way? Okay. Thank you.[7]

E. The Players

As we have stated, your case story is only as good as its sources. It must be told through what the jurors perceive to be credible players (attorneys, parties, witnesses) and exhibits. Ideally, your players would be flawless. However, in reality, for example, your story's protagonist may have a flaw or flaws, and your witnesses may likewise have some imperfections.

Additionally, when some of your potential jurors enter the courtroom, they bring with them biases for or against your players or the players on the other side of your case just based upon who the player is. For example, the juror may think that all large corporations are greedy or that all law enforcement officers are truthful witnesses or, as in *Brown v. Davis and Davis*, the wrongful death case discussed in Chapter 11, that truck drivers with wide loads are dangerous to others on the road.

You have at least two main goals when you question jurors about the players. First, you want to identify those jurors who harbor biases and whether they can set aside their bias and fairly decide the case. If they cannot, you may either be able to establish a challenge for cause or exercise a peremptory challenge. Second, you want to openly discuss any shortcomings your player has and precondition the prospective jurors to understand and not be antagonistic towards your player.

Here, we examine weaknesses and misconceptions against players in both civil and criminal cases. The suggested strategies and techniques for dealing with them can be applied to other weaknesses and misconceptions your players

---

7. *Id.* at 68.

may face in trial. Also, you can modify the patterns of questions in the example transcripts to your player's situation.

1. Bias For or Against a Player

Either the judge or counsel, following the court's directive, will identify for the prospective jurors the players in the trial—the lawyers, the clients and the witnesses that each side intends to call to testify—and ask whether any juror knows any of the them. If a juror indicates that she does, then the court will inquire about the connection and whether or not it will affect the juror's ability to serve as a fair and impartial juror. During your opportunity to address the jury, you want to follow up with questions about both the nature of the relationship and any potential favoritism or aversion towards either side that may exist because of a connection between the juror and a player. Certain connections between a prospective juror and a party, such as the prospective juror being a tenant of the plaintiff, may be grounds for a challenge for cause.

Bias Against a Player Example: In *United States v. Trinity Industries, Inc.*, a prosecution under the False Claims Act (see the earlier discussion of the case at pages 169–171) defense counsel inquired concerning whether members of the jury panel were acquainted with any of the plaintiff's 12 lawyers or members of their families. With each juror who was acquainted with a lawyer, counsel first learned about the connection and extent of the relationship and then got a commitment from the juror of a personal kind that the acquaintanceship with the plaintiff's lawyers would not interfere with their fair and impartial judgment. This technique can work with other players as well.

> MR. MANN: I need to know if you know any of these lawyers, and I'm going to name them—several of them. There's 12 of them that Mr. Harman has hired. And they are Sam Baxter, who spoke to you earlier; John Ward, who he mentioned; Kurt Truelove, who's from Marshall, and—okay. I'm going to let you raise your hands all at one time, and I'll take you each, okay? If that's okay? Is that all right?
>
> Kurt Truelove, Jennifer Truelove, Josh Maness, George Carpinello, Karen Dyer, Teresa Monroe, Nick Gravante, Steve Lawrence, Jeff Shelly, Wyatt Durrette.
>
> Now, and when I'm talking about them, I'm talking about people that you know work for them, their husbands or wives, their children, you know them, that's what I need to know. And can I go row by row? Did anybody know any of those lawyers on the first row?

Second row?

Yes, ma'am, Ms. Hagerty?

JUROR HAGERTY: I graduated with Kurt Truelove.

MR. MANN: Okay. And do I need to be concerned—does my client need to be concerned about that?

JUROR HAGERTY: No.

MR. MANN: Can we start out even—

JUROR HAGERTY: Yeah.

MR. MANN:—in this case? And do you socialize with him still, or you were classmates?

JUROR HAGERTY: No. We were classmates. We're friends on Facebook.

MR. MANN: Okay. All right. And—and so I don't—my client doesn't need to be concerned about that?

JUROR HAGERTY: No.

MR. MANN: All right. Thank you very much, Ms. Hagerty.

Anybody else know any of those lawyers?

Let's call it third row, this front row here, anybody know those lawyers?

Fourth row, starting with Mr. Toon?

JUROR TOON: Yes. I think Sam was the DA when I first went to work over at the Sheriff's Department and Jennifer, Josh—

MR. MANN: Okay.

JUROR TOON:—from over there.

MR. MANN: All right. So you know the drill. I'm going to ask you, can I—can I tell my client you're going to be fair—

JUROR TOON: Yes.

MR. MANN:—and do you believe you can be fair? Are there other cases you think it would be better that you'd be on, or you're fine with what you're hearing in this case?

JUROR TOON: I'm fine.

MR. MANN: All right. Thank you, Mr. Toon. Anybody else on that row?

All right. Mr. Morgan's row? Anybody on that row with Mr. Morgan?

Next row, Mr. Lewis, your—your row? Anybody on that row?

Next row, Ms. Parker's row?

And, yes, sir, we got to you.

Mr. Warren's row?

JUROR CLYNCH: I know the Trueloves.

MR. MANN: Okay. Mr. Clynch, should that be a concern that we have that we would start off behind them? Are you close enough with them where you go, hey, I don't know you, Mark Mann, and I know them and so I—I put more credence in what they say than what you would say?

JUROR CLYNCH: No, sir.

MR. MANN: Okay. So, again, I can tell my client that everything's fine, that you can be fair and impartial and we start off even?

JUROR CLYNCH: Sure.

MR. MANN: Thank you. Thank you, Mr. Clynch.[8]

2. Bias against Corporations

As a result of media coverage, movies such as *Wall Street*, personal experience, and other influences, some potential jurors hold a belief that large corporations are innately bad. The technique for addressing a bias against a corporate client is to readily acknowledge that the bias exists and seek a commitment from the jurors that they will not be swayed by it. This same approach can be used when the jurors potentially may have a bias against your client for whatever reason.

Plaintiff's Anti-Corporation Questioning Example 1: In *In re TFT-LCD (Flat-Panel)*, plaintiff's counsel dealt with the anti-corporate bias concern as follows:

MR. SILBERFELD: In your questionnaire, you were asked the question: Do you have any opinions about large corporations? And you said you have a negative opinion, that the corporate mentality is not conducive for what I consider good business, anyplace that has a boss or a boss or a boss or a boss is not a place to work for.

Do you remember that?

PROSPECTIVE JUROR ITO: I think a (sic) wrote a boss of a boss of a boss of a boss.

MR. SILBERFELD: Oh, yeah. Four bosses.

PROSPECTIVE JUROR ITO: Probably more than that. And those comments are based on my company being purchased by a corporation, and you get stuck with a structure where you have

---

8. Transcript of Proceedings at 102–05, *United States v. Trinity Indus., Inc.*, No. 2:12CV89-JRG E.D. (Tex. Oct. 13, 2014), App. 8.2.

multiple bosses, they don't know what you do. They don't seem to contribute anything to the end product. Yet they sort of have control over your life.

MR. SILBERFELD: So here we have three large firms involved in this case. Anything about that experience or your views about large corporations that causes you to either lean for or lean against any of the three parties here?

PROSPECTIVE JUROR ITO: I think this is separate.

MR. SILBERFELD: Okay. So you can take that experience, put it on the shelf for the duration of this case, and judge this case just on its facts here?

PROSPECTIVE JUROR ITO: Yes, I can.

MR. SILBERFELD: Okay. Wonderful. Thank you so much.[9]

In this example, the plaintiff did not learn any particularly helpful information about the juror. In fact, one might argue that this line of questioning exposed a potentially good juror for the plaintiff, highlighting for the defense where it might want to prioritize its strikes. However, one benefit to this line of questioning is that the plaintiff has gotten the juror to essentially say that she can be fair and impartial and set that personal experience aside. This makes it more difficult for the defense to get this juror excused for cause based on this potentially troubling personal experience.

Defense Anti-Corporation Questioning Example 1: In *United States v. Trinity Industries, Inc.*, a prosecution under the False Claims Act (see the earlier discussion of the case at pages 169–171), defense counsel confronted the possible bias that the prospective jurors might have against the corporate defendant.

MR. MANN: … Anybody else? I don't want to leave anybody out. Okay. One thing I need to ask each one of you to—to search in your heart is—and one thing that concerns me any time when I would be here representing somebody that—representing a large company that makes lots of money, okay? I need to know if you believe because this is a large company that makes lots of money, that they—you could not let them start out even with Mr. Harman who seeks lots of money.

Anybody have that feeling? You just say, look, you know, if it's a close call and I really kind of—it's kind of on the fence, I—I think I'll go with them instead of your company because it's a large company

---

9. Transcript of Proceedings at 68–69, *In re TFT-LCD (Flat-Panel)*, No. 07-MDL-1827 SI, 10-CV-4572, 10-CV-5452, 10-CV-4114 (N.D. Cal. July 22, 2013), App. 1.1.

and they've got lots of money and they can take care of this? Anybody have that feeling? And I'm not asking you in a cynical way at all. I—I really do want to know that if that's truly what you believe. Anybody? I see no hands.

So when I go talk to the president of the company during this trial, I can say that each one of you feels in your heart that you can be fair and impartial and you're not going to hold it against them? You're going to do like this Scale of Justice and have blinders on and say I'm just listening to the evidence? Is that true? Raise your hand if that's true. Give—give me an affirmative answer.

Thank you. I appreciate that.[10]

Plaintiff's Anti-Corporation Questioning Example 2: In *Costco Wholesale Corp. v. AU Optronics Corp.,* the antitrust example discussed at page 160, the plaintiff was not only a corporation but also a corporation that stood to gain from a jury award when none of its members would receive any of the awarded damages. Here's how plaintiff's counsel candidly faced the compound problem.

MR. BURMAN: ... First, I'm going to try to divide things into a couple of categories in many of these questions. The first one is whether your view of Costco, whether it's good or bad, whether you are a member or not a member, would cause you to ignore evidence presented by Costco, or presented by the defendants, for that matter.

Is there anybody who feels that their view of Costco would cause them to have a bias that would affect their ability to treat all of the evidence in this case fairly? Okay. Thank you.

Is there anything about your experience with Costco, good or bad, or your membership, that would cause you to be more skeptical or more believing of either side's witnesses, whether it's the Costco witnesses or the defense witnesses?

Was there anything about your experience with Costco, your membership in Costco, that would cause you to ignore or not to apply the judge's instructions when it comes time for the judge to instruct you on what the law is and how to evaluate the evidence in the case?

Now, if your experience with Costco is positive—and, of course, representing Costco, I hope it was positive—would that affect in any way your ability to be fair to both sides? Is there anyone who feels that

---

10. Transcript of Proceedings at 98–99, *United States v. Trinity Indus., Inc.,* No. 2:12CV89-JRG E.D. (Tex. Oct. 13, 2014), App. 8.2.

my experience with Costco is so positive I couldn't be fair to the other side in this case?

Some of you are members. And in this case, you'll learn that Costco is claiming that it should recover damages, significant damages, tens of millions of dollars that it should recover, the corporation should recover.

We are not claiming we are here to represent members. We are not going to suggest that members will benefit from the lawsuit. It is Costco that is bringing this case. Is there anybody who is a member of Costco or even not a member who would feel resentful about that, about the fact that Costco is pursuing this in its own stead in this case, it's making its own claim for damages? Anybody who would feel uncomfortable about that?[11]

Defense Anti-Corporation Questioning Example 2: The defendant in the Costco case likewise had a compound problem; AU Optronics, referred to as "AUO," had a prior conviction. Defense counsel, like plaintiff's counsel, acknowledged the situation and sought the prospective jurors' views and a commitment.

MR. RUSSONIELLO: But AUO was found guilty of price-fixing. And for purposes of this case, AUO admits and acknowledges that wrongdoing. Is there anyone who is sitting here now who would not be able to differentiate between what the company did in terms of its conduct and whether or not Costco is entitled to recover any damages as a result of it? Is there anyone that wouldn't be able to make that separation in their mind? Because at this point, there hasn't been any bridge between those two.[12]

The key in eliciting bias against corporate defendants is to provide venire members with many opportunities to disclose such biases. There are a variety of factors that could prevent jurors from disclosing such bias based on a single question addressing it. Perhaps their corporate bias does not comport with the specific question that was asked in jury selection. For this reason, defense attorneys should tackle the issue of corporate bias from several different angles in order to give prospective jurors as many opportunities as possible to indicate whether or not they have such anti-corporate biases.

---

11. Transcript of Proceedings at 232–33, *Costco Wholesale Corp. v. AU Optronics Corp.*, No. cv13-1207RAJ (W.D. Wash. 2014), App. 8.1.

12. *Id.* at 263–64.

3. Bias against the Defendant in a Criminal Case

Defendants in criminal cases are faced with a number of preconceived notions that the average person holds about the defense and the production of evidence at trial. Among them is a belief that, contrary to the law's requirement that the defendant is presumed innocent because the defendant is charged with a crime, the defendant must have done something wrong. Other misconceptions are that the defendant has a burden of proof and that the defendant should testify. Defense counsel should seek to not only uncover who among the prospective jurors holds any or all of these beliefs but also then disabuse them of the beliefs.

The trial strategy to accomplish these aims is to bring the beliefs to the surface, candidly concede that the beliefs are commonly held, show that they run contrary to the law, and ultimately obtain a commitment from the jurors to follow the law. In doing so, it is critical to maintain a tone and style of communication that is nonjudgmental. While it is important to obtain a commitment from jurors to follow the law, it is perhaps more important to have an open and honest discussion with jurors about their feelings about the law and the issues in this case. Asking for a commitment to follow the law could be perceived as finger-wagging, judgment, or may simply call for prospective jurors to offer the socially acceptable response rather than provide candid insights about their views of the issues. For this reason, it is important that counsel not reduce their jury selection strategy to simply asking for commitments without having a fuller discussion about jurors' opinions of the issues at hand. At the top of the list of misconceptions in a criminal case is that the defendant must have done something or he would not be in court.

Presumption of Innocence Example: Defense counsel in *People v. Harmon*, the domestic violence case, brought to the surface of the discussion the view that, at the outset of the trial, several prospective jurors rather than presuming the defendant Harmon innocent concluded that he would not be in court if he had not done something wrong. In essence, the fact that he had been charged and was in court was evidence against the defendant.

> MR. WILLIAMS: Okay. How many people when you walked into the courtroom yesterday and looked at Mr. Harmon thought, that's the innocent guy? Anybody think that? No hands.
>
> Our system—how many of you thought, like juror no. 14, well, he's here, he must have done something? Okay. Jurors No. 1, 3, 12, and 11 and Juror No. 7—8. That's right, eight, I'm sorry.
>
> Our system requires you to—it's kind of counterintuitive because you think, well, the guy's here, he must have done something or he

wouldn't be here. That's kind of our natural thinking. We don't come in and think, oh, he's the innocent guy. But that's what the law and the court system require us to do.

You all should be sitting here looking at Mr. Harmon like that's the innocent guy until the People prove their case beyond a reasonable doubt, and it's kind of counterintuitive and it's kind of hard to do that, but that's what the law requires you to do.

Do you think you can do that?

PROSPECTIVE JUROR No. 14: I'll try.[13]

4. Problematic Witnesses

Witnesses often come with baggage. It may be as little as a minor prior inconsistent statement or it may be a prior bad act or conviction of a crime. It may simply be a personality defect that influences others' perceptions of the witness. Whatever suitcase your witness carries, you should open it and show the contents to the jurors and determine whether they can still decide the case fairly and impartially. The earlier you do this the better; jury selection is your earliest possible opportunity. If opposing counsel reveals the baggage first, not only will the baggage be a problem but also the appearance that you were concealing it could give it greater weight.

Problematic Witness Example: In the *In re TFT-LCD (Flat-Panel)* case, counsel who represented defendant HannStar talked to the jurors about witnesses who worked for a company that had pled guilty and entered into cooperation agreements as follows:

MR. FREITAS: All right, Your Honor.

There will be evidence that will be presented in the case that will come from some of the parties who attended the crystal meetings. And, they will talk about what they saw, what they heard. And some of—some of them work or worked for companies that have made cooperation agreements with the government, or with private parties.

What's your reaction to the idea that some of the witnesses who will be testifying are employed by companies that have cooperation settlement agreements with the government or with private parties?

PROSPECTIVE JUROR MOYA: Um, I don't think I have a reaction to it. I—I think that's—happens in the normal course of events.

---

13. Transcript of Proceedings at 118–19, *People v. Harmon*, 2007 WL 5181456, 131–32 (2007), App. 3.2.

MR. FREITAS: You would listen to what they had to say and decide whether it was accurate or not, and—

PROSPECTIVE JUROR MOYA: Certainly, based on the evidence presented and what they say, yes.[14]

In sum, the method for dealing with a problematic witness is to first candidly concede that the baggage exists and in the process make the point that that alone should not determine the outcome of the case. In the *Flat Panel* case, attorney Freitas had already told the jury panel in his preliminary remarks that the defendant HannStar had done nothing wrong.

This approach can be applied no matter who the witness is and what bag the witness carries. For instance, in a criminal case, the fact that the victim in a robbery case had a prior conviction should not in and of itself keep the jurors from convicting the defendant if there is proof beyond a reasonable doubt. Another criminal case example is the criminal conspiracy case in which the government's prime witness is a co-conspirator who received immunity. The prosecutor would question the jurors about whether they could listen to the evidence and not prejudge it solely on the basis of the witness's conduct and the immunity agreement.

Client's Demeanor Example: In the wrongful death lawsuit in which a log skidder came off of a truck and landed on a car, killing the driver, counsel who represented the truck driver was faced with a client whose courtroom demeanor was troublesome. Counsel used the surrogate technique discussed at pages 217–221, candidly described his client's baggage and asked the jurors to decide the case based upon the evidence and not the client's baggage.

MR. DEFRANCO: Have any of you been subjected to rigorous cross-examination by an attorney? Anyone ever been a witness, raise your hands, ever been a witness?

THE COURT: Which question are we answering, rigorous cross-examination or witness?

MR. DEFRANCO: I apologize, Your Honor. Has anyone ever been a witness in any proceeding? Were you like a neutral witness or were you cross-examined?

MR. STAETTER: As a plaintiff.

THE COURT: And that's Juror No. 13.

MR. DEFRANCO: What kind of case was it?

---

14. Transcript of Proceedings at 145, *In re TFT-LCD (Flat-Panel)*, No. 07-MDL-1827 SI, 10-CV-4572, 10-CV-5452, 10-CV-4114 (N.D. Cal. July 22, 2013), App. 1.1.

MR. STAETTER: It was a sexual abuse case.

MR. DEFRANCO: Did part of that cross-examination make you angry?

MR. STAETTER: No. Uncomfortable, yes, but not angry.

MR. DEFRANCO: You understand different people react differently to being put on the spot? My last question to you all. My client's reaction to cross-examination and his comfort level with this whole process and what's going on is almost nonexistent, doesn't really understand what's going on here. Here is my question: Can you base your decision based on the evidence and not my client's ability to deal with this courtroom setting? Can you all do that for me?

Thank you very much. I appreciate it.[15]

Asking jurors whether they may be open to understanding that the client may react adversely to being put "on the spot" during cross-examination is one thing. However, the last question asks all the jurors to commit to the proposition that they will ignore the manner in which the client may testify. This question is objectionable in that it runs contrary to the court's jury instruction if the jury instruction states that the jury in judging a witness's credibility may consider "the manner of the witness while testifying."[16]

These examples of how to handle a witness's baggage can be applied to most situations. You may have a witness who is elderly and hard of hearing. Or a child witness who cannot understand abstract concepts. Or a client who has been severely injured and is disfigured. First, candidly explain the situation. Second, find out if the jurors can relate to it (empathize with it), and then get an assurance that the jurors will base their verdict on the evidence and not solely on the baggage.

5. Expert Witnesses

Among the players at trial are expert witnesses. When experts are going to testify, you can foreshadow that during jury selection, ascertain whether the prospective jurors have any views regarding experts, and determine whether they have knowledge regarding the particular field of expertise. Ultimately, your goals are to deselect those who cannot accept your expert's testimony as credible and to precondition the jury to be open to receiving expert testimony.

---

15. Transcript of Proceedings at 75–76, *Brown v. Davis and Davis*, No. 4:12 CV649-AGF (E.D Mo. 2014), App. 4.6.

16. Wash. Pattern Jury Instr. Civ. WPI 1.02 (6th ed.).

When exploring issues related to expert witnesses in jury selection, you should consider such factors as credentials, consulting fees, and methodology. Prospective jurors may have certain expectations for what constitutes an expert in a certain field, so counsel should identify these expectations in order to determine whether or not the retained expert will pass the test with jurors. For example, in a medical malpractice case, jurors may determine that experts who still practice in the field are more credible than some Ivy League professor who has published extensively on the topic, but has not actually practiced in some time.

Similarly, if the expert has an unusual fee structure or exorbitant rates, you may want to explore how that could influence jurors' views of her credibility. Finally, you may want to probe jurors' expectations for what methods an expert should use in a particular field to arrive at her conclusions.

Expert Testimony Example: In *In re TFT-LCD (Flat-Panel)*, defense counsel wanted to introduce the importance of expert testimony to the case and test the prospective jurors' receptivity to the testimony of an economist, and did this as follows:

> MR. FREITAS: Mr. Tanti, … Do you have any particular reaction to the idea of listening to testimony from economists, and since they are not here, I'll say apart from the fact that it might be pretty boring?
> PROSPECTIVE JUROR TANTI: No, I think it's good to get unbiased experts' opinions on things, and I'm curious what they have to say.
> MR. FREITAS: What is your general reaction to the idea that the parties will be presenting testimony from experts that they have retained to address the issues in the case?
> PROSPECTIVE JUROR TANTI: I'm sorry; can you repeat the first part?
> MR. FREITAS: Sure. Do you have any general reaction to the idea—
> PROSPECTIVE JUROR TANTI: No.
> MR. FREITAS:—to the idea that some the witnesses will be experts?
> PROSPECTIVE JUROR TANTI: That's expected.
> MR. FREITAS: You are willing to listen to what they say, and take it for what it's worth?
> PROSPECTIVE JUROR TANTI: Yes.[17]

---

17. Transcript of Proceedings at 75, *In re TFT-LCD (Flat-Panel)*, No. 07-MDL-1827 SI, 10-CV-4572, 10-CV-5452, 10-CV-4114 (N.D. Cal. July 22, 2013), App. 1.1.

The following two examples, one for the plaintiff and the other for the defense, come from *Jane Doe v. Robert Higgins,* the civil case involving sexual abuse of a child, found at pages 199–202.

Plaintiff's Psychologist Example: In *Jane Doe v. Robert Higgins,* plaintiff's counsel tells the jury about the expert testimony that the plaintiff expects to offer in its case in chief. Further, counsel discusses the particular fields of expertise to find out whether the jurors are familiar with them, whether they doubt the science, and whether they would be willing to render an award based on the expert testimony.

> MR. RECK: ... You're also going to hear testimony from experts. You're going to hear testimony from a psychologist. You're going to hear testimony from probably someone who is going to do some math calculations, and someone who is going to talk about psychological damage.
>
> The only thing that we can do at the end of this is to ask you to listen to that and render a verdict.
>
> That verdict, what we're going to be doing is asking you to apply what you heard from both the percipient witnesses and from the other witnesses, and award money damages.
>
> Is there anybody who doesn't believe that psychological damage exists?
>
> Okay. For example, now I'm going to ask you if a psychologist says to you that a person went through a trauma, emotional trauma when they were young, at the end of the trial if someone gives you an evaluation for that, says, this trauma occurred and there is a money valuation for that, are you comfortable awarding money damages in exchange for that trauma? Is that something that you feel you can follow through with if the facts dictated it?
>
> PROSPECTIVE JUROR: (No audible response.)
>
> MR. RECK: Good. Now anybody disagree with that statement? Is there anybody out here who says, you know, hey, I don't believe that there is such a thing as psychological damage. I don't believe a person can be hurt inside their head. Anybody think that that's not true?[18]

Defense Expert Versus Common Sense Example: Knowing plaintiff was going to call an expert in its case in chief, defense counsel questioned the

---

18. Transcript of Proceedings at 70–71, *Jane Doe v. Robert Higgins,* Cal. Super. Ct., No. YC052780, 2007 WL-5417657, 70–71 (2007), App. 10.1.

prospective jurors in order to determine whether they would abandon their common sense and accept the expert's testimony without question.

> MR. SPIVAK: Okay. You're going to hear from some people, quote, experts and they're going to have a bunch of letters following their name.
>
> Does anyone believe—here believe that just because someone has a degree that they have more knowledge than your common sense? Does anyone believe that?
>
> Mr. Soughton, why do you raise your hand in response to that question?
>
> PROSPECTIVE JUROR: They have looked at the topic in much more detail, looked at the literature, looked at the studies. Just have a broader knowledge base. I think you have to pay attention to that.
>
> MR. SPIVAK: I think that's a good response. What I'm trying to get at though, is when I hear somebody tell you that, I've researched, I've analyzed, I have looked at the reports, but they weren't—they weren't there at the particular time of the circumstance and they're using their expertise to try to convince you, correct?
>
> PROSPECTIVE JUROR: Correct.
>
> MR. SPIVAK: Okay. You don't throw your common sense out the window, correct?
>
> PROSPECTIVE JUROR: Hopefully not.
>
> MR. SPIVAK: I carry that hope as well.
>
> The—the question I am asking is: If you hear some expert testify to X, Y and Z, how many are going to automatically go, oh, he's an expert, we've got to go with his side of the case? Anyone going to raise their hand on that one?[19]

6. Bias against Other Types of Witnesses

While it is impossible to identify all of the different types of key witnesses who may be involved in a case and the common biases against them, it should not be difficult to identify the right issues to probe. Fundamentally, you want to probe for whether or not your client seems like the type of person or company to engage in the alleged conduct. In order to accomplish this, you should think about the common beliefs and experiences related to a particular profession. Talk to friends and family members to get their views. For example,

---

19. *Id.* at 103–04.

if you are defending a doctor in a medical malpractice case, think about the kinds of experiences and attitudes that are going to make jurors believe your doctor is the kind of doctor who commits malpractice. Perhaps your doctor is a chiropractor and some jurors have skeptical views of chiropractors. If your case involves an allegation of delayed care, you want to be on the lookout for prospective jurors who have had negative experiences where they felt they had to wait too long to receive medical attention.

As another example, consider an employment discrimination case. A defense attorney should consider the common beliefs and experiences that are more likely to make the allegations believable to a particular prospective juror. Maybe some jurors believe discrimination is common in this particular industry. Maybe they believe some conduct is indicative of a large environment in which discrimination occurs. Maybe they have witnessed retaliation in the workplace. This kind of powerful, personal experience can lead them to overestimate how common retaliation is in all workplaces. These experiences also become useful tools for filling evidentiary gaps in the case, which can create significant problems. The last thing that a defense attorney wants a juror to do in an employment discrimination case is to fill narrative holes or evidentiary gaps with their own personal experiences if those experiences align with the plaintiff's narrative.

F. The Evidence

1. Single Witness

Some cases are founded on the testimony of a single witness. For instance, sexual assault and domestic violence prosecutions often rely almost solely on the testimony of the victim. If your case is based primarily upon the testimony of one witness, you will want to determine if the prospective jurors will be able to render a verdict on your client's behalf under those circumstances and deselect any juror who would not be able to do so. In the process, you can explain that the law does not require more than one witness and seek a commitment that they will set aside any preconceived notion that the law requires more.

Single-Witness Example: In the domestic violence case, *People v. Harmon*, the prosecutor covered the single witness issue by utilizing a hypothetical to make the point as follows:

> MS. CORSA: Thank you.
> Good morning, everyone.

You've all heard the presumption of innocence and you all understand that we come to court in this case and the defendant comes with a clean slate, the presumption of innocence.

Does everyone understand that concept?

And can everyone wait and let me put on the evidence before you prejudge the case? Can everyone agree to do that?

And along those same lines, does everyone understand that in every criminal case every defendant comes to court with a presumption of innocence?

An example would be, suppose that a gunman were to come into the room right now, to the back of the courtroom and shot someone in the back row and we all see this happen and that person runs out but gets arrested out in the hallway.

If that person were brought to trial, that person would come to court with the same presumption of innocence. Does everyone understand?

And if we have — say there is a trial in that case and one of you is called to testify as to what you saw and you kind of — and you come and you take the stand and you testified as to what you saw in the back of the courtroom that day.

Does everyone understand that one witness is sufficient to establish a fact? Does everyone understand that? All heads are nodding.

Is there anyone here who would require that they need to hear from 10 jurors who saw the incident before they could find that that fact is established? Okay. No hands are raised.[20]

2. The CSI Effect

The "CSI Effect" is an example of the type of juror misconception about which judges and trial lawyers have been concerned. The CSI effect or syndrome has been described as the effect of the exaggerated portrayal of forensic science on crime television shows such as CSI: Crime Scene Investigation. According to the theory, jurors who view of CSI or its progeny have high expectations of forensic science evidence, and this causes them to acquit guilty defendants. The research on the CSI effect has led to mixed results. The most common finding is that jurors expect scientific evidence regardless of what kind of television shows they watch.

---

20. Transcript of Proceedings at 139–40, *People v. Harmon*, 2007 WL 5181456, 139–40 (2007), App. 3.2.

One study of the CSI effect determined that even though CSI viewers had higher expectations for scientific evidence than non-CSI viewers, this had little or no bearing on the respondents' propensity to convict. Nevertheless, Judge Donald E. Shelton, who conducted the study, observed:

> Our legal system demands proof beyond a reasonable doubt before the government is allowed to punish an alleged criminal. When a scientific test is available that would produce evidence of guilt or innocence—but the prosecution chooses not to perform that test and present its results to the jury—it may be reasonable for a jury to doubt the strength of the government's case. This reality may seem unreasonable to some, but that is not the issue. Rather, it is how the criminal justice system will respond to juror expectations.
>
> One response to this change in expectations would be to get the evidence that jurors seek. This would take a major commitment to increasing law enforcement resources and would require equipping police and other investigating agencies with the most up-to-date forensic science equipment. In addition, significant improvements would need to be made in the capacity of our Nation's crime laboratories to reduce evidence backlogs and keep pace with increased demands for forensic analyses.
>
> Another response would be to equip officers of the court (i.e., judges, prosecutors, and defense lawyers) with more effective ways to address juror expectations. When scientific evidence is not relevant, prosecutors must find more convincing ways to explain the lack of relevance to jurors. Most importantly, prosecutors, defense lawyers, and judges should understand, anticipate, and address the fact that jurors enter the courtroom with a lot of information about the criminal justice system and the availability of scientific evidence.
>
> The bottom line is this: Our criminal justice system must find ways to adapt to the increased expectations of those whom we ask to cast votes of "guilty" or "not guilty."[21]

One effective technique for eliminating juror expectations caused by the fictional portrayal of forensic science evidence is to deal with it during voir dire. Counsel can both seek an acknowledgement from the potential jurors that what they have seen and heard outside of court is merely fiction and gain a com-

---

21. Hon. Donald E. Shelton, *The "CSI Effect": Does It Really Exist?*, NATIONAL INSTITUTE OF JUSTICE (Mar. 17, 2008).

mitment from them that it has nothing to do with forensic science in the real world and the case they are to decide.

CSI Effect Example: In the domestic violence case used in the previous single-witness example, the prosecutor dealt with the *CSI* effect issue in this fashion:

> MS. CORSA: ...
>
> Is there anyone here—Well, anyone here watch shows like "C.S.I. Miami" or "Law and Order"? A few hands.
>
> Does everyone understand this is not an episode, a 40-minute episode, that you see on television? You're not going to hold me to that standard? We don't have scripts, not edited. We're not going to take and retake the scene if we don't like the way it looks.
>
> Anyone hold that against me? No DNA or surprise evidence. Anyone going to hold that against me? Thank you.
>
> I have no further questions.[22]

3. Just Circumstantial Evidence

You lack any direct evidence to prove your case. Instead, you are relying on circumstantial evidence. To you that is no problem; you know there is no difference between the two types of evidence. But, some prospective jurors harbor the misconception that circumstantial evidence is somehow deficient. This is a belief that has been engendered by fictional stories in books, movies, and television. This viewpoint creates a juror expectation of direct evidence. In other words, these jurors will not believe the allegations in the case unless they feel there is direct evidence proving the allegations. This frame of mind can be particularly concerning for a plaintiff, but may also impact a defendant where counterclaims are involved.

The court's jury instructions will explain circumstantial and direct evidence in this way:

> The evidence that has been presented to you may be either direct or circumstantial. The term "direct evidence" refers to evidence that is given by a witness who has directly perceived something at issue in

---

22. Transcript of Proceedings at 151, *People v. Harmon*, 2007 WL 5181456, 151 (2007), App. 3.2.

this case. The term "circumstantial evidence" refers to evidence from which, based on your common sense and experience, you may reasonably infer something that is at issue in this case.

The law does not distinguish between direct and circumstantial evidence in terms of their weight or value in finding the facts in this case. One is not necessarily more or less valuable than the other.[23]

During jury selection, you want to determine whether any of your jurors hold the belief that circumstantial evidence is not enough. An approach to getting the prospective jurors to the point where they will set aside any misconception about circumstantial evidence is to give them an analogy that illustrates that circumstantial evidence can be powerful evidence and get the jurors to agree that they will be receptive to circumstantial evidence and follow the law.

Several circumstantial evidence analogies exist, and every trial lawyer has their favorite. One analogy involves the mother who concludes her son ate the cookies, despite his denials, when she catches the child in the kitchen with cookie crumbs all over his face and an empty cookie jar. If the mother had seen the child eat the cookies it would be direct evidence, but the circumstantial evidence is equally strong evidence. Another favorite is about castaway Robinson Crusoe deciding that the island was inhabited when he saw the footprint in the sand. Further, you may wish to point out that circumstantial evidence can be stronger than direct evidence coming from a witness who is not credible.

Circumstantial Evidence Example: In *People v. Harmon*, the domestic violence case, the prosecutor relied upon another trial lawyer classic to explain direct and circumstantial evidence, adapting it to her one-witness case.

> MS. CORSA: There is a concept, you've all heard of circumstantial evidence and direct evidence. Does anyone here — has anyone not heard of circumstantial evidence, this concept? No hands are raised.
>
> I just want to illustrate this. Circumstantial evidence and direct evidence are two forms of evidence that you may hear in this case.
>
> Direct evidence would be, suppose you're in New York and you have this beautiful room overlooking central park. You check in that

---

23. Washington Pattern Jury Instruction Criminal No. 1.03 (2015).

evening and when you go to bed the streets are dry down below and the park is green.

When you wake up in the morning, the park is covered in this fresh blanket of beautiful white snow and the streets are covered in snow.

Circumstantial evidence, your observations would be circumstantial evidence that it snowed the night before. Does everyone understand that? Okay.

And direct evidence would be if you stood in the park while it was snowing and you actually saw the flakes fall onto the ground. That would be direct evidence.

And each of these types of evidence is sufficient and neither type of evidence is entitled to any greater weight than the other. Does everyone understand that? Okay.

And along those lines, and illustrated earlier, if one witness testified to their circumstantial observation of the street being dry the night before and there was snow on the ground the next morning, that sole witness would be sufficient to establish circumstantial evidence that it had snowed the night before.

Does everyone understand that? Is there anybody here that says, if I don't see the snow on the ground with my own eyes, I can't believe it. Anyone feel that way? No hands are raised.[24]

4. Conflicting Stories

Some cases involve the conflicting testimony of a few witnesses with little or no corroborating evidence for any witness. These cases, sometimes referred to as "he said/she said" cases, can be difficult for some jurors, leaving them unable to render a decision because they simply do not know who to believe.

There are a variety of ways to tackle this issue in jury selection, with the strategy depending largely on the type of claims in the case. For example, cases involving sensational claims, such as sexual abuse, may want to be more claim specific. Some jurors consider these types of claims so extraordinary that they find it hard to believe someone would ever lie about allegations of sexual abuse. These attitudes tend to favor the plaintiff, because the mere allegation alone constitutes enough evidence for these jurors. In less sensational cases, counsel may want to pose broader questions that simply ask jurors how they would go

---

24. Transcript of Proceedings at 149–51, *People v. Harmon*, 2007 WL 5181456, 131–32 (2007), App. 3.2.

about reconciling conflicting testimony in a case where there is independent evidence that definitively proves the case. The responses to these kinds of questions will help the attorneys for each side understand the kinds of evidentiary standards jurors are going to apply to the case.

Conflicting stories and mendacity are commonplace in the courtroom. However, novice prospective jurors are not accustomed to the phenomenon. Some potential jurors labor under the belief that witnesses do not fabricate. Some jurors may not feel that they are capable of judging the credibility of witnesses. A technique for dispelling such beliefs is to demonstrate to them that they are capable of performing the jurors' function of judging witness credibility because that is what they do in everyday life.

If you want to delve into this subject with the jurors, be on the lookout for a prospective juror who because of their job or community activities often settles disputes. It is particularly nice if you have someone who works with children, as the prospective juror in the following example did in supervising after-school programs.

Conflicting Stories Example: *People v. Edwards* was a murder trial. The defendant Allen Edwards claimed he acted in self-defense. Here, defense counsel discusses with a prospective juror how to use common sense and determine who is telling the truth when two people are telling conflicting stories.

> MR. HIZAMI: ... Now, Juror No. 3, you indicate that you work in some after school programs, right? I take it you deal with a lot of kids.
> PROSPECTIVE JUROR SEAT NO. 3: Yes.
> MR. HIZAMI: Have you ever had a situation where some kids come up to you and say we're in a fight and he started it.
> PROSPECTIVE JUROR SEAT NO. 3: Yes, all the time.
> MR. HIZAMI: Happens all the time. Okay. And what do you do to resolve that?
> PROSPECTIVE JUROR SEAT NO. 3: Well, it depends on the situation, I will handle differently. Sometimes you separate the two, talk to them, get both sides and come up with a solution. Sometimes, depending on because I' the boss, I can kind of let my staff deal with it. If it comes to me though, usually it's a big situation.
> MR. HIZAMI: And at times you have two different versions of the same event?
> PROSPECTIVE JUROR SEAT NO. 3: Yes.
> MR. HIZAMI: What do you use to make that decision?
> PROSPECTIVE JUROR SEAT NO. 3: My own judgment, kind of what I know of the kids. I usually will talk to other kids if I need to,

anybody who were witnesses. But a lot of the times, they get to me, they're going to tell me the truth, in my program.

MR. HIZAMI: And has anybody ever lied to you?

PROSPECTIVE JUROR SEAT NO. 3: Of course.

MR. HIZAMI: How do you know they're lying?

PROSPECTIVE JUROR SEAT NO. 3: Usually their facial expressions will give it away. A lot of the kids I've worked with, I know the kids well enough, I know when they're lying to me. Their body language will tell me sometimes.

MR. HIZAMI: So you use every day common experiences.

PROSPECTIVE JUROR SEAT NO. 3: Right.

MR. HIZAMI: Common sense.

PROSPECTIVE JUROR SEAT NO. 3: Right.

MR. HIZAMI: Would you be willing to do that in this case, use your common sense and everyday experiences to determine the credibility of the witnesses?

PROSPECTIVE JUROR SEAT NO. 3: Yes.

MR. HIZAMI: Would anybody not be able to do that that's a potential juror on this case?[25]

G. The Story

1. Sympathy

Because the stories told at trial are ones about deprivation or threatened deprivation, about loss, it is expected that members of the jury will feel sympathy for one side or the other or both. However, the court will instruct the jury along these lines:

> As jurors, you are officers of this court. You must not let your emotions overcome your rational thought process. You must reach your decision based on the facts proved to you and on the law given to you, not on sympathy, bias, or personal preference. To assure that all parties receive a fair trial, you must act impartially with an earnest desire to reach a proper verdict.[26]

---

25. Transcript of Proceedings at 71–73, *People v. Edwards*, No. BA305749 (Cal. 2007), App. 12.1.

26. WASHINGTON STATE PATTERN JURY INSTRUCTION, Civil No. 1.02 (2009).

When it is only natural for the jurors to be emotional and sympathize with the other side, the best course of action is to acknowledge that it is only human to feel that way, express your own sympathy, and to inquire of the jurors concerning whether it is still possible for the them to follow the law and not be swayed by sympathy or sidetracked by prejudice.

Sympathy Example: The wrongful death lawsuit *Brown v. Davis and Davis* (discussed at pages 183-187) involved a log skidder that came off of a truck and landed on a car, killing the driver. Defense counsel DeFranco, who represented the truck driver, raised the concern that the jurors would be sympathetic towards the widow and the two children and that that sympathy would sway them not to fairly consider the evidence and follow the law.

> MR. DEFRANCO: You've heard the basic facts of this case. Is there anyone here who does not already have sympathy for the situation of this wife and these two children? If you don't have sympathy, raise your hand.
>
> I don't mean this rhetorically. Is there any question that we all have sympathy for what happened here? My client is at fault. There's no question about it. We've admitted it, and it caused a death, and it's a tragic situation, it's a sympathetic situation. Does anyone not have sympathy for the situation and for the plaintiff and her two children?
>
> So here is my question: Can all of you put that sympathy aside and base your verdict, because you are going to give a verdict and it's going to be in her favor because we've already admitted fault and we've already admitted that we've caused damages. But the question is: Can you put your sympathies aside and decide the case based on the evidence you hear and more importantly, based on the law that the Judge is going to give you at the end of the case? Can you all do that for me?[27]

In this situation, defense attorneys should also probe for other experiences and thought processes that could result in jurors having strong emotional attachments to the plaintiff's case theory. For example, if it is a wrongful death case, the defense attorney may want to ask if anyone in the venire has recently lost someone close to them. A recent loss of a loved one naturally makes one

---

27. Transcript of Proceedings at 70–71, *Brown v. Davis and Davis*, No. 4:12 CV649-AGF (E.D Mo. 2014), App. 4.6.

more emotional and the plaintiff's story may turn into powerful reminders of that juror's own personal pain and sadness.

There are other ways to ask about how emotional jurors are. For example, using the forced choice format discussed earlier at pages 165–168, a defense attorney might ask a question such as:

> When it comes to making decisions, I've found there are two different types of people. Some people tend to make decisions with their heart, meaning they tend to be emotional decision-makers. Other people tend to make decisions with the head rather than their hearts and keep their emotions out of it. By a show of hands, how many of you are more like that first group and tend to be emotional decision-makers?

2. Prejudicial Pretrial Publicity

Your case story may conflict with the one told in pretrial publicity, and this can pose a major problem. According to one review of social science research, pretrial publicity leads to the development of a "story model." According to the review, negative publicity about a criminal (and to a lesser extent, a civil) case provides "a belief framework about the defendant's guilt." People exposed to this pretrial publicity have a story to make sense out of a particular event, and it is very difficult to remove that story.[28]

Media coverage can be particularly difficult due to the sensationalism that often takes place with the media's reporting on the story. Consequently, sensational claims that lack evidence are often given greater salience than less interesting facts tied to key issues in the case.

If the case is high profile and has received significant pretrial publicity, the best practice is to inquire about what the prospective jurors know of the case individually. This can be done with a customized questionnaire. Asking the jurors to indicate whether they have learned about the case through the media prior to jury selection but cautioning them not to reveal what they know to other members of the panel can also do it. Then, the court can inquire of those who indicated that they have seen pretrial publicity about the case individually and outside the presence of the rest of the jury panel. These approaches prevent other members of the panel from hearing about the case.

---

28. N. Steblay, et al., *The Effects of Pretrial Publicity on Juror Verdicts: A Meta-Analytical Review*, 23 Law and Human Behavior 219–35 (1999).

At pages 293–302 you will find extensive coverage of pretrial publicity as it pertains to motions for change of venue.

Pretrial Publicity Example: Let's return to *United States v. Trinity Industries, Inc.*, a prosecution under the False Claims Act (see the earlier discussion of the case at pages 169–171). Before counsel had an opportunity to question the jurors, the judge asked the panel about whether they had learned anything about the case through the media prior to jury selection. Jurors raised their hands, and the attorneys and judge noted who responded. Defense counsel followed up on earlier questioning on this subject. Note that in his questioning, he does not disclose what was in the media and thus inform the jurors who were not privy to that news. Note further that he obtained an assurance from each prospective juror that they would rely on the evidence produced in court and not outside sources.

> MR. MANN: ... You were asked early about—earlier about media coverage. And, yes, this has been in the media. And you may—some of you raised your hand and said that you knew something about it. What I really need to know is have any of you by either having media coverage, Internet, newspaper, whatever that might be, have any of you formed an opinion in this case about who's right and who's wrong? Have any of you? Would you raise your hand if you have?
>
> Okay. Can I just go row by row because I—I wrote your numbers down earlier who had heard some media. But did anybody on the front row raise your hand earlier?
>
> Mr. Taylor, did you? Mr. Taylor—could I get the microphone to Mr. Taylor, No. 5?
>
> Mr. Taylor, was it TV, radio, what?
>
> JUROR TAYLOR: Television.
>
> MR. MANN: Television. And—and by seeing that, did you form some opinions by listening to that?
>
> JUROR TAYLOR: No. It was just interesting.
>
> MR. MANN: Okay.
>
> JUROR TAYLOR: Not a problem.
>
> MR. MANN: And—and do you think that now that you're here and that you're going to see evidence in this case, that you can treat that fairly, or do you think that that would influence you in the case?
>
> JUROR TAYLOR: Yes, sir, I think I can treat it fairly.
>
> MR. MANN: Okay. Thank you, Mr. Taylor.
>
> Hold on to that just a minute. You can sit down, but just hold on to the microphone.

Anybody on the second row, did you have your hands raised earlier about the media coverage? So nobody on the second row has heard — knows anything about this case, except for what we've told you today; is that correct? All right.

Third row?

Yes, sir? Mr. Horton. My question will be what did you hear — I mean, not what, but what, television, radio, Internet?

JUROR HORTON: Television news stories and also some consumer reports.

MR. MANN: Okay. And did you — did you form an opinion then?

JUROR HORTON: Only to the fact that I didn't know what was causing the problem.

MR. MANN: Okay.

JUROR HORTON: Somebody said there was a problem.

MR. MANN: Okay.

JUROR HORTON: I couldn't figure out what they were talking about.

MR. MANN: Okay. And do — do we start off even in this case?

JUROR HORTON: Yes, sir.

MR. MANN: I mean, you're going to listen to the evidence? Will that influence you, what you heard?

JUROR HORTON: No, sir.

MR. MANN: Okay. Thank you, Mr. Horton.

Who else in the next row?

Ms. Beasley?

JUROR KERNAN: I read about it on the Internet and the newspaper. I didn't form an opinion one way or the other. They wasn't real specific about what all it was about.

MR. MANN: Okay. Mr. Kernan, so same question. The only thing — the thing that concerns me always, as you would all expect if this was your case on either side, is can — can you be fair? Can you?

JUROR KERNAN: I just have further questions about it.

MR. MANN: All right. And so you're going to wait and listen to form those questions and hopefully get those answers in this trial?

JUROR KERNAN: Exactly.

MR. MANN: Yeah. Thank you. Ms. Beasley, I think you raised your hand?

JUROR BEASLEY: Through the news and the media, not enough information to form an opinion.

MR. MANN: Okay. Thank you, Ms. Beasley. You anticipated my question.

Anybody else? I know there were maybe a few more hands. Yeah. Ms. Rogers?

JUROR ROGERS: Saw it on television, and I'm interesting in hearing the case.

MR. MANN: Okay. And what I would ask you is from what you've heard now, discount anything you've heard here today because you haven't heard any evidence, but from that television program, did you form any opinion in this case?

JUROR ROGERS: No, but I'd like to hear about it—hear about the case and, you know—

MR. MANN: Right.

JUROR ROGERS: But I'd like to—hear about it—hear about the case and, you know—

MR. MANN: Right.

JUROR ROGERS:—but I have no opinion on it. I'm open.

MR. MANN: Okay. You're open to both sides?

JUROR ROGERS: Ready to listen if I'm chosen.

MR. MANN: Okay. Thank—thank you, Ms. Rogers. And Mr. Wilson?

JUROR WILSON: Yes, I saw it on a television program, but I did not form an opinion.

MR. MANN: Okay. So you—you feel comfortable that you can sit and call balls and strikes in this case?

JUROR WILSON: Yes, sir.

MR. MANN: All right. Anybody else?

Mr. Adams?

JUROR KENNETH ADAMS: I saw it on 20/20 and Good Morning America.

MR. MANN: Okay.

JUROR KENNETH ADAMS: And plus, I'm a bus driver, and I— driving around rural routes and stuff, I'm seeing these barriers up—

MR. MANN: Okay.

JUROR KENNETH ADAMS:—and seen a couple of them—I think I heard someone earlier say something about they saw one— had seen one that had been glanced—

MR. MANN: Right.

JUROR KENNETH ADAMS:—not the head-on, but I—I haven't formed an opinion on it.

MR. MANN: Okay. Thank you, Mr. Rogers—Adams, I'm sorry.

JUROR KENNETH ADAMS: That's okay.

MR. MANN: Anybody else? Mr. Bryan?

JUROR GRAHAM: Graham.

MR. MANN: Graham. Okay.

JUROR GRAHAM: Yes, I saw it on television. But I'm looking at it a little bit different angle. We heard about a lot of car recalls, and having heard about some of these recalls, people trying to save 10 cents or whatever it might be on a part that's caused devastation, car wrecks, or what have you, I have a concern about that. And I guess I do have a little bit of opinion because I wondered if it was somebody saving money, putting lives in jeopardy for the bottom line, which is a dollar figure.

MR. MANN: Okay. All right. So besides wondering, have you formed an opinion on that?

JUROR GRAHAM: I don't know.

MR. MANN: Okay. All right. Thank you. Thank you.[29]

3. Special Knowledge

The jury panel may include a person who has experienced all or part of your case narrative or has expertise in an area pertinent to the case. Earlier, at pages 217–221, we discussed how counsel might call upon such a person to serve as a surrogate for the lawyer's client or witness to tell the story. Alternatively, counsel may not be looking out for those who may help the client's side but rather for those who have had a similar experience or have a relevant expertise and potentially could use that experience or knowledge in deciding the case to the client's detriment. Essentially, the concern is that, during deliberations, the juror with special knowledge will tell the rest of the jury a different story than what the evidence has shown.

Attorneys may sometimes find it difficult to determine which party a juror's expertise might favor. Where there are doubts or it is unclear, it makes the most sense to strike the prospective juror even though there is a chance her expertise could benefit your case. Personal expertise makes a juror a non-testifying expert, which has significant implications during jury deliberations. Other jurors may defer to this expertise and use it to fill gaps in the evidentiary

---

29. Transcript of Proceedings at 106–11, *United States v. Trinity Indus., Inc.*, No. 2:12CV89-JRG E.D. (Tex. Oct. 13, 2014), App. 8.2.

presentation. Even worse, a juror may appear to have expertise where he does not, but that appearance gives the juror unwarranted authority in the deliberation room to offer powerful views of the case.

Specialized Knowledge Example: This example is from *Jane Doe v. Robert Higgins,* the civil case involving sexual abuse of a child found at pages 199–202. Here, plaintiff's counsel asks prospective jurors about training in child sexual abuse, which is clearly a relevant area of inquiry. But, when it becomes apparent that counsel is attempting to use the juror to instruct the panel about the effects of child sexual abuse, the judge steps in to halt further questioning along those lines.

> MR. RECK: ... Is there anyone here who has any training in the effects of childhood sexual abuse? And by that I mean, has anyone ever been trained as a social worker, maybe some instruction came as a teacher, maybe a general you has some psychology classes, anything like that? That's what I want to talk about.
>
> Yes, Ma'am.
>
> PROSPECTIVE JUROR: I'm halfway through a graduate program with a Masters in psychology. Actually took the workshop and studied in school.
>
> MR. RECK: And does the Master's program have a specialization or is that a general psychology type of degree, how does that work?
>
> PROSPECTIVE JUROR: It's a master's in psychology with the idea of becoming a marriage and family therapist.
>
> MR. RECK: And in the course of that, some of your classes and coursework concern effects of childhood sexual abuse?
>
> PROSPECTIVE JUROR: In order to graduate you have to take three workshops, one on elder abuse, one on spousal abuse and one on child abuse. And I have to do the two-day on child abuse.
>
> MR. RECK: A two-day workshop?
>
> PROSPECTIVE JUROR: Uh-huh.
>
> MR. RECK: And in the course of that workshop, part of the training is that there are psychological changes that occur if one is abused as a child sexually, correct?
>
> PROSPECTIVE JUROR: Yes.
>
> MR. RECK: Anybody else have any training along those lines, even if it's not formal training?
>
> Yes, ma'am.
>
> PROSPECTIVE JUROR: In the course of educational experiences, there have been situations where we have worked with families and

children who have had different problems and we have worked through them. So there is an awareness, but not a direct study involvement.

MR. RECK: So this is something—

PROSPECTIVE JUROR: I am a teacher.

MR. RECK: How long have you been a teacher?

PROSPECTIVE JUROR: Forty-odd years, but I haven't been a practicing teacher for about 20 years and I have returned to it.

But I was—I taught the mentally retarded, nursery school, elementary school, and high school.

So I have a range of experience and I am back doing it again.

MR. RECK: Ms. Sax, have you ever been personally involved in any type of an allegation between a student and any school official regarding sexual activity?

PROSPECTIVE JUROR: No.

MR. RECK: And you've been aware of allegations or you've personally probably had some experience with students who were abused as children?

PROSPECTIVE JUROR: We just were aware of difficult situations, but they were very—I can say that I really have been in that regard, specifically there is an awareness when there is a situation in the school and everyone is made aware of it. So I was not directly involved none were any of my students.

MR. RECK: But you were aware there were some students who had been involved with some type of sexual abuse?

PROSPECTIVE JUROR: Family situations, yes.

MR. RECK: And did you ever witness the effects of that kind of abuse? Did you ever see those students?

PROSPECTIVE JUROR: Did I ever see those students, no.

MR. RECK: Can you understand that if children—If those students were sexually abused, there would be an effect on them, right?

THE COURT: Counsel, you're getting into the evidence in the case here. That's for the witnesses.

MR. RECK: Thank you, Your Honor ...[30]

---

30. Transcript of Proceedings at 77–79. *Jane Doe v. Robert Higgins*, Cal. Super. Ct., No. YC052780, 2007 WL-5417657, 77–79 (2007), App. 10.1.

Chapter 13

Evaluating Prospective Jurors

"Never forget, almost every case is won or lost when the jury is sworn."
Clarence Darrow

"To escape jury duty in England, wear a bowler hat and carry a copy of the Daily Telegraph."

John Mortimer,
English barrister and author of
Rumpole of the Bailey

"Jury selection isn't about selection. It's about getting rid of your nightmares. Anyone from law enforcement. Anyone from a law enforcement family. Anyone from a military family. No small business owners. No working class whites. No elderly blacks; they're tired of getting mugged. No one who knows anyone who was killed on 9-11. No one who listens to Fox News. No golfers. No bowlers. No sailors. And, absolutely no lawyers. You listenin' to me."

John Tuturro playing defense
counsel John Stone in the HBO
series *The Night Of* (2016)

A. Jury Selection Team

The jury panel is about to enter the courtroom. In the courtroom, you wait with your trial team. Your client sits beside you. If it is a criminal case and you are a prosecutor, the detective may be sitting with you. Your co-counsel and other parties on your side of the case and their counsel also may be present at your counsel table. You may have a jury consultant and/or an investigator in the courtroom. Your client and other team members are aware that the panel members will be watching everything that happens and every person in the courtroom. Your team members are dressed for court, and they are aware that it is critical they be on their best behavior, because the potential jurors will be observing facial expressions, body behavior, how you communicate with each other, everything.

Your team members have been assigned specific tasks. They are to watch and listen carefully to the prospective jurors and to evaluate them. As soon as the panel has been identified, you or a member of your team fills out the seating chart on paper and/or electronically and enters pertinent information about them. Throughout, jury selection notes are added to the chart about the jurors, especially a rating of each person as a suitable candidate for deselection.

Later, when you are questioning the jurors, it is difficult to pay close attention to everything. You need to focus on asking questions, encouraging open and honest responses, developing a rapport with jurors, and tracking information about the prospective jurors at the same time, and you may miss something. For example, when you are questioning a prospective juror in the jury box, another panel member outside your line of sight in the spectator section may be visibly expressing disapproval of your inquiry. This is why having assistance during jury selection is beneficial. Therefore, ideally, there would be multiple individuals at the table covering important tasks such as tracking verbal responses, tracking nonverbal responses of those not speaking, and maintaining a careful eye on who is in play and who is not.

Often the best times to concentrate on watching and listening to the panel members are when the judge and opposing counsel are questioning them, because then you are not engaged in questioning. Besides, you want to know not just how the potential jurors react to you and your case but also how they react to your opponent's case and opposing counsel.

B. Scouting Reports

How much information you have about the panel members depends upon four things:

1. whether you employed a jury consultant who helped you design the juror profiles, conduct trial simulations, and do a community attitude study and so on;
2. whether pretrial you knew the identity of the panel members and had the resources to investigate them;

3. whether, at a minimum, the court has provided you with a juror information form containing basic information about each prospective juror; and

4. whether the court had the prospective jurors fill out a customized jury questionnaire.

C. Telltale Factors

How the prospective jurors dress, how they interact with one another, the reading material they carry, their nonverbal communication and their verbal responses are all clues to whom they are as people and how they may view your case and your opponent's case. At the heart of your capacity to read them is your ability to apply what you have learned about people through your life experiences. This requires a deep understanding of the local community, its values, and its culture. A juror may look odd with their colored hair, facial hair, or tattoos in a Seattle or Portland, Oregon jury, but anyone who has spent meaningful time in the Pacific Northwest knows that colored hair, facial hair, and tattoos are quite common. In the Midwest, someone with this appearance may represent a counter-culture philosophy. In Seattle, he may be a six-figure, Microsoft programmer who lives in an upscale, suburban home and drives a Mercedes. In this sense, appearances and presentation can be deceiving if you do not understand the local culture.

1. Interaction with Others and Reading Material

How a person interacts with others on the panel can be telling. For instance, if the person is apart from others, that person may well be a silent loner or lone-wolf antagonist during deliberations. Alternatively, an outgoing person who interacts well with other panel members could be a good facilitator during deliberations and is more likely to exert influence over the entire group. This is why it is so important to watch jurors' behavior at all times, particularly during downtime and breaks. How they interact during these times can offer important insights into their personality.

What the panel member brought to read during waiting spells may give a clue as to the person's attitudes. A prospective juror who reads The Economist during breaks may have a higher need for cognition. The juror reading Foucault may be more skeptical of how power and money influences corporate decision-making. The possibilities are endless.

The key to effectively interpreting these kinds of factors lies in not developing firm opinions based on them. Remember that these kinds of factors are only indirect information. In other words, it is important to understand the many assumptions that you are making when you rely on these factors. They can be very useful in situations where voir dire is limited, but should not be determining factors in situations where attorneys have the opportunity to speak directly to jurors and learn about their personal experiences and beliefs. The latter are what are most important and most predictive of juror decision-making.

2. Nonverbal Communication

What a prospective juror says during jury selection is not enough in and of itself to guide you in assessing them. Studies have established that 60 to 65 percent of all communication is through nonverbal behaviors.[1] Therefore, the prospective jurors' nonverbal behavior is an important factor in assessing them. This is especially true, because some jurors conceal their true beliefs, saying what they think counsel or the judge wants to hear. Motivations to mask their real attitudes can be as simple as a desire to sit on the jury, or not.

One way to avoid misleading answers is to craft jury selection questions that do not suggest a correct or socially acceptable answer, but attention to nonverbal cues is still important even when the questions are appropriately worded.

Nonverbal communication includes: appearance, voice, posture, and movement. Nonverbal communication is not body language, which scholars of nonverbal communications agree does not exist because behavior is too complex, and unlike a language, it cannot be easily defined.[2]

Hale Starr and Mark McCormick in their seminal work *Jury Selection* explain why we understand the significance of nonverbal communication, the paradox that we nevertheless misunderstand it, and that a trained eye can interpret the messages sent by nonverbal communication as follows:

> There is no question that everybody sends and receives nonverbal communication all the time. Nor is there any question as to how much importance nonverbal communication can have for the receiver when it is decoded. There is, however, a primary contradiction contained in nonverbal communication.

---

1. Jeffrey T. Frederick, Ph.D, Mastering Voir Dire and Jury Selection 43 (3d ed. 2011).

2. Hale Starr & Mark McCormick, Jury Selection 26–29 (4th ed. 2009).

How is it that nonverbal communication is so important and yet is so misunderstood?

The answer is somewhat obvious. We all know nonverbal communication even if we do not know the technical terms or are not familiar with research on the subject, in the same way as a child knows and uses language before going to school and receiving formal instruction. We accept the fact that everyone learns how to talk but that some people later learn to talk more effectively and in more diverse situations. The same is true of nonverbal communication. We learn about nonverbal communication as we use it. Each of us knows that eye contact is important, that a touch can define a relationship, that how we dress carries a message about who and what we are. However, there are aspects of nonverbal communication in which we are not as successful simply because we have not become familiar with them or have not been made aware of their effectiveness. The person who has a trained awareness, who has been taught what to look for and where to look for it, will be a quicker, more efficient interpreter of nonverbal messages than the untrained or unaware.[3]

Dr. Jeffrey T. Frederick, Director of the Jury Research Services Division of the National Legal Research Group, Inc., has indicated that in order to evaluate jurors' behaviors, it is necessary to establish a baseline of anxiety and behavior against which to gauge changes in their behavior. The recommended baseline is the jurors' nonverbal communication early in jury selection when they answer questions about their backgrounds, because those questions produce the least anxiety. When you assess the potential juror's nonverbal behaviors, examine all verbal and nonverbal communication against that baseline. Also, examine the patterns of nonverbal behavior for consistency. Inconsistency between potential juror's answers and nonverbal communication should alert you to potential deception or other problem. When you detect some inconsistency, you can ask follow up questions to gain further insight into the person's views.[4]

As we previously mentioned, you and your team should observe the nonverbal communication of the panel members not just when they are speaking with you but also when they are listening to or speaking with the judge or opposing counsel. Notice how the person's behavior differs depending upon the person with whom they are communicating. If the person is sitting back with arms crossed when

---

3. *Id.* at 14–15, 26.

4. Jeffrey T. Frederick, Ph.D, Mastering Voir Dire and Jury Selection 58–59 (3d ed. 2011).

speaking with opposing counsel but is leaning forward and smiling when you question him, those are positive signals that the person is receptive to you.

In this section, we examine common nonverbal behaviors along with what they tell. It is critical that you examine the whole person, including what they say and all their behaviors. Rigidly interpreting body posture can lead counsel astray. For example, when a person uncrosses their legs and opens their hands and arms indicating that the person is receptive to you, the person may merely be stretching.

a. Body Behavior

i. Juror Posture

How a prospective juror sits and moves in their chair may tell you what they are thinking. While sitting back suggests resistance to the person or idea under discussion, sitting forward suggests the person is interested in what is being discussed or the person who is speaking. Leaning forward, however, does not necessarily mean the juror favors the person speaking; rather, the interest may be negative.[5]

Is the prospective juror open and receptive to you or closed off? Arms and hands open indicate that the person is receptive to the person talking and the person's ideas.[6] Conversely, crossed arms and/or legs suggest that the person is defensive or resistant to what is being said. Legs and arms crossed and a body turned from speaker indicates the person is not only defensive but also trying to get away.[7] On the other hand, if the person's legs are uncrossed and both feet on the floor, that suggests that the person is amenable to the person who is speaking.[8] Again, you must consider the totality of the person's verbal and nonverbal communication. A person with crossed legs and folded arms, but who is smiling at you, may be very friendly to you.

ii. Juror Movement

Dr. Frederick, in *Mastering Voir Dire and Jury Selection*, makes these observations about movement by prospective jurors:

In general, the more movement the potential juror exhibits, the greater the anxiety. These movements can involve the entire body (e.g.,

---

5. *Id.* at 43; *see also* MICHAEL MARCUS, TRIAL PREPARATION FOR PROSECUTORS 19-11 (2010).

6. MARCUS, *supra*, at 19-11.

7. FREDERICK, *supra*, at 47; MARCUS, *supra*, at 19-11.

8. MARCUS, *supra*, at 19.11.

shifting body postures) or more limited parts of the body (e.g., wring-
ing hands or tapping fingers). Gross movements such as repeatedly
shifting the body's weight ("fidgeting" or "squirming") reflect anxiety
or nervousness on the juror's part, the traditional reaction to being
placed on "the hot seat."[9]

When a person grooms, such as bushing hair back or straightening their
clothing, this also indicates anxiety.[10] A shrug of the shoulders can mean the
person is anxious. But, it may also mean that the person is qualifying an
answer, has a lack of commitment to what is being said or is indifferent.[11]

iii. Eye Contact

When a person is comfortable or interested in what another person has to
say, the person is likely to maintain moderate to high eye contact. However,
if the person is anxious, they may avert their eyes or blink. Steady eye contact
can mean the person is hostile, and increased eye contact can mean that the
person is being deceptive. As with other nonverbal behavior, consideration
must be given to the whole person, and cultural, gender and confidence differences may account for more or less eye contact.[12] For example, women tend
to gaze more at others than men, and self-confident people tend to gaze more
at others than dishonest or disinterested people.[13]

iv. Countenance

Reading a person according to their facial expressions is problematic. Dr.
Frederick, Ph.D., explains:

> Probably the cue that people rely upon most in their interactions with
> others is facial expressions. Frowning, smiling, looks of concern, or
> skeptical or incredulous expressions can reveal feelings about a
> situation or a person. The problem with facial expressions is that over
> the course of socialization, people learn to control their facial expres-
> sions more than other aspects of nonverbal communication. Potential
> jurors may smile or exhibit signs of interest even when their feelings
> are inconsistent with these expressions. However, unless a potential

---

9. FREDERICK, *supra*, at 45.
10. *Id.*
11. *Id.* at 48–49.
12. *Id.* at 49–50.
13. STARR & McCORMICK, *supra*, 29–35.

juror is particularly adept at controlling or manipulating nonverbal communication, inconsistencies between feelings and outward appearances will leak out. Leakage occurs in two areas: aspects of the facial expressions themselves and inconsistencies with other body cues.[14]

Cues that a smile is masking inconsistent feelings are the time it lasts and its appearance. If it is a fixed smile, lasting longer than a normal smile would, or an asymmetrical one, turning up on one side, then it may be hiding true feelings. Also, a smile can be belied by other verbal or nonverbal communication indicating disfavor towards the other person.[15] Also, look for the socially-conditioned response smile that is used when greeting others because that can hide true feelings. It can be spotted when the smile does not engage the eyes or muscles of the cheeks.[16]

Dr. Frederick provides some this advice for construing the smiling juror:

> The key to detecting the smiling juror lies in examining the consistency of his or her nonverbal cues. Are there wrinkles or crow's-feet at the outside corners of the juror's eyes that should accompany genuine smiling? Is there a softness to the eyes that is associated with positive feeling, or are the eyes hard, as would be consistent with the expression "eyes that looked daggers"? Is the smile asymmetrical (e.g., one side or the smile lifts up while the other side of the smile stays relatively flat or points downward)? Is the smile consistent with other nonverbal cues such as body orientation and posture? Always beware of the potential juror who smiles but angles his or her body away and maintains a rigid posture![17]

b. Voice and Manner of Speaking

In addition to what the prospective juror says, how the person says it is suggestive. Voice cues indicating that the prospective juror is anxious include a rising voice pitch and speaking rapidly.[18] Speech patterns can also indicate problems. For examples, if verbal hiccups, such as "ums," disrupt the potential juror's answers or if the juror fails to complete sentences, these mannerisms point to potential problems.

---

14. *Id.* at 50.
15. *Id.*
16. STARR & McCORMICK, *supra*, at 29–37.
17. FREDERICK, *supra*, at 51 (3d ed. 2011).
18. *Id.* at 55.

Talkativeness generally indicates a positive feeling towards the other person. The exception to this rule is when the speaker is using irrelevant information to camouflage the person's actual views.[19]

c. Verbal Responses

Just as you should compare and contrast a prospective juror's body behavior when relating to you with the person's body behavior when speaking to opposing counsel and the judge, you want to compare and contrast the juror's verbal responses to your questions with the responses to questions from opposing counsel and the judge. If the juror is reluctant to answer your questions but readily responds to opposing counsel, those are unfavorable indicators for your side.

Listen carefully for how the prospective jurors phrase responses to your questions, because phrasing may reveal that the person is disguising actual beliefs. For example, qualifiers, such as "I will try," in a potential juror's answer to a question about whether she could follow the court's instructions on damages, divulges reluctance on the person's part.

D. Bad Juror Profile

During your pretrial preparation, you developed profiles of the model bad (high risk) and best jurors. Now, during jury selection, you question and gather information from the jurors in an effort to uncover the characteristics of the model bad juror in the prospective jurors, and thus identify whom to deselect.

E. Group Dynamics

In terms of the group dynamic of jury deliberations, jurors can be categorized as the leader, outlier, opinionated, follower, alienator, and impartial. How do you identify these different types of jurors? Your life experience and common sense will tell you. Whom you represent determines which of these you want on or off your jury. In broad general terms, a plaintiff wants a group that will work together to reach a verdict, and a defendant wants discord.

---

19. *Id.* at 53–54.

1. Leader and Foreperson

Jurors tend to follow a leader. A leader does not always become the foreperson. A leader may not want to be the foreperson. For instance, we know lawyers who got on juries and did not want to serve as the foreperson even though they probably could have if they had wished. Rather, the lawyers wanted to observe the jury deliberation process from the inside without directing it as foreperson.

While a leader does not always become the foreperson, a leader often is chosen as the foreperson, and the foreperson certainly is influential during deliberations. Indeed, one study found that the foreperson consumes 25 percent of all the speaking done during deliberations.[20]

How do you spot the likely leader? Research shows that prior jury service is the best indicator of who will be selected as the foreperson. Even when not elected foreperson, the juror with prior experience may exert leadership, because the inexperienced jurors are likely to look to that person for some guidance.

Communication skills are another indicator of leadership. Strong leaders exhibit confidence, authenticity, likeability, and are well spoken. Finally, watch for interactions with other jurors. Friendly interactions also indicate leadership potential, because these interactions show that the juror is comfortable starting a conversation with strangers in an unfamiliar environment.

Life experiences are also good indicators. Therefore, when you question the prospective jurors, ask questions that will reveal what they do or have done in their work or in their outside activities. Watch for those who have held leadership positions, such as a management position in business or chairing a community organization. A prospective juror who has served as a leader before is a likely prospect to be a leader during deliberations.

Research of fifty actual civil jury trials and jury deliberations in Arizona provides some insight regarding who may be selected as the foreperson.[21] That research revealed that jurors with professional or managerial occupations were more likely to be selected as the foreperson. However, while prior jury service was not the predictor of who would become the foreperson, it was among the criteria that came into play in the selection. Further, the type of case could be

---

20. Strodtbeck F.L. & Lipinski, R.M., *Becoming First Among Equals: Moral Considerations in Jury Foreman Selection*, 49 J. OF PERSONALITY AND SOCIAL PSYCHOLOGY 927–36 (Oct. 1985), *available at* http://psycnet.apa.org/doi/10.1037/0022-3514.49.4.927.

21. Shari Seidman Diamond, et al., *Juror Discussions During Civil Trials: Studying an Arizona Innovation*, 45 ARIZ. L. REV. 1 (2003).

a predictor. For instance, in an antitrust case involving testimony of a statistician, an educational background in statistics was a contributing factor in determining that the person would be selected as the foreperson.[22]

Whether you want a particular leader on the jury obviously depends upon whether that person is someone you would like leading the jury. If you want the person on the jury, do everything you can to keep that person on the jury, such as not tipping off opposing counsel to your elation.

Then again, if a leader is likely to favor your opponent, that juror is likely to play a principal role during deliberations and can turn the jurors against your side. Deselecting that leader is of paramount importance.

2. Outlier

The outlier is a loner. The outlier doesn't play well with others. The outlier doesn't care for the coffee served in the jury room and brings their own. Plaintiff's counsel and the prosecutor prefer to have people who can work together and reach a verdict. They do not want the disharmony that an outlier brings to deliberations. For plaintiffs and prosecutors, it is critical that they deselect the outliers who are primary candidates to be holdouts.

Alternatively, defense counsel in criminal cases who would be satisfied with hung juries and mistrials are delighted to have outliers on their juries who are prone to disagree with the rest and be holdouts.

3. Opinionated

The opinionated prospective juror is one with a strong view that the juror wants the rest of the jury to accept. The opinionated juror may also be an outlier. This person may express the opinion during jury selection or stay quiet in hopes of getting on the jury and then imposing that view on the rest of the jury. An example of a stealth prospective juror is one who opposes the death penalty and remains silent during voir dire, wanting to get on the jury and nullify any potential death penalty verdict. Or, in a civil case, a juror who opposes large recoveries in lawsuits, and conceals those views during voir dire, hoping to be on the jury and prevent any high damages award. It's fine if the opinionated juror is on your side, but a disaster if the person is not. If the opinionated juror is on your opponent's side, it is essential that you deselect that person.

---

22. Shari Seidman Diamond, *Beyond Fantasy and Nightmare: A Portrait of the Jury*, 54 BUFF. L. REV. 717, 754–55 (2006).

The opinionated prospective juror will be easy to identify if the person speaks up during voir dire and expresses the view. On the other hand, the person may be impossible to identify if the person either remains silent or misrepresents. It is critical that you have a dialogue with the quiet jurors.

4. Follower

Followers tend to go along with whatever the rest of the jury decides. Generally, they are the type who are agreeable, easily swayed and avoid confrontation. You do not want to waste a peremptory challenge on a follower, even if they may have adverse opinions or experiences. Peremptory challenges are better spent on adverse jurors who exhibit leadership potential. Of course, you should not hesitate to strike an adverse follower if you find yourself in a situation where you have more peremptory challenges than you need.

5. Impartial

Impartial prospective jurors harbor no biases that would control them in their decision-making. They can be fair, impartial and follow the law. They are the type of people upon whom our justice system is founded.

F. Your Gut Reaction

Above all else, when it comes to deciding whom to deselect, trust your gut reaction. Trust your instincts. If you have a bad feeling about a prospective juror and how they relate to you, it is based upon your lifetime experiences and your understanding of people. For example, your reaction may be based upon your belief that the person was not candid when she answered your questions. Even if you cannot put your finger on why you are uneasy with the person, you should seriously consider exercising a peremptory challenge to that person.

The major caveat is that counsel must guard against exercising a peremptory strike due to implicit bias. Justice Steven C. Gonzalez of the Washington State Supreme Court discussed this concern as follows:

> Finally, a peremptory challenge can be based on unconscious racial bias. In other words, race can subconsciously motivate a peremptory challenge that the attorney genuinely believes is race-neutral. *See* lead opinion at 335–37. As one example among many, an attorney might

exercise a peremptory challenge based solely on his "gut feeling," unaware that the race of the challenged juror caused or substantially contributed to the gut feeling. As another example, an attorney might believe that the basis of her challenge is a prospective juror's answer to a particular question, unaware that she would neither have asked the question nor have brought the challenge against that prospective juror had he been of a different race. In such circumstances, the challenge is motivated at least in part by underlying racial bias, and thus, is racially discriminatory.[23]

---

23. *State v. Saintcalle*, 309 P.3d 326, 356 (Wash. 2013).

Chapter 14

Motions & Responses

> "[T]he Colonists believed in the concept that the community which had suffered injury should be allowed to judge those charged with the injury.... To this day, the interest of a community in trying those who violate its laws remains a central tenet of our judicial system."
>
> United States v. Dubon Otero,
> 76 F. Supp. 2d 161, 164 (D.P.R. 1999)
> (internal quotation marks and citations omitted)

> "Since the state trial judge did not fulfill his duty to protect Sheppard from the inherently prejudicial publicity which saturated the community and to control disruptive influences in the courtroom, we must reverse the denial of the habeas petition."
>
> Sheppard v. Maxwell,
> 384 U.S. 333, 363 (1966)

A. Potential Motions

Potential pretrial motions relating jury selection include:

- motion for change of venue;
- motion challenging the array;
- motion for additional peremptory challenges;
- motion for customized juror questionnaire and additional follow-up questioning;
- motion to prohibit opposing counsel from asking improper questions during jury selection; and
- motion to provide reasonable time for attorney questioning.

Throughout this chapter, we illustrate pretrial motions and responses to motions concerning jury selection with actual cases. The Boston Marathon bombing case is frequently used as an example. In that case, Dzhokhar Tsarnaev was convicted of 17 capital counts, and was sentenced to death on six of the counts. Defendant Tsarnaev never contested that he planted the pressure-cooker bomb at the 2013 Boston Marathon. On the other hand, the defense fiercely contested having the case tried in the United States District Court, Eastern Division of the District of Massachusetts (Boston); the way in which the jury pool was selected; and other matters pertaining to the selection of the jury. Judy Clarke, who had previously served as defense counsel in high profile capital cases including the Unibomber Ted Kaczynski, the Olympic Park Bomber Eric Rudolph, Jared Lee Loughner and Susan Smith—all of whom escaped the death penalty—principally represented the defendant. Assistant United States Attorney William Weintreb, Chief of the Anti-Terrorism and National Security Unit, was lead counsel for the prosecution.

Jury deliberations on sentencing in the Marathon bombing case took 14 hours, which some considered swift for such a complex case. A death penalty expert and commentator suggested that the quick verdict underscored that the grounds for appeal was "the failure to grant a change of venue ..."[1] Another news report at the time of the verdict stated:

> But experts say Tsarnaev does have a reasonably good chance of getting the death sentence set aside, based largely on his lawyers' repeated requests to move the trial out of Boston. The defense contended for months last year that the Boston community was too deeply scarred and that no local jury could give him a fair and impartial trial. The judge refused to hold a hearing on the matter, and an appellate court declined to intervene.[2]

With the Marathon bomber case and other actual cases as illustrations, this chapter explores jury selection issues that may be raised in pretrial motions and the legal arguments made by both sides. If you are planning to make or respond to the motions relating to jury selection, the descriptions of the motions and responses provided should be of value to you. Better still, the original motions, responses, supporting documentation and court decisions on the motions are in the Appendices, which are provided on the online sup-

---

1. *Jury Sentences Boston Marathon Bomber Tsarnaev to Death*, N.Y. Times (May 16, 2015).

2. Richard A. Serrano, *Tsarnaev Could Stay on Death Row for Years*, L.A. Times (May 18, 2015).

plement http://caplaw.com/jury. You can use these originals as templates for drafting your motions or responses.

B. Motion to Change Venue

Typically, a motion to change venue is brought in a case that has generated extensive publicity adverse to the moving party in the home venue. Examples of federal cases where motions for change of venue were made are the Enron case, in which Ken Lay and Jeffrey Skilling were prosecuted for securities fraud and other crimes; the Oklahoma City bombing case, in which Timothy McVeigh was prosecuted for bombing the Alfred P. Murrah Federal Building in downtown Oklahoma City killing 168 and injuring 680 others; and the Boston Marathon bombing case, in which Dzhokhar Tsarnaev was prosecuted for using a weapon of mass destruction that killed three spectators and injured 264 others.

While the Oklahoma City bombing case was moved to Denver, the motions to change venue in the Boston Marathon bombing and the Enron cases were denied. We draw upon the Boston Marathon bombing case for examples of both how to move to change venue and how to oppose a motion to change venue. Appendices 14.2–14.9 contain Boston Marathon bomber case motions to change venue, responses to those motions, a venue expert's report, and the court's orders.

It has been estimated that only about 15 cases in the federal court system have been moved to a different venue since the early 1960s.[3]

Changes of venue occur more often in state cases. To move a trial to another venue in a state is easier and less expensive, because the move can be made to another county rather than moving a trial from one federal circuit to another. Notable state cases involving motions to change venue are the 1991 Rodney King case in which four Los Angeles police officers were videotaped beating King, and the 2002 Beltway snipers case in which Lee Boyd Malvo and John Allen Muhammad were tried for shooting ten people in the Washington D.C. area. In both cases, the motions for change of venue were granted. In the King case, venue was moved to Simi Valley in Ventura County, and in the Beltway snipers case was moved to southeast Virginia.[4]

---

3. Michael Muskal, *Trial Venue Change as Sought in Boston Marathon Case is Rare*, L.A. TIMES, (Feb. 20, 2015), *available at* http://www.latimes.com/nation/la-na-venue-change-20150220-story.html.

4. *Id.*

Naturally, your case may call for a change of venue motion even though it does not rise to the high profile level of these cases.

1. Moving Party

a. Deciding Whether to Make the Motion

Even if the pretrial publicity has been hostile to your client, that does not mean that you will benefit if your motion for change of venue is granted. Instead, you could jump from the frying pan into the fire if the motion is granted. Are the other venues to which your case might be moved desirable places for you to try the case? The answer to this question may be easy if you and others that you consult are familiar with the demography of those other communities. For instance, you may prefer to have a pool of prospective jurors selected from a liberal, urban venue because it suits your client and the case rather than one picked in a rural community.

b. Venue Expert

To determine whether or not you should bring a motion to change venue, you may decide to employ a venue expert to assess the venue issues and to assist in the design of a survey of the current trial venue and alternative venues. In fact, many courts may require survey research or something similar before they will consider a change of venue motion. These courts want to see actual evidence of bias and prejudgment and would rather not rely on the attorney's arguments about the media coverage in the case. These surveys can be expensive. In the case of an indigent defendant in a criminal case, counsel will need to seek funding from the court to employ the expert and conduct a survey.

Your selection of an expert should be driven by whether the judge will give credence to the expert's opinion that venue should be changed. In that regard, the expert's qualifications are critical. Many change of venue experts are also jury consultants.

For example, the defense venue expert in the Boston Marathon bombing case was Edward J. Bronson, Professor Emeritus of Political Science at California State University, Chico. Bronson's declaration was filed in support of the defense motion for change of venue. Among Bronson's qualifications were the following: J.D. from the University of Denver; an L.L.M. from New York University; and a Ph.D. in Political Science, emphasizing Public Law, from the University of Colorado; previously qualified as an expert witness in nearly 300 cases; studied and did research on pretrial publicity for 44 years; developed, conducted, and evaluated surveys to measure the extent and nature of pretrial publicity; qualified over 100 times as an expert witness on change-of-venue motions in state and federal cases; authored the chapters on both venue and pretrial publicity in *California Criminal Law, Procedure & Practice* (15 ed. 2014); and was a member of a four-person group that was commissioned to write standards for venue surveys which have been published after being adopted by the American Society of Trial Consultants.[5]

c. Arguments for Change of Venue Motion

The Sixth Amendment to the United States Constitution guarantees the right to trial "by an impartial jury of the state or district wherein the crime shall have been committed." The Constitution's place-of-trial requirements, however, do not prevent transfer of the proceeding to a different district at the defendant's request if extraordinary local prejudice will prevent a fair trial, which is a "basic requirement of due process."[6]

In 1966, the United States Supreme Court decided *Sheppard v. Maxwell*.[7] Sam Sheppard had been convicted of murder in the second degree for beating his wife to death. The Court's landmark opinion held that Sheppard did not receive a fair trial due to the pervasive pretrial publicity, stating:

> [W]here there is a reasonable likelihood that prejudicial news prior to trial will prevent a fair trial the judge should continue the case until the threat abates, or transfer it to another county not so permeated with publicity.[8]

While the United States Supreme Court has reversed other convictions in cases such as *Sheppard v. Maxwell* where the press coverage corrupted the trial atmosphere and a presumption of prejudice arose, that presumption exists only in extreme cases. The Court stated in the Enron case—*United States v. Skilling*:

> Prominence does not necessarily produce prejudice, and juror *impartiality*, we have reiterated, does not require *ignorance*.... (Jurors are not required to be "totally ignorant of the facts and issues involved"; "scarcely any of those best qualified to serve as jurors will not have formed some impression or opinion as to the merits of the case."); ... ("[E]very case of public interest is almost, as a matter of necessity,

---

5. Appendix 14.1 Bronson Declaration.
6. *In re Murchison*, 349 U.S. 133, 136 (1955).
7. *Sheppard v. Maxwell*, 384 U.S. 333 (1966).
8. *Id.* at 362–63.

brought to the attention of all the intelligent people in the vicinity, and scarcely any one can be found among those best fitted for jurors who has not read or heard of it, and who has not some impression or some opinion in respect to its merits.").[9]

The Supreme Court, in the *Skilling* decision, distinguished the Enron case from the ones where the presumption of prejudice existed on three grounds. First, the venue for the Enron case was Houston, Texas with a large and diverse population, and that situation made it difficult to show that 12 fair and impartial people could not be found to sit on the jury. Second, the news stories, while hostile to Skilling, were not blatantly prejudicial against him. Third, four years had elapsed from when Enron went bankrupt and when the case went to trial, and the media coverage had significantly abated.[10]

In the wake of the landmark *Sheppard v. Maxwell* decision, the American Bar Association adopted standards for granting a motion for change of venue. Section 3.2(c), entitled "Standards for granting the motion," provides:

> A motion for change of venue or continuance shall be granted whenever it is determined that because of the dissemination of potentially prejudicial material, there is a reasonable likelihood that in the absence of such relief, a fair trial cannot be had. This determination may be based on such evidence as qualified public opinion surveys or opinion testimony offered by individuals, or on the court's own evaluation of the nature, frequency, and timing of the material involved. A showing of actual prejudice shall not be required.[11]

Federal court decisions on whether or not to grant a change of venue motion in a criminal case are governed by Federal Rule of Criminal Procedure 21(a), which provides:

> Upon the defendant's motion, the court must transfer the proceeding against that defendant to another district if the court is satisfied that so great a prejudice against the defendant exists in the transferring district that the defendant cannot obtain a fair and impartial trial there.

---

9. *United States v. Skilling*, 561 U.S. 358, 360, 381 (2010) (citations omitted).

10. *Id.* at 382.

11. The American Bar Association Project on Minimum Standards for Criminal Justice, Standards Relating to Fair Trial and Free Press (the Reardon Report) (1966), Section 3.2(c), Standards for granting the motion.

States have adopted similar rules covering the transfer of trials. For example, the California Rule provides:

> In a criminal action pending in the superior court, the court shall order a change of venue: (a) On motion of the defendant, to another county when it appears that there is a reasonable likelihood that a fair and impartial trial cannot be had in the county. When a change of venue is ordered by the superior court, it shall be for the trial itself. All proceedings before trial shall occur in the county of original venue, except when it is evident that a particular proceeding must be heard by the judge who is to preside over the trial.[12]

While all of these examples pertain to criminal cases, courts also consider change of venue motions in civil cases, though less frequently.

d. Social Science Research Supporting the Motion

A significant body of research has been done on the subject of the effects of pretrial publicity on jurors' consideration of evidence and decision-making. The defendant's venue expert may utilize those research findings to support the opinion that the venue should be changed. In the Boston Marathon bomber case, defense expert Edward Bronson offered findings from a review of social science research on the subject entitled N. Steblay, et al., *The Effects of Pretrial Publicity on Juror Verdicts: A Meta-Analytical Review* (hereafter "*Review*").[13]

According to Bronson, the Review examined 30 years of research on the effects of pretrial publicity (referred to as *PTP* in Bronson's report) including "44 empirical studies, representing 5,755 subjects, conducted by dozens of scholars using a variety of methodologies." The following is distillation of what Bronson extracted from the *Review* and included in his declaration, which may be found as Appendix 14.1 (found on the online supplement http://caplaw.com/jury).

- Quoting the Review in his declaration as follows: "Subjects exposed to negative PTP were significantly more likely to judge the defendant guilty compared to subjects exposed to less or no *PTP*."

---

12. CAL. PENAL CODE §§ 1033–1038 (West 2005); *see, e.g.*, WASH. ST. SUPER. CT. CRIM. R. 5.2(a)(2).

13. N. Steblay, et al., *The Effects of Pretrial Publicity on Juror Verdicts: A Meta-Analytical Review*, 23 LAW & HUMAN BEHAVIOR 219 (1999). For an updating study, see T. Daftary-Kapur & S. Penrod, *Are Lab Studies on PTP Generalizable? An Examination of PTP Effects Using a Shadow Jury Paradigm*, 26 THE JURY EXPERT 1 (2014).

- "Pretrial publicity leads to the development of a 'story model.'" The story model "provides the means by which negative publicity provides not just isolated fragments of information, but a belief framework about the defendant's guilt. Those exposed to *PTP* construct a story to make sense out of a particular event. Once that belief is formed, it is very difficult to dislodge."
- "Research has demonstrated the danger of 'conformity prejudice' — fear of community disapproval for rendering an unpopular verdict and has shown the limitations of voir dire to weed out jurors biased by such adverse publicity …"
- "It is not much of a leap to conclude that individuals with a close personal connection to the Boston Marathon and, thus to the bombings, will be less able to set aside preconceived notions regarding guilt and punishment. Thus, in this case, I believe that even a well conducted, probing voir dire by the parties and the Court, may well fail to surface bias and prejudice against Mr. Tsarnaev."

e. Survey

A survey of both the original venue and other potential venues can be conducted and used to support the motion. For example, in the Boston Marathon bombing case, Bronson, the defendant's venue expert, designed a survey of the Eastern Division of the District of Massachusetts (Boston) and four other venues that were selected because they were close, fairly accessible for witnesses, and could accommodate the trial. Bronson selected a California firm to conduct the survey.

The criteria that Bronson used to measure prejudice were: case awareness; case knowledge; prejudgment of the defendant's guilt; support for the death penalty if the defendant were convicted; and case salience.[14] The last factor, case salience, is the relevance that the case has to the lives of the people in the venue. Bronson argued that case salience is highly important in determining whether to change venue and that the Boston Marathon bombing case had "remarkably high salience in Boston because the Marathon attack was portrayed, and likely perceived as virtually a direct attack on Boston, its institutions, its traditions, and each of its residents."[15]

Based upon the survey results reported in his declaration, Bronson summarized his main conclusions as follows:

---

14. App. 14.1 at 26.
15. *Id.* at 24–25.

- "The pretrial prejudice to Mr. Tsarnaev's fair trial rights in the Boston area is extremely high;
- "While the prejudice in the three other divisions or districts surveyed, Springfield, Massachusetts; Manhattan, New York; and Washington, D.C., is somewhat high, the differences justify a change of venue;
- "Washington, D.C. is generally the least prejudicial venue; and
- "Springfield, Massachusetts is the site with prejudice closest to that in the Boston area."[16]

Change of Venue Motions Example: The Boston Marathon bombing case provides exemplars for a defense change of venue motion, and the defense's four motions are Appendices 14.2–14.5 found on the online supplement http://caplaw.com/jury. In the first motion, the defense argued that the adverse publicity gave rise to such a presumption of prejudice that voir dire could not produce a fair and impartial jury.[17] The initial motion relied upon preliminary survey findings that Boston ranked as the most prejudiced of the potential venues. The court denied the motion, stating that voir dire could adequately identify prejudice.[18]

The defense's second motion argued that the need for a change of venue had increased because the prejudicial publicity and "leaks" of non-public information continued after the first motion.[19] The defense's second motion relied heavily upon the defense's venue expert Bronson's declaration.

Jury selection began, and prospective jurors completed 1,373 juror questionnaires. The defense filed a third motion for change of venue contending that the responses in the questionnaires showed "that an extraordinary 85 percent of the prospective jurors either believe Mr. Tsarnaev is guilty, or have some self-identified 'connection' to the case or both" and "[s]tronger support for a finding of presumed prejudice in Boston is difficult to imagine, and the existing record precludes a fair trial in Boston."[20] Again, the trial court denied the motion. The defense twice sought relief from the First Circuit via mandamus, but both were denied.[21]

When voir dire produced provisionally qualified potential jurors and it was time for the parties to exercise peremptories, the defense brought a fourth mo-

---

16. *Id.* at 27.
17. App. 14.2 at 4, First motion.
18. App. 14.3 at 13, Memorandum in Support of Second Motion.
19. App. 14.3 at 2, Memorandum in Support of Second Motion.
20. App. 14.4 at 1, Memorandum in Support of Third Motion for Change of Venue.
21. App. 14.5 at 1, Fourth Motion for Change of Venue.

tion for change of venue. This motion was made to complete the record and was based on the total record.[22]

2. Responding Party

In responding to a defense motion to change venue in a criminal case, the government can rely on the Article III of the United States Constitution that provides that "[t]he trial of all Crimes ... shall be held in the State where the said Crimes shall have been committed," before a "jury of the State and district wherein the crime shall have been committed."[23] Further, the prosecution can argue that the United States Supreme Court in *United States v. Skilling* held that when Article III was considered together with the defendant's constitutional right to a trial, the defendant's request for change of venue should be granted only if "extraordinary local prejudice will prevent a fair trial."[24]

Appendices 14.6–14.9 are the government's responses to defendant Dzhokhar Tsarnaev's motions for a change of venue in the Boston Marathon bombing case. In the remainder of this section, we summarize the prosecution's responses to the defense change-of-venue motions. These summaries and the full original responses serve as examples of how the prosecution may argue against a change of venue motion.

a. Arguments against the Motions

To oppose a motion for change of venue, the prosecution can argue, as the government did in the Boston Marathon bombing case, that "the Supreme Court has made it nearly impossible to demonstrate that a jury pool has been so contaminated by negative pretrial publicity that a court cannot lawfully even attempt to seat an impartial jury using the traditional tools of jury questionnaires and voir dire."[25] The government in that case then argued that in only one case — *Rideau v. Louisiana*[26] — was the defense able to make the necessary showing. Further, the government in the Boston Marathon bombing case argued, "Since that case was decided (*Sheppard v. Maxwell*), over fifty years ago, hundreds of defendants in federal cases have moved for a change of venue based on claims of presumed prejudice; virtually every one of those motions

---

22. App. 14.5 at 1, Fourth Motion for Change of Venue.
23. U.S. Const. art. III, § 2, cl. 3.
24. *United States v. Skilling, 561 U.S. 358, 378 (2010).*
25. App. 14.6 at 1, Government's Surreply to Defendant's Motion for Change of Venue.
26. *Rideau v. Louisiana, 373 U.S. 723 (1963).*

has been denied, and to the government's knowledge, not a single such denial has been reversed on appeal."[27]

Response to Motion for Change of Venue Example: In the Boston Marathon bombing case, the prosecution's response to the defense survey and the expert's report that underpinned the defense motion for a venue change was to attack the expert's impartiality, the bases for the expert's opinion and the expert's analysis of the survey data.

Regarding defense expert Edward Bronson, the prosecution pointed out that he was a lifelong opponent of the death penalty who claimed he fought against it by testifying in death penalty cases.[28] Also, the government contended that in many of the highly publicized cases in which the motion was based on Bronson's report, the motion was denied. The prosecution argued, "[C]ourts often disagree with Mr. Bronson's media analyses and dismiss his use of polling data as unhelpful. They also reject many of his fundamental assumptions about jury behavior, which are at odds with established law. Courts generally hold instead that in determining whether it is possible to seat an impartial jury, a thorough voir dire of actual potential jurors is far more helpful and reliable than the opinions of a paid social scientist."[29]

The government argued that the publicity was neither as inflammatory nor as emotional as Bronson claimed, pointing out that his methodology captured articles that were hardly related to the case.[30] Also, the prosecution argued that Bronson's media analysis was unreliable and inaccurate. For instance, the government argued that anyone who actually lived in Boston and read the Boston Globe every day would know that Bronson's attestation that between April 1, 2013 and July 11, 2014, "the Globe published approximately [2,420 articles or] 5.2 articles per day referring to the bombing" was "absurd."[31] Further, the prosecution argued that only a small percentage of people responded to the defense survey and that the sampling was not representative.

In reply to the defense's "story model" of memory argument, which opines that once a wave of adverse publicity causes the public to have such a fixed view of a case that it cannot be dislodged, the prosecution contended that the courts have rejected the model.[32] The prosecution argued that the passage of

---

27. *Id.*
28. App. 14.6 at 2, Government's Surreply to Defendant's Motion for Change of Venue.
29. *Id.*
30. *Id.* at 10.
31. *Id.* at 8.
32. *Id.* at 14–16.

time between the negative publicity and the time of trial can cause the prejudicial effect of that publicity to dissipate, citing *Patton v. Yount*.[33] In *Yount*, the United States Supreme Court decided that the passage of time between the adverse publicity attending Yount's first trial and his second trial (after the original conviction was overturned) eliminated the presumption of prejudice.[34]

Another government argument made against changing venue in the Marathon bombing case was that public opinion polls are flawed and that the court should trust voir dire as a means of determining a prospective juror's fitness for jury duty.[35] The prosecution cited several cases holding that voir dire was more reliable than surveys in determining the effect of pretrial publicity.[36]

C. Motion Challenging the Array

1. Moving Party

In order to succeed in a challenge to the array of jurors summoned to jury duty, the moving party must establish three things:

(1) that the allegedly excluded group is a cognizable group;

(2) that the representation of that group in the pool is not fair and reasonable given the number of members of the group in the community; and

(3) that the underrepresentation is due to systematic exclusion of the group from the jury selection process.[37] Random selection from licensed drivers[38] has been an acceptable manner of selection of the jury pool.

---

33. *Patton v. Yount*, 467 U.S. 1025 (1984).

34. *Id.* at 1029–30.

35. App. 14.6 at 17–18, Government's Surreply to Defendant's Motion for Change of Venue.

36. *United States v. Haldeman*, 559 F.2d 31, 64 n.43 (D.C. Cir. 1976); *United States v. Rodriguez*, 581 F.3d 775, 785–86 (8th Cir. 2009); *United States v. Campa*, 459 F.3d 1121, 1145 (11th Cir. 2006); *United States v. Skilling*, Case No. 04-25 (S.D. Tex. Jan 19, 2005); *United States v. Mandel*, 431 F. Supp. 90, 100–01 (D.Md. 1977); *United States v. McVeigh*, 918 F. Supp. 1467, 1473 (W.D. Okla. 1996).

37. *Durren v. Missouri*, 439 U.S. 357, 364 (1979).

38. *Stanton v. State*, 648 So. 2d 638, 640 (Ala. Crim. App. 1994) (licensed drivers); *United States. v. Odeneal*, 517 F.3d 406, 512 (6th Cir. 2008) (registered voters); *United States v. Royal*, 174 F.3d 1, 6 (1st Cir. 1999) (same).

Motion Challenging the Array Example: In the Boston Marathon bombing case, the trial court granted defendant Tsarnaev's request for records maintained by the District of Massachusetts that the jury commission and Jury Commissioner for Massachusetts relied on in the selection process for both the grand jury and the petit juries during 2011–13.[39] The defense claimed that, based upon a review of those records, there were substantial violations of both the Jury Selection and Service Act (hereafter JSSA), 28 U.S.C. § 1861 et seq., and the Sixth Amendment of the United States Constitution fair cross-section of the community requirement. Based on those violations, the defense moved to dismiss the indictment in accordance with 28 U.S.C. § 1867(a), which provides that the defendant may move to dismiss "on grounds of substantial failure to comply with the provisions of this title in selecting the grand ... jury," and to stay the proceedings until the jury wheel was reconstituted to conform with those laws.

In support of the motion challenging the array, the defense argued that the three-step process for determining a violation of the cross-section requirement was met. First, the defense argued that persons over the age of 70 should be recognized as a distinctive group because age, like race, sex and national origin, is an immutable characteristic.[40]

Second, while the defense acknowledged that most courts including the First Circuit used an absolute disparity standard, which measures the difference between the percentage of members of the distinctive group in the relevant population and the percentage of group members on the jury, the defense contended a comparative disparity analysis should be applied and that such an analysis showed an under-representation of persons over the age of 70. Also, the defense argued that African Americans were under-represented.[41] Third and lastly, the defense argued that the systematic exclusion requirement was met because the District of Massachusetts Plan for Random Selection of Jurors (Jury Plan) permitted upon request the excuse of persons over the age of 70 years.[42]

The defense also argued that the Jury Plan was violated because replacement summonses were not sent out as required by the Plan when they were initially returned as "undeliverable."[43]

---

39. App. 14.10 at 1, Motion to Dismiss Indictment and Stay Proceedings Pending Reconstituting Jury Wheel to Conform with Statutory and Constitutional Requirements

40. App. 14.10 at 8–9, Motion to Dismiss Indictment and Stay Proceedings Pending Reconstituting Jury Wheel to Conform with Statutory and Constitutional Requirements.

41. *Id.* at 10–13.

42. *Id.* at 13–14.

43. *Id.* at 5–7.

2. Responding Party

In order to effectively reply to a motion challenging the array, the responding party should refute the defense's contentions that the cross-section requirement was violated through a systematic exclusion of a cognizable group.

Response to Motion Challenging the Array Example: The United States Attorney in the Boston Marathon bombing case responded to the defense arguments that the Massachusetts Jury Plan violated the cross-section requirements of the Sixth Amendment and JSSA with an argument that the cross-section requirement does not guarantee that the "venires ... [be] a substantially true mirror of the community."[44] It requires only that "the jury wheels, pools of names, panels, or venires from which juries are drawn must not systematically exclude distinctive groups in the community and thereby fail to be reasonably representative thereof."[45]

Further, the government's response argued that the Jury Plan met the three-stage process. Regarding the first stage, the government argued that persons over 70 years of age are not a distinctive group because a distinctive group is defined by "attitudinal representativeness"—the goal of jury selection is to seek a jury that represents the attitudes of the community in which the trial takes place. Also, the prosecution pointed out that "[e]very appellate court to consider this issue has held that an excluded age group is not 'distinctive' for Sixth Amendment purposes."[46] The government contended that the second step—under-representation—had not been shown, pointing first to the defense's acknowledgement that a two-percent disparity between the proportion of African Americans in the jury-eligible population and the proportion in the Qualified Jury Wheels did not establish a prima facie case of violation. Further the government argued that the First Circuit had rejected the proposed comparative disparity test.[47]

To meet the defense arguments that the Jury Plan was violated because replacement summonses were not sent out as required by the Plan, the government first traced the background of the Jury Plan. In 2005, the then U.S. District Court Judge Nancy Gertner concluded that African-Americans were

---

44. *Barber v. Ponte*, 772 F.2d 982, 997 (1st Cir.1985) (en banc).

45. App. 14.11 at 6, Opposition to Defendant's Motion to Dismiss Indictment and Stay Proceedings Pending Reconstitution of Jury Wheel (citing *Taylor v. Louisiana*, 419 U.S. 522, 538 (1975)).

46. *Id.* at 8–9.

47. *Id.* at 7.

unrepresented because, among other reasons, summons were often returned "undeliverable." Therefore, Judge Gertner ordered that summons be reissued based upon her holding that the JSSA, but not the Sixth Amendment, was violated. The First Circuit reversed, holding that neither the Constitution nor the JSSA were violated, but deciding also that the district court could revise the Jury Plan to comply with the statute. Therefore, the government argued, failure to resummons was not a violation, because under the First Circuit's decision, it was never required for compliance. Further, the government argued that although the law did not require reissuances of summons that were not delivered, the defense never proved a violation of the specialized draw requirement.[48]

D. Motion for Extra Peremptory Challenges

1. Moving Party

While the number of peremptory challenges allotted to each side is set by either statute or court rule, you may have grounds for requesting additional peremptory challenges. Chapter 3 Challenges to Prospective Jurors discusses the history of peremptories in the United States, the movement for their eradication, and the current trend toward symmetrical distribution of peremptories after the *Batson* decision.

Motion for Extra Peremptories Example: The defense in the Boston Marathon bombing case moved for ten additional peremptory challenges. In accordance with Federal Rule of Criminal Procedure 24(b)(1), each side has 20 peremptory challenges when the government seeks the death penalty. The defense contended that the statute created an advantage for defendants in all felony cases except a capital case, because for other felonies, the government has six peremptory challenges and the defense is given ten.[49] The defense stated, "[the] Rule would appear to create a perverse incentive for the government to seek the death penalty in precisely those cases where its proof is sufficiently weak that equalizing the number of challenges might increase the likelihood of conviction." The defense contended that to have the same 5:3 ratio given other felons, the defense should be given 13, and "[t]hus, the defendant's

---

48. *Id.* at 1–6.
49. FED. R. CRIM. P. 24(b)(2).

request for 10 additional challenges would not even restore him to the ratio of challenges guaranteed to all felony defendants in the federal courts—except where the government seeks the death penalty."[50]

Despite the express wording of Rule 24(b), the defense argued that the court has the inherent power to grant additional peremptories. The defense asserted that the Supreme Court implicitly approved the "granting of peremptory challenges to criminal defendants as a remedy to vindicate fair trial rights," and cited *Skilling v. United States*[51] as an example, because the trial court in that case had allotted the defendants jointly two extra peremptories.[52]

2. Responding Party

The response to the request for additional peremptory challenges can be founded on the language of the statute or court rule setting the number of peremptories granted to each side.

Response to Motion for Extra Peremptories Example: In the Boston Marathon bombing case, the prosecution relied upon the plain language of Federal Rule of Criminal Procedure 24(b) that granted 20 peremptory challenges to each side, pointing out that Congress allowed only one exception— when there are multiple defendants.[53] The prosecution also relied upon *United States v. Gullion* in which the defense sought additional peremptories due to pretrial prejudicial publicity. In *Gullion*, the First Circuit affirmed the district court's denial of the request, holding, "While Rule 24(b) permits extra peremptory challenges at the discretion of the court if there is more than one defendant, there is no authority in that rule for according extra challenges to a single defendant."[54] The prosecution pointed out that the additional peremptories awarded in *Skilling* were authorized by Rule 24(b).[55] The defense motion for additional peremptories was denied for the reasons argued by the government.[56]

---

50. App. 14.12 at 3, Defendant's Motion for Extra Peremptory Challenges.

51. *Skilling v. United States,* 561 U.S. 358 (2010).

52. *Id.* at 4.

53. App. 14.13 at 1, Opposition to Defendant's Motion for Additional Peremptory Challenges.

54. *United States v. Gullion,* 575 F.2d 26, 29 (1st Cir. 1978) (internal quotation marks and citation omitted); App. 14.13 at 2, Opposition to Defendant's Motion for Additional Peremptory Challenges.

55. App. 14.13 at 5, Opposition to Defendant's Motion for Additional Peremptory Challenges.

56. App. 14.13 at 5, Opinion and Order December 23, 2014.

E. Motion for Customized Questionnaire and Follow-Up Attorney Questioning

As we discussed at pages 102–105, customized juror questionnaires are utilized in both state and federal court. Here we discuss both requests for such questionnaires and opposition to them. In the Appendix you will find questionnaires from the following cases:

- *In re TFT-LCD (Flat-Panel)* trial—App. 4.2;
- O. J. Simpson robbery trial—App. 4.3;
- Boston Marathon bomber trial—App. 4.4;
- A capital murder trial—App. 4.5;
- An asbestos trial—App. 4.8; and
- People of California vs. Michael Jackson child molestation trial— App. 4.9

In this section, we use Engle Progeny cases to illustrate how to move for a customized juror questionnaire and follow-up questions and how to respond to the motion. Once again, we point out that the summaries here and the actual motion documents in the Appendices can be of value in planning to make or respond to a motion and in drafting those documents. We cover most but not every argument made by the parties in support of or opposition to the motion.

Howard Aaron Engle was the lead plaintiff in a class action lawsuit filed in 1994. The suit was brought on behalf of smokers alleging that the plaintiffs became addicted to nicotine and that the tobacco industry did not warn them of the danger. In 2000, the jury returned a verdict of $145 billion. Eventually, the verdict was overturned because the appellate court found the group was too disparate to be a certified as a class. The Florida Supreme Court decertified the group but permitted members of the group to file individual lawsuits; these individual cases are referred to as "Engle Progeny cases." Specifically, in this chapter, we refer to four of the Engle Progeny cases brought in the United States District Court, Middle District of Florida, Jacksonville Division, and we refer to them as the "Engle Progeny cases."[57]

---

57. Case 3:09-cv-10000-WGY-JBT, Document 1307, Filed 12/09/13, In re Engle Progeny Cases: *DeShaies v. R.J. Reynolds Tobacco,* Case No. 3:09-cv-11080.

1. Moving Party

a. Deciding Whether to Make the Motion

Two matters to consider when deciding whether or not to move for a customized juror questionnaire and follow-up questioning are: (1) whether your client will benefit from a questionnaire and (2) whether the court is likely to seriously entertain your motion.

First, assuming that you are concerned that the prospective jurors may harbor implicit biases, such as racial bias, that could distort their decision making against your client, consideration should be given to requesting an expanded juror questionnaire. As we cover in greater detail later, arguably general jury questioning fails to adequately uncover implicit bias, and a juror questionnaire is an efficient and effective way to do so.[58]

Second, do you have a chance of succeeding with your motion? The court already may have established practices that make the effort to get the court to use a customized questionnaire or to allow attorney questioning fruitless endeavors. For example, the court may have a practice of not permitting attorney questioning during voir dire, except to the extent that counsel may submit questions for the judge to ask. The court may already have a questionnaire that is ordinarily uses in your type of case. It is incumbent upon you to determine what the court's practices for jury selection are before you decide to make a motion for a questionnaire and additional attorney follow-up questioning. You do not want to unnecessarily take up the court's time with issues that the court has already decided in the judge's previous cases of the same type or have been resolved by appellate courts or uniformly decided adversely to your client by other judges in the judge's district.

b. Arguments for Juror Questionnaire and Attorney Follow-Up Voir Dire

To prevail with your motion, you must convince the court that an expanded juror questionnaire is warranted in your case and that the utilization of the expanded questionnaire will not overburden the court. Common justifications for an expanded questionnaire include media coverage and sensitive case issues.

---

58. *United States v. Shavers*, 615 F.2d 266, 268 (5th Cir. 1980); Case 3:09-cv-10000-WGY-JBT, Document 1307, Filed 12/09/13, In re Engle Progeny Cases: *DeShaies v. R.J. Reynolds Tobacco*, Case No. 3:09-cv-11080, Plaintiff's Motion for Juror Questionnaire and Attorney Follow-up Voir Dire at 15–17, App. 14.14.

For example, a judge may be more likely to allow an expanded questionnaire in a case involving sensitive claims such as sexual abuse than in an intellectual property case that does not involve sensitive issues.

In some cases, courts have adopted standard questionnaires for common litigation types. For example, in King County, Washington, some judges have adopted a standard, expanded questionnaire for asbestos cases due to the frequency of such claims.

Strong Biases Argument Example: In the Engle Progeny cases, plaintiffs' leadoff arguments for an expanded juror questionnaire and attorney follow-up questioning quoted Judge Edward Nichols to make the point that prospective jurors in the Engle Progeny cases harbored "deep seated biases against both parties—tobacco companies and smokers' families who seek recovery." Judge Nichols was quoted in part, as follows:

> I will say this, that I have tried three death penalty cases and did not have as many people who had as strong opinions in those cases as I have had in this case. Whether it be people who smoke and feel that it's a personal choice and say they aren't the right people for this jury or people who don't smoke and feel like cigarettes should be banned and say they are not the right person for this jury.
>
> The point is, it is very, very difficult to find a group of people, even 6 out of 150 who do not have some opinion, who do not have some information about the issues that are relevant in this case. I'm not suggesting in any way that the standards for challenges for cause should be loosened in these cases or that a different rule should apply; that's clearly not the case. I'm familiar with the case law and will apply it. I've tried cases for nearly 20 years, criminal, civil, every kind. The rules are the rules are the rules.
>
> I guess what I am trying to say is that ... these cases are ... challenging, difficult, different. They're challenging in many respects. In the context of trying to find a group of six jurors who have a sufficiently clean plate to satisfy both sides is a challenge ...[59]

Questionnaire Is Necessary Argument Example: Plaintiffs in the Engle Progeny cases argued that general voir dire questioning was not sufficient to reveal subconscious or unacknowledged bias, citing several federal cases, such as *United States v. Shavers*, for the proposition that general questions that are

---

59. App. 14.14 at 1–2.

"too broad" "might not reveal latent prejudice."[60] The plaintiffs argued that the opinions are supported by research "demonstrating that general voir dire presents serious problems for identifying biased jurors."[61] Also, the plaintiffs argued that the research suggests that prospective jurors are more candid and accurate when answering the questionnaire "than they do if required to respond to the same questions individually in front of a courtroom full of people, a process that prospective jurors often perceive as more intrusive and intimidating."[62]

Plaintiffs further argued that detailed questionnaires were the best way to detect latent biases and that defendants had made that argument to state courts in state Engle cases.[63]

Won't Overburden the Court Argument Example: Naturally, the trial court will be concerned about the amount of time and effort that will be dedicated to preparing, completing, reviewing and otherwise employing a juror questionnaire and allowing follow-up questioning.

Plaintiffs' counsel in the Engle Progeny cases proposed a questionnaire that was an edited version of a questionnaire used in another case with the edits designed to make the questions clearer.[64] Then, plaintiffs argued that use of that questionnaire and parties' voir dire "did not require substantially more resources or time to administer."[65]

If you are seeking an expanded questionnaire, it is important to make it as least burdensome on the court as possible. For example, you might consider offering to provide the blank copies of the questionnaire to the court rather than relying on the court to make enough copies for jurors. Similarly, you might offer to have your staff make copies of the completed questionnaires for you and the other side. These offers reduce the burden on the court and make it easier for the court to agree to your request.

Another way to reduce the burden on the court is to reach an agreement with your opposing counsel before raising the issue with the court. If both parties agree to a questionnaire in advance and agree to the particular questionnaire to be used, it makes it much easier on the court to allow it. However, if there is disagreement between the parties that the court would have to

---

60. *Id.* at 15 (citing *United States v. Shavers*, 615 F.2d 266, 268 (5th Cir. 1980)).
61. *Id.*
62. *Id.* at 21.
63. *Id.* at 17.
64. *Id.* at 18–19.
65. *Id.* at 23.

deal with in order to allow a questionnaire, the court may be disinclined to sort through such disagreement.

Follow-up Questioning Should Be Allowed Example: The arguments made for follow-up questioning are identical to those that can be made for attorney voir dire questioning regardless of whether there is a motion for a customized questionnaire.

In the federal Engle Progeny cases, plaintiff argued that under Federal Rule of Civil Procedure 47(a), a court has authority to allow attorney questioning of prospective jurors—the court "may permit the parties or their attorneys to make any further inquiry it considers proper, or must itself ask any of their additional question it considers proper." Beyond that, plaintiffs contended that voir dire questioning should be sufficient to allow a party to intelligently exercise challenges, citing language from several federal cases. For example, plaintiffs quoted *United States v. Brooks* to the effect that voir dire must provide "a reasonable assurance that any prejudice would be discovered if present."[66]

Further, plaintiffs argued that if the case involved controversy over which citizens are expected to harbor bias, more specific inquiry into jurors' opinions is required and that more individualized voir dire is called for in high pretrial publicity cases. Counsel argued that the Engle Progeny cases had received unusually extensive publicity and quoted statements made by prospective jurors during voir dire in previous Engle Progeny case jury selections.[67]

2. Responding Party

The response to the motion for a customized juror questionnaire can be framed around the concepts that an acceptable approach, short of introducing a questionnaire, already exists and that that alternative approach will save the court's time and lead to a fair and impartial jury.

An Expanded Questionnaire Is Unnecessary Example: To refute the plaintiffs' motion in the Engle Progeny cases for an expanded questionnaire, the defense contended that the plaintiffs were proposing an "outlier approach" to jury selection that had only been adopted by one federal judge in the *Smith* case.[68] The defense maintained that arguments for the approach proposed by

---

66. *Id.* at 3 (citing *United States v. Brooks*, 670 F.2d 148, 152 (11th Cir. 1982)).

67. *Id.* at 4–13.

68. Case 3:09-cv-13631-WGY-JBT, Document 68, Filed 12/20/13, In re: Engle Progeny Cases: *DeShaies v. R.J. Reynolds Tobacco*, Case No. 3:09-cv-11080, Defendants' Response to

the plaintiffs had been rejected in the vast majority of Engle Progeny cases tried since procedures were established in *Gollihue*, an earlier Engle Progeny case.[69]

Rather than expanding the juror questionnaire and having attorney follow-up questioning by the parties, the defense proposed that the court adhere to the acceptable jury selection method established in the *Gollihue* case. The *Gollihue* case jury selection procedures had three components. First, the court would use a concise written juror questionnaire patterned after the one used in *Gollihue*. Second, the federal judge, not counsel, would ask follow-up questions, incorporating acceptable suggestions by the parties. Third, the court would call a pool of 35 prospective jurors.[70]

Additionally, the defendants criticized the plaintiffs' proposed questionnaire, claiming that some of the questions were unnecessary and created confusion.[71]

Questioning by the Parties Is Unnecessary and Can Be Detrimental Example: In the Engle Progeny cases, the defense pointed out that the plaintiffs never objected in *Gollihue* after the court's sole questioning of the jurors without attorney participation and indeed the defense praised the judge in another case when only the judge questioned the potential jurors.[72]

The defense argued that party questioning should be avoided, because when plaintiffs were permitted to question jurors in the outlier *Smith* case, it led to "a truncated and skewed voir dire procedure that led to the dismissal of half the panel before the exercise of peremptory strikes."[73] Plaintiffs' questioning in *Smith* sought "a commitment that the jurors would side against the plaintiff, based on general skepticism toward smoking litigation."[74] The defense contended that the inquiry should have been more neutral and aimed at determining whether the prospective jurors could set aside their beliefs and decide the case based on the evidence and the law.[75]

Exclusive Judge Conducted Voir Dire Is Quicker and Better Example: In the Engle Progeny cases, the defense claimed that "the traditional federal ap-

---

Plaintiff's Motion for Juror Questionnaire and Attorney Follow-Up Voir Dire, App. 14.15 at 2.

69. *Id.* at 2, 5–6.
70. *Id.* at 3–4.
71. *Id.* at 15–17.
72. *Id.* at 6.
73. *Id.* at 10–11.
74. *Id.* at 10.
75. *Id.*

proach (voir dire conducted entirely by the Court) facilitates fair, even-handed, and efficient examination."[76] In support of the argument, the defense cited an empirical study that showed that when solely a judge conducts the voir dire, the jury is picked in fifty-eight percent of the time required for when attorneys asked questions.[77]

The defense sought to counter the plaintiffs' argument that defendants argued for more extensive voir dire in state court Engle Progeny cases by noting that state rules provide for attorney questioning. Further the defense noted that while jury selection in state court takes an average of two and a half days, it takes the federal court an average of three hours.[78]

F. Motion to Preclude Improper Questioning

1. Moving Party

If you anticipate that counsel will ask improper questions during jury selection and have a good faith basis for your belief (for instance, you have been in trial with counsel before, and he has asked improper questions), you can make a motion in limine to preclude counsel from asking certain types of questions during voir dire. You can support your brief with documentation of opposing counsel in another trial asking improper questions during jury selection, such as a transcript of a prior trial or the affidavit of someone who observed opposing counsel in a prior trial.

If you do not have a basis for your motion, you can still bring your motion in limine describing the types of questions that you want the court to prohibit opposing counsel from asking. When you bring a motion without a record to support your position, you can anticipate that opposing counsel may argue that the court should presume that counsel will behave appropriately and that your motion is premature. Opposing counsel may contend that jury selection should proceed, and the court should wait until an objection is made to a question and rule on it then. To counter this wait-and-see argument, you can cite Federal Rule 103(d), which states: "Preventing the Jury from Hearing Inadmissible Evidence. To the extent practicable, the court must conduct a jury trial so that inadmissible evidence is not suggested to the jury by any means."

---

76. *Id.* at 11.

77. *Id.* at 11 (summarizing Levit, Nelson, Ball & Chernick, *Expediting Voir Dire: An Empirical Study*, 44 So. CAL. L. REV. 916 (1971)).

78. *Id.* at 14.

You can argue that you are objecting to the question that counsel may ask because, just as it is impossible to unring a bell, it will be impossible to erase the improper question from the jurors' minds.

a. Improper Questions

Fed. R. Civ. P. 47(a) provides:

> The court may permit the parties or their attorneys to examine prospective jurors or may itself do so. If the court examines the jurors, it must permit the parties or their attorneys to make any further inquiry it considers proper, or must itself ask any of their additional questions it considers proper.

While this Rule provides that the judge may permit the attorneys to "make any further inquiry it considers proper," it does not explicitly explain what is proper or improper.

What is an improper question? As we have discussed in earlier chapters, while one judge may allow counsel to sell the case during jury selection, another may require that strict guidelines be followed, such as those found on pages 92–93. Assuming that you want the court to restrict voir dire questioning by opposing counsel, which means that the court will probably likewise limit the kinds of inquiries you make, you will have to convince the court that certain types of questions are improper and should be prohibited. To support your motion in limine, you may be able to draw upon your state's statutes, court rules, case law and/or even Judicial Standards.

i. Statutes or Court Rules

Your state statute may provide legal authority for your motion. For instance, Section 222.5 of the California Code of Civil Procedure provides: "[t]o select a fair and impartial jury in civil jury trials ... counsel for each party shall have the right to examine, by oral or direct questioning, any of the prospective jurors in order to enable counsel to intelligently exercise both peremptory challenges and challenges for cause." Further the Code provides "[t]he scope of the examination conducted by counsel shall be within reasonable limits prescribed by the trial judge in the judge's sound discretion." On point, Section 222.5 classifies as an improper question "any question that, as its dominant purpose, attempts to precondition the prospective jurors to a particular result, indoctrinate the jury, or question the prospective jurors concerning the pleadings and the applicable law."

Even if your state statute does not include a specific provision defining what improper questions are, you can argue that any questions that do not serve the court rule's or the statutorily defined purpose of voir dire (to select a fair and impartial jury) are improper and should not be permitted.

ii. Case Law

An example of case law restricting the type of questions counsel may ask is *People v. Williams*,[79] in which the California Supreme Court held:

> We reaffirm that it is not "a function of the examination of prospective jurors to educate the jury panel to the particular facts of the case, to compel the jurors to commit themselves to vote a particular way, to prejudice the jury for or against a particular party, to argue the case, to indoctrinate the jury, or to instruct the jury in matters of law." (*Rousseau v. West Coast House Movers, supra*, 256 Cal.App.2d 878, 882.) Therefore, a question may be excluded if it appears to be intended solely to accomplish such improper purpose. In addition, the court need allow only reasonable questions—although it cannot exclude questions proper in scope, it is free to require that they be phrased in neutral, nonargumentative form.

iii. Judicial Standards

Other authoritative sources may support the motion in limine. For example, California has Standards of Judicial Administration and Standard 3.25 that provides:

> In addition, some judges further advise attorneys to refrain from re-peating questions asked by the judge or other attorney; expounding on any theory of the case, evidence to be presented, or the law; referencing inadmissible or prejudicial matters; asking questions regarding a juror's knowledge about the law of the case; asking a juror to define legal terms; asking questions about the jurors conduct in the jury room if evidentiary or voting problems arise; asking questions as to how a juror would weigh a particular fact or circumstance; requesting a juror "tell me about yourself;" asking a juror to promise anything; phrasing statements in the form of a question; and addressing a juror by his or her first name.

---

79. *People v. Williams*, 29 Cal. 3d 392, 408, 628 P.2d 869 (1981).

b. Questions Designed to Indoctrinate

You could move to preclude opposing counsel from asking questions that are fashioned in such a way as to indoctrinate or educate the prospective jurors.

Indoctrination Examples: In *Villaverde v. Asbestos Corporation Limited*, an asbestos lawsuit, plaintiff made a motion in limine to preclude the defense from asking improper questions, specifically questions attempting to indoctrinate the jury during voir dire.[80] The motion was filed in the Superior Court of California for the County of San Francisco, and plaintiff contended that the California Code and the California case law previously discussed supported the motion. Appendix 14.16 is the Plaintiff's Motion in Limine, which can serve as a template if you wish to make a similar motion.

The following is an excerpt from the section in plaintiff's motion asking the court to preclude the defense from asking questions that are designed to educate the jury as to particular facts, to present evidence or to inject opinion of counsel:

> Such questions and/or statement might include, but are not necessarily limited to:

- *Has anybody had experience with a small business?*
  (This is an attempt to suggest or otherwise infer that a defendant is a small business).
- *The material at issue is (sic) this case is _____, which is _____ ... That's the product that's in issue.*
  (This is an attempt to summarize facts or insert evidence. Therefore, any statement like this should be precluded, especially one which misstates or mischaracterizes the facts of this case, such as when there are several products at issue).
- *There is going to be "sketchy" information presented about my client.*
  (Any statement similar to this posed by defense counsel equates to insertion of fact and opinion, as well as a mischaracterization of the evidence).
- *There will be evidence about the knowledge of the Navy and what the Navy knew. The defendant did not know about the dangers of asbestos.*

---

80. Plaintiff's Motion in Limine, *Villaverde v. Asbestos Corp. Ltd.*, Filed Mar. 5, 2013, App. 14.16.

- *Has anybody ever received a bill that was not theirs?*
- *Do any of the jurors believe, as I do, that _____?*

Plaintiff also sought to stop defense counsel from asking questions or making statements that would prejudice the plaintiff. Plaintiff set out these kinds of questions as follows:

Such questions and/or statements might include, but are not necessarily limited to:

- *Just because we used asbestos in our product, does that mean we are or were wrong?*
- *Just because we have been sued, does that mean we are wrong?*
- *Does anyone believe where there is smoke, there is fire?*
- *Just because we are here defending this case, does that mean we are wrong?*
- *Just because this case made it this far, does that mean the case must have some merit?*

c. Questions Introducing Improper Argument or Inadmissible Evidence

A motion in limine can be used to prevent opposing counsel from making improper arguments or introducing inadmissible evidence through voir dire questions.

Golden Rule and "Reptile Strategy" Example: In *Ernani v. City of Miami Beach*, plaintiff made a motion in limine to preclude the plaintiff from making "Golden Rule" arguments or employing the "Reptile Strategy" during voir dire.[81] The defense argued that plaintiff during voir dire would utilize the "Reptile Strategy" promulgated in David Ball and Don Keenan's book entitled, *Reptile: The 2009 Manual of the Plaintiff's Revolution* (2009), and attempt to argue that the jurors have the power to improve the safety of themselves and their families by rendering a verdict that would reduce or eliminate the dangerous conduct displayed by the defendant. The defense motion offered the following as the types of questions that fall within the Reptile Strategy:

Q: Aside and apart from money for damages, **how do you feel verdicts might affect community safety** or things like that?

---

81. Defense Motion in Limine, *Ernani v. City of Miami Beach*, S.D. of Fla., Filed Jan. 18, 2016, App. 14.17.

Q: Do you feel you are a person that could be asked to decide some rules about **community safety** and to make those decisions?

In the motion, the defense summarized the arguments in support of the motion to preclude the plaintiff from asking such questions, as follows:

> Having already established the underpinnings of the Reptile Strategy and its potential subliminal impact upon the minds of the prospective jurors and jury, the Plaintiff's counsel should be precluded from asking questions or making arguments based upon the premises of "personal safety" and/or "community safety" for at least four (4) reasons. First, such arguments are tantamount to "Golden Rule" arguments, which are not permitted under Florida law. Second, such arguments violate Florida's Model Jury Instructions (regarding not being swayed by sympathy or prejudice). Third, such arguments would undermine the Defendant's rights to due process and a fair trial. Fourth, arguments of "personal safety" and " community safety" are irrelevant and, to the extent they are relevant, should nonetheless be excluded because their relevancy is substantially outweighed by the danger of unfair prejudice, confusion of the issues and misleading the jury.

The full defense motion in limine in *Ernani v. City of Miami Beach* can be found in Appendix 14.17, and it can be used as a model for a motion in limine to prevent opposing counsel from injecting inadmissible evidence or improper argument into voir dire questioning.

Collateral Source Example: In the car-crash lawsuit *Huggins v. Esposito*, brought in the Eighteenth Judicial District, Sedgwick County, Kansas District Court, the plaintiff made a motion in limine to, among other things, prohibit defense counsel from referring to collateral sources of payment, including but not limited to Medicare benefits and unemployment benefits, by question or other means, which would include references during voir dire.[82] The plaintiff's argument was that under the collateral source rule, benefits received by the plaintiff that are independent of and collateral to the wrongdoer are not to diminish the damages recovered from the wrongdoer, and therefore, the defense

---

82. Defense Motion in Limine, *Huggins v. Esposito*, Eighteenth Judicial District, Sedgwick County, Kan. Dist. Ct., Filed May 10, 2016, App. 14.18.

should not mention collateral sources at trial. This plaintiff's motion in limine is Appendix 14.16.

G. Motion for Additional Time for Attorney Questioning

The judge may impose reasonable time limits for attorney questioning of the prospective jurors. But, the trial court cannot abuse its discretion and arbitrarily set time limits that interfere with counsel's right to ascertain hidden juror prejudgments. Also, the court should give counsel notice of the time limit at some fair time before commencement of trial. (See pages 27–29 for legal authority and further discussion.)

If you are concerned that the trial judge may not allot you sufficient time to question jurors, you may decide to approach the judge during a pretrial conference and informally request the time you believe is reasonable for you and opposing counsel to properly inquire of the prospective jurors. On the other hand, you may decide to file a trial brief, and in it, ask for the court to provide an extended period of time for attorney questioning.

Extra Time Motion Example 1: In *Wolf v. Mayo*, plaintiff provided the San Diego Superior Court with a pocket brief regarding jury selection in which counsel stated that it was impermissible for the trial court to set arbitrary time limits. The pocket brief cited California Code of Civil Procedure 222.5 as follows:

> ... The scope of the examination conducted by counsel shall be within reasonable limits prescribed by the trial judge in the judge's sound discretion. In exercising his or her sound discretion as to the form and subject matter of voir dire questions, the trial judge should consider, among other criteria, any unique or complex elements, legal or factual, in the case and the individual responses or conduct of jurors which may evince attitudes inconsistent with suitability to serve as a fair and impartial juror in the particular case. Specific unreasonable or arbitrary time limits shall not be imposed.
>
> The trial judge should permit counsel to conduct voir dire examination without requiring prior submission of the questions unless a particular counsel engages in improper questioning.

Besides the California Code, which provides persuasive authority for a reasonable amount of time for attorney questioning, the pocket brief cited California appellate decisions to the effect that arbitrary time limits should not be imposed on counsel. The *Wolf v. Mayo* pocket brief is in Appendix 14.19.[83]

Extra Time Motion Example 2: Even without the advantage of a statutory or court rule basis, such as California's statute, for arguing that the court should not set unreasonable or arbitrary time limits for attorney voir dire questioning, a persuasive argument can be made for an extended amount of time for attorney questioning when the nature of the case calls for it. *Dieter v. Children's Hospital* provides such an example.[84]

In *Dieter*, the plaintiff's attorney requested 45 minutes to question the prospective jurors. In the trial brief, counsel wrote:

> The parties are entitled to "considerable latitude" during good faith examination of prospective jurors to enable the parties properly to exercise both peremptory challenges and challenges for cause. *Oglesby v. Conger,* 507 P.2d 883, 885 (Colo. App. 1992). The trial court may not limit voir dire to the point of preventing the parties from intelligently exercising challenges. See *People v. Greenwell,* 830 P.2d 1116 (Colo. App. 1992). "Limitations in terms of time or content must be reasonable in light of the total circumstances of the case." *Minnesota v. Petersen,* 368 N.W.2d 320, 322 (Minn. App. 1985). Thus, if the circumstances of a case involve many emotional or prejudicial issues, extended time for meaningful voir dire is both appropriate and necessary for parties to effectively exercise both peremptory challenges and challenges for cause.

Plaintiff's counsel further argued that the nature of the case and the number and type of expert witnesses necessitated the requested extension of time. The case involved the slip-and-fall head injury of a parent in the defendant hospital's emergency where she had taken her child for treatment. The plaintiff's trial brief contended that the case would take five days to try and involved numerous "substantive and unique factual, medical and damages issues" that could not be explored in the normally allotted amount of time for counsel questioning during jury selection. The complete trial brief is in Appendix 14.20.

---

83. *Wolf v. Mayo*, 37-2014-00035743-CU-P A-CTL Super. Ct. of Cal., Nov. 2015, App. 14.19.

84. Plaintiff's Trial Brief, *Dieter v. Children's Hosp.*, Denver Dist. Ct., State of Colo., Filed Feb. 15, 2016, App 14.20.

Chapter 15

Assignments for Experiential Learning

"For the things we have to learn before we can do them, we learn by doing them."

Aristotle, *The Nicomachean Ethics*

"I hear and I forget. I see and I remember. I do and I understand."

Confucius

A. Experiential Learning

This chapter provides you with jury selection assignments that put you in the role of a lawyer preparing for and engaging in jury selection. By performing these assignments, you can gain the experience needed to be able to conduct an effective voir dire without any risk to a client. Your teacher may select as many of the assignments as are believed appropriate for your situation. For instance, many of the assignments may be utilized in a trial advocacy course that allots a significant number of class sessions on juror selection, or the assignments may be combined for a short course on jury selection.

This chapter also provides you with synopses of *Wingate v. Whitlatch*, an actual civil rights case, and *State v. Meagher*, a hypothetical domestic violence felony assault criminal case. Your teacher can select one or both of these cases to serve as the fact pattern for you to use in performing the assignments.

B. Law and Facts

Your teacher may decide that the law that governs voir dire is found in the statutes, court rules and case law in your jurisdiction. And your teacher may direct you to adhere to the procedures of a particular judge in your jurisdiction. In the alternative, your instructor may direct you to assume you are in a fictional venue and that you are following the Federal Rules of Evidence, Federal Rules of Criminal Procedure, federal codes governing voir dire and the ABA Model Rules of Professional Conduct.

Regarding the facts of the two cases, your instructor may change them to fit your situation. For instance the *Wingate v. Whitlatch* case involves an incident that took place in the city of Seattle, the lawsuit was commenced in state court and then removed to federal court. However, your teacher could turn it into a hypothetical case that involved an event in your jurisdiction and remained in state court. You can assume that both the alleged assault in the *State v. Meagher* case and the alleged civil rights violation in the *Wingate v. Whitlatch* case occurred last year.

For each assignment, your teacher will instruct you regarding the following: whether you are counsel in the civil or criminal case; which party you represent; and the law and facts that you can rely upon during your preparation and trial.

C. Teacher's Manual

Your instructor's Teacher's Manual contains teaching notes. It also includes supplementary materials for the course, such as: a syllabus for law school classes; a schedule of instruction for continuing legal education workshops; role-playing instructions for jurors; and other court documents.

D. Civil Rights Case Synopsis: *William F. Wingate v. Cynthia A. Whitlatch*

On July 9 at about 1:00 p.m., William Wingate, a 69-year-old black man, was walking in the Capitol Hill neighborhood of Seattle, Washington. Wingate was retired, having served as a military policeman and then worked thirty-five years as a bus driver. He was walking to get a newspaper to take to fellow church members who lived in assisted living. Wingate used his golf club as a cane just as he had for the past 20 years.

Seattle Police Officer Cynthia Whitlatch, a 49-year-old white woman and an Acting Sergeant with the Seattle Police department, drove her patrol car by Wingate and made a left turn. According to Whitlatch, when she made the turn, she heard a clang that she interpreted to be the golf club hitting the post of the stop sign at the intersection. Whitlatch contended that she looked in her mirror and saw a scowling Wingate swing the golf club across his body and down to the ground, which caused her to believe that Wingate was swinging the golf club at her. Whitlatch turned on her in-car video system, went around the block, drove up beside Wingate and stopped her patrol car.

Officer Whitlatch repeatedly asked Wingate to drop the golf club. Wingate did not drop or relinquish the golf club to Whitlatch. An angry exchange followed, and Wingate told Officer Whitlatch to call someone else to be a witness. Two backup Seattle Police Officers, Christopher Coles and Ben Archer, arrived at the scene. Wingate turned the golf club over to Officer Coles. Wingate told the two officers that he had done nothing wrong and that he did not know Whitlatch. Part of the interaction between Whitlatch and Wingate was captured on video, which can be viewed at the link in the footnote.[1]

Whitlatch arrested Wingate for harassment and obstruction. Officers Cole and Archer took him into custody. Wingate was transported to the King County jail, and in the process, he stumbled getting into the van and his back was wrenched. Wingate spent the night in the King County jail.

At the arraignment the next day, Wingate, on the advice of a Rule 9 intern with the King County Public Defender's Office, signed a dispositional continuance on the charge of Unlawful Use of a Weapon (if he violated no laws and possessed no firearm or weapon for two years, the charge against him would be dismissed). Then after 30 hours in custody, he was released. Whitlatch complained to the Assistant Seattle City Attorney's about his filing decision, expressing her displeasure that Wingate had just received a warning and she wanted him charged with a crime. Eventually, the charges against Wingate were dismissed upon the prosecutor's motion.

According to Wingate, his friends, his sister, his pastor and his treating physician he suffered from emotional distress as a result of the incident.

The Stranger, a Seattle newspaper, investigated the story and published several articles. *The Stranger* uncovered a Facebook post from Whitlatch which said in part: "… I am tired of black people saying poor poor me when other races and genders and homeless and gays suffer far more prejudice than any black man

---

1. http://www.thestranger.com/slog/archives/2015/01/28/seattle-police-jailed-elderly-man-for-walking-in-seattle-while-black.

does in America." Whitlatch's text messages and emails expressed similar views. The Office of Professional Accountability investigated the case, and its report was delivered to the Seattle Chief of Police. The Police Chief terminated Whitlatch for biased and overly aggressive policing, noting that Whitlatch said that she would do the same thing again if faced with the same circumstances. Whitlatch denied both any wrongdoing and that racial bias motivated her.

Initially, Wingate filed a complaint in King County Superior Court, but later defendant Whitlatch removed the case to United States District Court, Western District of Washington, Seattle. The complaint alleges that defendant Cynthia Whitlatch under 42 U.S.C. § 1983 violated Wingate's civil rights by depriving him of his right under the Equal Protection Clause of the Fourteenth Amendment to the United States Constitution to be free of racial discrimination. The complaint also alleges a state law claim for racial discrimination, as well as a claim for intentional infliction of emotional distress. Wingate sought punitive damages that the jury could award if they found Whitlatch's conduct malicious.

Among several pretrial motions ruled on by the Court, Judge Richard Jones denied defense motions in limine to exclude Whitlatch's Facebook post, emails, text messages, the OPA report and the letter terminating Whitlatch from the Seattle Police Department.

E. Domestic Violence Assault in the Second Degree Synopsis: *State v. Timothy Meagher*

Timothy Meagher, age 55, is charged with domestic violence assault in the second degree. Mr. Meager is a prominent Councilman for the city of Sequim and the owner of three apartment buildings in the city. He is currently slated as a candidate for reelection to the council.

On July 4th of last year, Meagher, who was divorced, lived with Elizabeth "Libby" Pierce, age 42, in the Pacific Shores neighborhood of the city of Sequim. Pierce was employed as a docent at the Sequim Art Museum. Meagher and Pierce were scheduled to attend an afternoon outdoors party at the Sequim Art Museum starting at 5:30 p.m. that day.

At 11:00 on the morning of July 4th, Meagher and Pierce were in the bedroom when Pierce confronted Meagher, telling him that she had seen sexting messages on his cell phone from Angela Porter. She accused Meagher of "having an affair with that slut Angela Porter." Porter was a city employee working for Meagher. And Pierce said that she "knew something was going on."

When Meagher picked up his cell phone from the bedside table, Pierce reached out to grab the phone in Meagher's hand. Meagher pulled back his right hand, and as he did, Pierce scratched Meagher's hand. The cell phone fell to the floor. Meagher grabbed both of Pierce's arms, lifted her off the floor and threw her against the wall. He put his hands around her neck, squeezing it until Pierce could not breathe. He then hit her in the face with his fist, and she fell to the floor.

Meagher went to the bedside table where he got a pistol from the drawer. He walked to Pierce, leaned down, and placed the muzzle of the handgun to Pierce's head. He told her that she should "stop being such a bitch" and that she "better keep your mouth shut about this or I'm done with you." When Meagher lowered the gun to his side, Pierce got to her feet and ran out of the bedroom, through the living room and out the front door.

Pierce ran across the street to the home of her friend Katherine Mitchel, who met her at the front door and let her into the house. Pierce was crying, and she told Mitchel that Meagher had just hit her in the face, choked her, knocked her down, and then pointed a gun at her head. Mitchel immediately locked the front door and called 911. At the same time, Meagher arrived at the house and began pounding on the front door. Mitchel shouted at Meagher that she was on the phone with the police and that he had better leave. The pounding on the door ended. Mitchel handed her cell phone to Pierce who told the operator what had just happened.

Within five minutes, three Sequim Police patrol cars arrived at the Mitchel residence. Officers Bennett, Cocoran and Oaks entered the Mitchel house. Pierce told them that she lived across the street with Councilman Meagher and that he had just punched her in the face, tried to suffocate her and pointed a gun at her. Officer Bennett remained with Pierce and Mitchel and took written statements of what had happened. Officer Bennett photographed a red mark on Pierce's left cheek where Pierce told the officer that Meagher had hit her. Officer Bennett also took pictures of her neck; there were no signs of physical injury. Dr. Alicia O'Brien is prepared to testify that the absence of apparent physical injury to Pierce's neck is not inconsistent with her having been strangled.

Officers Cocoran and Oaks crossed the street to the Councilman's house. Councilman Meagher came out the front door and met the officers on the front porch. Meagher told the officers that he and Pierce had quarrelled about messages on his cell phone. He said Pierce had scratched his hand when she tried to grab his phone and that she tripped while trying to take the phone and fell to the floor. He said she hit her face on the bedside table as she was going down to the floor. Meagher showed the scratch on his hand to the officers.

Meagher acknowledged that he owned a Glock 9mm, but denied pointing it at Pierce. Officer Oaks asked Meagher if he would consent to them entering the house to search. Meagher said he had nothing to hide and that he had a license to carry the weapon. Officer Oaks explained the Consent to Search form, and Meagher signed the form and let the officers into his home. The two officers and Meagher went to the bedroom where Meagher retrieved the handgun from a bedside table and handed it to Officer Oaks. Officer Oaks took into evidence both the handgun and Meagher's cell phone, which was sitting on the bedside table. Officer Oaks advised Meagher that he was under arrest for domestic violence assault, and the officers took him into custody.

At a preliminary appearance hearing, Meagher was released on bond, and the judge entered a no-contact order prohibiting Meagher from either verbally or physically contacting Pierce. The prosecutor charged Meagher with assault in the second degree, alleging that Meagher had assaulted Pierce both with a deadly weapon, the firearm, and by strangling her.

The Councilman's alleged domestic violence felony assault drew considerable media attention. It has been the lead story several times in the *Sequim Times* newspaper and on the local television station.

On the eve of trial, Elizabeth Pierce asked the deputy prosecutor assigned to the case to drop the charges against Councilman Meagher. Pierce recanted, saying that she fabricated the story because she was angry with the Councilman. She said that the injury to her face was a result of a struggle with Meagher when she tried to take his cell phone from him. She said she tripped, fell, and hit her face on the bedside table. Piece said that she had not been in contact with the Councilman and that he had not influenced her to ask that charges be dropped. The prosecutor's office declined to dismiss the charges against Meagher, and the case is going to trial.

Defense pretrial motions to exclude the 911 call and Pierce's initial statements to Mitchel from evidence were denied. Also, the court denied the defense motion to exclude Pierce's initial statements to the officers when they first arrived on the scene on the grounds that those statements to the officers were nontestimonial in nature and, therefore, not violative of the Confrontation Clause. Also, the court denied the defense motion to suppress the firearm and Meagher's cell phone, which was found to contain sexting between Meagher and Angela Porter. Elizabeth Pierce is a listed defense witness.

F. Experiential Learning Assignments

Assignment 1:
Lawyer Preparation: The Jury Selection Process —
The Jury Selection Binder

You are preparing for jury selection. In order to be ready for voir dire, you need to have a firm grasp of the law, rules and procedures that will be applied to your trial. With this knowledge, you can protect your clients right to the selection of a fair cross-section of the community, follow your trial judge's procedures and feel confident that you are prepared for voir dire.

As part of your preparation, you will create a Jury Selection Binder in which you can file in an organized fashion the law and other information that relates to the court's process for jury selection.

Preparation

Read: Chapter 2 and the teacher assigned statutes, rules, judicial procedures and so on that are applicable to jury selection in your jurisdiction.

Outside of class: Prepare a Jury Selection Binder containing the following: (1) the law relating to how the jury pool is selected: (2) the law concerning the qualifications of jurors to sit; (3) the law concerning the number of jurors necessary for your case; and (4) a summary of the law, if any, in your jurisdiction regarding the right to a public trial.

Submission: Turn in your Jury Selection Binder.

Assignment for Class

In class: Be prepared to discuss the jury selection process in your jurisdiction and particularly how it will be conducted in your case.

Assignment 2:
Lawyer Preparation: Challenges —
The Jury Selection Binder

You are preparing for jury selection by assembling the pertinent law and procedures into a Jury Selection Binder. In the binder, you file the law and other information that relates to the court's process for jury selection, and now you are concentrating on causal and peremptory challenges.

Preparation

Read: Chapter 3 and the teacher assigned statutes, rules, judicial procedures and other assigned reading that are applicable to jury selection in your jurisdiction.

Outside of class: Prepare a jury selection binder containing the following: (1) the law, if any, in your jurisdiction on actual and implied bias; (2) the law in your jurisdiction regarding coaxed rehabilitation; (3) the law concerning the number of peremptory challenges; (4) a summary of the *Batson* decision and the process for making and meeting a *Batson* challenge and any case law in your jurisdiction regarding *Batson*; (5) procedures for how peremptories will be exercised in your trial court, including the method used (struck method, jury box method, or other); (6) whether they will be exercised in the jury's presence; and (7) the trial judge's procedures for alternate jurors.

Submission: Turn in your Jury Selection Binder with these new materials.

Assignment for Class

In class: Be prepared to discuss causal and peremptory challenges in your jurisdiction and particularly how they would be exercised in your case.

Assignment 3:
Lawyer Preparation: Scouting and Objections—
The Jury Selection Binder

You are preparing for jury selection, and now it is time to scout the trial court, to determine the extent, if at all, you can conduct Internet scouting of the prospective jurors and to plan to make objections at trial. You will add this new information to your Jury Selection Binder.

Preparation

Read: Chapter 4 and other the teacher assigned readings that are applicable to jury selection in your jurisdiction.

Outside of class: Compile materials for your Jury Selection Binder as follows: (1) the trial judge's guidelines for attorney conduct during jury selection; (2) a seating chart for the judge's courtroom as well as a challenges chart; (3) the law in your jurisdiction, if any, restricting Internet research of prospective jurors; (4) your jurisdiction's juror pamphlet and other juror orientation information; (5) the court's basic juror information form; and (6) a list of jury selection objections along with legal authority for the objections.

Submission: Turn in your Jury Selection Binder with the new materials gathered for this assignment.

Assignment for Class

In class: Be prepared to discuss the informational material provided to prospective jurors; your trial judge's procedures for conducting jury selection; your seating and challenges charts; limitations, if any, on Internet research of prospective jurors, and objections that you may make during voir dire.

Assignment 4:
Jury Consultant

You are considering employing a jury consultant to assist you in preparation for jury selection and during voir dire.

Preparation

Read: Chapter 5.

Assignment for Class

In class: Be prepared to discuss how you might make the best use of a jury consultant.

Assignment 5:
Lawyer Preparation: Case Development for Trial

You are at that stage in your trial preparation when you need to analyze your case for strengths and weaknesses as well as for juror misconceptions. Also, you will prepare profiles of the best and worst jurors.

Preparation

Read: Chapters 4 and 9.

Outside of class: Analyze your case for strengths and weaknesses and likely juror misconceptions that would cause bias against your case. Develop your case theory, including your legal position and case narrative, and your case theme. Also, prepare written profiles of the best and worst jurors for your case.

Submission: Turn in your written descriptions of your best and worst jurors.

Assignment for Class

In class: Be prepared to explain: your legal theory; your persuasive case narrative; your case's strengths and weaknesses; and your case theme. Further, be ready to discuss what you envision to be the profiles of the best and worst jurors for your case.

Assignment 6:
Delivering Your Preliminary Remarks and Making a Favorable Impression

Time has come for you to prepare and perform part of your jury selection. Specifically, you will make your preliminary remarks to the jury panel. Your teacher will inform you concerning your trial judge's guidelines regarding what you may say in your opening remarks to the panel.

Preparation

Read: Chapters 6 and 7.

Outside of class: Draft a written script of the opening remarks that you intend to make to the panel.

Submission: Turn in your scripted opening remarks.

Assignment for Class

In class: Be prepared to deliver your opening remarks to the jury panel. Those remarks and how you present yourself should cause the prospective jurors to trust you and be receptive to your case.

Assignment 7:
Types of Questions and Questioning Strategies and Techniques

This assignment involves you in both crafting and asking the different types of voir dire questions and strategies and techniques that you can use in questioning prospective jurors. Your teacher will inform you concerning your trial judge's guidelines regarding what questions you may ask during voir dire.

Preparation

Read: Chapter 8.

Outside of class: Draft the following questions for your case: (1) questions to break the ice with the jurors and get them talking; (2) two forced-choice questions; (3) two scaled questions; (4) two hypothetical questions; (5) two questions designed to get a commitment; and (5) a catch-all concluding question.

Submission: Turn in your written questions.

Assignment for Class

In class: Be prepared to deliver and discuss the questions that you have drafted. Also, be prepared to talk about the few points upon which you want the venirepersons to focus.

Assignment 8:
Initial Remarks and Questions about
Your Legal Position

For this assignment, you will both draft and deliver initial remarks concerning your legal position. Also, you will draft and ask questions about your legal position. Your teacher will inform you concerning your trial judge's guidelines regarding what initial remarks you may make and the questions you may ask during voir dire about your legal position.

Preparation

Read: Chapter 10.

Outside of class: Draft both that portion of your initial remarks that deals with your legal position in the case and the questions that you plan to ask during voir dire concerning your legal position.

Submission: Turn in your written preliminary remarks and voir dire questions.

Assignment for Class

In class: Be prepared to deliver and discuss your preliminary remarks and questions concerning your legal position.

Assignment 9:
Initial Remarks and Questions about Your Case Story

This assignment involves you in drafting and delivering initial remarks concerning your case narrative as well as drafting and asking questions about it. Your remarks and questions should present your client and case in a positive light, tell a story of deprivation or threatened deprivation, utilize a visual, and, for the civil case, address damages. Your teacher will inform you concerning your trial judge's guidelines regarding what initial remarks you may make and the questions you may ask during voir dire about your case story.

Preparation

Read: Chapter 11.

Outside of class: Draft both that portion of your initial remarks concerning your case story and questions that you will ask about it.

Submission: Turn in your written preliminary remarks and jury selection questions as well as the visual that you will display during voir dire.

Assignment for Class

In class: Be prepared to deliver and discuss your preliminary remarks and questions concerning your case story.

Assignment 10:
Initial Remarks and Questions about Case Weaknesses and Juror Misconception

Your initial remarks and questions about your case weaknesses and juror misconceptions are critical, because you want to identify prospective jurors who are biased against your client or case so that you can deselect them. For this assignment, you will draft and deliver initial remarks and ask questions that focus on your case weaknesses and juror misconceptions. Your teacher will inform you concerning your trial judge's guidelines regarding what initial remarks you may make and the questions you may ask during voir dire about your case weaknesses and juror misconceptions that would cause a juror to be biased against your case.

Preparation

Read: Chapter 12.

Outside of class: Draft both that portion of your initial remarks concerning your case weaknesses and harmful misconception and questions that you will ask about them.

Submission: Turn in your written preliminary remarks and jury selection questions about case weaknesses and misconceptions.

Assignment for Class

In class: Be prepared to deliver and discuss your preliminary remarks and questions concerning your case weaknesses and misconceptions.

Assignment 11:
Jury Selection Including Evaluating the Prospective Jurors

Your final assignment is to engage in a full voir dire. Your teacher will assign you to the role of prosecutor or defense counsel for the criminal case or plaintiff's counsel or defense counsel for the civil case. You will engage in jury selection, including exercising challenges. Your teacher will inform you concerning your trial judge's guidelines regarding what initial remarks you may make and the questions you may ask during voir dire.

Preparation

Read: Chapters 4 and 13.

Outside of class: Draft an agenda for your jury selection.

Submission: Turn in your written agenda for jury selection.

Assignment for Class

In class: Be ready to engage in jury selection and to discuss your evaluations of the prospective jurors.

Jury Selection Checklist

Preparation for Jury Selection

❏ **Scout the trial court by asking these questions:**
- ✓ Will the court use a customized juror questionnaire?
- ✓ Are attorney preliminary statements permitted? (How much time is allotted for this?)
- ✓ Is counsel required to stand at a podium?
- ✓ Does the court permit attorney questioning of the jurors and to what extent?
- ✓ Can attorneys ask questions to the entire panel or only those seated in the box?
- ✓ What jury-selection method does the court use? (Jury box method? Struck method?)
- ✓ How are challenges for cause exercised? (In front of the panel? At sidebar? Other?)
- ✓ How are peremptory challenges exercised?
- ✓ How many peremptories will be allowed?
- ✓ How will jurors who are struck from the box be replaced? (Numerically? Or at random?)
- ✓ If one side passes when it is their turn to exercise a peremptory, do they lose that peremptory challenge, or are they simply limited to striking only new jurors in the box?
- ✓ If more than one party is on a side, how many peremptory challenges per party? Or are they joined in a challenge?
- ✓ Are any of the peremptories designated only for the alternate jurors?
- ✓ How will the alternate jurors be selected?

✓ What time or other limitations does the court impose on attorney questioning? (If the court has a time limit, how much time will each side receive?)

✓ What limitations does the court put on counsel's questioning? (No indoctrination? Other?)

✓ How does the jury select the presiding juror? (Some venues have statutes or rules that designate a particular seat number, such as seat number one, as the presiding juror.)

✓ Any other instructions on how the court would like jury selection conducted?

❑ **Scout the prospective jurors:**

✓ Access a list of prospective jurors pretrial, if one is available;

✓ Conduct an Internet search for information about the jurors;

✓ Investigate juror track records of prior jury service, if such records are available;

✓ Research community attitudes;

✓ Request a customized juror questionnaire;

✓ Employ a jury consultant to assist both pretrial and at trial; and

✓ Neither jury tampering nor ex parte contact with prospective jurors.

❑ **Assemble these materials into a Jury Selection Binder:**

✓ The law pertinent to jury selection;

✓ List of objections for voir dire;

✓ Judge's rules concerning voir dire;

✓ Paper and/or electronic (iJuror app) jury panel seating and challenges chart;

✓ Profiles of the good juror and bad juror;

✓ Motions in limine regarding jury selection or responses to the motions; and

✓ List of witnesses for the court to read to the prospective jurors.

❑ **Assemble and prepare the jury selection team:**

✓ Enlist the help of a jury consultant; and

✓ Prepare the client for voir dire.

❑ **Have an agenda for jury selection:**

✓ Preliminary remarks;

✓ General questions;

✓ Specific questions designed to uncover bias and gain commitments; and

✓ Concluding remarks.

Make a Favorable Impression

❑ Be authentic:
  ✓ Project sincerity;
  ✓ Be yourself;
  ✓ Be friendly; and
  ✓ Be a lawyer that the jurors can trust.

❑ Communicate nonverbally:
  ✓ Personal appearance shows professionalism;
  ✓ Make meaningful eye contact;
  ✓ Body behavior communicates sincerity, candor and an interest in what the prospective jurors have to say; and
  ✓ Be professional and civil in interactions with others.

Stimulate an Open Exchange

❑ Encourage an open conversation with preliminary remarks.

❑ Make a personal connection by sharing something about yourself.

❑ Be nonjudgmental, particularly if a juror says something negative.

❑ Adhere to the principles of a good conversation, including:
  ✓ Listen actively;
  ✓ Speak clearly and in plain English;
  ✓ Have a conversational tone; and
  ✓ Have something to say.

❑ Politely cut off the conversation dominators.

❑ Speak with the silent ones.

Preliminary Remarks

❑ Matters to cover in preliminary remarks:
  ✓ Introduction of self and client;
  ✓ Statement of the case theme;
  ✓ Statement of the legal position;
  ✓ Summary of the case story;

✓ Explanation of why an open exchange and candor are critical; and
✓ Alleviate concerns about being embarrassed.

Questioning Strategies and Techniques

❑ **Break the ice** by:
  ✓ Starting with an interesting question to an individual juror or
  ✓ Starting with an interesting, nonthreatening question to the panel.

❑ **Types of questions** to mine for useful information:
  ✓ Open-ended questions;
  ✓ Forced-choice questions;
  ✓ Scaled questions; and
  ✓ Hypothetical questions.

❑ **Subjects to cover with the questions** include:
  ✓ Legal theory; and
  ✓ Case narrative topics, such as nature of the incident; type of witnesses; location, etc.

❑ **Commitment questions** asking jurors to promise to follow the law, set aside bias and so on.

❑ **Concluding catch-all question** aimed at uncovering any bias not yet revealed.

Discussing Your Legal Position

❑ **In preliminary remarks** clearly and succinctly state your legal position.

❑ **When questioning the jurors about the legal theory,** ask:
  ✓ About bias against the legal position; and
  ✓ For a commitment to follow the law that states the legal theory.

Discussing Your Case Story

❑ **In preliminary remarks and questioning emphasize:**
  ✓ Your client is a good person or company; and
  ✓ Your client has been deprived or is threatened with deprivation.

❑ **Surrogate methodology** may be able to be used to tell the client's story.

❑ **Utilize visuals** to bring the story alive.

Handling Case Weaknesses and Juror Misconception

❑ Identify case weaknesses and juror misconceptions with a case analysis.

❑ Eliminate those weaknesses that you can with motions in limine.

❑ Question jurors about weaknesses and misconceptions, such as:
  ✓ A particular law;
  ✓ A player in the trial;
  ✓ Corporations;
  ✓ A defendant in a criminal case;
  ✓ A problematic witness;
  ✓ Expert witnesses;
  ✓ Single-witness cases;
  ✓ Conflicting stories; and
  ✓ A case based merely upon circumstantial evidence.

Evaluating Prospective Jurors

❑ Watch and listen for telltale factors:
  ✓ Attire;
  ✓ Interaction with others;
  ✓ Nonverbal communication; and
  ✓ Verbal responses.

❑ Group dynamics:
  ✓ Leader and foreperson;
  ✓ Outlier;
  ✓ Opinionated;
  ✓ Follower; or
  ✓ Impartial.

Motions Relating to Jury Selection

❑ Motion for change of venue;

❑ Motion challenging the array;

❑ Motion for additional peremptory challenges;

- ❑ Motion for **customized juror questionnaire;**
- ❑ Motion to **prohibit opposing counsel from asking improper questions** during jury selection;
- ❑ Motion to provide **reasonable time for attorney questioning;** and
- ❑ Motion to **permit counsel to question the panel.**

Appendix

These appendices can be found on the online supplement at http://caplaw.com/jury.

1.1—Jury Selection Transcript—*In re TFT-LCD (Flat-Panel)*, No. 07-MDL-1827 SI, 10-CV-4572, 10-CV-5452, 10-CV-4114 (N.D. Cal. July 22, 2013)

1.2—Jury Selection Transcript—*Retractable Techs., Inc. v. Becton, Dickinson and Company*, 2:08cv16 E.D. (Tex. Sept. 3, 2013)

3.1—Motion re Voir Dire Rehabilitation

3.2—Jury Selection Transcript—*People v. Harmon*, 2007 WL 5181456 (2007)

4.1—ABA Formal Opinion 466 Lawyer Reviewing Jurors' Internet Presence

4.2—Juror Questionnaire for *In Re TFT-LCD (FLAT-PANEL)*

4.3—Juror Questionnaire for OJ Simpson robbery trial

4.4—Juror Questionnaire Boston Marathon bomber trial

4.5—Juror Questionnaire capital murder trial

4.6—Jury Selection Transcript—*Brown v. Davis and Davis*, No. 4:12 CV649-AGF (E.D Mo. 2014)

4.7—Juror Questionnaire asbestos trial

4.8—People of California vs. Michael Jackson child molestation trial questionnaire

7.1—Jury Selection Transcript—*Ericson, Inc. v. D-Link Corporation*, 6:10cv 473E.D. (Tex. June 3, 2013)

14.12 — Defense Motion for Extra Peremptories — Boston Marathon bombing case

14.13 — Government's Opposition to Defense Motion for Extra Peremptories — Boston Marathon bombing case

14.14 — Plaintiff's Motion for Extended Questionnaire and Follow Up Questioning

14.15 — Defendants' Response to Plaintiff's Motion for Juror Questionnaire and Attorney Follow-Up Voir Dire

14.16 — Plaintiff's Motion in Limine, *Villaverde v. Asbestos Corp. Ltd.*, Filed Mar. 5, 2013

14.17 — Defense Motion in Limine, Golden Rule, *Ernani v. City of Miami Beach*, S.D. of Fla., Filed Jan. 18, 2016

14.18 — Defense Motion in Limine Collateral Source, *Huggins v. Esposito*, Eighteenth Judicial District, Sedgwick County, Kan. Dist. Ct., Filed May 10, 2016

14.19 — Motion re Time Limit — *Wolf v. Mayo* 37-2014-00035743-CU-P A-CTL Superior Court of California, Nov. 2015

14.20 — Plaintiff's Trial Brief, *Dieter v. Children's Hosp.*, Denver Dist. Ct., State of Colo., Filed Feb. 15, 2016

Index

qualifications, 43
questionnaire based, 56–58
ruling on, 59
strategies and techniques, 48–55
Challenge of jury selection, 3–4
Challenge to array motion, 302–305
Challenges to prospective jurors,
41–42
See cause challenge; *see also*
peremptory challenges
Checklists
court procedure, 88–89
jury selection, 335–340
Civility, 141
Clients
preparation for voir dire, 115–117
Coaxed rehabilitation, 54
Corporations, 209–211, 249–252
Courtroom, placement in, 34
Damages, 222–228
Death penalty, 59–61
Death qualification, 59–61
Defendant, criminal case
burden of proof, 253–254
presumption of innocence,
240–242, 253–254
right to remain silent, 241
Deselection of jurors, 4–5, 85–86
Difficult answers from jurors, 151–152
Embarrassing or personal matters, 172
Encourage to talk, 143–144
Engle Progeny cases, 307–313
Error, preservation of, 42
Ethics, *See* Rules of Professional
Conduct
Evaluating prospective jurors, 277–289
appearance, 279
body behavior, 282–284
interaction with others, 279–280
jury selection team, 277–278
leadership, 70–72, 286–287

nonverbal communication, 280–
282
reading material, 280
scouting jurors, 278–279, *See*
investigation of jurors
telltale factors, 279
verbal responses, 285
voice and manner of speaking,
284–285
Experienced jurors, 70–72
Experiential learning, 321–322
Expert witnesses, 256–259
Eye contact, 283
Focus groups, 126–127
Follower jurors, 288
Forced-choice question, 165
Frivolous lawsuits, 198–203
Goals of jury selection, 4–5, 85–87
case narrative, introduce, 5,
181–193
deselection, 4, 85–86
information, elicit useful, 4, 87,
143–157
impression of lawyer, 4, 87,
133–142
legal position, introduce, 5, 87
rapport, 144
weaknesses, deal with, 4, 87
Group dynamics, 285–288
follower, 288
impartial, 288
leader and foreperson, 286–287
opinionated, 287–288
outlier, 287
Gut reaction,288–289
Hardship, 30–31
Humanizing your client, 209–210
Humor, 135
Hypothetical question, 169
Ice breaking, 159–164
Impression of lawyer, 133–142
civility, 141–142